MY BEST OF CHESS
1908—1923

BY

ALEXANDER ALEKHIN

Docteur en Droit

TRANSLATED FROM THE ORIGINAL MSS (IN FRENCH) BY
J. DU MONT AND M. E. GOLDSTEIN

ISHI PRESS
INTERNATIONAL

My Best Games of Chess
1908-1923
by Alexander Alekhine

Introduction by Sam Sloan

Copyright © 2008 by Sam Sloan and
Ishi Press International

Introduction by Jerry Hanken copyright © 2008 by Jerry Hanken

First printed in 1927, translated from the original French manuscripts by J. DuMont and M. E. Goldstein.

Reprinted many times since by many different publishers

Current Printing September, 2008 by
Ishi Press in New York and Tokyo

All rights reserved according to International Law. No part of this book may be reproduced by any mechanical, photographic or electronic process nor may it be stored in a retrieval system, transmitted or otherwise copied for public or private use without the written permission of the publisher.

ISBN 0-923891-49-8
978-0-923891-49-7

Ishi Press International
1664 Davidson Avenue, Suite 1B
Bronx NY 10453
USA
917-507-7226

Printed in the United States of America

Introduction

Alexander Alexanderovich Alekhine was born in Moscow on October 31, 1892. According to Russian phonetics, his name should have been pronounced AL-YOK-IN, but he personally insisted that it be pronounced AL-YEKH-EEN.

By age 16, he was a master. In 1914, he played in the first major tournament of his career, the great tournament of St. Petersburg 1914, which was the strongest tournament in chess history up until that time. Alekhine finished in third place behind Lasker and Capablanca and ahead of Tarrasch, Marshall, Rubinstein, Nimzovitch, Bernstein, Blackburne, and many other famous players. Czar Nicholas II conferred the title "Grandmaster of Chess" upon Lasker, Capablanca, Alekhine, Tarrasch, and Marshall, after they took the top five places at St. Petersburg. As the title of "Grandmaster" was not previously known, Alekhine thereby became one of the first five grandmasters of chess.

In 1927, Alekhine became World Chess Champion by defeating Capablanca in a match. He lost the world title to Euwe in 1935 but won it back in 1937. He held the title of World Chess Champion from then until his death in 1946.

There have been many controversies involving Alekhine, including the controversy about the circumstances of his death. The official version was that he choked on a piece of meat or that he died of a heart attack. However, others say that he was murdered.

A bigger issue that still rages today concerns articles published under his name during World War II. Prior to the war, he was living in Paris. After France was overrun by the Germans, he escaped to Portugal. In March 1941, a series of articles supposedly by him appeared in the French publication *"Parisier Zeitung"*. Later, they were reprinted in Germany.

The questions raised by these articles include:

Introduction

1. Did Alekhine write the articles?

2. If so, when?

3. Was Alekhine anti-Semitic?

4. Was Alekhine a Nazi?

As to the first, it seems likely that Alekhine did write the articles. They discuss primarily the chess playing styles of his rivals, a subject Alekhine knew more about than anybody else. Those who have seen the articles say that they were in his handwriting. However, Alekhine claimed that they had been edited or modified by somebody else. Also, he seemed to be claiming that they were based on articles he had written in 1938 but that editorial changes had been made by others at a later date.

The third question is more relevant, but the answer is not so easy as one might suppose. Those who say that Alekhine was a Nazi and that his writings were anti-Semitic appear to have read little if any of the writing in the articles.

Here is perhaps the strongest example of an "anti-Semitic" quote from the articles:

> "Do the Jews, as a race, have a gift for chess? After 30 years' chess experience I would like to answer this question in the following manner: yes, the Jews have an exceptional talent for exploiting chess, chess ideas and the practical possibilities that arise. But there has not been up to now a Jew who was a real chess artist."

It is true that this statement can be regarded as anti-Semitic, until one considers the question: Who, in the view of Alekhine, was an example of "a real chess artist"?

Introduction

The answer to this question, it seems, was that only Alekhine himself was considered by Alekhine to be a real chess artist.

Indeed, the quotation above seems to be only mildly anti-Semitic compared to statements made by The Pope, various religious and political leaders and even by President Franklin D. Roosevelt during this same time period.

International Master Walter Shipman, who met Alekhine, says that more than any other grandmaster, Alekhine epitomized in physical appearance the features said to characterize the Nazi ideal of the "master race". Alekhine had blond hair, blue eyes and was very handsome, according to Shipman. Unfortunately, the black-and-white pictures of Alekhine that survive today do not reveal these features.

There are many articles accusing Alekhine of being a Nazi or anti-Semitic, but none of them have been able to provide exact quotes stronger than the one quoted above to prove their point. In short, it seems that Alekhine has been given a bum rap.

More than that, Alekhine disavowed the *"Parisier Zeitung"* articles even while World War II was still going on and while Alekhine was playing in tournaments in Germany and Poland.

The end of World War II proved tragic for Alekhine. He was invited to the London "Victory" Tournament in 1946. However, the Americans led by US Champion Arnold Denker refused to play if Alekhine was invited, on the ground that he had played in chess tournaments and had written articles for the Nazis. As a result, Alekhine was dis-invited to the tournament.

On March 24, 1946, only a few days after he had received the notice that he was no longer invited to the Victory tournament, Alekhine was found dead.

The very next day after his death, Alekhine, had he lived, would have received an invitation to play a match for the World Chess Championship against Mikhail Botvinnik.

Introduction

Subsequently, Grandmaster Arnold Denker often said that he deeply regretted the fact that he had protested the invitation of Alekhine to the London Victory tournament. Denker said that Alekhine had been his friend. Denker wrote, "Here I made a grave error. Alekhine had been my friend. You do not desert a friend. I should have stuck with him as he was dying in Lisbon and tried to find the facts, the pressures of war on him."

Another controversy concerning Alekhine concerns this book, *My Best Games of Chess 1908-1923*. On page 69, in a mere note, there is the famous *"Five Queens Game"*, the most famous game by Alekhine and one of the most famous chess games ever played.

But was it really played? Critics and researchers have suggested that it was not a real game but was a composition.

Researchers have found a substantially similar game played by Alekhine in 1915 with the same opening moves, but in that game Alekhine played black and white lost the game.

However, in defense of Alekhine, it must be pointed out that a careful reading of page 69 shows that he never said that he had played white or that he had won this game. He also never said that it was an actual official tournament game against a real human opponent. Players often played practice games against themselves, especially back then when there were fewer opponents and no computers. Those were still "played" games.

Here is the "fake" game:

1.e4 e6 2.d4 d5 3.Nc3 Nf6 4.Bg5 Bb4 5.e5 h6 6.exf6 hxg5 7.fxg7 Rg8 8.h4 gxh4 9.Qg4 Be7 10.g3 c5 11.gxh4 cxd4 12.h5 dxc3 13.h6 cxb2 14.Rb1 Qa5+ 15.Ke2 Qxa2 16.h7 Qxb1 17.hxg8=Q+ Kd7 18.Qxf7 Qxc2+ 19.Kf3 Nc6 20.Qgxe6+ Kc7 21.Qf4+ Kb6 22.Qee3+ Bc5 23.g8=Q b1=Q 24.Rh6 Qxf1 25.Qb4+ Qb5 26.Qd8+ Ka6 27.Qea3+ 1-0

Introduction

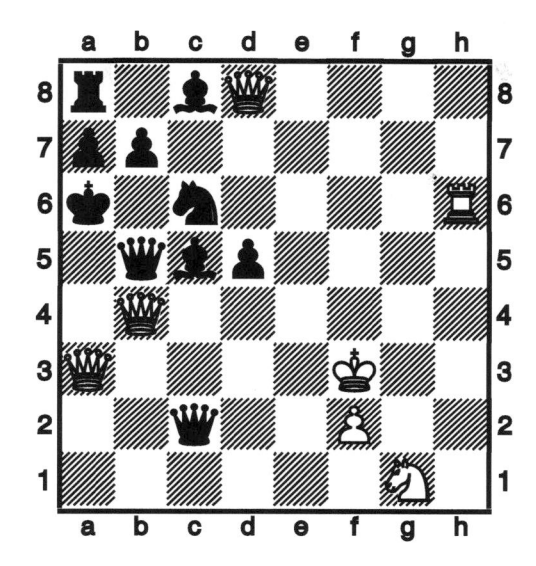

If this had been a tournament game between human opponents, it would certainly have been one of the main featured games in this book and not a mere note to an unrelated game.

Of course, had Alekhine said that this was merely analysis and not an actual game between two humans, it would not have gone down in chess history as one of the most famous games ever "played".

Alekhine was married four times, each time to a much older, wealthy woman. His last wife was Grace Wishard. She was born on October 26, 1876 in New Jersey and was the widow of Archibald Freeman, a wealthy English tea planter. Alekhine met her when she was among his opponents in a simultaneous chess exhibition in Tokyo. She was Jewish. They married in March 1934 at Villefranche-sur-Mer, near Nice, France. She died in March, 1956 and is buried next to him in the Cimetière du Montparnasse, Paris.

As each of his wives was older, they may have been too old to have children. However, there are reports that Alekhine

Introduction

fathered an illegitimate child in 1913 or 1914. Also, the book, *Alexander Alekhine's Chess Games, 1902-1946* by Robert G. P. Verhoeven and Leonard M. Skinner, includes a foreword by Alex A. Alejchin. He appears to be the son of the late World Champion, but by which wife is not made clear.

On one point on which every authority on chess agrees: This book, *My Best Games of Chess 1908-1923*, is the book that every chess master and grandmaster has read and studied and every aspiring chess master should be reading.

The author, a World Chess Champion, clearly explains the most complex and difficult concepts.

Grandmaster Reuben Fine wrote that Alekhine's collection of best games was one of the three most beautiful that he knew.

World Champion Garry Kasparov wrote, "Alexander Alekhine is the first luminary among the others who are still having the greatest influence on me. I like his universality, his approach to the game, his chess ideas. I am sure that the future belongs to Alekhine chess."

Bobby Fischer wrote, "He had great imagination. He could see more deeply into a situation than any other player in chess history. It was in the most complicated positions that Alekhine found his grandest concepts."

Chess Journalist Jerry Hanken writes, "The study of this book added nearly 400 points to my rating and made me a master."

Sam Sloan
Bronx New York
September 14, 2008

Introduction by Jerry Hanken, Original Life Master, former California Open Champion and President of The Chess Journalists Of America

INTRODUCTION TO
"MY BEST GAMES OF CHESS 1928 - 1923"
BY ALEXANDER ALEKHINE late Champion of the World
New addition edited by Sam Sloan

I agreed to write this introduction to this new edition of this great book because the book has meant so much to me. This book played a large part in my ultimate development as a Chess Master. In the winter of 1955, I was a graduate student at The University of Kansas in Lawrence Kansas. I was supposed to be doing work toward my M. A. in history and I had a teaching fellowship which required me to conduct ten one hour seminars in a core curriculum program studying Western Civilization through the great books and writers of the past. Students were required to read a great book a week and come to these 10 person "discussion groups" and pass a written test at the end of the Semester. The truth was that I read a lot of the books just before the classes so I could fake it as a "discussion leader". I had dropped most of my classes and my thesis never got started. I had trouble getting up for 3:00 PM classes. Why? Because I had fallen in with a degenerate den of chess players who often played at a friendly pizza parlor most of the night. They had dragged me to a couple of tournaments. I was completely hooked. My first published rating was 1562. I was convinced I could be better. Having tried a few books by Reinfeld and Chernev and not finding them that helpful in moving me up, I was frustrated. Was I blowing an education to be a bad chess player? That was a depressing thought, indeed.

Somehow, in the beginning of the year 1956, I came into possession of THE BOOK and from its first page, that sparkling Vienna game against B. Gregory, I knew I was onto something special.

I was renting a basement apartment near campus and it was January of 1956. I started to pour over the games and notes of Alekhine almost obsessively. I quit playing skittles all night and just barely kept my discussion groups going. I was faking it more and more with the works I had not read. Luckily, I had a good foundation from college and high school and had the same Cliff

Introduction by Jerry Hanken, Original Life Master, former California Open Champion and President of The Chess Journalists Of America

Notes most of the students were using, so I could just stay ahead of my students. I spent every spare hour in that dank basement playing over and over and re- playing the games and notes of the Great One. In April of 1956, four months after I received THE BOOK, I went to my second Kansas State Championship tournament. In the first, my introduction to tournament play in 1955, I had started OK but lost my last four of six. Since then, I had minus scores in 3 more tournaments. In round one in 1956 at the same Hutchison Kansas venue, I faced the white haired Carl Weberg, the reigning Champ from the last year who sported a Godlike 1960 rating --- and I beat him! It was a fine attacking game and the influence of The Great One was visible. I ended a mating attack with 4 consecutive pawn moves and a final King move! I was certain that my Great Mentor was watching from above and was pleased. (The game is in the old Chess Life newspaper in Jack Collins' column in June of 1956 and it has my notes, so it is my first published article. The title by Jack was "Hanken Beats Champion".) I didn't win the Championship as I lost one game to Dr. Wes Perkins, a Grad student in psychiatry at near by Menengers Clinic and an expert, the first I had ever played. My score was 4-2 and by the time the ratings came out, next year (Yes, that's how long it took then), I was rated 1947!

It was almost all this BOOK! I have never found anything quite like it since. The second volume was also quite good but it lacked the impact of this one on me. The World Champion has more than a mere game collection here. There are superb insights into all aspects of the game. For example, the intricate ending with Akiba Rubinstein, game 70, should be visited and revisited again and again. There is much to learn of the openings. The Great Master uses a very practical set of ways to start the game and he explains them lucidly. His sharp middle game skirmish with the great attacker Spielmann in game 11 is a joy to study. But they are all great to one degree or another and all instructive. Don't be put off by the descriptive notation. It simply means you shift your point of view of the board each move. It is not hard to get used to and delightful rewards await you as you start your journey through these riches. I won't keep you any longer. Just enjoy!

ALEXANDER ALEKHIN

BIOGRAPHICAL NOTE

Alexander Alexandrovitch Alekhin was born at Moscow on October 19th, 1892. When only sixteen he won the first prize in the Russian Amateur Chess Tournament held concurrently with the great St. Petersburg Tournament of 1909. Entering the Military School of St. Petersburg in 1909, his opportunities for tournament play were infrequent, but he succeeded in winning the first prize in three international events between 1909 and 1914.

Since the Revolution he has made Paris his permanent domicile and has recently obtained his Degree of Docteur en Droit at Paris.

His rapid rise to fame as a chess player since the war is well known, and he is now probably one of the three greatest living chess masters.

A short summary of his successes in tournament and match play is given overleaf.

SUMMARY OF RESULTS

The following tables summarise Alekhin's successes in tournament and match-play, the figures in the last four columns representing the number of games played, won, drawn, and lost respectively.

TOURNAMENTS

Date.		Prize.	Played.	Won.	Drawn.	Lost.
1909	St. Petersburg Amateur Tournament	1	16	12	2	2
1910	Hamburg	7 eq.	16	5	7	4
1911	Carlsbad	8 eq.	25	11	5	9
1912	Stockholm	1	10	8	1	1
1912	Vilna All-Russian Tournament	6 eq.	18	7	3	8
1913	St. Petersburg Quadrangular Tournament.	1 eq.	4	2	—	1
1913	Scheveningen	1	13	11	1	1
1913	St. Petersburg All-Russian Tournament	1 eq.	17	13	1	3
1914	St. Petersburg International Tournament	3	18	6	8	4
1914	Mannheim	1	11	9	1	1
1920	Moscow All-Russian Tournament	1	15	9	6	—
1921	Triberg	1	8	6	2	—
1921	Budapest	1	11	6	5	—
1921	The Hague	1	9	7	2	—
1922	Pistyan	2 eq.	18	12	5	1
1922	London	2	15	8	7	—
1922	Hastings	1	10	6	3	1

1923	Margate	2 eq.| 7	3	3	1
1923	Carlsbad	1 eq.| 17	9	5	3
1923	Portsmouth	1	12	11	1	—
1924	New York	3	20	6	12	2
1925	Paris	1	8	5	3	—
1925	Berne	1	6	3	2	1
1925	Baden-Baden	1 eq.| 20	12	8	—
1926	Hastings	2	9	8	1	—
1926	Semmering	2	17	11	3	3
1926	Dresden	1	9	5	4	—
1926	Scarborough	1	8	7	1	—
1926	Birmingham	—	5	5	—	—
1927	New York	2	20	5	13	2
	Totals		406	235	119	51

MATCHES

Date.		Played.	Won.	Drawn.	Lost.
1908	v. Blumenfeld	8	7	1	—
1911	v. Levitski	10	7	—	3
1921	v. Teichmann	6	2	2	2
1921	v. Sämisch	2	2	—	—
1923	v. Mufſang	2	2	—	—
1927	v. Euwe	10	3	5	2
	Totals	38	23	8	7

CONTENTS

	PAGE
BIOGRAPHICAL NOTE	v
SUMMARY OF RESULTS	vi & vii

PART I (1908-20)

CHAPTER I. ST. PETERSBURG AMATEUR TOURNAMENT, 1909

NO. OF GAME
1. ALEKHIN—GREGORY 1
2. VERLINSKI—ALEKHIN 4

CHAPTER II. INTERNATIONAL TOURNAMENT AT HAMBURG, 1910

3. SPEYER—ALEKHIN 6
4. ALEKHIN—YATES 9

CHAPTER III. INTERNATIONAL TOURNAMENT AT CARLSBAD, 1911

5. ALEKHIN—VIDMAR 12
6. ALAPIN—ALEKHIN 15
7. ALEKHIN—CHAJES 19
8. ALEKHIN—DUS-CHOTIMIRSKI 20

CHAPTER IV. INTERNATIONAL TOURNAMENT AT STOCKHOLM, 1912

9. ALEKHIN—MARCO 23
10. ALEKHIN—E. COHN 25
11. SPIELMANN—ALEKHIN 29

CHAPTER V. ALL-RUSSIAN MASTERS' TOURNAMENT AT VILNA, 1912

12. BERNSTEIN—ALEKHIN 32
13. NIEMZOVITCH—ALEKHIN 35
14. ALEKHIN—BERNSTEIN 37
15. LÖVENFISCH—ALEKHIN 40

CHAPTER VI. MASTERS' QUADRANGULAR TOURNAMENT AT ST. PETERSBURG, 1913

16. ALEKHIN—DURAS 43
17. ZNOSKO-BOROVSKI—ALEKHIN 45

CONTENTS

CHAPTER VII. INTERNATIONAL TOURNAMENT AT SCHEVENINGEN, 1913

NO OF GAME		PAGE
18.	OLLAND—ALEKHIN	48
19.	MIESES—ALEKHIN	50

CHAPTER VIII. ALL-RUSSIAN MASTERS' TOURNAMENT AT ST. PETERSBURG, 1913–14

20.	ALEKHIN—LÖVENFISCH	54
21.	ALEKHIN—NIEMZOVITCH	56
22.	VON FREYMANN—ALEKHIN	59
23.	NIEMZOVITCH—ALEKHIN	60

CHAPTER IX. INTERNATIONAL TOURNAMENT AT ST. PETERSBURG, 1914

24.	ALEKHIN—MARSHALL	64
25.	ALEKHIN—TARRASCH	66
26.	TARRASCH—ALEKHIN	69

CHAPTER X. INTERNATIONAL TOURNAMENT AT MANNHEIM, 1914

27.	DURAS—ALEKHIN	73
28.	FLAMBERG—ALEKHIN	77
29.	ALEKHIN—TARRASCH	79
30.	MIESES—ALEKHIN	82
31.	ALEKHIN—FAHRNI	84

CHAPTER XI. LOCAL TOURNAMENTS, EXHIBITION AND MATCH GAMES, SIMULTANEOUS AND CORRESPONDENCE GAMES, ETC.

32.	ALEKHIN—DE JONKOVSKI	87
33.	WJAKHIREFF—ALEKHIN	91
34.	WYGODCHIKOFF—ALEKHIN	93
35.	ALEKHIN—ROSANOFF	96
36.	BLUMENFELD—ALEKHIN	97
37.	ALEKHIN—VON FREYMANN	100
38.	POTEMKIN—ALEKHIN	102
39.	ALEKHIN—LÖVENFISCH	103
40.	ALEKHIN—LEVITSKI	105
41.	ALEKHIN—LEVITSKI	107
42.	DE RODZYNSKI—ALEKHIN	109
43.	ALEKHIN—PRAT	110
44.	ALEKHIN—ED. LASKER	111
45.	ALEKHIN—EM. LASKER	114
46.	ALEKHIN—ZUBAREFF	115
47.	EVENSSOHN—ALEKHIN	116
48.	ALEKHIN—FELDT	119
49.	ALEKHIN—GOFMEISTER	120
50.	ALEKHIN—A. RABINOVITCH	122
51.	GONSSIOROVSKI—ALEKHIN	124
52.	ALEKHIN—ISSAKOFF	125

PART II (1920-23)

CHAPTER XII. ALL-RUSSIAN MASTERS' TOURNAMENT AT MOSCOW, 1920

NO. OF GAME.	PAGE
53. E. Rabinovitch—Alekhin	129

CHAPTER XIII. INTERNATIONAL TOURNAMENT AT TRIBERG, 1921

54. Selesnieff—Alekhin	132
55. Alekhin—Bogoljuboff	137

CHAPTER XIV. INTERNATIONAL TOURNAMENT AT BUDAPEST, 1921

56. Alekhin—Sterk	140
57. Alekhin—Bogoljuboff	143
58. Steiner—Alekhin	145
59. Alekhin—von Balla	148

CHAPTER XV. INTERNATIONAL TOURNAMENT AT THE HAGUE, 1921

60. Yates—Alekhin	150
61. Alekhin—Rubinstein	153

CHAPTER XVI. INTERNATIONAL TOURNAMENT AT PISTYAN, 1922

62. Tarrasch—Alekhin	158
63. Alekhin—Selesnieff	160
64. Johner—Alekhin	162
65. Alekhin—Wolf	165
66. Treybal—Alekhin	168
67. Alekhin—Hromadka	171

CHAPTER XVII. INTERNATIONAL TOURNAMENT AT LONDON, 1922

68. Alekhin—Euwe	173
69. Alekhin—Yates	176
70. Rubinstein—Alekhin	179

CHAPTER XVIII. INTERNATIONAL TOURNAMENT AT HASTINGS, 1922

71. Alekhin—Tarrasch	183
72. Alekhin—Bogoljuboff	185
73. Bogoljuboff—Alekhin	187

CONTENTS

CHAPTER XIX. INTERNATIONAL TOURNAMENT AT VIENNA, 1922

NO. OF GAME		PAGE
74.	ALEKHIN—RÉTI	192
75.	KMOCH—ALEKHIN	196
76.	ALEKHIN—SÄMISCH	197
77.	ALEKHIN—KÖNIG	199
78.	ALEKHIN—TARTAKOVER	200

CHAPTER XX. TOURNAMENT AT MARGATE, 1923

79.	ALEKHIN—MUFFANG	205

CHAPTER XXI. INTERNATIONAL TOURNAMENT AT CARLSBAD, 1923

80.	ALEKHIN—RUBINSTEIN	208
81.	GRÜNFELD—ALEKHIN	212
82.	TARRASCH—ALEKHIN	215
83.	ALEKHIN—MARÓCZY	219
84.	WOLF—ALEKHIN	221
85.	ALEKHIN—CHAJES	223
86.	ALEKHIN—THOMAS	228

CHAPTER XXII. MAJOR OPEN TOURNAMENT AT PORTSMOUTH, 1923

87.	ALEKHIN—VAJDA	232
88.	ALEKHIN—WEST	235
89.	ALEKHIN—DREWITT	237

CHAPTER XXIII. EXHIBITION GAMES AND SIMULTANEOUS GAMES

90.	ALEKHIN—TEICHMANN	239
91.	ALEKHIN—TEICHMANN	241
92.	ALEKHIN—SÄMISCH (Berlin, 1921)	243
93.	ALLIES—ALEKHIN (Berlin, 1921)	245
94.	ALLIES—ALEKHIN (Basle, 1921)	248
95.	ALEKHIN—GOLMAYO	249
96.	TORRES—ALEKHIN	251
97.	ALEKHIN—SÄMISCH (Berlin, 1923)	253
98.	ALEKHIN—ALLIES (Antwerp, 1923)	255
99.	ALEKHIN—MUFFANG	259
100.	MUFFANG—ALEKHIN	261

INDEX OF OPENINGS **265**

INDEX OF NAMES **267**

MY BEST GAMES OF CHESS

PART ONE

CHAPTER I

ALL-RUSSIAN AMATEUR TOURNAMENT AT ST. PETERSBURG, FEBRUARY, 1909

GAME 1

VIENNA GAME

White : A. ALEKHIN.
Black : B. GREGORY.

1. P—K 4   P—K 4
2. Kt—Q B 3   Kt—K B 3
3. B—B 4   Kt—B 3

The best move is 3. .....Kt × P! (see game No. 41).

4. P—Q 3   B—Kt 5
5. B—K Kt 5   Kt—Q 5

This manœuvre is not to be recommended and, as the sequel shows, only results in the obstruction of the Q B. The best continuation is : 5. ......P—K R 3 ; 6. B×Kt, B×Kt ch ; 7. P×B, Q×B, etc., with equal chances.

6. P—Q R 3

The simplest, for now 6. ...... B—R 4; would be inferior because of 7. P—Q Kt 4, followed by 8. Kt—Q 5, etc. 6. P—B 4, P—Q 3 ; 7. Kt—B 3 was also worthy of consideration.

6. ......   B × Kt ch
7. P × B   Kt—K 3

Position after Black's 7th move.

8. P—K R 4 !

A strong move.

If instead 8. B—Q 2, P—Q 4 ; 9. P×P, Kt×P ; 10. Q—K 2, P—K B 3 ; whereas after 8. P—K R 4, P—K R 3 ; 9. B—Q 2, this manœuvre is not advantageous for Black, *e.g.*: 9. ....P—Q 4 ; 10. P×P, Kt×P ; 11. Q—K 2, Q—Q 3 ; (if 11. ....P—K B 3 ; 12. Q—R 5 ch ;) 12. Kt—B 3, P—K B 3 ; 13. Q—K 4, Kt—K 2 ; 14. P—Q 4, and White has the better game.

8. ......   P—K R 3

Clearly not 8. .....Kt×B; 9. P×Kt, Kt—Kt 1 ; because of 10. P—Kt 6 !

9. B—Q 2   P—Q 3
10. Q—B 3

The plan to advance the K Kt P, initiated by the last move, is somewhat perfunctory and devoid of real sting. The simple development by 10. Kt—K 2 followed by 11. Kt—Kt 3, would have given White the better game without any complications.

10. ......   B—Q 2
11. P—Kt 4   Q—K 2
12. P—Kt 5

Position after White's 12th move.

12. ......   Kt—Kt 1

Here Black should have availed himself of the opportunity to exchange his inactive K R, after which he would have had a satisfactory game; *e.g.*:

12. ....P×P; 13. P×P, R×R; 14. Q×R (if instead 14. P×Kt, R×Kt ch; 15. K—K 2, R×R!; 16. P×Q, R—K Kt 8!; and Black has the advantage), 14. ...... Kt—Kt 1; 15. Q—R 7, Castles; etc. Black could have repelled his opponent's somewhat hazardous advance by a manœuvre both precise and energetic; but, on the contrary, he justifies it by the inferior tactics adopted here.

13. R—Kt 1   B—B 3
14. Kt—R 3

The unsatisfactory development of this Knight is the direct outcome of the risky moves preceding it.

14. ......   K—Q 2

There was indicated: 14. .... P×P; 15. P×P, Castles; 16. Q—K 3, K—Kt 1; 17. R—Kt 1, with a complicated position which held chances for Black. The Black King would be safer on the wing than in the centre, where he will soon be exposed to a successful attack.

15. Q—Kt 4!

The intention being to bring the Knight into the centre after an exchange of Pawns at K B 5.

15. ......   R—K B 1

Preparing the counter-attack 16. ....P—B 4; which White will however refute by a pretty sacrifice; in any case Black's game was already compromised in consequence of the mistake on his 14th move.

16. P—B 4   P—B 4

If 16. ....P—K R 4; 17. Q—Kt 3, P×P; 18. Kt×P, Kt×Kt; 19. B×Kt, B×P; 20. Castles! etc. with a winning attack.

Position after Black's 16th move.

AMATEUR TOURNAMENT AT ST. PETERSBURG

17. P × B P !

The basic idea of this sacrifice, the consequences of which were not easy to determine, is to lure away the Black Q B. Furthermore White aims at the advance of his Q P (21st and 22nd moves) which is to make Black's Q Kt P indefensible.

| 17. ...... | B × R |
| 18. P × Kt ch | K—B 1 |

If 18. ....K—K 1 (K—Q 1 is evidently bad because of 19. Q—Kt 1, and 20. Q × P, threatening mate); 19. Q—Kt 1, P—Q 4; 20. B—Kt 5 ch, K—Q 1; (P—B 3; 21. B × P ch !) 21. B—Q 7 and White wins.

19. Q—Kt 1 !

The White Queen will, without loss of time, penetrate into the vitals of the hostile position.

| 19. ..... | P—B 3 ! |

An ingenious resource. If now 20. Q × B, P—Q 4; 21. B—Kt 3, Q × K P; and Black assumes the initiative. It is clear that after 19. ....P—Q Kt 3 or K—Kt 1, White, having captured the B, would have retained the attack, in addition to material advantage.

| 20. Q × P ! | P—B 4 |

The only way to prevent 21. R × P.

Position after Black's 20th move.

21. P—Q 4 !

Only this manœuvre can clearly demonstrate the soundness of the combination initiated by White's 17th move. Black cannot capture the Pawn, for after 21. ....K P × Q P ; 22. P × P, P × P ; 23. B—R 5 ! and mate cannot be prevented.

| 21. ...... | Q—Q B 2 |
| 22. P—Q 5 | |

Now the threat 23. R × P, is unanswerable. If 22. ....Q—Kt 1 ; 23. Q—R 4, R—Q 1 ; (or 23. ....Q—B 2 ; 24. R—Kt 5 ! followed by R—R 5, etc.) 24. R × P ! K × R ; (if Q × R ; 25. B—R 6 !) 25. Q—R 6 ch, K—B 2 ; 26. Q—B 6 mate.

22.	Kt—K 2
23. R × P	Q × R
24. B—R 6	B × P
25. P—B 4 !	

Winning another Pawn, the Black Bishop being held by the threat of 26. B—R 5 and mate next move.

25.	Q × B
26. Q × Q ch	B—Kt 2
27. Q × P	Kt—B 3
28. Kt P × P	Kt P × P
29. P—B 5 !	

The shortest way. Black is forced to capture the K B P, which involves the loss of a piece.

29.	R × P
30. Q—Q 7 ch	K—Kt 1
31. P—K 7	Kt × P
32. Q × Kt	K R—K B 1
33. Q—Q 6 ch	K—R 1
34. B × P	R (B 1)—B 3
35. Q—Q 8 ch	K—R 2
36. B—K 3	R—B 6
37. B × P ch	K—R 3
38. Q—Q Kt 8	Resigns

GAME 2

RUY LOPEZ

White :   *Black :*
B. VERLINSKI.   A. ALEKHIN.

1.	P—K 4	P—K 4
2.	Kt—K B 3	Kt—Q B 3
3.	B—Kt 5	P—Q R 3
4.	B×Kt	Q P×B
5.	P—Q 4	P×P
6.	Q×P	Q×Q
7.	Kt×Q	P—Q B 4
8.	Kt—K 2	B—Q 2
9.	P—Q Kt 3	

This move was played by Dr. Lasker in the first game of his match against Dr. Tarrasch (Düsseldorf, 1908). The latter continued : 9. ....B—B 3 ; 10. Kt—Q 2, B—K 2 ; 11. B—Kt 2, B—B 3 ; leading to an exchange of Bishops and the loss of his best chance—the conbined action of the two Bishops.

Position after White's 9th move.

9. ......   P—B 5 !

If Black fails to regain the Pawn thus sacrificed, he will have sufficient compensation in the dislocation of the White Pawn-position on the Queen-side. But, as the sequel shows, White cannot long maintain his advantage in material, which tends to prove the insufficiency of his last move. I consider that the reply 9. ....P—B 5 demolishes White's 9th move.

10.	P×P	B—R 5
11.	P—Q B 3	Castles

Position after Black's 11th move.

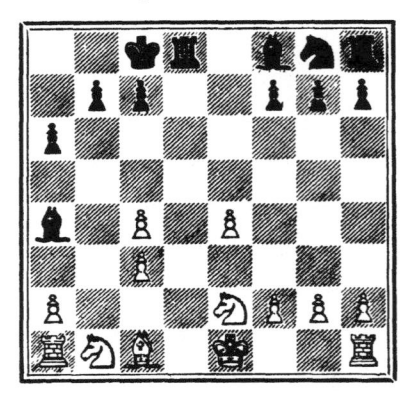

12. Kt—Q 2

Other moves would be no better ; *e.g.* : 12. Kt—Q 4, P—Q B 4 ; 13. Kt—Kt 3, R—K 1 ; 14. P—B 3, P—B 4 ; 15. Kt—Q 2, Kt—B 3 ; and Black has the better game. Or 12. Castles, B—B 7 ; 13. Kt—Q 2, Kt—B 3 ; 14. Kt—K Kt 3 (if 14. P—B 3, B—B 4 ch ; followed by 15. ....B—Q 6), B—B 4 ; and Black wins back his Pawn with an excellent game.

12.	......	B—B 7
13.	P—B 3	

13. Castles leads into the second variation shown above.

13. ......   B—B 4

Opposing 14. Kt—Q 4 (to which the reply is 14. ....R×Kt ! ; etc.) and forcing White to lose precious time to counteract the action of this Bishop.

14.	P—Q R 4	Kt—B 3
15.	B—R 3	

The blockade of Black's K B will be seen to be insufficient. The following variation offered better chances of a draw: 15. Kt—Q 4, B×Kt; 16. P×B, R×P; 17. B—Kt 2, R—Q 6, although in this case Black's pressure on the Q file would have been very harassing.

15.	B—K 6!
16. Kt—K B 1	B—R 2
17. P—R 5	

If 17. P—B 5 at once, then 17. ....B×R P.

17.	R—Q 6
18. P—B 5	K R—Q 1
19. K—B 2	

White could have held out longer by: 19. B—Kt 4, R—Q 8 ch; 20. R×R, R×R ch; 21. K—B 2, Kt—Q 2; 22. Kt (B 1)—Kt 3, R×R; 23. Kt×R, Kt×P; 24. B×Kt (if 24. K—K 1, Kt—Kt 6; followed by 25. ....P—Q B 4), B×B ch; 25. Kt—Q 4, P—Q Kt 3; 26. P×P, P×P; but the issue would not have been in doubt, as Black remains with his two Bishops and a passed Pawn.

The text-move gives Black the chance of an elegant finish.

| 19. ...... | Kt—Q 2 |
| 20. Kt—K 3 | |

See Diagram.

| 20. ...... | Kt×P! |

Threatening mate in 5 should White capture the B, *e.g.*: 21. Kt×B, Kt×P dbl. ch; 22. K—K 1, R—Q 8 ch!; 23. R×R, B—B 7 ch!; 24. K—B 1, R×R ch; 25. Kt—K 1, R×Kt mate.

Position after White's 20th move.

| 21. Kt—Q 4 | B—Kt 6 |

This wins the Q B P, for if 22. K R—Q B 1, or B—Kt 2, then 22. ....R (Q 6)×Kt (Q 5); followed by 23. ....Kt—Q 6 ch and Black wins.

| 22. K—K 2 | R×P |
| 23. B—Kt 2 | |

White could have avoided the loss of a piece by 23. Kt (Q 4)—B 5, which, however, would not have influenced the result.

23.	R×Kt ch!
24. K×R	Kt—K 3
25. R—R 3	

Or 25. K R—Q 1, B×R; 26. R×B, Kt×Kt; 27. B×Kt, B×B ch; 28. R×B, R×R; and the end-game is easily won for Black.

25.	Kt×Kt
26. K—B 4	B—B 4
27. K R—R 1	Kt—K 7 ch
28. K—Kt 4	B—K 3 ch
White resigns.	

CHAPTER II

INTERNATIONAL TOURNAMENT AT HAMBURG
JULY, 1910

GAME 3

FRENCH DEFENCE

White :	Black .
A. SPEYER.	A. ALEKHIN.

1. P—K 4   P—K 3
2. P—Q 4   P—Q 4
3. Kt—Q B 3   B—Kt 5

This move is far better than its reputation. Its object is to simplify the position, at any rate in the variation usually adopted by White, starting 4. P×P, a simplification which allows Black more easily to evolve a plan of development. It has been adopted with success at various times by Niemzovitch.

4. B—Q 2

This idea is interesting but does not produce any advantage if Black makes the correct reply. The most usual move is here 4. P×P, the consequences of 4. P—K 5, P—Q B 4 appearing to be rather in Black's favour (compare Dr. Lasker—Maróczy, New York, 1924).

See Diagram.

4. ......   Kt—K 2 !

Simplest, for the complications

Position after White's 4th move.

resulting from 4. ....P×P; 5. Q—Kt 4 would give White attacking chances : *e.g.* :

I. 5. ....Kt—K B 3; 6. Q×Kt P, R—Kt 1; 7. Q—R 6, Q×P; 8. Castles Q R, threatening 9. B—K Kt 5.

II. 5. ....Q×P; 6. Kt—B 3, Q—B 3; 7. Q×K P, followed by Castles Q R with good attacking chances for White.

5. P×P

White was threatened with : 5. ....P×P and 6. ....Q×P.

5. ......   P×P
6. Q—B 3

This is not a normal developing move. As the sequel will show, most of the White pieces will find themselves on unfavourable squares. It might have been better to play 6. B—Q 3 followed by 7. K Kt—K 2; 8. Castles, etc.

6. ......   Q Kt—B 3
7. B—Q Kt 5

compulsory after the last move.

7. ......   Castles
8. K Kt—K 2   B—K B 4

....The Black pieces, on the other hand, are well placed for concerted action.

9. Castles Q R

White's object in playing 6. Q—B 3 was to Castle on the Queen's side; this is a strategic error, however, for on the King's side White has no prospect which might compensate for Black's attack on the Queen's side. 9. R—Q B 1, followed by 10. Castles, was certainly not so bad.

9. ......   P—Q R 3 !

White's K B must be eliminated in order to allow a Black Knight to occupy Q B 5.

10. B—Q 3   B×B
11. Q×B   Kt—R 4 !
12. P—Q R 3

White takes advantage of the opportunity to force the exchange of one of Black's attacking pieces, for 12. ....B—Q 3 fails on account of 13. Kt×P, unmasking the White Bishop.

12. ......   B×Kt
13. B×B   Kt—B 5
14. Q R—K 1

Position after White's 14th move.

14. ......   Kt—B 3

Strategically, the game is already won by Black, but the latter here makes a slight tactical error, which allows his opponent to exchange Queens. The simple plan of attack to lead to an easy win would be: P—Q R 4 followed by P—Q Kt 4—5, etc. *The decision of the game could and should have been brought about by a direct attack on the King.*

15. Kt—B 4   Q—Q 3

Against any other move, White's reply 16. Q—B 3 would have been still more awkward for Black.

16. Q—B 3   Q R—Q 1

The plausible K R—Q 1 would have been wrong, for then 17. Kt×P, and if Q×Kt; 18. R—K 8 ch, etc. However, White now succeeds in exchanging Queens.

17. Kt—Q 3   P—Q R 4 !

....Better late than never!

18. Q—B 4

Else Black's attack would become irresistible.

18. ......   Q×Q ch

If 18. ....Q—Q 2 ; White could already try a counter-demonstration with 19. P—K R 4 followed by R—R 3.

19. Kt × Q   P—Q Kt 4

This advance remains strong even after the exchange of Queens, for the White Bishop is very badly placed.

20. Kt—Q 3   R—Kt 1
21. Kt—K 5

There does not appear to be any other method of saving the Pawn. But after the exchange of Knights Black finds fresh resources for the attack, with the aid of his Q B P.

21. ......   Kt (B 3) × Kt
22. P × Kt   P—Q B 4 !

Less good would have been : 22. ....P—Kt 5 ; 23. P×P, P×P ; 24. B—Q 4, R—R 1 ; 26. P—Q Kt 3, etc.

23. P—Q Kt 3

again the only chance against the threat of P—Kt 5, etc.

Position after White's 23rd move.

23. ......   P—Q 5 !

The winning move, for this Pawn will exert a decisive pressure in the ensuing Rook end-game. Should White avoid the exchange of pieces by 24. B—Kt 2, Black obtains a winning advantage by : 24. ....Kt—Kt 3 followed by P—R 5.

24. P × Kt   P × B
25. R—K 3

Compulsory, for after 25. P×P, R×P ; this move would not be feasible because of 26. ....K R—Kt 1.

25. ......   P—Kt 5
26. P—Q R 4   Q R—Q 1

Position after Black's 26th move.

For the better appreciation of this end-game, it may be pointed out that White cannot here offer the exchange of both Rooks ; *e.g. :*

27. R—Q 1, R × R ch ; 28. K × R, R—Q 1 ch ; 29. R—Q 3, R × R ch ; 30. P × R, P—Kt 4 ; 31. P—R 3, P—R 4 ! 32. P—Kt 3 (if 32. P—B 3, P—R 5 ;), P—Kt 5 ! followed by K—B 1, K 2, K 3 and K × P winning.

White's subsequent moves are therefore forced.

27. K R—K 1   R—Q 5
28. R—K 4   R × R
29. R × R   R—Q 1
30. P—K 6

If 30. R—K 2 Black would win a Pawn by 30. ....R—Q 5.

30.	P×P
31. R×P	R—Q 7

After this incursion by the Black Rook the remainder of the game is purely a matter of technique.

32. R—K 5	R×P
33. K—Kt 1	R—B 8 ch
34. K—R 2	R—B 8
35. R×P	R×P ch
36. K—Kt 1	R—Kt 7 ch
37. K—B 1	R×P
38. R—Q Kt 5	

to parry the threat of P—Kt 6.

38.	K—B 2
39. P—B 5	K—K 3
40. P—B 6	K—Q 3
41. P—B 7	K×P
42. R×R P	R×P
43. R—Q Kt 5	R—Q Kt 7
44 P—R 5	K—B 3
45. R—Kt 8	K—B 4
46. P—R 6	R—Q R 7
47. R—B 8 ch	K—Kt 4
48. R—Kt 8 ch	K—B 5

White resigns.

GAME 4

QUEEN'S GAMBIT DECLINED

White :	*Black :*
A. ALEKHIN.	F. D. YATES.
1. P—Q 4	P—Q 4
2. P—Q B 4	P—K 3
3. Kt—Q B 3	Kt—K B 3
4. B—Kt 5	B—K 2
5. Kt—B 3	Q Kt—Q 2
6. P—K 3	Castles
7. Q—B 2	

This move, followed by Castles Q R, was very fashionable from 1903 to 1911 until Teichmann, in a well-known game against Rotlevi (Carlsbad, 1911) proved its inferiority. In itself the move 7. Q—B 2 is not bad, but if Black should make the best reply, 7. ....P—B 4, White, instead of castling, should play 8. R—Q 1.

The position is then identical with that of the fourth and tenth games of the Capablanca-Lasker match (with transposition of moves) and offers chances to both White and Black.

7.	P—Q Kt 3

After this reply Castles Q R affords White very good chances of attack, for the Pawn at Q Kt 3 hinders an immediate counter-attack by Black, obstructing Q R 4 and Q Kt 3 for the Queen and Q Kt 3 for the Knight.

8. P×P	P×P
9. B—Q 3	B—Kt 2
10. P—K R 4 !	

An important move preventing the liberating move 10. ....Kt—K 5, which would be playable if White at once Castled Q R.

10.	P—B 4
11. Castles Q R	P×P

If 11. ....P—B 5 White would have seized the initiative by 12. B—B 5, P—Q R 3 ; 13. P—K 4.

12. K Kt×P

By this move White wishes to secure possibilities of attack against the isolated Q P, as shown for instance in the following variation : 12. ....Kt—K 4 ; 13. B×Kt, Kt×B ch ; 14. Q×Kt, B×B ; 15. K—Kt 1 followed by 16. R—Q B 1, 17. P—K Kt 3 and 18. K R—Q 1. Instead of 12. K Kt×P White could equally well have played 12. P×P.

12.	R—K 1

Probably played so as to be able to withdraw the Bishop to K B 1 if White attacks it by Kt—B 5, but this manœuvre loses time for Black. He should have tried for a counter-attack on the Queen-side by P—Q R 3 and P—Q Kt 4 without delay.

13. K—Kt 1

To stop Black from making the embarrassing reply 14..... Kt—K 4, threatening to take the K B with check, after the intended 14. P—K Kt 4.

| 13. ...... | P—Q R 3 |
| 14. P—K Kt 4 | P—Kt 4 |

This move, played after mature consideration, nevertheless shows itself insufficient, because of a Rook sacrifice by White on his 22nd move, which Black could scarcely have foreseen at this stage of the game.

Nevertheless, if Black instead of the text-move had played 14. .... Kt—B 1 White would equally have secured a clear advantage by 15. K R—Kt 1, P—Kt 4 ; 16. Kt—B 5.

15. B × Kt	Kt × B
16. P—Kt 5	Kt—K 5
17. Kt × Kt	P × Kt
18. B × K P	B × B
19. Q × B	B × P

Now Black has obtained the position he played for with 14. ....P—Kt 4.

Position after Black's 19th move.

20. Kt—K 6 !

This combination will ultimately force Black to give up a Pawn, thus allowing White to gain the victory after an interesting end-game.

| 20. ...... | Q—K 2 |
| 21. P × B | P—R 3 |

Forced, for after 21. ....P—Kt 3 ; White has an immediate win by 22. R × P ! Q × Kt ! ; 23. Q—K R 4, Q—K 5 ch ; 24. Q × Q, R × Q ; 25. Q R—R 1, etc. This is the crux of the attack inaugurated by 16. P—Kt 5.

| 22. P × P | Q × Kt |
| 23. Q—Q 4 ! | |

If White exchanges Queens at once the Black Rook recaptures at K 3, where it would be well posted. The object of the text-move is to force the Rook to recapture at K 5, a less favourable square.

23.	Q—K 5 ch
24. Q × Q	R × Q
25. P × P	K × P

With an extra Pawn and the better position White should certainly win. However, the Rook-ending which now follows presents certain technical difficulties

26. Q R—Kt 1 ch	K—B 3
27. R—R 6 ch	K—K 2
28. R—Q B 1	R—R 2
29. R (B 1)—B 6 !	P—R 4

Black's last moves were compulsory. 29. ....R—K 3 would have been disastrous because of 30. Q R × R ch followed by R—R 7 ch, etc.

30. R—R 6	R × R
31. R × R	P—R 5
32. R—Q Kt 6	R—K 4
33. K—B 2	R—B 4 ch
34. K—Q 3	K—Q 2

If 34. ....R—Q 4 ch ; then 35. K—K 4, R—Q B 4 ; 36. P—R 3,

followed by 37. P—B 4 ; 38. K—Q 4, etc.

| 35. P—R 3 | R—B 4 |

....To play K—B 2

36. P—B 4	K—B 2
37. R—K R 6	R—Q 4 ch
38. K—B 3	P—B 4

By this move, which is his last chance, Black prevents 39. P—K 4.

| 39. R—K 6 ! | K—Q 2 |

Position after Black's 39th move.

This is the most interesting phase of the ending. At first sight an exchange of Rooks seems of doubtful value, for after 40. R—K 5, R ×R ; 41. P ×R, K—K 2 ! White cannot play 42. K—Q 4, because of 42..... K—K 3. On the other hand the variation 42. K—Kt 4, K—K 3 ; 43. K ×P, K ×P ; etc., only leads to a draw, the Black B P queening one move later than the White Q P. The end-game, however, is won by White, thanks to a little artifice.

40. R—K 5 !	R ×R
41. P ×R	K—K 2
42. K—Q 3	K—Q 2
43. P—K 4	P—B 5
44. K—K 2 !	

Forcing Black to attack the Pawn.

| 44. ...... | K—K 3 |

If now 45. K—B 3 ?, K ×P ; and Black wins ! White's next move settles the question.

| 45. K—B 2 ! | Black resigns. |

CHAPTER III

INTERNATIONAL TOURNAMENT AT CARLSBAD
JULY—AUGUST, 1911

GAME 5

FOUR KNIGHTS' GAME

White: Black:
A. ALEKHIN. DR. VIDMAR.

1. P—K 4   P—K 4
2. Kt—K B 3   Kt—Q B 3
3. Kt—B 3   Kt—B 3
4. B—Kt 5   B—Kt 5
5. Castles   Castles
6. B×Kt   Kt P×B

After the better move: 6. .... Q P×B; White can either obtain an easy draw by 7. Kt×P, R—K 1; 8. Kt—Q 3, B×Kt; 9. Q P×B, Kt×P; 10. Q—B 3, or he can attempt a King-side attack by 7. P—Q 3 followed by Kt—K 2, Kt—Kt 3, P—K R 3, Kt—R 2, P—K B 4. But in my opinion Black can repel this attack, for he has two Bishops and good chances of a counter-attack on the Queen's file.

7. Kt×P   Q—K 1

After 7. .... R—K 1; 8. P—Q 4, B×Kt; 9. P×B, Kt×P; 10. Q—B 3, etc. White obtains a slight advantage.

8. Kt—Kt 4

Here the following line is considered stronger: 8. Kt—Q 3, with the continuation 8. ....B×Kt; 9. Q P×B, Q×P; 10. R—K 1, Q—K R 5; 11. Q—B 3, and 12. B—B 4. It is, however, uncertain whether this line of play is sufficient to prevail against a correct defence. The fault lies in the variation 6. B×Kt, which, in this opening, proves to be dull and lifeless.

8. ......   Kt×P

With 8. Kt×Kt; 9. Q×Kt, P—Q 4; 10. Q—R 4, B×Kt; 11. Kt P×B (threatening 12. B—R 3), Q×P; 12. Q×Q, P×Q; etc., Black could bring about a draw. The complications which he seeks with the text-move turn out to his discomfiture.

See Diagram.

9. Kt—R 6 ch!

With this unexpected sally, White completely assumes the initiative. It would have been relatively better for Black to remove the audacious Knight, though in that case also White's game would have remained superior after: 9. ....P×Kt; 10. Q—Kt 4 ch, K—R 1: 11. Q×Kt, Q×Q; (or 11. ....B×Kt; 12. Q×Q, R×Q; 13. Q P×B, etc.) 12. Kt×Q, B—K 2; 13. P—Q 3, P—K B 4; 14. Kt—B 3, P—B 5; 15. R—K 1 followed by R—K 4.

Position after Black's 8th move.

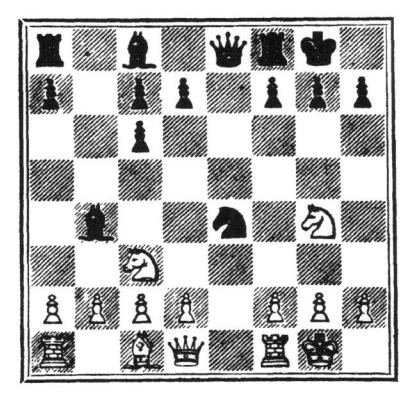

9. ......   K—R 1
10. R—K 1

This pin which, on the previous move, would not have been favourable because of the reply: 9. .... P—Q 4; (threatening 10. ....B × K Kt, etc.) now causes Black serious difficulties.

10. ......   P—Q 4
11. P—Q 3   Q—K 4

The alternative was: 11. .... Kt × Kt; 12. P × Kt, B—K 2; 13. Q—R 5, B—K 3; 14. P—K B 4, etc. with good prospects for White.

In giving preference to the text-move, Black probably did not sufficiently consider the consequences of 16. R—Kt 1.

12. P × Kt   P—Q 5
13. P—Q R 3   P × Kt
14. P × B   P × P
15. Kt × P ch

Here White had the choice between the variation in the text and the equally good continuation 15. R—Kt 1, with the sequel: 15. .... Q—K 3; (if P × B (Q); 16. Kt × P ch and Kt × Q) 16. R × P, P × Kt; 17. R—Kt 3, and Black, forced to prevent B—Kt 2 ch followed by R—Kt 3 ch, will thus lose the K R P.

However, I gave the preference to the text-move both because I did not wish to give Black any chance of counter-action on an open K Kt file opposite the castled White King, and because the consequences of Kt × P ch seemed to be simpler and equally certain.

15. ......   K—Kt 1

Position after Black's 15th move.

16. R—Kt 1!

With this move White secures an advantage in material. Indeed, Black has nothing better than to bring about an ending with Bishops of different colour, for the variation 16. ....P × B (Q); 17. Kt × Q, Q—K B 5; 18. Kt—Q 3, etc., leaves him not the slightest chance. On the contrary, White has chances of further gain, based not only on the possession of an extra Pawn, but also on the clear majority of Pawns on the King-side. On the Queen-side Black's extra Pawn is quite a negligible quantity, as two of his Pawns are doubled.

16. ......   R × Kt
17. B × P   Q—K Kt 4
18. Q—Q 3

Preventing 18. ....B—R 6.

18. ......   B—K 3
19. B—Q 4

Threatening 20. R—Q 1, etc. Black's only choice lies between the exchange of Queens or the loss of another Pawn.

19. ......   R—Q 1
20. Q—K 3

Position after White's 20th move.

20. ......   Q—Kt 4

In the hope of creating complications with the Queens on the board. After 20. ....Q × Q ; 21. B × Q, P—Q R 3 ; White would have an easily won game, *e.g.* : 22. K R—Q 1, K R—Q 2 ; 23. R × R, R × R ; 24. P—K B 3, K—K 1 ; 25. R—R 1, B—B 5 ; 26. K—B 2 followed by K—K 1, R—R 3, R—B 3, R—B 5, P—Q B 4, etc.

21. B × R P   Q—R 5
22. P—Q B 3   B—B 5
23. B—Q 4

He could have occupied the Q R file now, but White is in no hurry, his opponent having no means of preventing this manœuvre.

23. ......   R—R 1
24. Q—Q 2   P—R 3
25. P—R 3   Q—Kt 4

Else White would play 26. Q—Kt 2 followed by R—R 1.

26. R—R 1   R—R 5
27. Q—B 2   R × R
28. R × R   B—Q 6
29. R—R 8 ch   K—R 2
30. Q—R 2   Q—K R 4

If 30. ....B—B 5 ; 31. Q—R 7 followed by Q or R—Kt 8, etc.

31. Q—K 6

The Queen's irruption into the adverse position decides the game in a few moves.

Position after White's 31st move.

31. ......   B—B 8

Black has no satisfactory defence and so he can without danger indulge in this little pleasantry.

32. R—R 5   Q—Q 8
33. K—R 2   B × P

The last chance. If White takes the Rook he loses his Queen by Q—R 8 ch, Q × P ch, and Q—B 6 ch, etc.

34. K×B	Q—B 6 ch
35. K—Kt 1	R—B 5
36. R—R 8	

Threatening mate in three, commencing with 37. Q—Kt 8 ch.

36.	R—B 2
37. Q—Kt 4	Q—Q 6
38. R—K B 8	Black resigns.

GAME 6

THREE KNIGHTS GAME

White :	Black :
S. ALAPIN.	A. ALEKHIN.
1. P—K 4	P—K 4
2. Kt—K B 3	Kt—K B 3
3. Kt—B 3	B—Kt 5

This variation (an inverted Lopez) has often been played, with success, by Pillsbury. It seems sufficiently strong to equalize the position.

4. Kt×P	Q—K 2

The most normal continuation is 4. ....Castles ; 5. B—K 2, R—K 1 ; 6. Kt—Q 3, B×Kt ; 7. Q P×B, Kt×P ; 8. Castles, P—Q 3 ; with an equal game. However, 4. ....Q—K 2 is equally good.

5. Kt—Q 3	B×Kt
6. Q P×B	Kt×P
7. B—K 2	P—Q 4

This last move is not at all in the spirit of the opening, as it allows White to undouble his Pawns immediately. He should have played 7. ....Castles ; 8. Castles, P—Q 3.

8. Castles	Castles
9. Kt—B 4	

See Diagram.

9.	P—Q B 3

Forced, as 9. ....R—Q 1 ; would be bad on account of 10. Kt×P !, Q—K 4 ; (or Q—Q 3 ; 11. P—

Position after White's 9th move.

Q B 4, etc.) 11. P—Q B 4, P—Q B 3 ; 12. B—B 4, Q—K 3 : 13. B—Kt 4 !, P—K B 4 ; 14. B×P, and if then Q×B ; 15. Kt—K 7 ch and the Black Queen is lost. Now White assumes the initiative.

10. P—B 4	P×P
11. B×P	B—B 4
12. Q—K 2	

Not 12. R—K 1 because of 12. ....Q—B 4.

12.	R—K 1
13. R—K 1	

This pin on the King's file is very troublesome for Black.

13.	Q—Q 2

After 13. ....Q—B 1 ; White could by 14. Q—R 5 provoke the weakening 14. ....P—K Kt 3.

14. B—K 3	P—Q Kt 4

To be able at last to bring out the Q Kt (via R 3).

15. Q R—Q 1	

White has played the opening well, but this is slightly weak, and he loses the positional advantage he has acquired. The text-move appears to be good, as it brings into play a non-developed piece without loss of time. But it allows Black to bring his Q Kt to a more favourable square than Q R 3. The logical sequence would have been : 15. B—Kt 3, Kt—R 3 ; 16. Q R—Q 1, Q—B 2 (or B 1) ; 17. Q—R 5 and White has the better game.

15. ......   Q—B 2
16. B—Q 3

More promising would have been B—Kt 3.

16. ......   Kt—Q 2

Position after Black's 16th move.

17. P—K B 3

Here White seems to pursue a will-of-the-wisp. The simplest and best plan would have been to try to equalize and to play for a draw, *e.g.* . 17. P—K Kt 4, B—Kt 3 ; 18. Kt×B, R P×Kt ; 19. B×Kt, R×B ; 20. B—Kt 6 !, R×Q ; 21. B×Q, R×R ch ; 22. R×R, etc.

17. ......   Kt—Q 3
18. P—K Kt 4

White thinks quite erroneously that Black cannot exchange Bishops without losing a piece.

18. ......   B×B
19. Q×B

Position after White's 19th move.

19. ......   Kt—K 4 !

The soundness of this move rests on the following main variation : 20. Q×Kt, Kt×P ch ; 21. K—B 2, Q×Q ; 22. R×Q, Kt×R ; 23. R—Q 2 !, P—Kt 3 ; 24. R—K 2, R×B ; 25. K×R, R—K 1 ch ; 26. K—Q 2, Kt—B 6 ch ; 27. K—B 3, R×R ; 28. Kt×R, P—Q B 4 ; etc. To avoid this losing line of play, White is reduced to a retreating manœuvre which will cost him a Pawn.

20. Q—B 1   Kt (Q 3)—B 5
21. B—B 1   Q—R 4

This threatens 22. ....Kt×P ch ; and so White must submit to the loss of the R P. Against that, however, the Black Queen, after capturing the R P, will momentarily be out of play, which will give White the necessary time to inaugurate a counter-attack.

22. R—K 2   Q×P
23. Q R—K 1

Now Black is under compulsion to provide against 24. P—Kt 3, winning a piece.

23. ......   P—B 3
24. Kt—Q 3   R—K B 1
25. P—Kt 3   Kt—Q 3
26. Kt×Kt   P×Kt
27. Q—Kt 2

INTERNATIONAL TOURNAMENT AT CARLSBAD

Threatening R × P, as now White's Q B P is covered by the Queen.

27. ......   Q R—K 1

Position after Black's 27th move

28. P—K B 4!

Conscious of his chances, White is wanting in neither energy nor astuteness. Indeed, he has prospects of a draw. Much less strong would have been: 28. R × P, R × R; 29. R × R, Q—R 8; 30. R—K 1, Q—B 3; 31. R—B 1, P—Q R 4; giving Black a clear advantage.

28. ......   P—K 5

The only move. If 28. ....P × P; 29. R × R, Kt × R; (or R × R; 30. R × R ch, Kt × R; 31. Q × P, etc.) 30. Q × P, Q—R 8; 31. Q—K 6 ch followed by 32. Q × Kt and White wins.

29. P—B 5   Q—R 8

The only way to bring the Queen back into play.

30. Q—Kt 3

The object of this move is clear; it aims at keeping out the adverse Queen. However, it gives Black the chance of a counter-attack. Better would have been: 30. B—B 4, Q—Q 5 ch; 31. K—R 1 (not 31. Q—B 2 because of 31. ....P—K 6; followed by Kt—K 5; and Black has the better game.) Kt—Kt 2; 32. R × P, R × R; 33. Q × R, Q × Q; 34. R × Q, K—B 2, with good prospects of a draw for White in spite of Black's majority of Pawns on the Queen's side.

30. ......   Kt—B 2
31. P—B 3

Position after White's 31st move.

31. ......   P—Kt 5!

The beginning of the final attack. By sacrificing his K P, Black easily brings his Queen into the centre of the Board, where, in co-ordination with the Knight, her action proves deadly, as the White King's position is dangerously exposed by reason of the advance of his Pawns.

32. B—Kt 2

Had White played 32. B—Q 2, the sequence would have been the same, with the difference that the Black Knight would have entered via K 4 instead of Kt 4.

32. ......   Q—R 4
33. R × P   R × R
34. R × R   Q—Q 4
35. R—K 2

A trap. If 35. ....Q×Kt P; 36. P×P, Q×P; 37. Q—Q B 3, Q× P ch; (or if....Q×Q; 38. B×Q, with an easy draw) 39. R—Kt 2, Q—Q 8 ch; 40. K—B 2 and White wins.

35. ......   Q—Q 8 ch
36. Q—K 1   Q×P
37. P×P   Kt—Kt 4

The entry of the Knight should have decided the game in a few moves.

38. Q—B 3   Kt—R 6 ch
39. K—B 1

The only move, for, if 39. K—R 1, Q—Q 4 ch; and if 39. K—Kt 2, Kt—B 5 ch; winning in either case.

39. ......   Q—Q 8 ch
40. Q—K 1   Q—Q 4

Threatening Q—R 8 mate, which can only be prevented by R—K 4.

41. R—K 4.

Position after White's 41st move.

41. ......   Kt—Kt 4

This move wins ultimately, but the logical sequel to the attack initiated by 31. ....P—Kt 5; would have been 41.....P—K R 4;

42. Q—B 3 (there evidently is nothing better), R×P ch; 43. P×R, Q×P ch; 44. K—Kt 2, Q×R ch; 45. K×Kt, Q—Kt 5 mate. The text-move allows White to struggle on for some time.

42. Q—B 3   R—B 3!
43. R—Q 4   Q—R 8 ch
44. K—K 2   Q×P ch
45. K—Q 1   P—K R 4!
46. R—Q 7

Evidently threatening R×P ch, etc.

46. ......   Kt—B 2

Position after Black's 46th move.

47. P—K Kt 5

A desperate venture which only results in the loss of White's Kingside Pawns. The trap is as follows: 47. ....Q—Kt 8 ch; 48. Q—K 1, Q×Q ch; (or Q×P; 49. Q—K 8 ch, etc.); 49. K×Q, R×P; 50. P—Kt 6, etc.

47. ......   Q—Kt 8 ch
48. Q—K 1   R—Q 3 ch!

leading to an easily won end-game.

49. R×R   Q×Q ch
50. K×Q   Kt×R
51. P—B 6   P×P
52. B×P

Evidently 52. P×P was no better, as the Pawn could not be defended.

52.	K—B 2
53. B—Q 4	P—R 3
54. K—K 2	K—Kt 3
55. K—Q 3	

or 55. B—B 6, Kt—K 5, etc.

55.	K×P
56. B—K 5	Kt—B 4
57. K—B 4	P—R 5
58. B—R 2	K—Kt 5
59. K—B 5	K—R 6
60. B—B 7	K—Kt 7
61. K×P	P—R 6
62. K—Kt 6	Kt—Kt 6
63. K×P	P—R 7
64. P—Kt 5	P—R 8=(Q)
65. P—Kt 6	Kt—K 5
66. P—Kt 7	Kt—B 4 ch

White resigns.

GAME 7

ENGLISH OPENING

White : *Black :*
A. ALEKHIN. O. CHAJES.

1. P—Q B 4	P—K 3
2. P—K 4	P—Q B 4

Simpler and better would be 2. ....P—Q 4 ; 3. K P×P, P×P ; 4. P—Q 4, Kt—K B 3 ; leading to a good variation of the French Defence. After the text-move White can obtain a very good game by 3. Kt—K B 3, Kt—Q B 3 ; 4. P—Q 4, etc.

3. Kt—Q B 3	Kt—Q B 3
4. Kt—B 3	P—K Kt 3

The right move here is : 4. .... Kt—Q 5 (as played in a game Alekhin—Leonhardt in the same tournament), after which Black obtains at least an even game. The text-move weakens the Black squares and White takes advantage of it in an energetic manner.

5. P—Q 4	P×P
6. Kt×P	B—Kt 2
7. K Kt—Kt 5 !	

This demonstrates the weakness of Black's fourth move. Now, in order to protect his Q 3, he must lose a *tempo* with his Bishop.

7.	B—K 4
8. P—B 4	

In order to reply to B—Kt 1 ; by 9. P—Q B 5, etc., thus permanently blocking the position.

Position after White's 8th move.

8.	P—Q R 3

Black attempts to bring about complications which would turn to his advantage upon the slightest mistake on White's part.

9. P×B	P×Kt
10. B—B 4	P×P
11. B×P	

White has now a splendid development and threatens 12. Kt—Kt 5 (after possibly 11. .... Q—Kt 3) or 12. Castles K R with an attack on the K B file.

11. ......   R—R 4

Directed against 12. Kt—Kt 5, which would now be countered by 12. ....R×Kt; 13. B×R, Q—R 4 ch; etc. It also threatens: 12. ....P—Q 4.

12. Castles!   P—Q Kt 4

12. ....Kt×P; would be disastrous because of 13. B×Kt, R×B; 14. Q—Q 6! followed by Kt—Kt 5, etc.

Position after Black's 12th move.

13. P—Q Kt 4!

This combination, both elegant and sound, gives White a winning attack. The temporary sacrifice of two minor pieces for a Rook will allow the White Queen to enter decisively into the game. The point is the 17th move, R—Q Kt 1.

13. ......   Q—Kt 3 ch
14. K—R 1   Kt×Kt P
15. B×Kt P   R×B

It is clear that Black has no alternative.

16. Kt×R   Q×Kt

Position after Black's 16th move.

17. R—Q Kt 1!

This pin is decisive, as Black cannot relieve it, *e.g.*: 17. ....Q—B 4; 18. R—B 1, or 17. ....Q—B 5; 18. Q—R 4, or again 17. ....Q—R 4; 18. B—Q 2, winning in each case.

17. ......   B—R 3
18. Q—Q 6

Played not with a view to an immediate capture of the Q Kt, but in order to prevent 18. ....Kt—K 2; because of 19. Q×Kt, Q×Q; 20. R×Q, B×R; 21. R—Kt 8 ch, etc.

18. ......   P—B 3
19. K R—B 1   Q—Q 6

Now the Knight must be taken.

20. R×Kt   P—Kt 4
21. R—Q 4   Q—Kt 4
22. P—Q R 4   Q—Kt 2
23. R—B 7   Q—Kt 8 ch
24. R—Q 1   Black resigns.

GAME 8

ENGLISH OPENING

White: *Black:*
A. ALEKHIN.   F. DUS-
                 CHOTIMIRSKI.

1. P—Q B 4   P—K 4
2. Kt—Q B 3   Kt—K B 3
3. P—K Kt 3

With this move White obtains a favourable variation of the Sicilian Defence with the additional advantage of having a move in hand.

3.	P—Q 4
4. P×P	Kt×P
5. B—Kt 2	B—K 3
6. Kt—B 3	P—K B 3

This move weakens the position of Black's Q B and will cause Black many difficulties. 6. .... Kt—Q B 3, the natural move, was far better.

| 7. Castles | Kt—B 3 |

In playing 6. ....P—K B 3; Black most probably intended continuing 7. ....P—Q B 4, but noticed in time that this advance would be downright bad because of the reply 8. Q—Kt 3 threatening 9. Kt×P. After the text-move 8. Q—Kt 3 would not have the same sting because of the defence: 8. ....B—Q Kt 5.

| 8. P—Q 4 | |

After the exchange of Black's K P, which is now compulsory, the weakness of 6. ....P—K B 3 becomes manifest.

8.	P×P
9. Kt—Q Kt 5 !	B—Q B 4
10. Q Kt×Q P	Kt×Kt
11. Kt×Kt	B—B 2

The alternative was: 11. ....B×Kt; 12. Q×B, Castles; 13. R—Q 1 and the White Bishop exercises an overwhelming pressure on Black's game. The text-move is, however, hardly better, because it deprives Black of the chance of Castling.

See Diagram.

| 12. Q—R 4 ch ! | K—B 1 |

Compulsory, for if 12. ....P—B 3; then 13. Kt×P, etc.; and if

Position after Black's 11th move.

12. ....Q—Q 2; 13. Q×Q ch, K×Q; 14. R—Q 1, threatening 15. P—K 4, and Black's position would be even more compromised than as actually played.

13. R—Q 1	Q—K 2
14. P—K 4	Kt—Kt 3
15. Q—B 2	B×Kt

Relatively best, for White threatened to win a piece by Kt—B 5.

| 16. R×B | P—Q B 4 |
| 17. R—Q 3 | P—Kt 4 |

Black decides on this desperate advance in the hope of getting his K R into action. Naturally the weakness caused thereby will open new avenues of attack for White.

| 18. B—K 3 | |

Here 18. P—Kt 3, was to be considered, as White can then retain his two Bishops, *e.g.*: 18. ....P—B 5; 19. P×P, Kt×P; 20. R—Q B 3, R—B 1; with 21. ....K—Kt 2 to follow. But in this variation Black has more resources than in the actual game.

18.	Kt—B 5
19. Q R—Q 1	Kt×B
20. R×Kt	K—Kt 2
21. P—K 5 !	

The beginning of an attack which leads to a speedy win.

21. ......   Q R—Q 1

Disastrous would be 21....P × P; 22. Q R—K 1, etc. But 21. .... K R—K 1; leaving the Black King a refuge at R 1, would have given Black better chances of defence.

22. Q R—K 1!

Insufficient to win would have been: 22. R×R, R×R; 23. P × P ch, Q × P; 24. B × P, R—Q Kt 1; etc. Now White threatens 23. P × P ch, Q × P; 24. B × P, R—Q Kt 1; 25. R—K 7, etc.

22. ......   P—Kt 3
23. P—B 4

White's main threat is to establish a very strong passed Pawn by 24. P—K 6, followed by P—B 5.

23. ......   P × B P
24. P × P   P × P
25. R—Kt 3 ch!

The check was essential at this precise moment in order to prevent Black's B—Kt 3. He could not play it now because of 26. P—B 5 winning a piece. The Black King must therefore take flight to a square where he will be exposed to attack.

25. ......   K—B 1
26. P × P

Position after White's 26th move.

26. ......   Q—K 3

Black has no longer a sufficient defence, *e.g.*: 26. ....B—Kt 3; 27. R×B!, P×R; 28. Q×Kt P, Q×P; 29. R—B 1 ch, followed by R—B 7 ch and White wins. Or 26. ....B—K 3; 27. R—B 1 ch, K—K 1; 28. B—B 6 ch, B—Q 2; 29. Q—Kt 2 and White wins.

27. B—R 3   Q—B 5
28. Q—B 2   Q—Q 5

Or 28. ....K—K 1; 29. P—K 6, B—Kt 3; 30. P—K 7, R—Q Kt 1; 31. R—K B 3, B—B 2; 32. R×B, followed by B—Q 7 ch and White wins.

29. P—K 6   Q × Q ch
30. K × Q   R—Q 7 ch
31. K—K 3   R × Kt P
32. R—K B 1   R × Q R P
33. R × B ch K—K 1
34. R—Q Kt 7 R—R 6 ch
35. K—K 4   R × R
36. P × R   R—B 1
37. B—Kt 4   Black resigns.

CHAPTER IV

INTERNATIONAL TOURNAMENT AT STOCKHOLM
JUNE, 1912

GAME 9

PHILIDOR'S DEFENCE

White :	Black :
A. ALEKHIN.	G. MARCO.

1. P—K 4	P—K 4
2. Kt—K B 3	P—Q 3
3. P—Q 4	Kt—K B 3
4. Kt—B 3	Q Kt—Q 2

Marco's favourite defence, which I also have adopted on several occasions (compare game No. 47), but I have since come to the conclusion that against logical and sound play it is not altogether satisfactory.

5. B—Q B 4	B—K 2
6. Castles	

Sacrificial combinations commencing 6. Kt—Kt 5 or 6. B×P ch turn to Black's advantage.

6.	Castles

After Castling, Black's development becomes laborious and he has not the slightest chance of a counter-attack. It seems to be more in the spirit of the defence to play : 6. .... P—K R 3 followed by P—B 3, Q—B 2, Kt—B 1, P—K Kt 4 and Kt—Kt 3. This system was adopted successfully by my opponent in several recent tournaments (Yates—Marco, The Hague, 1921 ; Wolf—Marco, Pistyan, 1922). This line of play forces White to play with great care, for Black's manœuvre on the Kingside may develop into a serious attack.

7. Q—K 2	P—B 3
8. P—Q R 4 !	

In this variation it is essential once and for all to prevent Black's P—Q Kt 4.

8.	P—K R 3

The anxiety to provide against Kt—Kt 5 or B—Kt 5 is natural enough, but the resultant weakening of the King's position may have unfortunate consequences, as the bad development of the Black pieces does not warrant this move.

9. B—Kt 3	

After 9. B—K 3 Black could have played 9. ....Kt×P, followed by P—Q 4. By preventing this manœuvre, the text-move maintains White's supremacy in the centre. However B—R 2 would have been still better (see Bogoljuboff v. Niemzovitch, Stockholm, 1920).

9.	Q—B 2
10. P—K R 3	

To prevent Black from playing Kt—Kt 5 in reply to 11. B—K 3.

10. ......   K—R 2

Black adopts an unsound plan in an already difficult position. The development of the Queen-side by P—Q Kt 3, B—Kt 2 and Q R—Q 1, followed by an attempt to stabilize matters in the centre by P—Q B 4, would have been more to be recommended.

11. B—K 3   P—K Kt 3
12. Q R—Q 1 K—Kt 2

All this laborious manœuvring aims at getting the K R into play. But Black will not have even this meagre satisfaction, as White, now fully developed, will initiate a direct attack on the Black King.

13. Kt—K R 2!   Kt—K Kt 1

If 13. ....Kt—R 4; then 14. Q—Q 2, followed by P—Kt 4 and P—B 4, etc.

14. P—B 4   P—B 3

Position after Black's 14th move.

15. Q—Kt 4!

The strongest continuation of the attack. The plausible 15. P—B 5 would be less energetic, *e.g.*: 15. ....P×Q P; 16. B×P, Kt—K 4; 17. B×Kt, B P×B!; 18. Q—Kt 4, B—Kt 4; and Black's position is defensible. After the move in the text Black has nothing better than to sacrifice the K Kt P, which will give him the necessary time to exchange the White K B. If on move 9 White had played B—R 2 Black would not have even this small resource.

15. ......   P×Q P
16. B×P   Kt—B 4
17. P—B 5!   Kt×B

Or 17. ....P—Kt 4; 18. B×Kt followed by Q—R 5 and wins.

18. Q×P ch   K—R 1
19. P×Kt   B—Q 2

If now 20. Kt—Kt 4? the White Queen is lost by 20. ....B—K 1.

20. Q—Kt 3   R—B 2
21. Kt—Kt 4

threatening 22. P—K 5, etc.

21. ......   Q—Q 1
22. Kt—K 2!

This Knight now journeys to Kt 6 and decides the game in a few moves.

22. ......   R—Kt 2
23. Kt—B 4   Q—K 1
24. Q—R 4   Q—B 2
25. R—Q 3

Here White could have won a second Pawn by Kt×R P, but he prefers to play for a mate.

25. ......   K—R 2
26. Kt—Kt 6

See Diagram.

26. ......   R×Kt

Frustrating White's intended combination, which would have terminated the game brilliantly. The threat was: 27. R—B 4 followed by 28. Kt×R P, Kt×Kt; 29. Q×Kt ch; K×Q; 30. R—R 4 ch, K—Kt 4!

Position after White's 26th move.

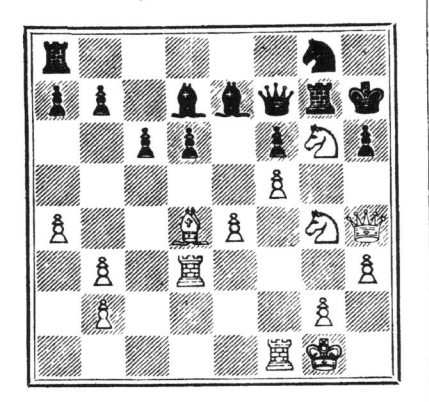

31. B—K 3 or R—Kt 3 mate. This threat could only be parried by giving up the Exchange, which anyhow leaves Black without hope.

27. P×R ch	Q×P
28. B×B P	B×Kt
29. B×B	R—K 1
30. R×P	Q—Kt 2
31. B—B 6	Kt×B
32. K R×Kt	Black resigns

GAME 10

SCOTCH GAME

White:	Black:
A. ALEKHIN.	E. COHN.

1. P—K 4	P—K 4
2. Kt—K B 3	Kt—Q B 3
3. P—Q 4	P×P
4. Kt×P	Kt—K B 3
5. P—K 5	

An innovation which has little to commend it. First of all Black can force a draw by 5. ....Kt×P; 6. Q—K 2, Q—K 2; 7. Kt—B 5, Q—K 3; 8. Kt—Q 4, Q—K 2, etc. Furthermore he can attempt to play for a win by 7. ....Q—Kt 5 ch; 8. Kt—B 3, P—Q 3; 9. Kt—K 3, B—K 2 and it seems doubtful if White can work up an attack sufficient to compensate for the Pawn he has sacrificed. Black could and should have captured the Pawn.

5. ......   Q—K 2

On the contrary this move brings about a complicated game which finally will turn to White's advantage.

6. P—K B 4	P—Q 3
7. B—Kt 5	B—Q 2
8. B×Kt	P×B
9. Castles	P×P

9. ....Kt—Kt 5 at once would not be good because of 10. P—K 6, etc.

10. P×P	Kt—Kt 5
11. Kt—Q B 3	

Now 11. P—K 6 would be a mistake because of B×P; 12. Kt×B, Q×Kt; 13. R—K 1, B—B 4 ch, etc.

11. ......   Q—R 5

With this move Black expects to obtain the advantage, as 12. ....Kt—B 3 seems bad on account of 12. ....B—B 4 ch. After 11. ....Kt×K P; White obtains a promising attack by 12. B—B 4, P—B 3; 13. Kt—K 4, etc.

Position after Black's 11th move.

12. Kt—B 3 ! !

This move spoils Black's attack. If 12. ....B—B 4 ch ; 13. K—R 1, Kt—B 7 ch ; 14. R × Kt, Q × R ; 15. Kt—K 4 and White wins the Queen. This is the combination which White had in mind when he played 11. Kt—Q B 3.

12. ......   Q—R 4

After 12. ....B—B 4 ch ; 13. K—R 1, White would gain an important *tempo* by Kt—K 4, etc.

13. Kt—K 4   B—K 2

Naturally not 13. ....Kt × K P ; because of 14. Kt × Kt, followed by 15. Kt—B 6 ch, etc.

14. Q—Q 4 !

Defending the K P and preventing R—Q 1, which would leave the Q R P unprotected.

14. ......   B—K 3
15. B—Kt 5 !

After this move, Black cannot avoid the loss of a Pawn.

15. ......   B × B
16. Kt (K 4) × B

Position after White's 16th move.

16. ......   Castles K R

There is hardly anything better. If 16. ....Kt × R P ; 17. Kt × B, Kt × Kt ch ; 18. R × Kt, P × Kt ; 19. R—Q 1, and White wins.

17. P—K R 3   Kt—R 3
18. Q—K 4

winning the Q B P.

18. ......   B—B 4
19. Q × P   Q—Kt 3
20. Q × Q   B × Q

Black's game is not yet hopeless, as his opponent is not likely to obtain a passed Pawn very speedily, and he has an isolated Pawn. On the other hand it is admittedly an advantage for the end-game to have a Bishop. For this reason White attempts, and with success, to add to his material advantage by complicated combinative play.

21. Kt—Q 4 !

The first aim of this move is to stalemate Black's two minor pieces. In addition the White Knight at Q 4 protects the Q B P, for if now 21. ....P—Q B 4 ; 22. Kt—B 6, B × P ; 23. K R—B 1 followed by R × P, White would obtain a passed Pawn on the Queen's side without any difficulty.

21. ......   Q R—Kt 1
22. P—Q Kt 3   K R—K 1

This ill-timed demonstration against the K P, which cannot be taken because of Kt—B 6, suggests a new plan for White. This consists in luring the Rooks away from the first rank and taking advantage of the unfavourable position of the minor pieces in order to create mating threats.

23. Q R—Q 1   R—Kt 3

The logical sequence of the preceding move.

24. P—B 4   R × P

Position after Black's 24th move.

25. P—B 5 !!

Black probably expected 25. Kt (Q 4)—K 6, upon which 25. ....R—Kt 1 yielded a sufficient defence. Now the Rook is forced to abandon the Knight's file, for after 25. .... R × B P ; White's reply would be : 26. Kt (Q 4)—K 6 and after 25. .... R—Kt 2 ; the answer would be : 26. Kt—B 6, R—K 1 ; 27. Kt—K 7 ch, K—B 1 (if 27. ....K—R 1 ; 28. Kt × B ch, B P × Kt ; 29. R—Q 7, etc.) ; 28. Kt × B ch, R P × Kt; 29. R—Q 7, R—K 2 ; 30. R—Q 8 ch, R—K 1 ; 31. Kt—R 7 ch, K—K 2 ; 32. R (Q 7)—Q 1 ! and Black cannot avoid the threatened mate without serious loss in material. The following moves are therefore compulsory.

25.	....	R—R 3
26.	Kt (Q 4)—K 6	K—R 1
27.	R—Q 8 ch	Kt—Kt 1
28.	Kt × Q B P	

Not 28. K R—Q 1, R (R 3) × Kt ; 29. Kt × R, P × Kt ; etc.

28.	......	R × R P
29.	K R—Q 1 !	

This is clearer than the variation 29. Kt × P ch, B × Kt ; 30. R × B, R—K 8 ch ; 31. K—R 2, R (K 8)—K 7 ; 32. R (B 7)—B 8, R × P ch ; 33. K—R 1, P—R 3 ; 34. R × Kt ch, K—R 2 ; in which Black has chances of a draw.

29.	......	P—B 3

The only move.

30.	R × Kt ch	K × R
31.	R—Q 8 ch	B—K 1
32.	Kt × B	

Threatening mate in two.

32.	......	K—B 1
33.	Kt—Q 6 ch	K—K 2
34.	R—K 8 ch	K—Q 2
35.	R × R	P × R

After all these complications the situation is now cleared up. With two Knights for a Rook, White should have no difficulty in winning as he has a passed Pawn in addition.

36.	Kt—B 4	K—B 3
37.	Kt—K 4	R—R 8 ch

In order to advance the King without being exposed to Kt—B 3 ch, winning a Rook.

38.	K—B 2	K—Q 4
39.	K—B 3	

White, still under the spell of a series of problem-moves, shows a desire to continue in the same strain by seeking extraordinary combinations for the end-game. A simple way of winning was : 39. Kt (B 4)—Q 2, followed by 40. K—K 3, with the threat of 41. Kt—Kt 1, and 42. Kt (Kt 1)—B 3 ch.

39.	......	P—Q R 4
40.	K—K 2	

Pretty, but scarcely logical. Here also 40. Kt (B 4)—Q 2 was sufficient in order to win.

40.	......	P—R 5 !

Naturally, not 40. ....K × Kt ; because of 41. P—B 6, after which

Black is compelled to give up the Rook for the passed Pawn. The text-move aims at simplification and a draw.

Position after Black's 40th move.

I had not provided against this advance as I thought that the following variation, which is not unlike an end-game study, would ensure the win: 41. P—Q Kt 4, K×Kt (B 5); 42. P—B 6, K×P; (or if R—R 7 ch; 43. K—Q 1!, K—Q 4; 44. Kt—B 3 ch, etc.); 43. Kt—B 3! and wins. I noticed in time, however, that on move 41 Black could capture the Kt at K 4, because after 42. P—B 6, R—Q B 8 the other Knight would not be supported by the Q Kt P. A draw was easily forced by: 41. Kt—B 3 ch, K×P; 42. Kt×P ch, K—Q 5; 43. Kt (R 4)—Kt 2, etc. But playing for a win at all cost I adopted another line, the consequences of which proved highly dangerous to my game.

41. Kt (B 4)—Q 2   P—R 6
42. P—Q Kt 4

White has obtained two passed Pawns, but the Black Q R P will cost him a piece.

42. ......   R—Q B 8
43. K—Q 3   P—R 7
44. Kt—Q Kt 3   R—Q 8 ch!

Gaining a most important *tempo* by which Black obtains prospects of an advantage. When playing my 41st move I had expected P—R 8 (Q); 45. Kt×Q, R×Kt; 46. Kt—B 3 ch, followed by K—B 4; with an ending similar to that which occurred in the game, but there only through a mistake on the part of my opponent.

45. K—B 2   P—R 8=Q
46. Kt×Q   R×Kt
47. Kt—B 3 ch

Position after White's 47th move.

47. ......   K—B 3

The decisive mistake. He should have played 47. ....K—B 5!; 48. P—B 6, R—R 6; 49. Kt—K 4, R—R 2; and the White Pawn being stopped, Black could have brought his material advantage to bear. Now White benefits from this lucky gift and forces a win.

48. K—Q 3   R—K B 8
49. P—Kt 3

Securing Q B 4 for the King.

49.	P—R 4
50. K—B 4	P—R 5
51. P—Kt 5 ch	K—Q 2
52. P×P	R—B 5 ch
53. K—Q 5	R×P
54. P—B 6 ch	K—B 2
55. K—B 5	R×P

There is nothing to be done.

56. P—Kt 6 ch	K—Kt 1
57. Kt—Kt 5	Black resigns

GAME 11

KING'S BISHOP OPENING

White : R. SPIELMANN.   *Black :* A. ALEKHIN.

1. P—K 4	P—K 4
2. B—B 4	Kt—K B 3
3. P—Q 4	P×P
4. Kt—K B 3	B—B 4

After 4. ....Kt×P; 5. Q×P, etc. White obtains a very strong attack for the Pawn he has given up. On principle, in the opening, I never try to obtain such an advantage in material. It can only be had at the cost of time and of delay in development, which often proves fatal.

5. Castles

After 5. P—K 5 Black would naturally play 5. ....P—Q 4; etc.

5.	P—Q 3
6. P—B 3	

White insists on playing a gambit at all cost!

6.	P—Q 6

After 6. ....P×P; 7. Kt×P, followed by 8. B—K Kt 5, White has a splendid development. The text-move, giving back the Pawn, hinders the rapid and efficacious development of the White forces.

It conforms to the general principle enunciated above regarding the danger of winning a Pawn in the opening.

7. Q×P	Kt—B 3
8. P—Q Kt 4	

This last move weakens the Queen's side. The reason why White plays it notwithstanding, is that in the quiet variation : 9. B—K Kt 5, P—K R 3; 10. B—R 4, B—K Kt 5; 11. Q Kt—Q 2, Kt—K 4 ; Black has an easy game.

8.	B—Kt 3
9. P—Kt 5	Kt—Q R 4
10. P—K 5	

This advance forces Black to play with circumspection on account of the King's exposed position. It also frustrates the threat of 10. .... Kt×B, which, in conjunction with Castles, would give Black the better game.

10.	P×P
11. Q×Q ch	K×Q
12. B×P	P—K 5
13. Kt—K 5	B—Q B 4 !

Essential, for White threatened 14. B—R 3 with good prospects of attack. Failing this possibility, White must abandon the offensive and develop his backward pieces.

14. Kt—Q 2	R—B 1

Threatening to win a piece by 15. ....B—Q 3, etc.

15. Q Kt—B 4	Kt×Kt
16. B×Kt	K—K 2
17. B—Kt 5	B—Q 3 !

Forcing White to play 18. P—B 4, which eliminates the possibility of opening the King's file eventually by P—B 3.

18. P—B 4	B—K B 4 !
19. P—Kt 4	

The object of this move is to force the Bishop from the Diagonal Q Kt 1—K R 7. In fact, without this move Black, by playing P—K R 3, would secure a retreat for the Bishop at K R 2, rendering his passed Pawn invulnerable and very embarrassing for White. At the same time the text-move presents serious drawbacks, since it dangerously weakens the King-side.

19. ...... B—K 3
20. K R—K 1

White has the following variation in view: 20. ....B×Kt; 21. P×B, B×B; 22. R×P! etc., with advantage. That is why he does not play 20. Q R—K 1, for in this variation the K R would be *en prise* to the B at Q B 4.

Position after White's 20th move.

20. ...... P—K 6!

Now the inferiority of White's position, weakened by the advance of Pawns on both wings, becomes obvious.

21. B—Q 3

It would have been somewhat better for White to get rid of Black's K P by playing 21. K—Kt 2. There would have followed: 21. ....B×Kt; 22. P×B, B×B; 23. R×P, K—B 2; 24. P×Kt, P×P; etc., but the end-game would still have been in Black's favour.

21. ...... K—K 1!

This move, relieving the Bishop's pin, allows not only the defence of the K P by Kt—Q 4, but also attacks White's K Kt P.

22. P—K R 3 Kt—Q 4

Now two more Pawns are attacked, demonstrating the inconvenience of having advanced them prematurely.

Position after Black's 22nd move.

23. P—B 5

By 23. B×P, White could momentarily have avoided material loss, but, after 23. ....Kt×K B P; 24. B×Kt, R×B; etc. his position remained precarious if not desperate. This is why he prefers to attempt a sacrificial combination in order to recover the initiative.

23. ...... B×Kt
24. P×B   B×P
25. B×P

Threatening the gain of the Exchange by 26. B—Kt 6 ch,

INTERNATIONAL TOURNAMENT AT STOCKHOLM

Position after White's 25th move.

25. ......   Kt—B 5 !

The only way to ensure success definitely. Neither 25. .... R—B 6 ; 26. B—Kt 6 ch, followed by 27. R—K B 1 ; nor 25. ....Kt—K 2 (which move Spielmann probably anticipated); 26. Q R—Q 1, B × R ; 27. R—Q 7, B—Kt 5 ; 28. B × Kt, followed by B—Kt 6 ch, would have been sufficient.

Now White is lost.

26. Q R—Q 1   B × R
27. R—Q 7

A last hope. If now 27. ....Kt—K 7 ch ; 28. K—Kt 2, R—B 7 ch ; 29. K—R 1, B—Kt 5 ; White would continue with 30. R × Kt P, threatening mate in three, and Black would have to be content with a draw by perpetual check.

27. ......   B—Kt 5 !
White resigns.

CHAPTER V

ALL-RUSSIAN MASTERS' TOURNAMENT AT VILNA, SEPTEMBER, 1912

GAME 12

QUEEN'S GAMBIT DECLINED

White :   *Black :*
Dr. O. S. Bernstein.   A. Alekhin.

1. P—Q 4   P—Q 4
2. Kt—K B 3   Kt—K B 3
3. P—B 4   P—B 3
4. P—K 3

In answer to 4. Kt—B 3, I have, on several occasions, successfully played 4. ....P×P ; and if 5. P—K 3, P—Q Kt 4, followed by P—Kt 5; or if 5. P—Q R 4, B—B 4 !, etc., as in the game against Rubinstein, London, 1922. After the text-move Black can play 4. ....B—B 4 ; 5. Q—Kt 3, Q—Kt 3 ; with a good game.

4. ......   P—K Kt 3

Played for the first time by Schlechter in a match-game against Lasker at Berlin, 1910. However, this system has little to commend it, as in this position the Bishop at K Kt 2 has for once not much scope, whilst the Q B, although not shut in by the K P, has no useful squares of development.

5. Kt—B 3   B—Kt 2
6. B—Q 3   Castles
7. Q—B 2   Kt—R 3
8. P—Q R 3

Up to now the position is identical with that in the game mentioned before. But on the next move Schlechter played 8. ....P×P ; followed by P—Q Kt 4 and P—Kt 5, after which his Queen's side naturally became very weak.

8. ......   Kt—B 2

After this move Black's position is constrained, but without any weak point. He can now hope to free his position by gradual stages.

9. Castles   B—K 3
10. P×P

If 10. P—Q Kt 3, R—B 1 ; 11. B—Kt 2, P—B 4 ; and if then 12. P×B P, P×B P, followed by ....Kt—R 3, and Black has a satisfactory game.

10. ......   K Kt×P !

The correct reply. After 10. ....P×P ; White would obtain the advantage by seizing the Q B file and by exploiting the lack of mobility of the Black pieces.

11. P—R 3

The object of this move is to prevent 13. ....B—Kt 5; after 12. P—K 4, Kt×Kt; 13. P×Kt. But Black takes advantage of this moment's respite to start operations in the centre on his own account.

| 11. ...... | Kt×Kt |
| 12. P×Kt | P—Q B 4 ! |

The position now recalls a variation of Grünfeld's defence : 1. P—Q 4, Kt—K B 3 ; 2. P—Q B 4, P—K Kt 3 ; 3. Kt—Q B 3, P—Q 4 ; etc., which was in fashion in recent Master Tournaments, with this difference in White's favour, however, that the Black Knight is at Q B 2 instead of Q B 3 or Q 2.

| 13. R—Kt 1 | R—Kt 1 |
| 14. R—Q 1 | |

If 14. P—K 4, then 14. ....P×P ; 15. P×P, Q—Q 3 !, etc., with a good game, *e.g.* : 16. P—Q 5, B—Q 2 ; or 16. P—K 5, Q—Q 2 ; followed by K R—B 1.

It is clear that the capture of the Q B P either now or on the preceding move would not be to White's advantage, because of Q—Q 4.

| 14. ...... | P—B 5 |

With this move Black allows his opponent to dominate the centre squares in order to gain an advantage on the Queen-side. More prudent and sufficient to equalize would have been 14. ....Q—Q 3 followed by K R—B 1.

| 15. B—K 2 | P—Q Kt 4 |

Not 15. ....P—B 4 ; because of 16. Q—R 4 !

| 16. Kt—Q 2 | |

After this unnecessary withdrawal Black takes the initiative. It was essential to have played 16. P—K 4, which would have been followed by 16. ....Q—Q 3 ; 17. B—K 3, P—Q R 3, with chances for both sides.

Position after White's 16th move.

| 16. ...... | P—B 4 ! |

Permanently taking hold of the centre, as his Q 4 is definitely secured. From the strategic point of view this consideration is of paramount importance.

| 17. B—B 3 | B—Q 4 |
| 18. P—K 4 | |

Essential in order to develop the Q B at last, but too late to improve White's game.

| 18. ...... | B—Q R 1 ! |

In order to bring his Knight to Q 4 and to prevent the White Knight from reaching Q B 5 via K 4.

| 19. Kt—B 1 | P×P |
| 20. B×P | Kt—Q 4 |

Now Black dominates the board and can, at will, undertake an attack on either wing.

If White play 21. Kt—Kt 3 (if 21. Kt—K 3, Kt×P ; etc., as in the game) Black would play 21. ....Q—Q 3, tying the Q B to the defence of the Q R P, and then P—Q R 3 ; following by the doubling of the Rooks on the K B file with an overwhelming advantage in position.

21. B—Kt 5

This move, plausible as it may seem strategically, is refuted by the combinative play which follows.

Position after White's 21st move.

21. ......   Kt × P !

If White replies B × B, then follows: 22. ....Kt × Q R ; 23. B—K 4, Kt × P ; followed by P—Kt 5 and Black has won the Exchange. White therefore choses the better alternative.

22. B × Kt P !   Q—Q 4 !

Not 22. ....Kt × Q R ; 23. B × P ch, K—R 1 ; 24. Q—Kt 6, Q—K 1 ; (otherwise Q—R 5, etc.) ; 25. Q × Kt, and White has a Pawn and prospects of an attack for the loss of the Exchange.

23. B × P ch   K—R 1
24. P—B 4

Evidently compulsory.

24. ......   Kt × Q R
25. R × Kt   Q × Q P ch
26. K—R 1

If 26. K—R 2, then 26. .....R × P ; 27. B × R, Q × B ch ; 28. K—R 1 (or 28. Kt—Kt 3, B—K 4 ; etc.) R—K B 1 ! (threatening Q × Kt ch ;

and mate in three), with a winning position for Black.

26. ......   Q—B 6 !

The simplest way of forcing the exchange of Queens, as Black now threatens Q × P ch.

27. K—R 2   Q × Q
28. B × Q   P—K 4

At first sight this appears to be risky on account of White's three passed Pawns on the King's side, but Black had worked out that his Queen-side Pawns would queen first. The variation 28. ....B—K B 3 ; 29. B—R 6, followed by P—Kt 4, and Kt 5 promised no more than the text-move.

29. P—B 5   B—K B 3
30. B × B ch

If now 30. B—R 6, R—Kt 1 ; 31. P—Kt 4, P—R 4, and the White Pawns are stopped. White therefore decides to mobilize the Knight and to initiate a direct King-side attack with his remaining pieces.

30. ......   R × B
31. Kt—K 3   P—R 4
32. R—Q 1

If 32. Kt × P, Black wins easily by 32. ....R—B 3 ; 33. Kt—K 3, R—B 6 ; 34. R—K 1, R × P ; etc.

32. ......   R (B 3)—B 1

In order to seize the Queen's file at once, White's few checks being of no consequence.

33. R—Q 6   Q R—Q 1
34. R—R 6 ch   K—Kt 2
35. R—Kt 6 ch K—B 2
36. Kt—Kt 4

My opponent, who was in the running with Rubinstein for the first prize in this tournament, offers a maximum of resistance and discovers unexpected resources in a desperate position. Now mate in two is threatened.

Position after White's 36th move.

36. ......   R—Q 7 !

This move, the climax of the manœuvre initiated by 32. .... K R—B 1, not only parries the mating threat but unexpectedly wins the Q B, which has no flight-square. It is the end.

37. Kt×P ch   K—K 2
38. B—Kt 1   R—Kt 7
39. R—K 6 ch   K—Q 1
40. R—Q 6 ch   K—B 1
41. P—K R 4   R×B
42. P—Kt 4   P—B 6
43. R—Q 3   P—Kt 5
44. P×P   P×P

White resigns.

GAME 13

QUEEN'S PAWN GAME

White :   Black :
A. NIEMZOVITCH.   A. ALEKHIN.

1. P—Q 4   P—Q 4
2. Kt—K B 3   P—Q B 4
3. B—B 4   Kt—Q B 3
4. P—K 3   Kt—B 3

Here 4. ....Q—Kt 3 would be premature on account of 5. Kt—B 3.

5. Kt—B 3

Now, however, this move is out of place. The usual line of play 5. P—B 3 followed by 6. B—Q 3 is certainly better.

5. ......   B—Kt 5

Equally satisfactory would be 5. ....P—Q R 3 followed by 6. .... B—Kt 5.

6. B—Q Kt 5   P—K 3
7. P—K R 3   B—R 4

This move will allow White to weaken the adverse position on both wings. Black had two ways of obtaining a good game :

I.—7. ....B×Kt ; 8. Q×B, P—Q R 3 ; 9. B×Kt ch, P×B etc.

or II.—7. ....P×Q P ; 8. P×P, B—R 4 ; 9. P—K Kt 4, B—Kt 3 ; 10. Kt—K 5, Q—Kt 3 ; 11. P—Q R 4, B—Kt 5.

8. P—K Kt 4   B—Kt 3
9. Kt—K 5   Q—Kt 3

Of course not 9. ....R—B 1, because of 10. Kt×Kt, followed by 11. B—Q R 6, etc. However, 9. ....Q—B 1 would have been more prudent.

10. P—Q R 4 !

Very strong, as Black has no time to play P×P followed by B—Kt 5, because of 11. P—R 5, etc. Therefore he is compelled to yield the square at Q Kt 5 to his opponent.

10. ......   P—Q R 4
11. P—R 4   P—R 4

This move is relatively better than P—R 3, as it forces White to make an immediate decision on the King's wing.

12. Kt×B   P×Kt
13. Kt P×P

The variation 13. P—Kt 5, Kt—K Kt 1 ; 14. Q—Q 3, K—B 2 ;

15. R—K R 3, looks stronger than it really is, as Black can resist the attack by bringing his K Kt via K 2 to K B 4.

The text-move makes things easy for Black. His K Kt P, it is true, is weakened, but, on the other hand, he obtains excellent prospects in the centre.

  13. ...... Kt P × P
  14. Q—K 2 Castles

The King's position on the Queenside will be quite safe, as the White Bishop can easily be eliminated.

15. Castles Q R !

A very pretty trap.

Position after White's 15th move.

15. ...... B—Q 3

Black discovers in time the adversary's subtle plan : 15. ....P × P ; 16. P × P, Kt × P ; 17. R × Kt, Q × R ; 18. Q × K P ch, Kt—Q 2 ; 19. Q—B 6 ch !!, P × Q ; 20. B—R 6, mate. The text-move eliminates all danger.

  16. B × B R × B
  17. B—Q 3

White has not sufficiently weighed the consequences of this move; in particular he has not realized that the Knight will have no time to settle down at Q Kt 5, and consequently Black will obtain an important advantage. Better would be : 17. B × Kt, P × B ; 18. K R—Kt 1, R—Q 2 ; etc., but in this case also Black's game is superior.

  17. ...... P—B 5 !

Dislodging the Bishop and initiating a combined attack on both wings.

  18. B—Kt 6

Naturally not 18. Kt—Kt 5, P × B ; 19. Kt × R ch, K—Q 2, followed by K × Kt, etc.

  18. ...... Kt—K 2
  19. K R—Kt 1 Q—Kt 5
  20. K—Q 2

Position after White's 20th move.

  20. ...... R—Kt 3 !

An amusing reply to White's trap on the 15th move. Black in his turn threatens mate by a Queen sacrifice, a Roland for an Oliver ! 21. .... Kt × B ; 22. R × Kt, Q × Kt P ; 23. R—Q Kt 1, Q × Kt ch ; 24. K × Q, Kt—K 5 mate. In addition the text-move allows the Queen to co-operate in a decisive action against the tracked White Bishop.

21. P—B 3

Evading the threat.

21. ......   R—K R 3
22. B—B 7

Hapless Bishop, with only one square on which to shelter !

22. ......   Kt—B 4
23. Q—R 2   Q—K 2 !
24. Kt—Kt 5

A desperate move. After 24. B—Kt 6 Black would win at once by 24. ....Kt×R P, threatening, if 25. Q×Kt, to win the Queen by 25. ....Kt—K 5 ch. In giving up the Bishop, White has a vague hope of complications resulting from the Queen reaching Q Kt 8.

24. ......   Q×B
25. Kt—R 7 ch   K—Q 2
26. Q—Kt 8   Kt—Q 3

Black could have continued with 26. ....Q—K 1. But his objective, which he indeed succeeds in achieving, is the capture of the White Queen.

27. R—Kt 5   Kt (B 3)—K 1
28. Q R—K Kt 1   R—K B 3

Not, of course, 28. ....Q×P ; because of 29. R×P ch.

29. P—B 4   P—Kt 3
30. K—B 1   Q—R 2
31. P—B 3   Q—B 2
32. K—Kt 1   Q—K 2

Taking advantage of the fact that White cannot capture the K Kt P because of the pin by 33. ....Q—R 2, etc.

33. K—R 2   R—B 1
34. Kt—Kt 5   Kt×Kt
35. P×Kt   Kt—B 2
36. Q—R 7   Q—Q 3

If now 37. R×Kt P, Kt×P ; 38. R—Kt 7 ch, K—B 3 ; 39. Q×P, R—R 3, and the Queen is lost.

White resigns.

GAME 14

SICILIAN DEFENCE

White :   *Black :*
A. ALEKHIN.   DR. O. S. BERNSTEIN.

1. P—K 4   P—Q B 4
2. Kt—K B 3   P—K 3
3. Kt—B 3

I am now convinced that the best move here is 3. B—K 2, in order to be able to play P—Q B 4 if Black adopts the Paulsen variation (P—Q R 3 and Q—B 2 ; etc.).

3. ......   P—Q R 3
4. P—Q 4   P×P
5. Kt×P   Q—B 2

This defence, adopted frequently of late by Sämisch, forces White to play with circumspection.

6. B—K 2   Kt—K B 3
7. Castles   B—K 2
8. P—B 4   Kt—B 3

Threatening 9. ....Kt×Kt ; 10. Q×Kt, B—B 4, winning the Queen, and consequently preventing 9. P—K 5.

9. K—R 1

Was 9. B—K 3 more simple ? However, the King is better placed at R 1 and in a close game like the Sicilian the loss of time entailed is of no great consequence.

9. ......   P—Q 3
10. B—B 3   B—Q 2
11. B—K 3   Castles K R
12. Q—K 2

A position typical of Paulsen's system. At the moment the White pieces have the superior mobility, but subsequently the open Q B file may become an important factor in Black's favour.

12. ......   Q R—B 1

It would have been preferable to occupy this file with the K R as the King-side is not threatened at present. Probably Black's operations on the Queen-side would be more efficacious if supported by both Rooks.

13. Q—B 2

An important move which prevents 13. ....Kt—Q R 4, to which White's reply would be 14. Kt × P, and if P × Kt; 15. B—Kt 6 regaining the piece. Therefore Black is compelled to lose a *tempo* in order to make this manœuvre with the Q Kt possible.

13. ......   P—Q Kt 4
14. Kt—Kt 3   Kt—K 1

After this last move, which shuts in the K R, White's advantage becomes manifest. Black had nothing better than to acknowledge the error of his 12th move by playing 14. ....R—Kt 1; followed by 15. ....K R—B 1. The move Kt—K 1 should only have been played in case of absolute necessity.

15. Q R—Q 1   R—Kt 1
16. R—Q 2

Played in anticipation of 16. .... Kt—R 4, as White foresees the coming attack. The text-move does not aim at doubling the Rooks on the Queen's file, but rather at defending the Q R P later on with the K R.

16. ......   Kt—R 4
17. Kt × Kt   Q × Kt

See Diagram.

18. P—K 5 !

With this unexpected move White assumes the initiative. It would be to Black's disadvantage to reply: 18. ....P—Q 4; because of:

I.—19. B × P !, P—Kt 5; 20. B—Kt 3, P × Kt; 21. R × B, etc.

Position after Black's 17th move.

II.—19. B × P !, P × B; 20. Kt × Q P, Q—Q 1; 21. B—B 5, B × B; 22. Q × B and Black has no defence against the numerous threats.

III.—19. B × P !, P × B; 20. Kt × Q P, B—Q 1; 21. B—B 5, B—K 3; 22. B × R, K × B; 23. Q—B 5 ch, K—Kt 1; 24. P—B 5, B × Kt; 25. Q × B, with an evident advantage in position.

IV.—19. B × P !, P × B; 20. Kt × Q P, B—Q 1; 21. B—B 5, B—K 3; 22. B × R, K × B; 23. Q—B 5 ch, K—Kt 1; 24. P—B 5, B × P; 25. P—Q Kt 4 and wins.

V.—19. B × P !, P × B; 20. Kt × Q P, B—Q 1; 21. B—B 5, B—K 3; 22. B × R, K × B; 23. Q—B 5 ch, K—Kt 1; 24. P—B 5, Q × R; 25. P × B, and wins.

On the other hand the move actually chosen is merely a makeshift, offering the adverse Knight a particularly useful square.

18. ......   P—Kt 5
19. Kt—K 4   P—Q 4
20. Kt—B 5   B—Q Kt 4
21. R—R 1

See note to White's 16th move.

21. ......   Kt—B 2

ALL-RUSSIAN MASTERS' TOURNAMENT AT VILNA

By this move Black cuts off the retreat of his own Queen. White, by an energetic demonstration, takes immediate advantage of this injudicious manœuvre. Q — Q 1 or Q—B 2 would certainly have been better, although in any case Black's position would remain very precarious.

Position after Black's 21st move.

22. P—Q R 4 !

Threatening to win the Queen by 23. Kt—Kt 3. Black must submit to the loss of the Exchange, for after

I.—22. ....P×P e. p.; 23. R×R P, Q—Kt 5; 24. P—B 3, Q—B 5; 25. B—K 2, his Queen is lost, and after

II.—22. ....B×Kt; 23. B×B, K R—B 1; 24. P—B 3, B×P; 25. B—Q 1, P×P; 26. P—Q Kt 4, White wins equally.

22. ...... B—B 5

Black hopes to obtain some chances still by bringing his Knight to Q B 5 after pushing on the Pawn to Q Kt 6, but White does not leave him time to consummate this manœuvre.

23. Kt—Q 7

Not 23. P—Q Kt 3 because of 23. ....B—Q Kt 4 !, etc.

23.	P—Kt 6
24. Kt×Q R	R×Kt
25. P—B 3	Kt—R 1
26. B—K 2 !	

Preparing the coming attack on the Black King's position.

26.	R—Q B 1
27. P—B 5	B×B
28. R×B	B—B 4
29. R—K B 1	B×B
30. R×B	Q—Kt 3
31. P—R 5	Q—B 3
32. R—B 3	

Simpler would have been : 32. P—B 6, P—Kt 3 ; 33. Q—R 4, Q—K 1 ; 34. R—R 3, P—R 4 ; 35. Q—Kt 5, Q—B 1 ; 36. R×P, etc.

32.	P×P
33. R×P	Kt—B 2
34. R×P	Kt—K 3

Position after Black's 34th move.

35. Q—R 7 !

Threatening 36. R×P ch, Kt×R; 37. Q—B 7 ch, K—R 1 ; 38. Q—B 8 ch, R×Q ; 39. R×R mate. If however White plays at once 35. R×P ch, then K×R and there is no more than a draw.

35.	P—R 3
36. R—K 7	Q—B 5

Black has no adequate defence against 37. R (B 1)—B 7.

37. R (B 1)—B 7   Q—K 5 !

Hindering 38. R × P ch and threatening P—Q 5 himself.

38. Q × P   R—B 3

The reply to 38. ....R—B 5 is 39. Q × Kt ! etc.

39. Q—B 1

again threatening R × P ch.

39. ......   K—R 2
40. R—B 6 !

The finishing stroke, for if 40. ....Kt—Q 1 ; 41. R—Q 6, and if 40. ....Q × P ; 41. Q—Q 3 ch and wins.

40. ......   P—Q 5
41. R (B 6) × Kt   R × R
42. R × R   P × P
43. P × P   P—Kt 7
44. R—Q Kt 6   Q—B 7
45. P—R 6   Q—B 8
46. Q—Kt 1   Black resigns.

GAME 15

RUY LOPEZ

White :   *Black :*
H. LÖVENFISCH.   A. ALEKHIN.

1. P—K 4   P—K 4
2. Kt—K B 3   Kt—Q B 3
3. B—Kt 5   P—Q R 3
4. B—R 4   Kt—B 3
5. Q—K 2

Alapin's move. Without being bad it leaves Black various ways of equalizing the game.

5. ......   B—K 2

Equally good is 5. ....P—Q Kt 4 followed by 6. ....B—B 4 (see game No. 16).

6. P—B 3   P—Q 3
7. P—K R 3

This move, which is apparently played in order to prevent the pinning of the K Kt, by 7. ....B—Kt 5, would be understandable were it White's intention to play P—Q 4, which requires the free manœuvring of the Kt. As will be seen later on, however, White has only P—Q 3 in view and so this precautionary measure is superfluous. The move would be more logical after Black's B—Kt 5, so as to be clear from the first as to that Bishop's intentions.

7. ......   B—Q 2
8. P—Q 3   Castles
9. B—B 2

In order to avoid the possible threat of Kt—Q 5 ; etc.

9. ......   K—R 1 !

The timid manner in which White has played the opening allows Black at once to formulate a plan of attack.

10. Castles   Kt—Kt 1

Played, apparently, in order to continue with P—B 4. White prepares for this eventuality by placing the R on the King's file so as to obtain compensation in the centre by P—Q 4.

11. R—K 1   Q—K 1

Black pursues his concealed objective.

12. P—Q 4   P—B 3 !

In accordance with the principle that *an advance on the wings is only possible after the position in the centre is stabilized.*

13. Q Kt—Q 2

See Diagram.

13. ......   P—K Kt 4 !

The logical reaction against 7. P—K R 3 (see also game No. 18). The opening of the K Kt file after 14. ....P—Kt 5 ; 15. P × P, B × P ; would evidently be to Black's advantage. To avoid this threat

ALL-RUSSIAN MASTERS' TOURNAMENT AT VILNA 41

Position after White's 13th move.

White is compelled to weaken the position of his King still more.

14. P—Q 5

After 14. P—K Kt 4, P—K R 4 !, White would still be forced to block the centre.

14. ......   Kt—Q 1

The inactivity of this Knight and of the K B are the only drawbacks in Black's position.

15. P—K Kt 4   P—K R 4
16. Kt—R 2   Kt—R 3
17. Kt (Q 2)—B 1

Position after White's 17th move.

17. ......   P—B 3 !

Taking the initiative on the Queen's side also, Black still further improves his game, *e.g.* :

I.—18. P—Q B 4, P—Kt 4 ; 19. P—Kt 3, Kt—Kt 2 ; 20. B—K 3, P×Q P ; 21. B P×Q P, P—B 1 followed by Kt—Q B 4, etc.

II.—18. Kt—K 3, R P×P ; 19. R P×P, P×P ; 20. Kt×P, Kt—K 3 followed by Kt—B 5, etc.

18. Kt—Kt 3

An unsuccessful attempt to force the exchange or to compel the advance of Black's K R P.

18. ......   B P×P
19. K P×P   Q—B 2 !

Position after Black's 19th move.

Gaining an important *tempo*, which will allow Black, should White defend his Q P, to break up the centre by P—B 4, *e.g.* : 20. P—Q B 4, P×P ; 21. P×P, P—B 4 ; 22. P×P, Kt×P ; 23. Kt×Kt, B×Kt ; 24. B×B, Q×B ; etc., with advantage for Black. White prefers to avoid this threat by a manœuvre, whose drawback is a considerable weakening of his K B 5 and consequently of the Pawn which is to occupy that square.

20. Kt—B 5   Kt×Kt
21. B×Kt

Equally after 21. P×Kt the reply 21. ....Q—R 2 would be very strong.

21.	B×B
22. P×B	Q—R 2 !
23. Q—K 4	Kt—B 2
24. Kt—B 1	Kt—R 3
25. Kt—K 3	R—K Kt 1
26. K—Kt 2	

Anticipating the threat: 26. .... P—Kt 5 and 27. ....P—Kt 6 ; etc.

26.	B—Q 1 !

The entry of this Bishop into the game marks the turning point. Black now threatens 27. ....P—Kt 4 followed by 28. ....B—Kt 3 ; etc.

27. P—Q R 4	P—Q R 4

Securing the diagonal Q R 2—K Kt 8 for the Bishop. By attempting to counteract the threat B—Kt 3 and B—B 4, White allows his opponent to adopt a different line of play which leads to a win just as easily.

28. P—Q Kt 4	P×P
29. P×P	B—Kt 3
30. Kt—B 4	

This move, which aims at giving up two pieces for a Rook, is White's best chance and can be refuted only by energetic attacking play. If 30. R—B 1, Black wins easily by 30. ....P—Kt 5 ; 31. P—R 4, B×Kt ; 32. P×B, P—Kt 6 ; followed by Kt—Kt 5.

30.	B—Q 5
31. B—Kt 2	Q R—Q B 1

Black could also play 31. .... B×B followed by Kt×P, but the move in the text is more decisive.

32. Q R—B 1	R×Kt
33. R×R	B×B
34. Q—B 2	

White had based his hopes upon this position when giving up a piece. Indeed, after 34. ....B—Q 5 ; 35. R—B 7, R—Kt 2 ; 36. R×R, Q×R ; 37. Q—B 8 ch, K—R 2 ; 38. R—Q B 1, etc., he had still some chances.

Position after White's 34th move.

34.	Kt×P !

The beginning of the end. Should White capture the Bishop, Black wins by 35. ....Kt—R 5 ch ; 36. K—R 1, Q—Q 6 ; 37. R—B 3, Q×P ch ; 38. P—B 3, Kt×P.

35. R—B 7	Q—Kt 3

If now 36. Q×B, P—Kt 5 ; and Black wins.

36. R—B 8	P—Kt 5

The commencement of the mating combination.

37. R×R ch	K×R
38. Q×B	

Or 39. Q—B 8 ch, K—R 2 ; 40. Q×P ch, K—R 3 and wins.

38.	P×P ch
39. K×P	

The flight of the King to B 1 would have allowed the following pretty ending : 39. K—B 1, Q—Kt 7 ch ; 40. K—K 2, Q—K 5 ch; 41. K any, Q×R ch followed by P—R 7.

After the text-move Black announced mate in five as follows :

39.	Q—Kt 5 ch
40. K—R 2	Kt—R 5
41. P—B 4	Kt—B 6 ch
42. K—R 1	Q—R 6 ch
43. Q—R 2	Q×Q mate

CHAPTER VI

MASTERS' QUADRANGULAR TOURNAMENT AT ST. PETERSBURG, APRIL, 1913

GAME 16

RUY LOPEZ

White : A. ALEKHIN.
Black : O. DURAS.

1. P—K 4   P—K 4
2. Kt—K B 3   Kt—Q B 3
3. B—Kt 5   P—Q R 3
4. B—R 4   Kt—B 3
5. Q—K 2   P—Q Kt 4

This move, in conjunction with the next one, affords Black the simplest method of equalizing the game.

6. B—Kt 3   B—B 4
7. P—Q R 4 !

The opening of the Q R file is of great moment in this variation. Black cannot prevent it, for if : 7. ....P—Kt 5 ; 8. B × P ch, K × B ; 9. Q—B 4 ch, P—Q 4 ; 10. Q × B, Q—Q 3 ; 11. Q × Kt !

7. ......   R—Q Kt 1
8. P × P   P × P
9. P—Q 3

After 9. Kt—B 3, Black could simply Castle, for after 10. Kt × Kt P, P—Q 4 ! and he obtains an attack fully equivalent to the Pawn sacrificed. After the text-move White can eventually play P—B 3 and bring his Knight to K 3 or K Kt 3 via Q 2 and K B 1.

9. ......   P—Q 3
10. B—K 3   B—Kt 5

Here Black could have obtained an even game by forcing the exchange of White's only well posted piece, the K B, by 10. ....B—K 3. It is clear that White would not have reaped any advantage by exchanging at K 6 and Q B 4, as Black would have had command of the centre, thanks to his Pawn position and the two open files.

11. P—R 3   B—R 4

Consequent but not best. 11. .... B—K 3 was even now preferable and would have brought about variations similar to those resulting from the immediate development of the B at K 3.

12. Q Kt—Q 2   Castles
13. Castles K R Kt—Q 5

This offer to exchange is premature, and, as will be seen, gives White a marked positional advantage. Relatively better would have been 13. ....Q—K 2 followed by Kt—Q 1—K 3, although in either case Black has the inferior game.

14. B×Kt   B×Kt

Forced, for otherwise the Black Bishop would have been in jeopardy, e.g.: 14. ....B×B; 15. P—Kt 4, B—Kt 3; 16. Kt×B, P×Kt; 17. P—K B 4, etc., or 14. ....P×B; 15. P—Kt 4, B—Kt 3; 16. Kt—R 4, followed by P—K B 4, with advantage to White in either variation.

15. Kt×B   P×B

Position after Black's 15th move.

16. P—K 5!

The beginning of a strong attack against Black's K B 2, weakened as it is by the premature exchange of Black's K B. Furthermore it is interesting to observe how important it is for White's attack to have the open Q R file.

16. ......   Q—K 2

Besides this move and the sequel it implies, Black had a further choice of two lines of play:

I.—16. ....P×P; 17. Q×P, Q—Q 3; 18. Q×Q, P×Q; 19. K R—K 1 with advantage to White; or

II.—16. ....K R—K 1; 17. P—K 6!, P×P; 18. B×P ch, K—B 1 (if K—R 1; 19. Kt—Kt 5); 19. P—Q Kt 4!, B×P (if B—Kt 3; 20. K R—K 1, etc.); 20. Kt×P, R—Kt 3!; 21. Q—B 3!, B—B 6; 22. Kt—B 6!, R×Kt; 23. Q×R, B×R; 24. R×B, and White has the better game.

17. K R—K 1   Q R—K 1
18. Q—Q 2   P×P

Forced, as P—K 6 was threatened.

19. R×P   Q—Q 3
20. Q—Kt 5!

Forcing a further exchange which brings the Knight into decisive action.

20. ......   R×R

It is clear that 20. ......P—R 3 would have achieved nothing after 21. Q—B 5.

21. Kt×R

Already threatening mate after Kt×P.

21. ......   Q—Kt 3

Relatively best. 21. Kt—Q 2 would not be sufficient, e.g.: 21. ....Kt—Q 2; 22. Kt×P!, R×Kt; 23. R—R 8 ch, Kt—B 1; 24. Q—B 5!, Q—K 2; 25. B×R ch, Q×B; 26. Q×B and wins. The move in the text removes the immediate threat, for now 22. Q—B 5, would be insufficient as a preliminary to the Kt sacrifice, as Black could prepare a fresh defensive position by 22. ....P—Kt 3, followed by K—Kt 2, etc.

22. P—Kt 4!

But this somewhat hidden preparation of the Kt sacrifice wins at once, as Black is compelled to make a reply which will render his position still more precarious.

22. ......   B—Q 3

If 22. .....P—Kt 3, then 23. Q—R 6 threatening either Kt×B P or R—R 8; and if 22. ....B—K 2; 23. Kt—Q 7!, Kt×Kt; 24. Q×B, Q—Q 3; 25. Q×Q, P×Q; 26. R—R 5, R—Kt 1; 27. R—R 7, R—Q 1; 28. R—Kt 7 and wins.

Position after Black's 22nd move.

23. Kt×P !   R×Kt
24. Q—B 5 !

The point of the manœuvre started with 22. P—Kt 4 ! Against the double threat of 25. B×R ch, followed by 26. P—Kt 5, or else 25. Q—K 6 Black has no defence.

24. ......   P—Kt 3

If 24. .....Q—B 3 ; 25. P—Kt 5, Q—Q 2 ; 26. B×R ch, K×B (if Q×B ; 27. P×Kt), 27. Q—B 3 ; and White wins.

25. Q—K 6   K—Kt 2
26. Q×R ch   K—R 3
27. B—K 6 !   Black resigns.

GAME 17

RUY LOPEZ

White :   *Black :*
E. ZNOSKO-BOROVSKI. A. ALEKHIN.

1. P—K 4   P—K 4
2. Kt—K B 3   Kt—Q B 3
3. B—Kt 5   P—Q R 3
4. B—R 4   P—Q 3
5. P—Q 4   B—Kt 5

5. B—Q 2 is better. The variation in the text, favoured by Marshall, is not favourable to Black should White, as in the game Réti—Spielmann, Berlin, 1920, adopt the continuation 6. P—Q 5, P—Q Kt 4 ; 7. P×Kt, P×B ; 8. P—B 4 !

6. B×Kt ch

White also obtains a good game by this move, but allows Black some counter chances.

6. ......   P×B
7. P×P   P×P
8. Q—K 2

It is clear that after exchange of Queens Black would protect his K P by 8. ....R×Q, threatening mate if White plays 9. Kt×P.

8. ......   B—Q 3
9. B—K 3   Kt—K 2
10. P—K R 3   B—R 4
11. Q Kt—Q 2   Castles

Black could equally play 11. .... P—B 3 in order to withdraw his Bishop to B 2 in case of need. But he considered that White would not find the time necessary to increase his pressure on the King's side on account of Black's counter-attack on the opposite wing, and in the centre.

12. P—K Kt 4   B—Kt 3
13. P—K R 4

If 13. Kt—R 4, Kt—Q 4!; 14. Kt×B, Kt×B; 15. Q×Kt, B P× Kt, with good prospects.

13.	P—B 3
14. P—R 5	B—B 2
15. Kt—R 4	Q—Kt 1!

The Black Queen enters into the game very effectively through this outlet.

| 16. P—Kt 3 | Q—Kt 5! |
| 17. P—K B 3 | |

The opening of the K Kt file would here be without effect: 17. Kt—B 5, Kt×Kt; 18. Kt P×Kt, Q—B 6! and White, to avoid the loss of his Q B P without any compensation, must decide to Castle on the Queen's side, whereupon his opponent would mate in two by 19. ....B—R 6 ch.

Position after White's 17th move.

| 17. ...... | K R—Q 1! |

Stronger than 17. ....Q—B 6, whereupon White would obtain an equivalent in position sufficient for the Pawn sacrificed, by 18. K—B 2!, Q×B P; 19. K R—Q B 1, Q—Kt 7; 20. Kt—B 4!, Q×Q ch; 21. K×Q, etc.

18. K—B 2

After 18 Castles (K R) the ensuing reply, 18. ....B—B 4, would be still stronger.

18.	B—B 4
19. Kt—B 1	R—Q 3
20. B×B	Q×B ch
21. Kt—K 3	Q R—Q 1
22. K R—Q 1	Q—B 6!

Undoubling the Q B P by force, and in this way removing the only weakness in his position.

23. R×R

If 23. Kt—B 1, Black would reply simply 23. ....P—R 4, and White could only defer the exchange of Rooks, which must be made sooner or later.

| 23. ...... | P×R |
| 24. R—Q 1 | P—Q 4! |

The most energetic. In exchange for the Q R P Black obtains a strong passed Pawn in the centre and besides, White's Q R P is a most noticeable object of attack.

| 25. Q×P | P—Q 5 |
| 26. Kt (K 3)—B 5 | |

As this Kt can no longer be assisted by the other pieces, its inroad on B 5 loses much of its efficacy.

26.	Kt×Kt
27. Kt×Kt	Q×Q B P ch
28. Q—K 2	Q—B 4
29. Q—Q 3	

29. Q—Q 2! would be a little better, with the double threat 30. R—Q B 1 followed by R×P and Kt—K 7 ch, and 30. P—Kt 5. But in this case also Black would secure an advantage in position by 29. ....Q—B 1!

| 29. ...... | B—K 3 |

In order to be able to dislodge the Kt, at need, by P—Kt 3, but White prefers to withdraw it himself to maintain the defence of his seriously weakened left wing.

QUADRANGULAR TOURNAMENT AT ST. PETERSBURG

30. Kt—Kt 3	R—R 1
31. R—Q 2	Q—Kt 5!
32. R—B 2	P—Q B 4
33. Kt—B 1	

Position after White's 33rd move.

33.	P—B 5!

This temporary Pawn-sacrifice will allow the Black pieces to break through into the hostile camp, and to co-operate in a direct attack against White's King, an attack which will become irresistible thanks to the passed Pawn, which fixes the White pieces on the other wing.

34. P×P	R—R 6
35. Q—Q 2	Q—B 4
36. K—Kt 3	

After 36. K—Kt 2, B×B P Black would be threatening to capture the Knight with check.

36.	B×B P
37. Q—B 1	R—B 6!
38. R×R	P×R
39. Kt—K 3	

Directed against the threatened Q—Kt 8 ch.

39.	B×P
40. Q—B 2!	B—K 3
41. Kt—Q 1	

Else Black would win easily with his passed Pawn.

41.	Q—Kt 8 ch
42. K—R 4	P—Kt 4 ch!

In conjunction with the following move this is the shortest road to victory.

43. P×P e. p.

Position after White's 43rd move.

43.	P—R 4!

This Pawn now shares in the attack and settles the result outright. White is helpless against the threat: 44. ....Q—R 8 ch; 45. K—Kt 3, P—R 5 ch; 46. K—B 2, Q—R 7 ch. On the other hand 43. ....P×P would not have been so strong, for White could have still defended himself by 44. Q—K 2!, K—Kt 2; 45. K—R 3!

44. Kt—K 3	Q×Kt
45. Q—R 4	Q—B 7 ch
46. K—R 3	P—R 5
47. Q—K 8 ch	K—Kt 2
48. Q—K 7 ch	K×P

White resigns.

CHAPTER VII

INTERNATIONAL TOURNAMENT AT SCHEVENINGEN, AUGUST, 1913

GAME 18

RUY LOPEZ

White : *Black :*
Dr. A. G. Olland. A. Alekhin.

1. P—K 4   P—K 4
2. Kt—K B 3   Kt—Q B 3
3. B—Kt 5   Kt—Q 5

This old variation is not quite correct from a theoretical standpoint. The best line of play for White seems to be : 4. Kt×Kt, P×Kt ; 5. Castles, P—Q B 3 ; 6. B—B 4, Kt—K 2 (or P—K Kt 3) ; 7. P—Q 3 followed by 8. P—Q B 3 !

4. B—K 2

The fact that White yields the two Bishops to the opponent at the commencement of the game is certainly not calculated to refute Bird's variation, as he does not obtain the slightest compensation.

4. ......   Kt×B
5. Q×Kt   P—Q 3
6. P—Q B 3

Even 6. P—Q 4 would not compel Black to surrender the centre, because after 6. ....P—Q B 3 ! ; 7. P×P, P×P, his K P would be defended by the threat Q—R 4 ch.

6. ......   P—Q B 3
7. P—Q 4   Q—B 2
8. B—K 3   Kt—B 3
9. Q Kt—Q 2

White has now developed all his minor pieces, but they have only a very limited range of action, whilst the white squares are weak on account of the premature exchange of the K B. On these grounds Black has already the better game.

9. ......   B—K 2
10. P—K R 3

In order to limit the action of Black's Q B. But, as experience has many a time shown, the advance of the K R P facilitates the formation of a direct attack on the King by the opponent.

10. Castles K R, and if 10. .... B—Kt 5 ; 11. Q—Q 3, etc., was comparatively better.

10. ......   P—Q Kt 3 !

With the double object of opening the diagonal Q R 3—K B 8 for the Q B and, in the event of the obstruction of this diagonal, blocking the centre before undertaking operations on the King-side.

The correctness of this plan is clearly shown in the course of the game.

INTERNATIONAL TOURNAMENT AT SCHEVENINGEN

11. Castles K R   P—Q R 4
12. P—B 4

If 12. K R—K 1, Black would be satisfied with B—R 3, followed by Q—Q, whereas he now avails himself of the opportunity to launch the attack which he intended.

12. ......   P—Q B 4 !
13. P—Q 5

The opening of the Q file would clearly be to Black's advantage.

13. ......   P—R 3 !
14. P—R 3

A counter-attack on the opposite wing. It is not difficult to foresee that it will not materialize as quickly as Black's direct attack against the adverse King.

14. ......   P—K Kt 4
15. P—Q Kt 4

If 15. Kt—R 2, then 15. ....P—R 4 ; 16. B×Kt P, Kt×Q P ; 17. B×B, Kt—B 5 !, etc. with good attacking chances.

15. ......   P—Kt 5
16. R P×P   B×P
17. P×B P   Kt P×P
18. Q—Q 3   Q—Q 2 !

White's ensuing combination could have been prevented by 18. ....Q—B 1, but Black, having assessed it at its proper value, seeks, on the contrary, to provoke it.

19. B×B P !

Ingenious and seemingly correct, for after 19. ....P×B ; 20. Kt× P followed by P—B 4, White's Pawns would become formidable. Unfortunately for White, Black is by no means compelled to accept the sacrifice.

19. ......   B×Kt

Not at once 19. ....R—K Kt 1 because White could answer very energetically 20. Kt×P !, Black's Queen not having the resource of occupying the square K Kt 5. By the move in the text Black retains this option.

20. Kt×B

Position after White's 20th move.

20. ......   R—K Kt 1 !

The quiet refusal of the Greek Gift sets off in striking fashion Black's superiority in position.

If 21. B—K 3 (21. B—Kt 6, Q—R 6 !) Black would have continued his attack in the following manner : 21. ....R×P ch ; 22. K×R, Q—Kt 5 ch ; 23. K—R 2, Q×Kt ; 24. R—K Kt 1, Kt—Kt 5 ; 25. R×Kt, Q×R ; 26. R—K Kt 1, Q—R 4 ch ; 27. K—Kt 2, P—B 4 ! ; 28. P×P, K—B 2, after which White's position would rapidly become untenable.

This is the reason why White prefers by a fresh sacrifice to obtain two passed centre-Pawns whose advance will certainly threaten to become very dangerous.

21. Kt×P   P×Kt
22. B×B   Q—Kt 5 !

E

It was very important not to concede White time to play P—B 3, thus allowing his Rooks to defend the Kt P. This would have rendered the prosecution of the attack very difficult for Black.

23. P—Kt 3	K×B
24. P—Q 6 ch	K—B 1
25. K R—K 1	P—R 4 !

This advance of the R P comes just in time to thwart the intentions of the opponent.

26. Q R—Q 1

Threatening 27. P—Q 7 followed by Q—Q 6 ch and Q×P, etc.

26.	R—Q 1
27. P—B 5	P—K R 5
28. R—K 3	P×P
29. P×P	

Or 29. R×P, Q×P, and Black wins easily.

| 29. ...... | Kt—R 4 |

Position after Black's 29th move.

30. P—Q 7

There is nothing else to be done. For example, if 30. R—Q 2, Q—R 6; 31. R—K Kt 2, Q×R ch. and if 30. K—B 2, then 30. ....R—Kt 3 !, etc. Nevertheless, the text-move loses still more rapidly.

30.	Kt×P
31. Q—Q 6 ch	K—Kt 2
32. Q×P ch	K—R 2
33. K—B 2	Q×R
34. R×Kt	Q—Q 7 ch
35. K—B 1	R×R
36. Q—B 5 ch	R—Kt 3
37. P—B 6	Q—B 8 ch
38. Resigns	

GAME 19

CENTRE GAME

White :   *Black :*

J. MIESES.   A. ALEKHIN.

1. P—K 4	P—K 4
2. P—Q 4	P×P
3. Q×P	

It is quite evident that such displacements of the Queen at an early stage in the opening are not likely to reap any advantage. However, Black is compelled to play with precision, so that his opponent may have no time to start an attack against the King-side or even in the centre. For, no doubt, the White Queen installed at K Kt 3 (via K 3) would exercise a pressure on Black's King-side if he eventually Castles on that side.

| 3. ...... | Kt—Q B 3 |
| 4. Q—K 3 | B—K 2 |

Black could also have played Kt—B 3, for the following variation is mere bluff and eventually turns to Black's advantage : 5. P—K 5, Kt—K Kt 5 ; 6. Q—K 4, P—Q 4 !; 7. P×P e. p. ch., B—K 3 ; 8. B—Q R 6 (or 8. P×P, Q—Q 8 ch !), Q×P ; 9. B×P, Q—Kt 5 ch ! 10. Q×Q, Kt×Q.

5. B—Q 2	Kt—B 3
6. Kt—Q B 3	Castles
7. Castles	P—Q 4 !

INTERNATIONAL TOURNAMENT AT SCHEVENINGEN

This advance, which at first sight appears somewhat risky, in view of the position of White's Q R, will on the contrary allow Black to extract the maximum return from his advanced development. 7. ....P—Q 3; would result in almost a close game and White would find time to complete his neglected development.

8. P×P   Kt×P
9. Q—Kt 3   B—R 5 !

Providing without loss of time against the threat 10. B—K R 6. Black's advantage is now evident.

10. Q—B 3   B—K 3

The sacrifice initiated by this move is full of promise and on the other hand devoid of risk, for Black will have an equivalent in material for his Queen. It would, however, have been more logical to adopt the following variation: 10. ....Kt × Kt ; 11. B × Kt, Q—Kt 4 ch ; 12. B—Q 2 (else 12. ....B—Kt 5), Q—Q B 4 ! ; 13. B—K 3, Q—Q R 4 ; which would have given Black a dominating position without such complications as defy exact calculation.

11. B—K 3 !

Calling for the subsequent combination, for 11. ....Q Kt—K 2 ; would be bad because of 12. Kt × Kt, followed by 13. Q—R 5, and 14. P—Q B 4, etc.

See Diagram.

11. ......   Kt×Kt !

Black obtains Rook, Knight, and Pawn for his Queen while maintaining the superior position. The sacrifice is therefore fully justified. Much less strong would be: 11. .... Q Kt—Kt 5 ; 12. P—Q R 3, Kt×Kt; 13. R×Q, Kt (Kt 5)—R 7 ch ; 14. K—Q 2, Kt—Kt 8 ch ; 15. K—K 1, and the two Black Knights would find themselves in a tragi-comical situation.

Position after White's 11th move.

12. R×Q   Kt×P ch
13. K—Kt 1   Q R×R
14. B—K 2   Kt (R 7)—Kt 5
15. Kt—R 3   K R—K 1

Essential as a basis for all the subsequent combinations.

16. Kt—B 4

16. R—Q 1, B—Q 4 ; 17. Q—R 5, B—B 3 was no better, as Black now threatens 18. ....B—K 5.

Position after White's 16th move.

16. ......   B—B 4
17. R—Q B 1   P—K Kt 3

52 MY BEST GAMES OF CHESS

Preparing the combination Kt × P followed by Kt (B 3)—Kt 5, etc. which at present would not be sufficient, e.g.: 17. ....Kt × P; 18. R × Kt, Kt—Kt 5; 19. Kt—Q 3!, R—K 5; 20. Kt × Kt!, etc.

18. P—Kt 4

In order to exchange the dangerous Black Bishop.

18. ......   B—K 5
19. Q—R 3   B—B 3
20. B—B 3

White seems to be able to disentangle his forces now; but nevertheless Black's position still remains very strong, even after the unavoidable exchange.

20. ......   B × B
21. Q × B   Kt—K 4
22. Q—K 2

It is clear that the capture of the Q Kt P would entail a rapid disintegration through the combined action of the K B and the Q R, the latter seizing the open Q Kt file.

Position after White's 22nd move.

22. ......   P—B 4!

A very important move which puts renewed vigour into Black's attack. White in particular threatened to force further simplifications by 23. P—B 3, Kt (Kt 5)—Q 6; 24. Kt × Kt, Kt × Kt; 25. R—Q 1, etc.

By his last move Black frustrates this plan, and, if necessary, aims at posting a Knight at Q 6 by P—B 5, etc. As White cannot reply 23. B × P, because of 23. ....Kt (K4)—Q 6; 24. Q × R ch, R × Q; 25. Kt × Kt, Kt—B 3, etc., weakening his right wing, he has to attempt a counter-attack which Black allows him no time to develop.

23. R—Kt 1   P—B 5
24. P—R 4   Kt—Q 4

The renewed complications resulting from this move required the most exact calculations.

25. Kt × Kt   R × Kt
26. P—B 4

If 26. P—Kt 5, B—Kt 2; 27. R—Q 1, then 27. ....R—Kt 4; 28. B—Q 4, R—K 3, etc., also to Black's advantage.

26. ......   Kt—Q 6!

Black takes immediate advantage of the weakening of the White Bishop resulting from 26. P—B 4.

27. Q—B 3

If White had taken the Knight the sequel would have been: 27. ....R × P; 28. R—Kt 3, B—Q 5!; 29. Q—Q B 2 (not 29. Q × R, P × Q; 30. B × B, R—K 8 ch; 31. K—R 2, P—Q 7! and wins), B × B; 30. Q × P, R (K 1)—Q 1; with the better game. However, this variation is more favourable than the one chosen by White, after which Black can force the win by a fresh sacrifice.

See Diagram.

27. ......   R—Q Kt 4!

Decisive! Now White has to take the Knight, for after 28. P—Kt 3, R—Q R 4; 29. P × Kt, Black could force the win by 29. ....P × Kt P;

INTERNATIONAL TOURNAMENT AT SCHEVENINGEN

Position after White's 27th move.

Position after Black's 30th move.

30. K—B 1, B—B 6 ; 31. K—Q 1, R—R 8 ch, etc. A curious position, for although Black has only a Rook for the Queen, White is without resource.

28. P×Kt	R×P ch
29. K—B 1	P×P
30. K—Q 1	

30. R—Kt 2, R—B 1 ch ; 31. K—Q 1, etc., is merely an inversion of moves.

30. ...... R—Q B 1 !

See Diagram.

Against the threat 31. .....R (B 1) —B 7, White's only defence was 31. R—Kt 2. But it was in no way sufficient for a draw, despite the opinion of all the critics who annotated the game at the time it was played, and in this case Black would have won as follows : 31. ....R—Kt 8 ch ; 32. K—Q 2, R—Kt 6 ; 33. K—Q 1 (or A), B—B 6 ! ; 34. B—B 1, B—Kt 5 ! and White is helpless against the threats 35. .... P—Q 7 ; and 35. ....R—Kt 8.

A. 33. K—K 1, R—B 8 ch ; 34. K—B 2 (or 34. B×R, P—Q 7 ch), B×P ch and wins.

This analysis shows the correctness of the sacrifice initiated on move 11, and the soundness of the final combination.

31. P—Kt 5	R (B 1)—B 7 !
32. K—K 1	R—Kt 8 ch
33. Q—Q 1	B—B 6 ch
White resigns.	

CHAPTER VIII

ALL-RUSSIAN MASTERS' TOURNAMENT AT ST. PETERSBURG, JANUARY, 1914

GAME 20

RUY LOPEZ

White :   *Black :*
A. ALEKHIN.   H. LÖVENFISCH.

1. P—K 4   P—K 4
2. Kt—K B 3   Kt—Q B 3
3. B—Kt 5   P—Q R 3
4. B—R 4   Kt—B 3
5. Q—K 2   B—K 2
6. P—B 3   P—Q Kt 4
7. B—Kt 3   Castles

An unusual move. The usual line of play commencing 7. ....P—Q 3 is Black's best.

8. P—Q R 4

But White does not answer with the strongest move, and thereby allows Black to equalize the game. He should play 8. P—Q 4 (but not 8. B—Q 5 because of 8. ....B—Q 3!) 8. ....P—Q 3 (or 8. ....P×P ; 9. P—K 5, R—K 1 ; 10. Castles, etc.); 9. P—Q 5, Kt—Q R 4 ; 10. B—B 2 followed by Q Kt—Q 2 and P—Q R 4, thereby fully justifying 5. Q—K 2.

8. ......   P—Q 4 !

The right reply.

9. R P×P

The answer 9. K P×P would, of course, be unfavourable for White after 9. ....P—K 5 !

9. ......   Q P×P

This is very tempting and leads to very interesting complications, from which, however, White succeeds in emerging with advantage. By playing 9. ....B—K Kt 5 !; 10. P—Q 3 ! (if 10. P×Kt, P×P), Q P×P ; 11. Q P×P, P×P ; 12. R×R, Q×R ; 13. Castles. Black would have secured equality at least.

Position after Black's 9th move.

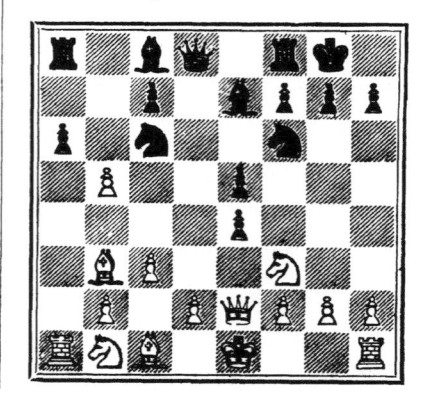

54

10. Kt—Kt 5 !

White in this manner wins a Pawn to the detriment of his development. He had, however, foreseen that Black's pressure would be only temporary, since he could not in the long run maintain his Pawn at K 5.
The whole variation is based on the fact that Black cannot now play 10. .... B—K Kt 5 on account of 11. Kt × B P ! (not 11. P—B 3, P × B P ; 12. P × B P, P × P ; 13. R × R, Q × R ; 14. P × B, Kt—R 4 ! with advantage to Black) ; 11. .... R × Kt ; 12. Q — B 4 ! and White wins at least the Exchange ; not, however, 12. B × R ch, K × B ; 13. Q—B 4 ch, B—K 3 ; 14. Q × Kt, B—Q 4 ! and Black wins.

10. ......   Kt—R 2 !

This is Black's best chance.

11. P × P

Of course 11. Kt × K P would be inadequate, because of 11. .... Kt × P !

11. ......   B—K B 4
12. B—B 2

The key of the adverse position, Black's Pawn on K 5, must be attacked as quickly as possible.

12. ......   Q—Q 4
13. P—B 4

Thus enabling his Q Kt to be developed ; but on the other hand the text-move renders the squares Q 5 and Q Kt 5 available to Black's Knight now occupying Q R 2.

13. ......   Q—Q 5

After the interesting continuation 13. .... Q—B 3 the danger White would run is more apparent than real, *e.g.*: 13. .... Q—B 3 ;
14. Kt—B 3, P—K 6 ; 15. B × B, Q × Kt P ; 16. R—B 1, Q × Kt (or 16. .... P × B P ch ; 17. R × P, Q × Kt ; 18. P—Q 4, etc.) ; 17. B P × P, Q—R 5 ch ; 18. K—Q 1 and White has the advantage.

14. Kt—B 3   B—K Kt 5
15. Q—K 3   Kt—B 3 !

Being unable to defend his K P any longer, Black attempts to rid himself of the dangerous White Q R P, a plan which he later on abandons, with very serious consequences.

16. Kt (Kt 5) × K P
                      Kt—Q Kt 5 !
17. Kt × Kt ch   B × Kt

The variation 17. .... P × Kt ; 18. B—Kt 1 ! (but not 18. B—K 4 because of 18. .... P—K B 4) was no better.

18. B—K 4   Q × P

This continuation of the attack at all cost will be countered by a sacrifice on the 20th move, whereby White will secure a decisive advantage on the Queen-side. After 18. .... R × P ; 19. R × R, Kt × R ; 20. P—Q 3, Kt—Kt 5 ; 21. Castles, Black would have retained some drawing chances by reason of the weakness of White's Pawns on the Queen-side.

19. P—R 7 !

The despised Pawn now becomes formidable.

19. ......   K R—Q 1
20. P—Kt 3 !

By this sacrifice White is enabled to Castle, and he thereby puts an end to the hostile attack. Black cannot reply 20. .... Kt—Q 6 ch because of 21. K—B 1, etc.

20.	Q×P
21. Castles	Kt—B 7

A little better, but insufficient to save the game, was 21. ....P—B 3 etc.

Position after Black's 21st move.

22. Q—B 5 !

The decisive move. If 22. .... Kt×R ; 23. B×R, R×B ; 24. Q—B 6 ! and wins. Much less effective was 22. B×R, Kt×Q ; 25. B—Q 5, Kt×B ; 26. P—R 8=Q, Kt×Kt ; 25. P×Kt, Q×P, and Black with his two Bishops has a very fine game, apart from the fact that he has two Pawns for the Exchange.

22.	P—B 3

As hopeless as every other move.

23. R—Kt 1	Q—K 3
24. B×Kt	B—K 2
25. Q—Kt 6	Q—Q 2
26. R—R 1	P—K B 4
27. B—R 4	K R—Q B 1
28. B—R 3	B—Kt 4
29. B—B 5	B×P
30. Kt—Q 5 !	B—K 7
31. Kt—K 7 ch	K—R 1
32. Kt×R	R×Kt
33. B×P	Black resigns

GAME 21

RUY LOPEZ

White :   *Black :*
A. ALEKHIN.   A. NIEMZOVITCH

1. P—K 4	P—K 4
2. Kt—K B 3	Kt—Q B 3
3. B—Kt 5	P—Q R 3
4. B—R 4	Kt—B 3
5. Castles	Kt×P

The most analysed variation of the Ruy Lopez. In the latest practical tests the results are somewhat in White's favour, and it occurs less and less in master-play.

6. P—Q 4	P—Q Kt 4
7. B—Kt 3	P—Q 4
8. P×P	B—K 3
9. P—B 3	B—K 2
10. Q Kt—Q 2	

After 10. B—K 3, Castles ; 11. Q Kt—Q 2, Kt×Kt ; 12. Q×Kt, Kt—R 4 ; Black has a satisfactory game. Less recommendable, however, are : 11. ....P—B 4 ; 12. P×P e. p., Kt×P ; 13. Kt—Kt 5 ! etc. ; and 11. ....B—K Kt 5 ; because of 12. Kt×Kt, P×Kt ; 13. Q—Q 5 !, etc. (see game No. 91).

10.	Kt—B 4

Better would have been 10. .... Castles ; 11. B—B 2, P—B 4 ; 12. P×P e. p., Kt×P (B 3) ; although in this case also White's game after 13. Kt—Kt 3 (not 13. Kt—Kt 5, because of 13. ....B—K Kt 5 ; 14. P—B 3, B—B 1 !, etc.) is somewhat preferable.

11. B—B 2

See Diagram

11.	B—Kt 5

11. ....Castles, would be insufficient because of Bogoljuboff's ingenious innovation in his game against Réti (Stockholm Tournament, 1920):

ALL-RUSSIAN TOURNAMENT AT ST. PETERSBURG 57

Position after White's 11th move.

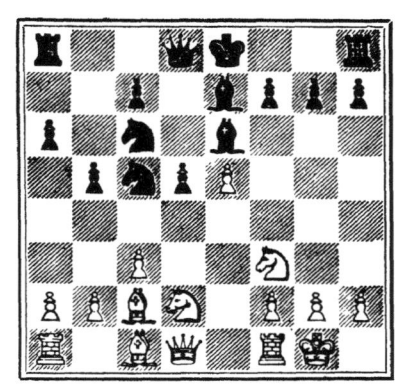

12. Kt—Q 4 !, Kt×P ; 13. P—K B 4, B—Kt 5 ; 14. Q—K 1, B—R 5 ; 15. Q×Kt, R—K 1 ; 16. Kt—B 6, Q—Q 2 ; 17. P—B 5 !, and White must win.

| 12. R—K 1 | Castles |
| 13. Kt—Kt 3 | Kt—K 5 |

If 13. ....Kt—K 3 (Janowski—Lasker, Paris, 1913) White obtains a fine attacking game after 14. Q—Q 3. The text-move is an innovation which is refuted in the present game.

14. B—B 4 !

Not 14. B×Kt, P×B ; 15. Q×Q, R×Q ; 16. R×P, R—Q 8 ch ; 17. Kt—K 1, B—K B 4 ; 18. R—K 2, B—Q 6 ; 19. R—K 3, B—Kt 4 ; whereas with the text-move White threatens to win a Pawn.

14.	P—B 4
15. P×P e. p.	Kt×P (B 3)
16. Q—Q 3	Kt—K 5

This Pawn sacrifice will ultimately prove insufficient ; but Black's position was already beset with difficulties. If, for instance, 16. ....B—R 4 ; then 17. Kt—R 4 ! with a great positional superiority.

| 17. B×P | Q—Q 2 |

Obviously Black cannot afford 17. ....Q×B ; because of 18. Q×P ch, etc.

| 18. Kt—K 5 ! | Kt×Kt |
| 19. B×Kt | B—R 5 |

It is clear that Black cannot capture the B P with the R because of 20. R×Kt.

| 20. B—Kt 3 | B×B |
| 21. R P×B | B—B 4 |

At first sight this move seems to create difficulties for White, for instance after 22. Q—K 2, the manœuvre 22. ....B—Kt 5 ; would force the White Queen back to Q 3.

Position after Black's 21st move.

22. Q—Q 4 !

This definitely ensures an advantage, since the threat of Kt×Kt P by Black is illusory, *e.g.* : 22. ....Kt×Kt P ; 23. Kt—B 5, Q—Q 3 ; 24. B—Kt 3 ! and wins. Consequently Black is now forced to look after his weak point, Q 4.

| 22. ...... | K R—Q 1 |

Q R—Q 1 would have been slightly better, but the game was lost in any event.

| 23. Q R—Q 1 | Q—B 2 |

Renewing the threat of 23. .... Kt×Kt P.

24. Kt—Q 2 !

To this move Black cannot reply with 24. ....Kt×Kt P, because of 25. B—Kt 3; nor is 24. ....Kt×Kt feasible, on account of the following variation: 25. B×B, Kt—B 5; 26. B—K 6 ch, K—R 1; 27. B×P!, Kt×P; 28. R—Kt 1, Kt—B 5; 29. B×R! and wins.

24. ...... Kt×B P

A desperate sacrifice. But similarly after 24. ....B—Kt 3; 25. B—Kt 3, Kt—B 3; 26. Kt—B 3, the win was only a question of technique.

25. B×B	Kt×R
26. R×Kt	Q×Kt P
27. B—K 6 ch	K—R 1
28. B×P	Q R—B 1
29. Kt—K 4	Q—R 5
30. P—Q Kt 3	R—B 3
31. Q—B 2	

More straightforward would have been: 31. B×R!, R×Q; 32. P×R, and the passed Pawn would have become irresistible. But once the Queens are exchanged the ending could not present any difficulties for White.

| 31. ...... | Q—R 4 |
| 32. Q—B 3 | Q×Q |

Evidently forced.

33. P×Q	P—Kt 3
34. R—Q 2	R—Kt 3
35. P—B 4	P×P
36. P×P	R—Kt 8 ch
37. K—B 2	P—Q R 4
38. P—B 5	R—B 8
39. P—B 6	K—Kt 2

See Diagram.

40. B—B 4 !

Position after Black's 39th move.

Winning the Exchange as well, for after 40. ....R—Q B 1; 41. R—Q 7 ch, K—R 3; 42. B—Q 5, or if 40. ....R×R; 41. Kt×R, followed by 42. P—B 7 and Black loses at once.

40.	R×B
41. R×R	R×P
42. R—Q 7 ch	K—R 3
43. K—Kt 3	R—B 5

Or if 43. ....R—B 7; 44. P—B 4, R×P; 45. Kt—Kt 5 and the mate cannot be avoided.

44. Kt—B 2 !

Position after White's 44th move.

ALL-RUSSIAN TOURNAMENT AT ST. PETERSBURG 59

44. ...... K—Kt 4

If 44. ....R—Q R 5 ; 45. Kt—Kt 4 ch, K—R 4 !; 46. R—Q 5 ch, P—Kt 4 ; 47. R—Q 6 and mate to follow. Or 44. ....P—Kt 4 ; 45. Kt—Kt 4 ch, followed by 46. Kt—K 5 ch and White wins.

45. R—Q 5 ch   K—B 3
46. R × P   Black resigns.

GAME 22

QUEEN'S GAMBIT DECLINED

White :   *Black :*
S. von Freymann.   A. Alekhin.

1. P—Q 4   P—Q 4
2. Kt—K B 3   Kt—K B 3
3. P—B 4   P—K 3
4. B—Kt 5

This move is of doubtful value, for it allows the following reply, hit upon by Duras. It is better to play 4. Kt—Q B 3 first.

4. ......   P—K R 3 !

After this move White has nothing better than to take the Knight, leaving his opponent with two Bishops, for if the Bishop retreats, the acceptance of the Gambit is in favour of Black.

5. B—R 4   P × P

More precise would have been 5. ....B—Kt 5 ch; followed by P × P; as then the Gambit Pawn could be held by P—Q Kt 4, etc.

6. Q—R 4 ch

The only way of regaining the Pawn. Black threatened 6. ....B—Kt 5 ch ; followed by 7. ....P—Q Kt 4.

6. ......   Q Kt—Q 2
7. Q × B P   P—B 4
8. Kt—B 3   P—R 3

With the intention of developing the Q B on the long diagonal, a plan which White, as the sequel shows, will be unable to frustrate.

9. P—R 4

A scheme based on insufficient means. Evidently 9. P—K 3 would have been better, although in any case Black's position was preferable.

9. ......   P—Q Kt 4 !

Black still persists, for if 10. R P × P, R P × P ; the White Queen and Rook would both be *en prise*.

10. Q—Q 3   P—B 5
11. Q—Kt 1

Position after White's 11th move.

11. ......   B—Kt 2 !

A Pawn sacrifice, the object of which is to obstruct White's development through pressure on White's Q B 3.

12. P × P

It would have been preferable to decline the offer of a Pawn. But in any event, even after 12. P—K 3, Q—Kt 3 ; White's position would have remained distinctly inferior.

12.	P×P
13. Kt×P	B—Kt 5 ch
14. Kt—B 3	P—Kt 4
15. B—Kt 3	Kt—K 5
16. Q—B 1	

All White's last moves were obviously forced.

| 16. ...... | Kt—Kt 3 |

Threatening 17. ....Kt—R 5.

17. R×R	Q×R
18. Kt—Q 2	Kt×Kt (Q 7)
19. K×Kt	Q—R 7!

Initiating the deciding manœuvre. Black again threatens 20. ....Kt—R 5; and does not allow his opponent the respite he needs to disentangle his position by 20. P—K 3.

| 20. K—Q 1 | Q—Kt 6 ch |
| 21. Q—B 2 | |

Now the Black Q B P will move straight on to Queen.

| 21. ...... | B×Kt |
| 22. P×B | |

Position after White's 22nd move.

| 22. ...... | B—K 5! |

Simple and immediately decisive.

| 23. Q×Q | P×Q |
| 24. P—K 3 | |

Or 24. K—B 1, Kt—B 5; and mates in a few moves.

| 24. ...... | P—Kt 7 |

White resigns.

GAME 23

FOUR KNIGHTS' GAME

White : *Black :*
A. NIEMZOVITCH. A. ALEKHIN.

1. P—K 4	P—K 4
2. Kt—K B 3	Kt—Q B 3
3. Kt—B 3	Kt—B 3
4. B—Kt 5	Kt—Q 5!

Rubinstein has, in my opinion, made one of his finest contributions to the theory of the openings in the discovery and analysis of the variations springing from this move.

White, if he does not wish to run the risk of dangerous complications resulting from the capture of the proffered Pawn, has nothing better than 5. Kt×Kt, P×Kt; 6. P—K 5, P×Kt; 7. P×Kt, Q×P (not 7. ....P×P ch; 8. B×P, Q×P; 9. Castles with an irresistible attack); 8. Q P×P, B—K 2!; 9. Castles, Castles with approximately an equal game.

The present game affords a typical example of the dangers to which White exposes himself when seeking the demolition of the Rubinstein variation.

5. B—B 4

Alternatives are:

I.—5. Castles, Kt×B; 6. Kt×Kt, P—B 3; 7. Kt—B 3, P—Q 3; 8. P—Q 4, Q—B 2.

II.—5. Kt×P, Q—K 2; 6. Kt—B 3, Kt×B; 7. Kt×Kt, Q×P ch; 8. Q—K 2, Q×Q ch; 9. K×Q, Kt—Q 4; 10. P—B 4, P—Q R 3; and in neither case does White have any advantage.

ALL-RUSSIAN TOURNAMENT AT ST. PETERSBURG

5.	B—B 4
6. Kt × P	Q—K 2 !
7. Kt—Q 3	

After 7. Kt—B 3 Black would also have obtained a strong attack by 7. ....P—Q 4 ! On the other hand, it is clear that White cannot capture the K B P with the Kt, because of 7. ....P—Q 4 ! nor with the B, because of 7. ....K—Q 1, followed by 8. ....P—Q 3.

7.	P—Q 4 !

The point of this variation.

8. B × P

Or 8. Kt × P, Kt × Kt ; 9. B × Kt, P—Q B 3. If 8. Kt × B, P × B and Black has the advantage.

8.	Kt × B
9. Kt × Kt	Q × P ch
10. Kt—K 3	B—Q 3
11. Castles	B—K 3

Now the sacrifice of the Pawn is greatly compensated by the superiority in development secured by Black.

White finds himself confronted with great difficulties resulting from the fact that his Knights lack points of support in the centre.

12. Kt—K 1	Castles (Q R)

To profit as quickly as possible by the open files in the centre.

13. P—Q B 3	Kt—B 4
14. Q—B 2	

14. P—Q 3 at once would be a little better, although in this case Black would also maintain a good attacking position by 14. ....Q—K R 5 ; 15. Kt—B 3, Q—R 4.

Now Black demolishes the hostile position by a series of moves, apparently quite simple and by that very fact difficult to discover.

Position after White's 14th move.

14.	Q—K R 5 !

More plausible was 14. ....Q—K B 5, provoking 15. P—K Kt 3 and allowing Black to carry on the attack by the advance of the K R P. But the continuation 15. P—K Kt 3, Q—Kt 4 ; 16. P—Q 4, Q—B 3 ; 17. Kt (K 1)—Kt 2 or Kt—Q 3 seems to give White adequate defensive resources.

It is for this reason that Black sought to make the direct attack against the King coincide with a strong pressure on the centre.

To attain this latter end it was of paramount importance to compel White to weaken the K file by the advance of his K B P.

15. Kt—B 3

Now 15. P—K Kt 3 would be faulty, on account of 15. ....Q—R 6.

15.	Q—K B 5

Threatening 16. ....Kt—R 5.

16. Kt × Kt	B × Kt
17. P—Q 3	Q—K Kt 5

Threatening 18. ....Q—R 4 ; followed by 19. ....B × P and 20. ....B × P ch.

18. Kt—Q 4   Q—R 4
19. P—K B 4

Black has thus attained the goal which he had in view on his 14th move.

19. ......   K R—K 1
20. P—Q Kt 4

If 20. B—Q 2, Black would maintain his advantage by 20. ....B—B 4 ; 21. Q R—K 1, R—K 7 !, etc.

20. ......   P—Q B 4 !

Thus forcing the exchange of White's only active piece.

21. Kt × B   Q × Kt

Threatening 22. ....P—B 5.

22. Q—Q 2   B—B 2
23. R—B 3

All this is compulsory.

23. ......   P × P
24. P × P

Position after White's 24th move.

24. ......   P—K Kt 4 !

After this move Black regains his Pawn at least, and maintains his superiority in position.

25. P × P

If 25. B—Kt 2, which was, however, better, the continuation would have been 25. ....P × P ; 26. Q—B 3, K—Kt 1, and Black would have won the weak Q P in the end. The text-move causes a speedy collapse.

25. ......   Q—K 4
26. B—Kt 2   Q × P ch
27. K—B 1

Position after White's 27th move.

27. ......   B—Kt 6 ?

This premature move allows White to secure a draw. The game was easily won by 27. ....Q—R 8 ch ; 28. K—B 2, Q—R 5 ch ; 29. K—B 1, B—Kt 6 !! ; after which White would have nothing else than 30. Q—B 3 ch, K—Kt 1 ; 31. Q—B 5, P—Kt 3 !; 32. Q—Kt 1, R × P ! ; 33. R × R, Q—B 5 ch ; 34. R—B 3, Q—B 5 ch and mate next move.

28. B—Q 4 !

And now behold Black himself reduced to seeking a drawing variation ! The following sacrifice answers this purpose.

ALL-RUSSIAN TOURNAMENT AT ST. PETERSBURG

28.	......	R×B !
29.	Q—B 3 ch	K—Kt 1
30.	Q×R	B—K 4
31.	Q—Q 7	R—Q B 1
32.	R×P !	

By this threat of mate White eliminates all danger. Unfortunately for him, he allows himself to be intoxicated by a mirage of victory; but, by reason of the exposed position of his King, this conception bears great risks in its train.

32.	......	Q—R 8 ch
33.	K—B 2	Q—R 5 ch

Naturally not 33. R—B 7 ch, because of 34. K—K 3 and wins.

34.	K—K 2	Q—R 4 ch
35.	P—Kt 4	

This move is altogether too venturesome, and merely gives Black fresh chances.
After 35. K—B 1 Black would have nothing better than the draw by 35. ....Q—R 8 ch, etc.

35	......	Q—R 7 ch
36.	K—B 3	Q—Kt 6 ch
37.	K—K 4	

Forced, for if 37. K—K 2, Q—Kt 7 ch, followed by 38. ....B×R or R—B 7 ch according to circumstances, and Black wins.

37.	......	B—B 2

Threatening Q—K 4 ch followed by Q×R.

38.	R—Q B 1	Q—Kt 7 ch
39.	K—K 3	B—Kt 3 ch

Position after Black's 39th move.

40. P—Q 4

This loses at once. The only reply was 40. R—B 5, with the continuation 40. ....R—Q 1 ; 41. Q—B 5 ! (else 41. ....Q—Kt 6 ch), R—K 1 ch ; 42. K—Q 4, Q—Kt 7 ch ; 43. K—B 4, Q×R P ch ; 44. K—B 3, and Black, having to reckon with the threat R×P ch, could still not force the win.

40.	......	R—Q 1 !

Decisive.

41. R—B 7

If the White Queen moves, Black would win by 41. ....B×P ch, followed by 42. ....Q—K B 7 ch, etc.

41.	......	Q—Kt 6 ch
42.	R—B 3	Q—K 8 ch
43.	K—Q 3	Q—Q 8 ch
44.	K—K 3	B×R

White resigns.

CHAPTER IX

INTERNATIONAL TOURNAMENT AT ST. PETERSBURG, MAY, 1914

GAME 24

PETROFF'S DEFENCE

White :   *Black :*
A. ALEKHIN.   F. J. MARSHALL.

1.	P—K 4	P—K 4
2.	Kt—K B 3	Kt—K B 3
3.	Kt × P	P—Q 3
4.	Kt—K B 3	Kt × P
5.	P—Q 4	P—Q 4
6.	B—Q 3	B—Q 3
7.	P—B 4	

This variation of the Petroff does not cause Black any difficulty. White could secure better chances by 3. P—Q 4 (Steinitz), or 5. Q—K 2 (Lasker), or even 5. Kt—B 3.

7.	......	B—Kt 5 ch !
8.	Q Kt—Q 2	Kt × Kt

This exchange, which allows White quite an appreciable advantage in development, appears hardly justified. The correct line of play was 8. ....Castles ; 9. Castles, B × Kt !; 10. B × B, B—Kt 5, with at least an equal game.

9.	B × Kt	Q—K 2 ch
10.	Q—K 2	Q × Q ch

It is interesting to notice that this plausible exchange is later on shown up as a decisive mistake. Black must first play 10. ....B × B ch ; 11. K × B, Q × Q ch ; 12. B × Q, P × P ; 13. B × P, Castles ; after which White would have maintained a slight superiority in position, but Black's game would still remain very defendable.

11.	K × Q	B × B
12.	K × B	B—K 3

If now 12. ....P × P, then 13. K R—K 1 ch ! with still greater effect than in the actual game, White having preserved his Bishop for the attack against his opponent's undeveloped game.

13.	P × P	B × P
14.	K R—K 1 ch	K—Q 1
15.	B—K 4 !	B × B

Forced, for if 15. ....P—Q B.3 White would win a Pawn at once by exchange of Bishops, followed by 17. R—K 5.

16.	R × B	R—K 1

This move was absolutely necessary to prevent the threatened doubling of White's Rooks on the K file.

INTERNATIONAL TOURNAMENT AT ST. PETERSBURG

17. Q R—K 1	R × R
18. R × R	Kt—B 3

Position after Black's 18th move.

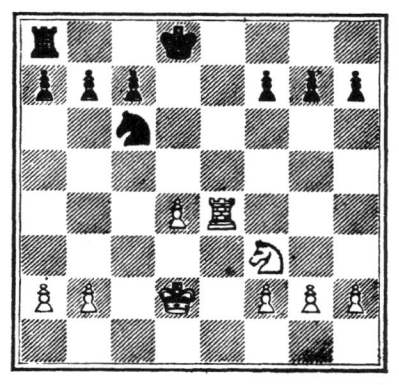

19. R—Kt 4 !

The winning manœuvre. On the other hand, 19. Kt—Kt 5 was insufficient, on account of 19. .... K—Q 2 ! Now Black is going to lose a Pawn by force.

19.	P—K Kt 3
20. R—R 4 !	K—K 2

Best in the circumstances, for after 20. ....P—K R 4 ; 21. P—K Kt 4 followed by 22. P × P White would establish a passed Pawn.

21. R × P	R—Q 1
22. R—R 4	R—Q 4
23. R—K 4 ch !	

Forcing the retreat of Black's King, for after 23. ....K—B 3 ; 24. K—B 3, the threat 25. R—K 8 would have been very dangerous for the opponent.

23.	K—B 1
24. K—B 3	R—K B 4

Contemplating ....Kt—Q 4 ; to cause White the maximum of technical difficulties.

25. R—K 2	P—R 3

If 25. ....Kt—K 2 White would have replied 26. R—K 5 and the continuation of the game would scarcely be modified.

26. P—Q R 3	Kt—K 2
27. R—K 5 !	R—B 3

After the exchange of Rooks, Black could no longer save the game.

28. K—Q 3

Preparing 29. R—Q B 5, which Black prevents by his reply, but at the cost of a new weakness at Q B 2 which White will proceed to exploit without delay.

28.	P—Kt 3
29. R—K 2	

White, as we see from the sequel, proposes to sacrifice a Pawn in order to occupy the 7th rank with his Rook and thus to obtain a passed Pawn. This manœuvre is the shortest and surest means of securing the victory.

29.	Kt—Q 4
30. K—K 4	Kt—B 5

Or 30. ....R—K 3 ch ; 31. Kt—K 5, Kt—B 3 ch ; 32. K—B 3 and White dominates the board.

31. R—B 2	Kt × P
32. Kt—K 5 !	

Not at once R × P on account of 32. ....R—B 5 ch followed by 33. ....R × Kt, whereas now, since White threatens 33. Kt—Q 7 ch, Black cannot save his Q B P.

32.	K—K 1
33. R × P	R × P
34. Kt—B 4 !	

A very important move. The Knight is going to be posted on Q Kt 7, where it will guard the advance of the passed Q P.

34.	P—Q Kt 4	48. R—K 8 ch	K—B 2
35. Kt—Q 6 ch	K—B 1	49. R—K 2	P—B 4
36. P—Q 5	P—B 3	50. K—Q 5	K—B 3
37. Kt—Kt 7 !	Kt—B 5	51. K—Q 4	P—B 5
38. P—Kt 4	P—Kt 4	52. K—K 4	K—Kt 4
39. P—Q 6	Kt—K 3	53. R—Q B 2	P—B 6
		54. R—Q 2	K—R 5
		55. K—B 4	Black resigns.

Position after Black's 39th move.

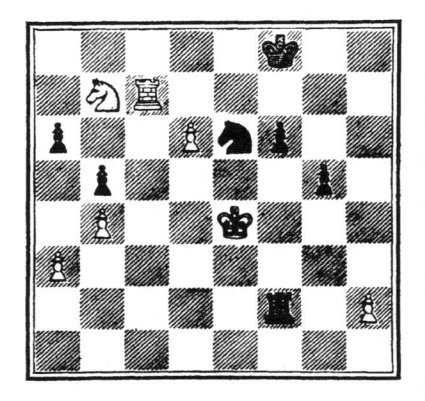

40. K—Q 5 !

The *coup de grâce*. White's Rook cannot be captured on account of 41. P×Kt, R—B 7; 42. Kt—B 5 ! Similarly, after 40. ....R—K 7 White would win easily by 41. K—B 6, Kt—Q 5 ch ; 42. K—Kt 6, etc., so, as a last resource, Black attempts to exploit his King-side Pawns after the sacrifice of the Rook for the passed Pawn. But this manœuvre is foredoomed to failure.

40.	Kt—B 5 ch
41. K—B 6	R×K R P
42. Kt—B 5	

Preventing the sacrifice of Black's Knight for the Pawn, and winning a whole Rook.

42.	R—Q 7
43. R—B 8 ch	K—B 2
44. P—Q 7	Kt—K 3
45. Kt×Kt	K×Kt
46. P—Q 8=Q	R×Q
47. R×R	P—Kt 5

GAME 25

FALKBEER COUNTER-GAMBIT

White :   *Black :*
A. ALEKHIN.   DR. S. TARRASCH.

1. P—K B 4	P—K 4
2. P—K 4	

From's Gambit accepted offers White at best only an equal game.

2.	P—Q 4
3. K P×P	P—K 5
4. P—Q 3	Kt—K B 3

At the time the present game was played the variations springing from this move were considered advantageous for White, thanks especially to analyses by the late Simon Alapin.

Recently, however, Dr. Tarrasch succeeded in invalidating this opinion, introducing in his game against Spielmann at Mährisch-Ostrau, 1924, an improvement of great importance (see note to Black's 6th move).

5. P×P	Kt×K P
6. Kt—K B 3	B—K B 4

An innovation which the sequel shows to be insufficient. The correct line of play, demonstrated by Dr. Tarrasch in the game mentioned, is 6. ....B—Q B 4 ; 7. Q—K 2, B—B 4 !, and if 8. P—K Kt 4? then 8. ....Castles !, with a winning sacrificial attack.

7. B—K 3

This move deprives Black of his best chance on the diagonal Q R 2 —K Kt 8, and leaves him without compensation for the Pawn he has given up.

7. ......   P—Q B 3
8. B—B 4   P—Q Kt 4

Trying to keep his opponent busy lest he secure his position definitely by Castling.

9. B—Kt 3

White could play equally well 9. B—K 2, P—Q R 3; 10. P—Q R 4 !, P—Kt 5; 11. P×P, Q×Q ch; 12. B×Q, Kt×P, etc., but the combination based on the text-move offered better prospects.

9. ......   P—B 4

Position after Black's 9th move.

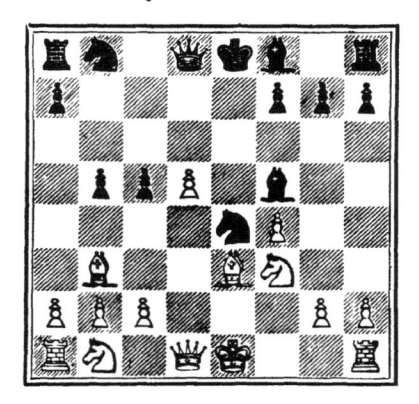

10. P—Q 6 !

Bringing about an advantageous simplification in view of his extra Pawn. The Q P cannot be captured by the Black Queen on account of 11. Q×Q, followed by B—Q 5, etc.

10. ......   P—B 5
11. Q—Q 5   Kt—Q 2
12. Q×B   Kt×P
13. Q—Q 5   B—K 2
14. Castles   Castles
15. Kt—B 3   Kt—B 3
16. Q—Q 2   P×B

Just in time, for White threatened 17. Kt×P, etc.

17. R P×P

White's advantage in material is in no way diminished by his having a doubled Pawn, for he will always be in a position to obtain a passed Pawn by advancing his Q B P.

17. ......   P—Kt 5
18. Kt—Q 5   Kt—B 4
19. Kt×B ch   Q×Kt

White has still a slight weakness in the centre, which he will subsequently eliminate by holding and strengthening his Q 4.

20. K R—K 1   K R—Q 1
21. B—Q 4 !   Kt×B
22. Kt×Kt   Q—B 4
23. Q R—Q 1

Intending to play P—B 3 once the Black Rooks are doubled on the Queen's file.

23. ......   R—Q 4
24. P—R 3   Q R—Q 1

Position after Black's 24th move.

25. P—B 3

After this move White's position is invulnerable. Black is forced to adopt a waiting policy, which is all the more distressing as he is minus a Pawn.

White's next moves aim at unpinning the Knight, which will take a decisive part in the final onslaught when the White Rooks are doubled on the King's file.

25. ......   P—K R 3
26. Q—Q 3   Q—Q 3
27. Q—B 3   Kt—R 4

An inoffensive demonstration which cannot hinder White's plans.

28. R—K 4   Kt—B 3

Of course not 28. ....P—B 4, because of 29. R—K 6.

29. R—K 3   Kt—R 4
30. R—K B 1   Kt—B 3
31. R (B 1)—K 1

To be able to play 32. R—K 5, in answer to 31. ....Kt—R 4.

31. ......   Q—B 4
32. K—R 2   R—Q B 1
33. R (K 1)—K 2

A subtle preparation to the following attacking move.

33. ......   K—B 1
34. R—K 5 !

Now Black cannot play 34. .... P×P; 35. P×P, Q×P; because of 36. R—Q B 2.

34. ......   R (B 1)—Q 1
35. Kt—B 5

Threatening amongst other things 36. P—B 4, R×R; 37. P×R, followed by 38. P—K 6, etc.

35. ......   Q—Kt 3
36. Q—Kt 3   Kt—R 4
37. Q—R 4

Threatening mate in three by 37· R—K 8 ch !, etc.

See Diagram.

37. ......   R×R

A desperate move in an untenable dosition. Against 37. Kt—B 3,

Position after White's 37th move.

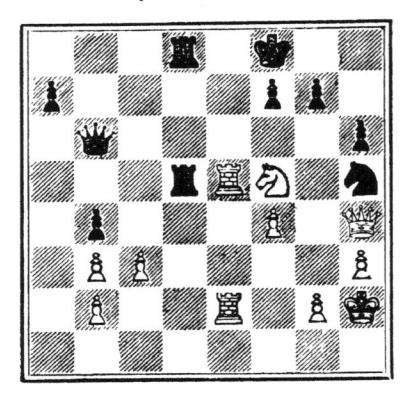

recommended by Dr. Tarrasch in the Tournament book as providing a sufficient defence for the time being, White had prepared the following pretty winning combination: 38. Kt×R P !, P×Kt ; 39. R—K 6 !, P×R (alternatives are :
I.—39. ....R (Q 4)—Q 3 ; 40. Q×Kt, R×R ; 41. R×R.
II.—39. ....R (Q 1)—Q 3 ; Q×P ch and mate in two).

40. Q×Kt ch, K—Kt 1 ; 41. R×P, R (Q 4)—Q 3 ; 42. Q—Kt 6· ch, K—R 1 (or 42. ....K—B 1 ; 43. Q—B 5 ch, K any ; 44. R—K 7, etc.) ; 43. Q×P ch, K—Kt 1 ; 44. Q—Kt 6 ch, K—R 1 ; 45. Q—R 5 ch !, K—Kt 1 ; 46. R—K 7 ! and mate is unavoidable. Such a finale would have given the game a good chance of a brilliancy prize.

38. P×R   R—Q 8
39. R—K 3

White could also have captured the Kt and then brought his King to R 4. The text-move is still more simple and hinders 39. ....P—Kt 3, which would prove disastrous for Black after 40. Q—K 7 ch, K—Kt 1; 41. Q—K 8 ch, K—R 2 ; 42. Q×P ch, K—R 1 ; 43. Kt—K 7 ! and wins.

39. ......   Q—Kt 3
40. Q×P ch   Black resigns

GAME 26

FRENCH DEFENCE

White: Black:
Dr. S. Tarrasch.   A. Alekhin.

1. P—K 4   P—K 3
2. P—Q 4   P—Q 4
3. Kt—Q B 3   Kt—K B 3
4. B—Kt 5

The variation 4. P×P, P×P ; 5. B—Kt 5, recommended by Svenonius, brings White no advantage at all after 5. ....Kt—B 3, which is favoured by the author and was successfully tried by Bogoljuboff v. Mieses (Berlin, 1920).

4. ......   B—Kt 5
5. P×P

This variation has gradually fallen into desuetude of late years. Players prefer to aim at a rapid King's side attack by : 5. P—K 5, P—K R 3 ; 6. B—Q 2, B×Kt ; 7. P×B, Kt—K 5 ; 8. Q—Kt 4, K—B 1 ! ; 9. P—K R 4 !, etc. But the latest master-practice, and particularly some of Dr. Tarrasch's games, tend to show that here too Black disposes of sufficient resources from the defensive point of view. Interesting, too, is Tchigorin's continuation : 5. P—K 5, P—K R 3 ; 6. P×Kt, P×B ; 7. P×P, R—Kt 1 ; 8. P—K R 4, P×P ; with the improvement 9. Q—Kt 4 ! instead of 9. Q—R 5. A game played by the author in Moscow, 1915, continued as follows :

9. ......   B—K 2
10. P—K Kt 3 !   P—Q B 4
(10 ....B—B 3 was better.)
11. Kt P×P   P×P

See Diagram.

12. P—R 5 !   P×Kt
13. P—R 6   P×P
14. R—Kt 1   Q—R 4 ch
15. K—K 2   Q×P
16. P—R 7   Q×R
17. P×R=Q ch   K—Q 2

Position after Black's 11th move in Sub-Variation

18. Q×B P   Q×P ch
19. K—B 3   Kt—B 3 !
20. Q (Kt 4)×P ch   K—B 2
21. Q—B 4 ch   K—Kt 3
22. Q (K 6)—K 3 ch   B—B 4
23. P—Kt 8=Q   P—Kt 8=Q

Position after Black's 23rd move in Sub-Variation.

In this extraordinary position White won by a *coup de repos* :

24. R—R 6 ! !

Threatening 25. Q—Q 8 mate, for if now :

24. ......   Q×B
25. Q—Kt 4 ch   Q—Kt 4
26. Q—Q 8 ch   K—R 3
27. Q (K 3)—R 3 ch

and mates in two moves (*See Diagram.*

Final Position in Sub-Variation

This position is certainly unique of its kind!

5.	Q×P
6. B×Kt	B×Kt ch
7. P×B	P×B
8. Kt—B 3	P—Q Kt 3

Here the fianchetto is very strong, inasmuch as White, as has been demonstrated by a St. Petersburg amateur, cannot reply with a King's fianchetto without inconvenience.

9. P—Kt 3

To this Black could have replied: 9. ....Kt—Q 2!, the idea being to wait for 10. B—Kt 2, and then to prevent White from castling on the King-side by 10. ....B—R 3!, for 11. Kt—R 4 is not to be feared because of 11. ....Q—Q R 4! This important innovation casts doubt on the value of White's fifth move.

9. ......   B—Kt 2

But with this simple move he equally obtains a perfectly safe game.

10. B—Kt 2	Q—K 5 ch
11. K—Q 2	

White had nothing better than to propose the exchange of Queens by 11. Q—K 2, although in that case also Black had somewhat the better game on account of the possibility of an attack against the centre by P—Q B 4. The text-move, just as 11. K—B 1 (Réti—Bogoljuboff, Berlin, 1920) is insufficient, in view of the exposed position of his King. Black at once assumes the initiative and keeps it to the end.

11. ......   Q—Kt 3

The only move to parry the threat 12. Kt—R 4, but amply sufficient.

12. Kt—R 4	Q—R 3 ch
13. P—B 4	Kt—B 3!

Threatening 14. ....Castles Q R; followed by 15. ....P—K 4, etc. and forcing the White King to retreat once more.

14. Q—K 2	Castles Q R
15. K—B 1	K—Kt 1

Threatening 15. ....P—K 4, which at present would not be so good because of 16. P—Q 5, P×P; 17. Q—Kt 4 ch, followed by Q×P.

16. K—Kt 2   Kt—R 4!

The exchange of Bishops is essential in order to allow Black's Rook to participate in the attack via Q 4.

17. B×B	Kt×B
18. Q R—Q 1	R—Q 4
19. P—B 4	

In conjunction with R—Q 3 this provides comparatively the best means of defence, but White misses a fine point on the following move.

19.	R—Q R 4
20. Kt—Kt 2	

He should have played 20. R—Q 3 at once, so as to be able to defend himself with 22. R—Kt 3, etc., after 20. ....R—Q 1; 21. K R— Q 1, Q—B 1! Now Black's reply will no longer leave him time for this.

Position after White's 20th move.

20. ......   R—Q 1!

For if now 21. R—Q 3, then 21. ....Q—B 1, with the very strong threat 22. ....R×P! followed by 23..... Q—R 6 ch; 24..... Q × P ch; 25. ....Q—R 8 ch; and 26. ....Q×R. Confronted with these difficulties, White is compelled to weaken his position in the centre.

21. Kt—K 3   Q—B 1
22. P—B 5

Obstructing the Queen's diagonal, but not for long, unfortunately for White.

22. ......   P×P
23. P—Q 5   P—B 5!

This Pawn can be taken only by the Knight, for if 24. Q×P, Q—R 6 ch would win a piece.

24. Kt×P   Q—Kt 5 ch
25. K—R 1   Q—B 6 ch
26. Kt—Kt 2   R—Q 3!

Far stronger than the simple gain of a Pawn by Q R×P; as now White has not sufficient defence against the doubling of Rooks on the Q R file, feasible as it is even should White play 27. R—Q 3.

27. Q—B 4

Position after White's 27th move.

27. ......   R (Q 3)—R 3!

Forcing the exchange of both Rooks for Queen and two Pawns, which, in view of the exposed position of the White King, leads to an evidently favourable ending.

28. P×P

Clearly the Queen cannot be captured because of mate in two.

28. ......   P×P
29. K—Kt 1   R×P
30. Q×R (R 2) R×Q
31. K×R   Q×B P
32. Q R—Q B 1 Q—Q 7
33. K—Kt 1   Kt—Q 3

The entry of the Knight into the game should have decided the game in a few moves.

34. R—B 2   Q—Kt 5
35. R—Q 1   Kt—Kt 4
36. R—Q 8 ch   K—Kt 2
37. R (B 2)—Q 2 P—K 4

Black, thinking the game won in any case, makes no effort to find the shortest way. More energetic is 37. ....P—Q R 4 !, White being without resource against this advance.

38. P×P	P×P
39. K—B 1	Kt—Q 5
40. R—Q 3	Q—K 8 ch
41. R—Q 1	Q—K 5
42. R—Q 3	Q—R 8 ch

Here again 42. ....P—Q B 4, followed by 43. ....P—B 5 ; led to a more speedy victory. It goes without saying that the capture of White's last Pawns was also sufficient.

43. R—Q 1	Q×P
44. K—Kt 1	Q×P
45. R—Q 3	Q—K 8 ch
46. K—R 2	P—K R 4
47. R—K 8	Q—K 5
48. R—Q B 3	Kt—Kt 4
49. R—B 5	Q—Kt 5 !

See Diagram.

With the last move, which threatens 50. ....Kt—B 6 ch ; 51. K—R 1, Q—R 6, mate, Black ensures the gain of the Exchange. Had White wished to play on, the

Final Position.

only alternative would have been 50. R (K 8)×P, Kt—B 6 ch ; 51. R×Kt, Q×R ; 52. R×P, after which Black wins in the following manner : 52. ....K—B 3 ; 53. R—R 4, K—Kt 4 ; 54. R—R 5 ch, P—B 4 ; 55. R—R 4, P—R 4 ; 56. R—K B 4, Q—B 7 ! ; 57. K—R 3, Q—Kt 7 ! and the White Rook must leave the fourth rank, after which Black wins easily by 58. ....Q—Kt 6 ch ; followed by 59. ....P—R 5 ; etc.

White resigns.

CHAPTER X

INTERNATIONAL TOURNAMENT AT MANNHEIM, JULY, 1914

GAME 27

RUY LOPEZ

White: Black:
O. DURAS. A. ALEKHIN.

1. P—K 4   P—K 4
2. Kt—K B 3   Kt—Q B 3
3. B—Kt 5   P—Q R 3
4. B×Kt   Kt P×B

Though unusual, this variation appears to me eminently practicable. In any case it has the advantage of not allowing White the majority of Pawns on the Queenside as happens after 4. ...Q P×P; 5. P—Q 4, P×P; 6. Q×P, Q×Q; 7. Kt×Q, etc.

5. P—Q 4

White would obtain no advantage from 5. Kt×P, Q—Kt 4; etc.

5. ......   P×P
6. Q×P   Q—B 3 !

A new move and probably the best. Black concludes that his somewhat cramped position will be more easily defendable after the exchange of Queens, and the sequel confirms the correctness of his judgment.

7. Castles

Conforming to the preceding note, White should have avoided the exchange of Queens. There was, for instance, to be considered 7. P—K 5, Q—Kt 3; 8. Castles, for after 8. ....Q×P ?; 9. Kt—B 3 he would have obtained an advantage in development compensating for the Pawn sacrificed.

7. ......   Q×Q
8. Kt×Q   R—Kt 1

To hinder the development of White's Q B.

9. Kt—Kt 3

After 9. P—Q Kt 3, Black could have given up a Pawn by P—Q B 4 and P—B 5 ! as in game No. 2, with good attacking chances.

9. ......   Kt—K 2 !

Far better than the plausible 9. ....Kt—B 3, after which White would have obtained a fine game by 10. B—B 4, P—Q 3; 11. R—K 1, with the threat of 12. P—K 5, etc.

10. B—Q 2

An attempt to oppose the development of Black's K B, but Black circumvents this plan by the manœuvre which follows.

10. ......   Kt—Kt 3
11. B—B 3   Kt—B 5 !

Threatening 12. ....Kt—K 7 ch followed by Kt × B, thus gaining the necessary time for the development of the K B.

12. R—K 1   B—K 2
13. Q Kt—Q 2

It can be seen that 13. B × P, R—Kt 1 ; followed by R × P ch would be to Black's advantage.

13. ......   Castles
14. Kt—B 4

Position after White's 14th move.

14. ......   R—K 1

Up to the present Black has played very carefully and obtained an entirely satisfactory game ; but his last move is perhaps too risky, for it allows White to prevent the advance of Black's Q P for a long time. It is true that after 14. .... P—Q 3 ; White could force a draw (but no more) by 15. Kt (B 4)—R 5, B—Q 2 ; 16. Kt—Q 4, R—Kt 3 ; 17. Kt—B 4, Q R—Kt 1 ; 18. Kt—R 5, etc. But from the theoretical point of view, this result was not to be disdained for Black in a Lopez.

15. Kt (B 4)—R 5   B—B 1
16. Q R—Q 1   P—Q B 4
17. P—K 5 !

Again opposing 17. ....P—Q 3 (prepared by Black's last moves), to which White would now reply 18. P × P, R × R ch ; 19. R × R, P × P ; 20. R—K 8 with a winning position.

17. ......   Kt—K 3
18. Kt—B 4

White has achieved his object, which was to prevent definitely the advance of Black's Q P. Black's position, though very restricted, is easy to defend, as it has no weaknesses. White's only threat would consist eventually in an advance of the King-side Pawns. By his next move Black seeks to obviate this danger.

18. ......   P—R 3 !

Preparing P—Kt 4 which would secure the square K Kt 3 for the King.

19. P—K R 4

After 19. P—Kt 3, Black would have obtained the advantage by 19. ....Kt—Kt 4 ; 20. R—K 3, B—Kt 2 ! ; 21. R × P, Kt—B 6 ch ; 22. K—B 1, Kt × P ch ; 23. K—K 2, Kt—Kt 5 ; 24. K R—Q 3, Q R—B 1, etc. The text-move was played in the hope—shown to be illusory by the sequel—of developing an attack by doubling the Rooks on the K R file.

19. ......   B—K 2
20. P—Kt 3   P—Kt 4 !
21. P × P   P × P
22. Kt (Kt 3)—R 5

The two adversaries pursue their respective plans with consequence. However White, through not taking into account a very hidden resource of his opponent's, initiated by a Pawn sacrifice on the 24th move, will see his chances diminish.

INTERNATIONAL TOURNAMENT AT MANNHEIM

22.	K—R 2 !
23. K—Kt 2	K—Kt 3
24. R—K R 1	

As will soon be seen, 24. P—R 3 ! was necessary, after which, however, Black could have occupied the K R file and eased his defence by exchanging one Rook. The text-move gives him the long awaited opportunity to take the initiative.

Position after White's 24th move.

24. ...... Kt—Q 5 !

An unexpected sacrifice which White is compelled to accept, for after 25. R—Q 2, Kt—Kt 4 ; 26. R—Q 3, Kt × B ; 27. R × Kt, P—Q 4 !, or 25. Kt—K 3, P—Q 3 !, Black would have obtained the superior game without difficulty.

| 25. B × Kt | P × B |
| 26. R × P | B—Kt 5 |

Indirectly threatening the K P and the Q Kt P. That is why White should have played 24. P—Q R 3.

27. Kt—Kt 3

The only move to preserve the extra Pawn temporarily.

27. ...... P—Q 4 !

The point of the sacrifice is only apparent now. White cannot play 28. P × P e. p., B—Kt 2 ch ; 29. P—B 3, R—K 7 ch ; 30. K—B 1, Q R—K 1, with a winning position for Black.

28. Kt—K 3 P—Q B 4 !

Stronger than 28. ....R × P ; 29. P—R 3, B—Q 3 ; 30. Kt × P, B—Kt 2 ; 31. K R—Q 1, with uncertain result.

29. R × P !

His best chance. If 29. R (Q 4)—Q 1, P—Q 5; 30. Kt—B 4, B—Kt 2 ch; 31. P—B 3, B—Q 4, followed by R × P, would secure a decisive advantage for Black.

29. ...... B—Kt 2
30. P—Q B 4 !

Not 30. P—K B 4 because of 30. ....P—B 5 ; and Black wins.

30. ...... R × P

Position after Black's 30th move.

31. P—R 3 !

An ingenious resource which allows White to save the Exchange, at first sight irretrievably lost.

31.	B×P !
32. Kt—R 5	B×R ch
33. P×B	

Position after White's 33rd move.

After the excitement of the last moves the situation is clear at last. Black, although forced to give back the Exchange because of the threats Kt—B 6, Kt—B 4 or P×B, secures the gain of a Pawn and retains excellent chances for the ensuing ending.

33.	R×Kt !
34. P×R	R×P ch
35. K—B 3	P—B 4 !

The only move to preserve the advantage, for now White can neither play 36. Kt—B 4, because of 36. ....P—Kt 5 ch followed by 37. ....R—Kt 5 ; nor 36. P—Q 6, because of 36. ....P—Kt 5 ch ; 37. K—B 4, P—B 5 ! : threatening B—Q 3 mate.

36. P—Kt 4

In order to bring his King into the centre and to obtain some chance with the two passed Pawns.

| 36. ...... | P×P ch |
| 37. K—K 4 ! | |

Not 37. K×P, on account of 37. ....P—B 5.

| 37. ...... | R—Kt 5 ch |
| 38. K—Q 3 | |

The alternative 38. K—K 5 would only occasion loss of time, Black continuing 38. ....P—B 5 ; 39. K—Q 4, B—Kt 7 ch, etc.

38. ...... B—Kt 7

Black has just time to bring back the Bishop to stop the dangerous White Queen's Pawn.

| 39. P—Q 6 | B—B 3 |
| 40. R—K B 1 | |

Position after White's 40th move.

40. ...... P—Kt 6 !

The deciding move, based on the following variation : 41. P—Q 7, R—Kt 1 ; 42. Kt—B 6, P—Kt 7 ; 43. R×B ch (or 43. R—any, R—Kt 2 !), K×R ; 44. Kt×R, K—K 2 ; 45. Kt—B 6 ch, K×P ; 46. Kt—K 5 ch, K—K 3 ; 47. Kt—B 3, P—Kt 5 ; 48. Kt—Kt 1, K—K 4 ; and Black evidently wins.

| 41. P—Q 7 | R—Kt 1 |
| 42. R—Q 1 | |

This offers no better chances for White than the preceding variation.

42.	P—Kt 7
43. K—K 2	R—Kt 7 ch
44. K—B 3	R—Q 7
45. R—K Kt 1	R × P
46. R × P	

The remainder is only a question of technique.

46.	R—Q 6
47. R—Q B 2	R—B 6
48. R × R	B × R
49. Kt—B 4	P—R 4
50. Kt—Kt 6	B—Kt 5

Now the Black King will move to the Queen's side and escort his passed Pawns to Queen.

White resigns.

GAME 28

RUY LOPEZ

White:	Black:
A. FLAMBERG.	A. ALEKHIN.
1. P—K 4	P—K 4
2. Kt—K B 3	Kt—Q B 3
3. B—Kt 5	P—Q R 3
4. B—R 4	Kt—B 3
5. Castles	Kt × P
6. P—Q 4	P—Q Kt 4
7. B—Kt 3	P—Q 4
8. P × P	B—K 3
9. P—B 3	B—K 2
10. R—K 1	

The best line of play for White is, in my opinion: 10. Q Kt—Q 2, Castles; 11. B—B 2 or 11. Kt—Q 4.

| 10. ...... | Castles. |
| 11. Q Kt—Q 2 | Kt—B 4 |

In order to reply to 12. B—B 2 with Tarrasch's move, 12. ....P—Q 5 !

12. Kt—Q 4

But this is hardly better than 12. B—B 2. Speaking generally, in this variation 10. R—K 1 appears to be loss of time.

12.	Kt × Kt
13. P × Kt	Kt—Q 6
14. R—K 3	Kt—B 5 !

Much better than 14. ....Kt × B; after which White is able to exercise a pressure on the open Q B file, which would justify the line of play he has adopted.

15. B—B 2

With the intention of preventing 15. ....P—Q B 4 by the threat: 16. P × P, followed by 17. B × P ch, and 18. Q—B 2 ch.

Position after White's 15th move.

| 15. ...... | P—Q B 4 ! |

Yet as the following variation shows, the move is quite playable: 16. P × P, B × P; 17. B × P ch, K × B; 18. Q—B 2 ch, K—Kt 1; 19. Q × B, P—Q 5; 20. R—K 4, R—B 1; 21. Q—R 3, Q—Kt 4 !; 22. P—K Kt 3 (or 22. Q—K Kt 3, Q × Q; followed by 23. ....Kt—Q 6; and wins); 22. ....Kt—R 6 ch; followed by 23. ....R × B, and Black wins.

16. Kt—Kt 3

In order to block up the position in the centre (for 16. ....P × P; 17. Kt × P would not be to Black's advantage) and then to attempt a King-side attack. But the majority of Pawns on the Queen-side which Black secures with his next move constitutes, as will be seen later, a far more potent weapon than his opponent's problematic chances on the King-side.

16. ......   P—B 5
17. Kt—Q 2   P—B 4

This and the following move are dictated by motives of a purely defensive character. Black wishes to consolidate his King's position before attempting a decisive action on the Queen-side.

18. Kt—B 1

18. P×P e. p., B×P ; 19. Kt—B 3, B—Kt 5 would be insufficient.

18. ......   R—B 2 !

An excellent defensive move which, in case of need, reserves the square K B 1 for the Black Knight and which, at the same time, protects his K Kt 2. 18. ....Kt—Kt 3 would be less good, for after 19. R—K R 3, Black could not have played 19. ....P—B 5 because of 20. R×P !

19. R—K Kt 3   Kt—Kt 3
20. P—B 4   P—Q R 4
21. B—K 3   P—Kt 5
22. Kt—Q 2   Q—Kt 3

Opposing for the moment 23. Q—R 5, because of the reply : 23. ....Kt×B P ; 24. B×Kt, Q×P ch ; 25. B—K 3, Q×Kt P, with the better game.

23. Kt—B 3

Of course not 23. Kt×P, P×Kt ; 24. P—Q 5, B—B 4 ; and Black wins.

23. ......   B—Q 2

Preparing 24. ....P—R 5, and aiming eventually at posting the Knight at K 3.

24. Kt—Kt 5

After 24. B—R 4, B×B ; 25. Q×B, Kt—B 1, followed by 26. ....Kt—K 3, Black's game remains preferable.

24. ......   B×Kt
25. R×B

This exchange implies further loss of time and brings the Rook still farther away from the threatened sector.

25. ......   P—R 5
26. K—R 1

In order to play 27. Q—R 5, impossible hitherto because of 26. ....Kt×B P, etc. It would have been better, however, for White to retire the Rook to Kt 3 and to resign himself to the defensive.

26. ......   Kt—K 2

Providing once and for all against White's 27. P—Kt 4, which, if played on the previous move, would have been disastrous for White, e.g.: 26. P—Kt 4, P×P ; 27. P—B 5, Kt×P.

27. Q—R 5

A last attempt which will be refuted by an energetic counter-demonstration by Black on the other wing.

27. ......   P—Kt 6
28. P×P   B P×P
29. B—Q 3

See Diagram.

29. ......   P—R 6 !

The passed Pawn which Black obtains by this temporary sacrifice wins the game in a few moves.

30. R×P   R×R
31. P×R   P—Kt 7
32. Q—Q 1

White begins a general retreat, but it is far too late !

Position after White's 29th move.

32.	R—B 1 !
33. R—Kt 3	R—R 1
34. B—Q Kt 1	R × P
35. B—Kt 1	R—R 8
36. R—Q B 3	B—R 5 !

The final manœuvre. This Bishop is to be posted at Q Kt 4 *without loss of time.*

37. Q—Q 3

Or 37. Q—K 1, B—Kt 4.

37.	B—Kt 4
38. Q—Q 1	Q—R 3 !

Final Position.

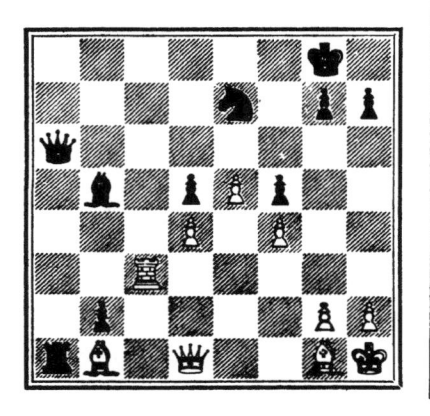

White has no resource against the threat : 39. ....R × B ! ; 40. Q × R, Q—R 8. If 39. R—Q Kt 3, Q—R 5 ! ; if 39. R—B 2, B—R 5 ; and if 39. R—K 3, B—R 5 followed by 40. ....B—B 7 and wins.

White resigns.

GAME 29

GIUOCO PIANO

White :   *Black :*
A. ALEKHIN.   DR. S. TARRASCH.

1. P—K 4	P—K 4
2. Kt—K B 3	Kt—Q B 3
3. B—B 4	B—B 4
4. P—B 3	Q—K 2

This ancient defence is better than its reputation, but it demands particularly accurate opening play on the part of Black.

5. P—Q 4   B—Kt 3

5. ....P × P would be quite illogical, for after 6. Castles, White would obtain a very strong attacking game.

6. Castles   P—Q 3

The most usual move, but not the best. With 6. ....Kt—B 3 attacking the K P, Black could gain valuable time by compelling White to make a defensive move.

7. P—Q R 4	P—Q R 3
8. B—K 3	

In a game Gunsberg—Alekhin, in the St. Petersburg Tournament, 1914, White continued here : 8. P—R 5, but after 8. ....Kt × R P ; 9. R × Kt, B × R ; 10. Q—R 4 ch, P—Kt 4 ; 11. Q × B, P × B ; he did not secure sufficient compensation for the sacrifice of the Exchange.

8. ......   B—Kt 5

As the sequel will show, this Bishop was needed for the defence of the Q Kt P. Therefore it would have been better to play first 8. ...,Kt—B 3.

9. P—Q 5   Kt—Kt 1

The intention is to protect later on the Pawn at Q Kt 3 by Q Kt—Q 2, in the event of White playing Q—Kt 3 after exchanging the Bishops.

10. P—R 5 !

Less good would have been 10. B×B, P×B, as the open Q B file would give Black sufficient prospects to compensate for the weakness of his Queen-side Pawns.

The text-move forces Black either to retire his Bishop to R 2, which would leave his Q R badly placed after 11. B×B, R×B ; or to open White's K B file, thus giving the latter the initiative on both wings.

10. ......   B×B
11. P×B   Kt—K B 3
12. Q Kt—Q 2

If 12. Q—Kt 3, then 12. ....B—B 1.

12. ......   Q Kt—Q 2
13. Q—K 1

More simple would have been 13. P—Kt 4, followed by 14. Q—K 1, etc. The text-move, however, can hardly be said to be inferior and, in fact, results in luring his opponent to retire his B to B 1, a somewhat peculiar manœuvre which will give White further possibilities of attack.

13. ......   Kt—B 4
14. Q—Kt 1 !

Not 14. Q—Kt 3, because of 14. ....P—K R 4 !, etc.

14. ......   B—B 1

Better was 14. ....Castles K R ; after which White would have continued his advance on the Queen-side, e.g. : 15. P—Kt 4, Q Kt—Q 2 ; 16. B—Q 3 and by 17. P—B 4. After the text-move Black's game becomes very precarious.

15. P—Q Kt 4   Q Kt—Q 2
16. Kt—R 4 !

In order to open a file on the Queen-side by 17. P—Kt 5, should Black play 16. ....Kt—B 1. But Black, with his next move, prefers to create a first weak point on the King-side.

16. ......   P—K Kt 3
17. Q—K 1   P—B 3

This counter-attack in the centre complicates the game. After 18. ....P×P ; 19. P×P, P—K 5 ; Black secures the square at K 4. Against that White will be able to exercise pressure on the opposing K P, and will, sooner or later, post his Knight at Q 4. In the end the insecure position of Black's King will be the deciding factor in White's favour.

18. K Kt—B 3   P×P
19. P×P   P—K 5

Position after Black's 19th move.

20. Kt—Kt 5 !

INTERNATIONAL TOURNAMENT AT MANNHEIM 81

An unexpected move. Instead of playing this Knight at once to Q 4, White takes five moves, but the Knight arrives there with decisive results ! The idea is to provoke a further weakening of Black's position by the attack on the K P. Had White played 20. Kt—Q 4, at once, Black would have obtained a satisfactory position after 20. .... Kt—K 4 ; 21. R—B 4, Castles !, and White could not capture the K P because of 22. .... Kt×Kt ; 23. R×Kt, P—B 4 ; etc., or 21. Q—R 4, Kt×P !

20. ......   P—R 3

If now 20. .... Kt—K 4 ; 21. B—Kt 3 !, B—B 4 ; 22. B—R 4 ch, K—B 1 ; 23. B—B 2 !, and White has the advantage.

21. Kt—R 3

21. Q—R 4 was not feasible because of 21. .... Kt—R 2.

21. ......   Q—K 4

Black over-estimates the efficacy of this counter-attack. He should, after all, have played 21. .... Kt—K 4 ; and the continuation would have been : 22. Kt—B 4, B—B 4 ; 23. P—R 3, P—R 4 ; 24. B—Kt 3, R—Q B 1 ; 25. P—B 4, followed by Kt—K 2 and Kt—Q 4 with the better prospects for White.

22. R—B 1 !

Only the B P had to be defended, for Black would gain no advantage from capturing the Q P, e.g. : 22. .... Kt×P ; 23. B×Kt, Q×B ; 24. Kt—K B 4, Q—B 3 ; 25. P—B 4 ! followed by 26. P—Kt 5, and White regains the Pawn with a dominating position.

22. ......   Kt—Kt 5

Only leading to a further weakening of the position, for Black will not be able to play P—B 4. Somewhat better would be 22. .... Castles.

23. Kt—B 4 !   P—K Kt 4
24. P—R 3   K Kt—B 3

Forced, for if 24. .... P×Kt ; 25. P×P, followed by 26. P×Kt, would spell immediate disaster for Black.

25. Kt—K 2   Kt×P

Seeking some sort of compensation for his precarious position, which, it is clear, could not be held for long in any way.

26. B×Kt   Q×B
27. Kt—Q 4 !

Position after White's 27th move.

27. ......   Q—K 4

After 27. .... Castles, there were many threats for Black, as for instance 28. R—B 5, Kt—K 4 ; 29. P—B 4 ! or 28. .... Q—R 7 ; 29. R—R 1, Q—Kt 7 ; 30. Kt—B 4 !, winning the Queen in either case.
If 27. .... Kt—B 1, the sequel would have been 28. Q—K 2 ! (threatening Kt—B 4 and Q 6), B—K 3 ; 29. P—B 4, Q—K 4 ; 30. P—B 5, P—Q 4 ; 31. P—B 6 !, P×P ; 32. Q R×P, followed by 33. R×Q R P, and the passed Pawns on the Queen-side would win easily.

After the text-move White wins easily by a direct attack on the Black King's position.

28. Kt—B 4   Q—Q 4
29. Kt—B 5! K—B 1
30. Kt(B 5)×Q P R—K R 2
31. R—Q 1   Q—B 3
32. R—Q 4!

More simple and direct than combinations starting with Kt×B P. Now Black has no move.

32. ......   P—Kt 4
33. P×P e. p. B—Kt 2
34. Kt—R 5   Black resigns

GAME 30

GIUOCO PIANO

White :   *Black :*
J. MIESES.   A. ALEKHIN.

1. P—K 4   P—K 4
2. Kt—K B 3 Kt—Q B 3
3. B—B 4   B—B 4
4. Kt—B 3   P—Q 3
5. P—Q 3   B—K 3

A good way of avoiding the symmetrical variations springing from 5. ....Kt—B 3.

6. Kt—Q 5

This plausible move, however, allows Black a series of favourable exchanges. The best continuation at this stage is 6. B—K 3!

6. ......   Kt—R 4!
7. B—K 3

If 7. B—Kt 3 there would likewise follow 7. ....Kt×B, and 8..... P—Q B 3. dislodging White's advanced Knight with advantage.

7. ......   Kt×B
8. P×Kt

If 8. B×B, then 8. ....Kt×P.

8. ......   B×B

Taking advantage of the fact that White cannot recapture with the Pawn, because of 9. ....P—Q B 3.

9. Kt×B   Kt—B 3
10. Q—Q 3

10. Kt—Q 2 would be a little better. After the text-move Black provokes a weakening of the hostile Queen-side.

10. ......   Kt—Q 2!
11. P—Q Kt 4

If now 11. Kt—Q 2, then 11..... Kt—B 4; 12. Q—K 2, Q—R 5! also to Black's advantage.

11. ......   P—Q R 4!
12. P—B 3   Castles
13. Castles K R

Position after White's 13th move.

13. ......   P—K Kt 3!

Having assumed the initiative on the Queen-side, Black by this move prepares an advance on the other flank. This advance aims at either the formation of a strong centre after 14. ....P—B 4; 15. P×P, P×P; or at the decisive attack resulting from the opening of the K Kt file after the blockade by 14. ....P—B 5, which sooner or later forces White's reply P—K B 3.

INTERNATIONAL TOURNAMENT AT MANNHEIM 83

14. Kt—Q 2	P—B 4
15. P—B 3	P—B 5
16. Kt—Q 1	

Not 16. Kt—Q 5 on account of 16. ....P—B 3. After the text-move White's Knights have an extremely limited range of action.

16.	P—K Kt 4
17. Kt—B 2	P—R 4
18. P—R 3	Kt—B 3
19. K R—Q 1	Q—K 2

Black could definitely have prevented White's next move by 19. ....P—Kt 3, but this precaution seemed needless to him, since the variation resulting from 20. P—B 5 leaves him with a Pawn to the good in the end-game.

20. P—B 5

Compelling the opponent to modify his plan of attack—but at what a cost ! It is true that without this diversion Black would ultimately have shattered the enemy position by P—Kt 5, after the preparatory moves K—R 1, R—K Kt 1, R—Kt 3, Q—Kt 2 and R—K Kt 1.

20. ...... R P × P

There was equally to be considered the line of play 20. .... Q P × P; 21. Kt—B 4, B—B 2 !; 22. Kt × R P (or 22. P × R P, Q—K 3), P × P. But in the variation adopted in the text Black's material advantage will be still more readily exploited in the end-game.

21. P × Q P   Q × P !

At first sight Black does not seem to have gained very much, for after 22. P × P, Q × P White would obtain good counter-chances by 23. K R—Kt 1. The finesse of the variation selected does not become apparent until Black's 24th move.

22. P × P	R × P
23. R × R	Q × Q !
24. Kt × Q	B × R

Position after Black's 24th move.

And now White cannot take the K P on account of 24. R—Q 1 !, threatening B—Kt 6, and forcing the gain of the Exchange. The ensuing end-game still offers Black some technical difficulties, because of the weakness of his K P, but he makes certain of victory by a farsighted pinning combination.

25. R—R 1	R—Q 1
26. R × B	R × Kt
27. Kt—B 4	R—Q 5
28. R—Q B 2 !	

Position after White's 28th move.

84   MY BEST GAMES OF CHESS

28. ......   Kt—K 1 !

The most difficult move in the whole game, for other defences of his Q B P would be inadequate, e.g. :

I.—28. ...P—B 3 ; 29. P—Kt 5 !, P×P ; 30. Kt×P, and Black's material advantage would be illusory.

II.—28. ....Kt—Q 2 ; 29. Kt—R 5, P—Kt 3 ; 30. Kt—B 6, and the strong position of this Knight would give White good drawing chances.

After the text-move Black threatens P—Kt 4.

29. P—Kt 5

Threatening 30. P—Kt 6 and 31. Kt × K P.

29. ......   P—Kt 3
30. Kt × K P

Forced, for if 30. K—B 2, then 30. ....P—Kt 5 ! White now expects to find sufficient compensation for his lost Pawn in the entry of his Rook at Q B 6.

30. ......   R—Kt 5
31. R—B 6   R × Kt P
32. R—Kt 6 ch   Kt—Kt 2
33. R × K Kt P   P—R 5 !

The point of the whole combination ! White's pieces are paralysed and 34. Kt—B 7, the sole way to free White, is temporarily impossible because of 34. ....R—Kt 8 ch. White therefore selects the continuation :

34. K—B 2   R—B 4
35. K—K 2
       See Diagram.
35. ......   K—R 2 !

White would reply to the plausible move 35. ....P—Kt 4 by 36. Kt—B 7 ! and would then be out of all his difficulties. The text-move, on the contrary, removes this last resource. In fact, if now 36. Kt—B 7, R × R ; 37. Kt × R ch, K—Kt 3,

Position after White's 35th move.

winning the Knight. And against any other reply by White the Q Kt P would go straight on to Queen.

White resigns.

GAME-31

FRENCH DEFENCE

White :	Black :
A. ALEKHIN.	H. FAHRNI.

1. P—K 4   P—K 3
2. P—Q 4   P—Q 4
3. Kt—Q B 3   Kt—K B 3
4. B—Kt 5   B—K 2
5. P—K 5   K Kt—Q 2
6. P—K R 4 !

This energetic move has been especially played in off-hand games by the ingenious Paris amateur, M. Eugène Chatard, and previously by the Viennese master, A. Albin.

It was during the present game that it was introduced for the first time in a Master Tournament.

6. ......   B × B

6. ....Castles, adopted on several occasions in international

tournaments in recent years, was refuted by Bogoljuboff in his game against Spielmann at Vienna, 1922, which continued 7. B—Q 3, P—Q B 4; 8. Kt—R 3!, R—K 1; 9. Kt—Q Kt 5, P—B 4; 10. Kt—Q 6, P×P; 11. Kt×R, Q×Kt; 12. B—Kt 5·! and White should win.

6. ....P—Q B 4, and if 7. Kt—Kt 5 then 7. ....P—B 3, seems somewhat better.

7. P×B Q×P
8. Kt—R 3 Q—K 2

After 8. ....Q—R 3 Black's Queen would be in a precarious position, and in this case White could gradually have strengthened his position by 9. P—K Kt 3 and 10. B—Kt 2.

9. Kt—B 4 Kt—B 1

White refutes this plausible move by an enterprising attack, but against any other reply he would have obtained ample compensation for the Pawn sacrificed.

A particularly interesting continuation has been suggested here by Bogoljuboff: 9. ....P—Q R 3; 10. Q—Kt 4, P—K Kt 3; 11. Castles, P—Q B 4; 12. Q—Kt 3!, Kt—Kt 3; 13. P×P, Q×P; 14. B—Q 3, Q—B 1.

Position after Black's 14th move in sub-variation.

15. B—K 4!! and White's Knight will force its way into the hostile camp via K 4 or Q 5, with decisive effect.

10. Q—Kt 4!

Threatening both 11. Q×Kt P and 11. Kt×Q P! Black's reply is therefore compulsory.

10. ...... P—K B 4
11. P×P e. p. P×P
12. Castles

White is again threatening 13. Kt×Q P, his King having removed from the King's file.

12. ...... P—B 3
13. R—K 1 K—Q 1

There is no other way to develop the Queen-side. If 13. ....B—Q 2 the sacrifice of the Knight at Q 5 would once more be decisive.

14. R—R 6!

In order to tie up Black's pieces still more, on account of the pressure on his K B P. From now onwards all Black's moves are forced.

14. ...... P—K 4
15. Q—R 4 Q Kt—Q 2
16. B—Q 3

Threatening among other moves 17. B—B 5.

16. ...... P—K 5
17. Q—Kt 3!

An essential preliminary for the ensuing sacrifice. White now threatens to win off-hand by 18. Kt×Q P. Black cannot play 17. ....Q—Q 3, for after 18. B×P!, P×B; 19. R×P! he would be defenceless against the threat 20. Q—Kt 7!

17. ...... Q—B·2

The only resource!

Position after Black's 17th move.

18. B×P!

This sacrifice, which must be accepted by the opponent, wins the game in a few moves.

18. ...... P×B
19. Kt×P R—K Kt 1

If 19. ....Q×P; 20. Kt×P!, Kt×Kt; 21. Q—Kt 7! and wins.

20. Q—Q R 3!

If 20. Kt—Q 6 Black could still have defended himself by 20. .... Q×P, seeing that White's discovered checks do not lead to mate.

But after the text-move he has no longer an adequate defence.

20. ...... Q—Kt 2

If 20....Q—K 2; 21. Q—R 5 ch, P—Kt 3; 22. Q—B 3 and wins.

21. Kt—Q 6! Kt—Kt 3

Position after Black's 21st move.

22. Kt—K 8!

Forcing the win of the Queen, or else mate, *e.g.*: 22. ....Q—Q 2; 23. Kt×P; or 22. ....Kt—B 5; 23. Q—B 5, Q—B 2; 24. R×P.

22. ...... Q—K B 2
23. Q—Q 6 ch

and mates in two moves.

CHAPTER XI

LOCAL TOURNAMENTS, EXHIBITION AND MATCH GAMES, SIMULTANEOUS AND CORRESPONDENCE GAMES, ETC.

GAME 32

KIESERITSKI GAMBIT
(RICE GAMBIT)

Played by correspondence in Russia, 1908–1909.

White :   *Black :*
A. ALEKHIN.   W. DE JONKOVSKI.

1. P—K 4   P—K 4
2. P—K B 4   P × P
3. Kt—K B 3   P—K Kt 4
4. P—K R 4   P—Kt 5
5. Kt—K 5   Kt—K B 3
6. B—B 4   P—Q 4
7. P × P   B—Q 3
8. Castles

This move, suggested by Professor I. L. Rice, has not, truth to tell, any theoretical value, since Black can revert to a variation of the Kieseritski Gambit, not unfavourable for him, by 8. ... Castles. Moreover, he runs no risks in accepting the temporary sacrifice of the Knight, since White, as Master practice has shown, cannot hope for more than a draw after a long and difficult struggle. However, as the position arising from the sacrifice offers the two adversaries a multitude of very complicated tactical possibilities, it lends itself to the wish of players eager for combinations, and still more particularly to those who desire to devote themselves to the detailed analyses required by correspondence play.

8. ......   B × Kt
9. R—K 1   Q—K 2
10. P—B 3

Not 10. P—Q 4 on account of B × P ch.

10. ......   P—Kt 6

With this move Black attempts the refutation of the Knight-sacrifice by a violent counter-attack. He had also the choice between 10. ....P—B 6 (tried in the match Lasker—Tchigorin at Brighton, 1904) and Jasnogrodski's move, 10. ....Kt—R 4 !, which is in my opinion the strongest move.

11. P—Q 4   Kt—Kt 5
12. Kt—Q 2   Q × P
13. Kt—B 3

See Diagram.

13. ......   Q—R 3

Threatening to win the Queen by Kt—B 7. After 14. R × B ch, Kt × R ; 15. P × Kt, B—Kt 5 White has not sufficient compensation for the lost Exchange, and 14. Q—K 2 (if 14. Q—Q 2, Kt—K 6 !) would be demolished by 14. ....Castles ; 15.

Position after White's 13th move.

Position after Black's 15th move.

P×B, Kt—B 7 ; 16. K—B 1, Q—R 8 ch ; 17. Kt—Kt 1, Kt—R 6 !

There consequently remains nothing better than to attempt the following diversion :

14. Q—R 4 ch   B—Q 2
15. Q—R 3

This move was also played by Professor Rice, in a consultation game at New York, which resulted in a draw. In a game between Lipschutz and Napier played about the same period, the continuation was : 15. Q—Kt 4, Kt—Q B 3 ! ; 16. P×Kt, B×B P ; 17. B—Kt 5, Castles Q R ; 18. B×B, P×B ; 19. P×B, Kt—B 7 ; 20. K—B 1, Q—R 8 ch ; 21. Kt—Kt 1, Kt—R 6 ! ; 22. Q—B 5 (if 22. P×Kt, P—B 6), P—B 6 ! ; 23. P×P, Kt×Kt, and wins.

But at Q R 3 also White's Queen remains out of play for a very long time.

15. ......   Kt—B 3 !

See Diagram.

16. P×Kt

White has no choice. After 16. P×B, Q Kt×P, followed by Castles Q R, Black's attack would become irresistible.

16. ......   B×B P
17. P—Q 5

Clearly forced.

17. ......   B×Q P

Very ingenious. It is probable, however, that the simple variation, 17. ....B—Q 2 ; 18. Q—B 5 !, P—K B 3 ! ; 19. P—Q 6, P—B 3 ; leaving Black two Pawns ahead in a defendable position, was preferable.

The text-move leads to extremely interesting complications most difficult to fathom.

18. B×B   Q—Kt 3 ch
19. Kt—Q 4   Castles Q R

Having brought his King into safety, Black has a splendid attacking position and White, to avoid immediate disaster, must decide to sacrifice some of his material.

20. R×B

Reckoning on the variation 20. ....Kt×R ; 21. Q—Kt 3, Q×Q ; 22. B×Q, Kt—Kt 3 ; 23. B—Q 2, which would give White excellent drawing chances. But Black replies by another surprise-move.

Position after White's 20th move. *Position after Black's 25th move.*

20. ......   R×B !

A very long-headed combination by means of which Black attempts to force a win when a Rook and Bishop to the bad.

21. R×R   Q—K R 3
22. Kt—B 3

After 22. Q×P, Q—R 7 ch ; 23. K—B 1, Q—R 8 ch ; 24. K—K 2, Q×P ch ; 25. K—Q 3, Q×R ; 26. Q—R 8 ch, K—Q 2 ; 27. Q×R, Black would have at least a draw by perpetual check: 27. ....Kt—K 4 ch ; 28. K—B 2, Q—K 5 ch ; 29. K—Kt 3, Q—Q 4 ch, but he could also have attempted to utilise his dangerous passed Pawns on the King-side by playing 27. ....P—B 6.

22. ......   Kt—B 7
23. K—B 1   R—K 1 !

Threatening 24. ....Q—R 8 ch ; 25. Kt—Kt 1, Q×Kt ch ; 26. K× Q, R—K 8, mate.

24. B×P !

The only resource to escape the deadly coils which are enveloping him more and more.

24. ......   Q—R 8 ch !
25. Kt—Kt 1   Kt—Kt 5

26. R—K R 5 !

This sacrifice is the simplest and surest way of saving the game. By playing 26. R—K 5 White would expose himself to fresh dangers without the slightest chance of a win, as the following very interesting variations show :

26. R—K 5, Kt—R 7 ch ; 27. K—K 2, R—Q 1 ! (preventing the flight of White's King to the Queenside) ; 28. B×P !, Q×P ch ; 29. B—B 2, Q—Kt 5 ch ; 30. K—K 3 (if 30. K—K 1, Q—Kt 7 ! ; 31. K—K 2, Q—Kt 5 ch, and Black has already a draw), 30. ....P—K B 4.

See Diagram.

And against the threat 31. .... Q—Kt 4 ch ; 32. K—K 2, Q—Q 7 mate, White has only the two following defences :

I.—31. Q—K 7, P—B 5 ch ; 32. K—K 4, Q—Kt 7 ch ; 33. K×P, Q×B ch, and Black has at least perpetual check, for the White King cannot go to Kt 5 because of mate in three by Q—Kt 6 ch, Q—Kt 5 ch and Q—Kt 3.

II.—31. Q—Kt 4, Q—Kt 4 ch ; 32. Q—B 4, Kt—Kt 5 ch ! (stronger than 32. ....R—Q 6 ch) ; 33. K—B 3, Kt×R ch ; 34. Q×Kt, Q—Kt 5 ch ; 35. K—K 3, P—B 5 ch ;

Position after Black's 30th move in sub-variation arising on White's 26th move.

Position after Black's 27th move.

28. K—Kt 1 !

36. K—K 4, Q—Kt 7 ch ; 37. Kt—B 3, Q×B, etc., with good winning chances, as White cannot protect both his King and his Queen-side Pawns.

These variations demonstrate the extraordinary vitality of the attack initiated by Black on his 20th move.

| 26. ...... | Q×R |
| 27. Kt—R 3 | Q—Kt 4 ch |

Equally the tempting manœuvre 27. ....Kt—R 7 ch ; 28. K—Kt 1, Kt—B 6 ch ; 29. K—R 1, R—Kt 1 !, threatening 30. ....Q×Kt ch and 31. ....P—Kt 7 mate, would lead only to a draw against a correct defence, *e.g.* 30. B×Kt P, R×B ; 31. Q—B 8 ch, K—Q 2 ; 32. R—Q 1 ch, K—B 3 ; 33. Q—K 8 ch, K—Kt 3 ; 34. Q—K 3 ch, K—R 3 ; 35. Q—Q 3 ch ! (if 35. Q—K 2 ch, P—Kt 4 !; 36. Q—B 1, Kt—R 5 and Black must win), K—Kt 3 ! (not 35. ....P—Kt 4, because of 36. Q—Q 7 !, threatening mate in three moves) ; 36. Q—K 3 ch, K—R 3 ! (if 36. ....P—B 4 ; 37. R—Q 6 ch, K—R 4 ; 38. R—K R 6, Q—B 4 ; 39. Kt—Kt 1 and wins) ; 37. Q—Q 3 ch and the game is a draw.

28. P—B 4 would allow White to preserve his material, but would leave Black winning chances, *e.g.* : 28. P—B 4, Q×P ch ; 29. K—Kt 1, Q—Q 5 ch ; 30. K—R 1, Kt—B 7 ch ; 31. Kt×Kt, P×Kt ; 32. B—Kt 3 (or A), Q—B 3 ; 33. R—K B 1, Q—R 3 ch ; 34. B—R 2, R—K 8 ; 35. Q—Q 3, Q—B 8 and wins.

(A) Or 32. Q—K Kt 3, Q×P (if 32. ....R—K 8 ch ; 33. R×R, P×R=Q ch ; 34. Q×Q, Q×B ; 35. Q—K 8 mate) ; 33. R—K B 1, Q×P and Black should win.

28.	Q—Kt 3 ch
29. K—R 1	Kt—B 7 ch
30. Kt×Kt	Q×Kt

Not 30. ....P×Kt ; 31. R—K B 1, Q—K B 3 ; 32. P—K Kt 3 and wins.

| 31. B×Kt P | Q×B |
| 32. Q×P | |

The fluctuating struggle has ended in a peaceful finish with equal forces. Black rightly contents himself with perpetual check, for the only possible attempt to win, 32. ....R—K 5, is easily refuted by 33. K—Kt 1 !

32.	R—K 8 ch
33. R×R	Q×R ch
34. K—R 2	Q—R 5 ch
35. K—Kt 1	Q—K 8 ch

Drawn game.

GAME 33

VIENNA GAME

Played by correspondence in Russia, 1908.

White:	Black:
A. WJAKHIREFF.	A. ALEKHIN.
1. P—K 4	P—K 4
2. Kt—Q B 3	Kt—K B 3
3. B—B 4	Kt—B 3
4. P—Q 3	B—Kt 5
5. K Kt—K 2	

This game was played before the stronger move 5. B—Kt 5 was introduced into master practice by Mieses.

5.	P—Q 4
6. P×P	Kt×P
7. B×Kt	Q×B
8. Castles	Q—Q 1

This retreat is preferable to 8. ....B×Kt, as played by Dr. Bernstein against myself in Paris (February, 1922). The continuation was 9. Kt×B, Q—Q 1; 10. P—B 4, P×P; 11. B×P, Castles; 12. Kt—Kt 5! by which White obtained the advantage and ultimately won.

9. Kt—Kt 3

In a game Mieses—Tchigorin (Monte Carlo, 1902) White continued 9. P—B 4, Castles; (better is 9. ....P×P; 10. B×P, Castles; 11. Kt—K 4, B—K 2); 10. P—B 5, with advantage for White.

9.	Castles
10. P—B 4	

Now this move is not so good, for Black by his reply will assume the initiative on the King-side.

10.	P—B 4
11. Q Kt—K 2	Q—R 5
12. K—R 1	B—Q 3

Opposing the manœuvre Kt—Kt 1—B 3, etc.

13. P—Q 4

White, with the inferior game, tempts Black to play for a passed Pawn, which would give White chances of counter-attack in the centre.

13. ......   P—K 5

Nowadays, I should have adopted the simple variation: 13. ....P×Q P; 14. Kt×Q P, Kt×Kt; 15. Q×Kt, B—K 3; or 15. ....B—Q 2, followed by B—B 3. But my lack of experience was a poor shield against the temptation of an attack with brilliant sacrifices; and though my anticipations were realized, it was solely due to the defective strategy adopted by my opponent.

14. P—B 4	R—B 3
15. P—B 5	R—R 3
16. P—K R 3	B—B 1
17. Q—Kt 3 ch	K—R 1

Position after Black's 17th move.

18. Q—B 3

A grave error of position judgment, which gives up the very important square at Q 5. 18. P—Q 5 was absolutely necessary, e.g.: 18. ....Kt—K 2 or Q 1; 19. B—K 3, with a good position in the centre. The move in the text leaves Black with a marked advantage.

18. ......   Kt—K 2!

Of course not 18. ....B—K 3 because of 19. P—Q 5!, etc.

19. B—K 3   B—K 3
20. B—B 2   Q—B 3
21. P—R 3

The Pawn advance on the Queenside (see also White's 23rd and 26th moves) leads to nothing, as there is no threat. But White's game is so much compromised by his 18th move that it is hardly possible to suggest a valid plan of defence.

21. ......   B—Q 4

Threatening 22. ....P—K 6, followed by R×P ch, etc. The square Q 4 has to be occupied precisely by the B, as the Knight has another and a very important rôle to play.

22. B—K 3   Kt—Kt 3
23. P—Kt 4   Kt—R 5
24. K—Kt 1

To any other move Black would reply, as in the game, with 24. .... Kt—B 6, blocking up the King in the corner square, exposed to most violent attacks, such as Q—R 5, threatening Q×P ch!, etc.

24. ......   Kt—B 6 ch!
25. K—B 2

For the capture of the Knight spelt disaster, e.g.: 25. P×Kt, P×P; 26. Kt—B 1, R×P; 27. K—B 2 (or B—B 2), Q—R 5; and Black wins.

Position after White's 25th move.

25. ......   Q—R 5!

A rather peculiar position; Black's intention is to play R—Kt 3 and B—K 2, followed by R×Kt!; Kt×R; Q×Kt ch!; K×Q, B—R 5 mate, and White has no satisfactory defence against this threat!

26. P—Kt 5   R—Kt 3
27. K R—B 1 B—K 2!
28. K—B 1

As White sees it is impossible to oppose the threat shown above, he seeks compensation in the capture of the Black Knight. But Black's attack still remains strong and will lead to a new mating position.

28. ......   R×Kt
29. Kt×R

If 29. B—B 2. Kt—Q 7 ch; 30. K—Kt 1 (or if K—K 1, R×Q), R×P ch; 31. K×R, P—K 6 ch; 32. K—Kt 1 (or R 2), Q×B mate.

29. ......   Q×Kt
30. B—B 2   Q—R 7
31. P×Kt   P×P
32. R—B 2   R—K 1!

The initial move in the combination which is to prevent the White King from taking refuge on the Queen-side.

33. B—K 3

If 33. B—Kt 1, Q—Kt 6; followed by B—R 5, etc.

33.	Q—R 8 ch
34. B—Kt 1	B—R 5 !
35. R—K R 2	

Now Black's Queen is lost, but the loss allows the Black Pawn to administer the *coup de grâce*.

Position after White's 35th move.

| 35. ...... | Q—Kt 7 ch ! |
| 36. R × Q | P × R mate |

GAME 34

RUY LOPEZ

Played by correspondence in Russia, 1908–1909.

White :   Black :
K. WYGODCHIKOFF. A. ALEKHIN.

1. P—K 4	P—K 4
2. Kt—K B 3	Kt—Q B 3
3. B—Kt 5	P—Q R 3
4. B—R 4	Kt—B 3
5. Castles	B—B 4

This move, suggested in 1908 by the Danish master Möller, is in my opinion much better than its reputation as, up to the present, it has in no way been refuted and the few games in which it has been adopted rather tend to militate in its favour.

6. Kt × P

White could also play 6. P—B 3, to which the best reply is 6. .... B—R 2 ; as in a game Yates—Alekhin (Hastings, 1922), which continued as follows : 7. P—Q 4, (interesting would be 7. R—K 1, Kt—K Kt 5 !; 8. P—Q 4, P × P ; 9. P × P, Kt × Q P !; 10. Kt × Kt, Q—R 5 !; with a winning attack), Kt × K P ; 8. Q—K 2, P—B 4 ; 9. P × P, Castles ; 10. Q Kt—Q 2, P—Q 4 ; 11. P × P e. p., Kt × Q P ; 12. B—Kt 3 ch, K—R 1 ; 13. Kt—B 4, P—B 5 ; 14. Kt (B 4)—K 5, Kt × Kt ; 15. Kt × Kt, Q—Kt 4 ; 16. B—Q 2, B—R 6 ; 17. B—Q 5, Q R—K 1 ; 18. K R—K 1, R—K 3 !; 19. Q—Q 3, and now Black, who played the surprise move 19. ....B—K 6 !?, finally obtained only a draw, whereas he could have won a Pawn simply by 19. ....B × P ; followed by 20. ....R × Kt.

| 6. ...... | Kt × Kt |
| 7. P—Q 4 | Kt × P ! |

Position after Black's 7th move.

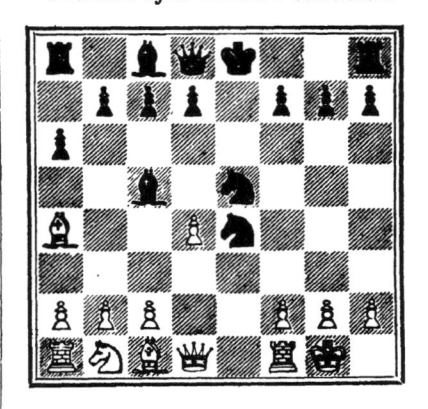

8. R—K 1

After 8. P × B, Kt × Q B P ; 9. Q—Q 4 or Q 5, Q—K 2 !; 10. B—

B 4, P—K B 3; (Dr. Groen—Alekhin, Portsmouth, 1923) White has not sufficient compensation for his Pawn.

If 8. Q—K 2 (Takacs—Alekhin, Vienna, 1922), then 8. ....B—K 2; 9. Q×Kt, Kt—Kt 3; 10. P—Q B 4, Castles; 11. Kt—B 3, P—K B 4; with good attacking chances. The continuation of this interesting game was 12. Q—B 3, Kt—R 5; 13. Q—Q 3, P—Q Kt 4; 14. B—Kt 3, K—R 1; 15. B—B 4, Kt—Kt 3; 16. B—Q 2, B—Kt 2; 17. K R—K 1, P×P; 18. B×P, P—Q 4; 19. B—Kt 3, P—B 4!; 20. P×P, P—Q 5; 21. Kt—R 4, B—K 5; 22. Q—B 4, B—Kt 4; 23. Q—Q B 1, B×B; 24. Q×B, Kt—R 5; 25. P—B 3, B×P; 26. P—Kt 3, and Black could have won at once by the sacrificial combination: 26. ....P—B 5; 27. P×Kt, Q×P; for after 28. B—B 2, P—Q 6!; 29. B×P, Q R—Q 1, is decisive.

8.	B—K 2
9. R×Kt	Kt—Kt 3
10. Kt—B 3	Castles
11. Kt—Q 5	B—Q 3!

It was most important to preserve this Bishop. Now that Black has overcome most of the opening difficulties, he must in the sequel obtain at least an equal game.

12. Q—B 3

To 12. P—Q B 4, Black had the powerful reply 12. ....P—K B 4; 13. R—K 1, P—B 4!, etc.

12. ......   P—K B 4

But in this position this advance is premature. White gains an important *tempo* by playing his K B to Kt 3 and Black loses the chance of playing P—Q B 4. The correct play was 12. ....P—Kt 4; 13. B—Kt 3, B—Kt 2, etc., with very good chances for Black.

13. B—Kt 3!   K—R 1

Evidently the Rook could not be captured because of mate in four: 14. Kt—K 7 dbl disc ch, K—R 1; 15. Kt×Kt ch, P×Kt; 16. Q—R 3 ch, Q—R 5; 17. Q×Q mate.

14. R—K 2   P—B 5

In preparation for 15. ...P—B 3. If 14. ....Q—R 5; 15. P—K R 3, Q×Q P; 16. P—B 3, Q—B 4; 17. B—K 3, Q—B 3; 18. B—Q 4, etc., with a strong attack.

15. P—B 4   P—B 3

Aiming at the Rook sacrifice on move 17. Insufficient would be 15. ....Q—Kt 4; 16. P—B 5, Kt—R 5; because of 17. Q—Kt 3! or 15. ....P—Q B 4, because of 16. B—B 2, a move which is threatened in any event.

16. P—B 5   B—Kt 1
17. Kt—Kt 6

Position after White's 17th move.

17. ......   P—Q 4!!

This Rook sacrifice is absolutely sound, and White would have been better advised not to accept it and to play 18. Kt×B! (not 18. B—B 2 at once because of 18. ....Q—Kt 4!; etc.), Q×Kt; 19. B—B 2! with a slight advantage.

It is easy to understand that White was tempted to capture the Rook, considering that Black's strong attack which follows was not obvious.

18. Kt×R   Kt—R 5

Position after Black's 18th move.

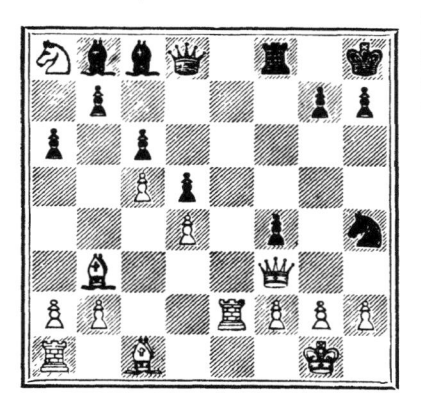

19. Q—B 3

Naturally not 19. Q—R 5, because of 19. ....P—K Kt 3; 20. Q—R 6, Kt—B 4; followed by 21. Kt×P; etc.

If 19. Q—Q 3! there would have been interesting complications. The probable line of play would have been: 19. ....B—B 4; 20. Q—Q B 3 (if 20. Q—Q 1, Q—Kt 4!), P—B 6; 21. R—K 3! (if 21. P×P, Q—B 3; 22. P—B 4, B—Kt 5), P×P; 22. P—B 3!, Q—Kt 4! (threatening B×P ch), 23. R—K 5, B×R!; 24. B×Q, B×Q P ch; 25. Q×B, Kt×P ch; 26. K×P, Kt×Q; 27. Kt—Kt 6, B—K 5 ch; 28. K—Kt 3, R—B 6 ch; 29. K—R 4, B—B 4! and mate in a few moves.

The text-move in some ways facilitates Black's attack, as he now has a serious threat comprising a Queen sacrifice.

19. ......   P—B 6
20. R—K 5

Compulsory. After the plausible reply 20. R—K 3, the continuation would be 20. ....Q—Kt 4!; 21. P—Kt 3, B×P!; 22. R P×B, Q×P ch; 23. P×Q, P—B 7 ch; 24. K—B 1, B—R 6 ch and Black wins.

20. ......   B×R
21. P×B   Kt×P!

Threatening Q—R 5—R 6.

22. Q—Q 4   Q—Q 2

Black could also win by 22. ....Kt—B 5!; 23. B×Kt, Q—R 5!; etc., but the variation adopted is equally decisive.

23. P—K 6

A desperate move. But after 23. K—R 1, Q—R 6, White had no defence against 24. ....Kt—K 8!, etc.

23. ......   Q×P
24. B—Q 2

Position after White's 24th move.

24. ......   Q—Kt 3!

Stronger than 24. ....Q—R 6; 25. B—B 3, R—Kt 1; 26. Q—K 5, Kt—B 5; 27. Q—Kt 5, and

Black cannot play 27. ...B—Kt 5; because of 28. B×P ch! with perpetual check.

25. B—B 2

If instead 25. K—R 1, then 25. ....Kt—K 8; or if 25. K—B 1, B—R 6; and Black wins.

25.	Q×B
26. K—R 1	Q—Kt 3
27. R—K Kt 1	

The only resource.

| 27. ...... | B—R 6 |
| 28. Kt—Kt 6 | |

Position after White's 28th move.

| 28. ...... | Kt—B 5! |

This manœuvre, prepared by Black's last few moves, is immediately decisive, for after the exchange of Queens and the loss of the Exchange White's game remains absolutely without resource.

29. R×Q	B—Kt 7 ch
30. R×B	P×R ch
31. K—Kt 1	Kt—K 7 ch
32. K×P	Kt×Q
White resigns.	

GAME 35

QUEEN'S FIANCHETTO DEFENCE

Local Tournament in Moscow,* September, 1908.

| *White*: | *Black*: |
| A. ALEKHIN. | W. ROSANOFF. |

1. P—K 4	P—Q Kt 3
2. P—Q 4	B—Kt 2
3. Kt—Q B 3	P—K 3
4. Kt—B 3	P—Q 4

A move which is not in the spirit of the opening selected by Black, for it restrains the action of the Q B. More logical would have been: 4. ....B—Kt 5; 5. B—Q 3, P—Q 3; followed by Kt—Q 2 and Kt—K 2.

| 5. B—Kt 5 ch | P—B 3 |
| 6. B—Q 3 | Kt—B 3 |

Relatively better would have been 6. ....P×P; 7. Kt×P, Kt—B 3; leading into a variation—in truth not very favourable for Black—of the French Defence. White takes advantage of this move by commencing an immediate attack on the Black King's position.

| 7. P—K 5 | K Kt—Q 2 |
| 8. Kt—K Kt 5! | |

Threatening 9. Kt×K P, P×Kt; 10. Q—R 5 ch, followed by B—Kt 5 ch, etc.

| 8. ...... | B—K 2 |

If 8. ....P—K R 3; 9. Kt×K P, P×Kt; 10. Q—R 5 ch, K—K 2; 11. Q—R 4 ch, and White wins.

9. Q—Kt 4

Much better than 9. Q—R 5, after which Black would have had a sufficient defence by 9. ....P—Kt 3; 10. Q—Kt 4, Kt—B 1; etc. After the text-move Black has nothing better than: 9. ....B×Kt;

* First prize.

10. B×B, Q—B 2 ; 11. B—R 4 !, P—Kt 3; 12. Kt—K 2, P—Q B 4; 13. P—Q B 3, and White has a fine attacking position.

9. ...... Kt—B 1

This allows of a sacrificial combination.

10. Kt×R P ! R×Kt

If 10. ....Kt×Kt ; 11. Q×Kt P, etc.

11. B×R Kt×B
12. Q×Kt P Kt—B 1

At first sight it would appear that White has a simple win by advancing his K R P after P—K Kt 3, after which it would cost Black at least a piece by the time it reached K R 7. But Black in that case could, by a counter-attack in the centre, hinder that plan or else obtain compensation elsewhere.
E.g.: 13. P—K Kt 3, P—Q B 4 ; 14. P—K R 4 (or 14. Kt—K 2, Kt—B 3 ; 15. P—Q B 3, P×P ; 16. P×P, B—R 3 ! followed by Kt—Kt 5), P×P ; 15. Kt—K 2, P—Q 6 !; 16. P×P, P—Q 5 ; 17. R any, B—R 3, etc.

There is only one way for White to obtain an immediate win from his advantage in position.

Position after Black's 12th move.

13. P—K R 4 !—

A surprise move, the first link in the chain of the ensuing combination, in the course of which Black will have to give up his Queen.

13. ...... B×P
14. R×B ! Q×R
15. B—Kt 5

Black, being unable to keep the White Queen from K B 6, with a double threat of mate at K 7 and Q 8, is compelled to give up his Queen for the Bishop.

15. ...... Q—R 8 ch
16. K—Q 2 Q×P
17. Q—B 6 Q×B ch
18. Q×Q

The rest is only a matter of routine.

18. ...... Kt—Kt 3
19. P—B 4 Kt—K 2
20. R—R 1 Kt—Q 2
21. Kt—Q 1 Kt—K B 1
22. Kt—K 3 B—B 1
23. Kt—Kt 4 B—Q 2
24. R—R 8 Kt—Kt 3
25. Kt—B 6 ch K—Q 1
26. Q×Kt !

The simplest, White remaining with an extra Rook.

Black resigns.

GAME 36

PHILIDOR'S DEFENCE

Second game of the match played at Moscow. October, 1908.
(*Result* +7, =1, —0)

White :	Black :
B. BLUMENFELD.	A. ALEKHIN.

1. P—K 4 P—K 4
2. Kt—K B 3 P—Q 3
3. P—Q 4 Kt—Q 2

More correct is Niemzovitch's move: 3. ....Kt—K B 3, as the variation 4. P×P, Kt×P; 5. B—Q B 4, P—Q B 3 presents no difficulties at all for Black. But after the text-move White can adopt the Schlechter variation: 4. B—Q B 4, P—Q B 3; 5. Kt—B 3, B—K 2; 6. P×P, P×P; 7. Kt—K Kt 5, B×Kt; 8. Q—R 5!, which gives him a slight advantage for the endgame.

4. P—Q Kt 3

After this move Black has no surprises to fear and can quietly attend to his development.

 4. ......   P—Q B 3
 5. B—Kt 2   Q—B 2
 6. Q Kt—Q 2

Intending to attack the K P a third time with Kt—B 4 and so to force his opponent to modify the arrangement of his Pawns. Black frustrates this plan in a very simple manner.

 6. ......   Kt—K 2

This Knight is to be posted at K Kt 3, and, whilst assuring from that square the defence of the K P, is to await an opportune moment to establish itself at K B 5, a square which has been left weak by White's development of his Q B at Kt 2.

7. B—K 2

It would certainly have been better to forestall Black's threat by 7. P—Kt 3, followed by B—Kt 2, especially as the Bishop's action from K 2 is practically nil.

 7. ......   Kt—K Kt 3
 8. Castles   B—K 2
 9. P—Q R 4

Loss of time. In this position 9. ....P—Kt 4 was not to be feared.

 9. ......   Castles
10. Kt—B 4   R—Q 1

In the Hanham variation of Philidor's Defence the Queen's file is of as paramount importance as the King's file in the exchange variation of the French Defence.

11. Q—B 1

The White Queen very reasonably evades the uncomfortable opposition of the adverse Rook. It would, however, have been more urgent to prevent the exchange of the K B, which might subsequently have proved most useful, by first playing 11. R—K 1, followed by B—K B 1. Black immediately exploits this slight strategical error.

11. ......   Kt—B 5
12. R—K 1   Kt×B ch
13. R×Kt   P—B 3

In the absence of a White K B, the weakening of the White squares, resulting from the advance of Black's K B P, is no longer dangerous.

14. Kt—R 4   Kt—B 1

Black's Q Kt now aims at K B 5.

15. Kt—K 3   Kt—K 3
16. P×P

White realizes that he can no longer hinder the opening of the Queen's file and this is tantamount to a condemnation of his opening strategy. Certainly the continuation: 16. K Kt—B 5, B—B 1; 17. P—Q B 3, P—K Kt 3; 18. Kt—Kt 3, Kt—B 5; 19. R—Q 2, B—K 3; 20. Q—B 2, Q—B 2; etc., was even less attractive than the variation actually adopted.

16. ......   Q P×P
17. Kt (R 4)—B 5
    See Diagram.

17. ......   B—Kt 5!

A well thought-out manœuvre which aims at the permanent command of the Queen's file. It at once

LOCAL TOURNAMENTS, ETC.

Position after White's 17th move.

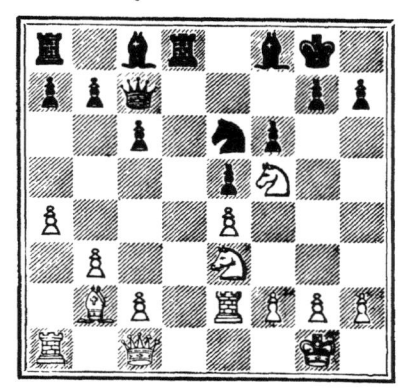

threatens : 18. ....Kt—B 5 ; and hence provokes the reply 18. P—Q B 3, and, in consequence, the weakening of White's Q 3.

18. P—Q B 3

The alternatives were :

I.—18. P—Kt 3, Kt—Kt 4.

II.—18. P—K B 3, Kt—B 5 ; 19. R—B 2, B×Kt ; 20. P×B (if 20. Kt×B, B—B 4 ; 21. Kt—K 3, Q—Kt 3 ; 22. P—R 5 !, B×Kt ; 23. P×Q, B×Q ; 24. R×B, P×P ; with an extra Pawn), B—B 4 ; and Black, threatening as he does 21. ....Kt—Q 4 and Q—Kt 3, must win.

| 18. ...... | Kt—B 5 |

Gaining a precious *tempo* which will allow Black to bring his Q R rapidly into play after 19. ....B× Kt. Had Black played 18. .... B—B 1, White had an easy defence by 19. R—Q 2, Kt—B 5 ; 20. R×R, Q×R ; 21. Q—Q 1, etc.

19. R—Q 2	B×Kt
20. Kt×B	B—B 4
21. P—Q Kt 4	

Without this precaution, Black, after 21. ....P—Q R 4, would have secured his B in a dominating position on the diagonal Q R 2—K Kt 8.

| 21. ...... | B—B 1 |
| 22. R×R | |

White has no choice, and control of the Queen's file is definitely lost.

22.	R×R
23. Q—B 2	Q—Q 2
24. R—K B 1	

To free the White Queen, at present immobilized by the threat of mate at Q 1.

| 24. ...... | Q—Q 6 ! |
| 25. Q—Kt 3 ch | |

After 25. Q×Q, R×Q ; 26. Kt—Kt 3, P—Q B 4 ; 27. P×P, B×P ; followed by R—Q 7, etc., White's position would be hopeless.

| 25. ...... | K—R 1 |
| 26. Kt—Kt 3 | |

Evidently compulsory. Black now dominates the board.

| 26. ...... | P—K R 4 |

But this is not the shortest way to win. More direct would have been 26. ....Kt—K 7 ch ; 27. Kt×Kt, Q×Kt ; 28. B—B 1, Q×P ; 29. Q—B 7, P—Q B 4 ! ; 30. P×P, B×P ; 31. Q—B 7, B—Kt 3 ; and Black, with a fine position and an extra Pawn, must win easily.

Position after Black's 26th move.

27. B—B 1

White, in his turn, does not adopt the best continuation and thus lets slip his last chance : 27. P—R 4 ! after which Black cannot play 27. ....P—K Kt 4 ; which would considerably weaken his King's position, e.g. : 27. P—R 4 !, P—K Kt 4 ; 28. Q—B 7 !, B—Kt 2 ; 29. P×P, P×P ; 30. B—B 1, etc. In this case Black would have contented himself with 27. ....Kt—K 7 ch ; 28. Kt×Kt, Q×Kt ; 29. B—B 1, Q×P ; 30. Q—B 7, P—Q B 4 ! ; 31. Q×R P ch, K—Kt 1 ; with a advantage sufficient to win, but at the cost of some technical difficulties.

27. ......   P—R 5 !

The end, so to speak, plays itself.

28. B×Kt   P×B
29. Kt—B 5

If now 29. ....Q×K P ; then 30. Kt×R P with some defensive possibilities. But Black's reply destroys his opponent's last illusions.

Position after White's 29th move.

29. ......   P—R 6 !

Decisive, as the following variations show.

I.—30. P—B 3, Q—K 7 ! ; 31. P×P, R—Q 7 ; and wins.

II.—30. P×P, Q×K P ; 31. Kt—Q 4, R—Q 4 ! and wins, for if 32. P—B 3, Q—K 6 ch ! followed by R×Kt.

III.—30. R—K 1, Q—Q 7 ! ; 31. R—K B 1, Q—K 7 and wins.

30. Q—K 6   P×P
31. K×P

A desperate move. If 31. R—K 1, Q×B P ; 32. R—Kt 1, Q—B 7 ; 33. R—K 1, R—Q 8 (the simplest) ; 34. R×R, Q×R ch ; 35. K×P, Q—Kt 5 ch ; 36. K—B 1, B×P ; 37. Q—B 8 ch, K—R 2 ; 38. Q×Kt P, P—R 4 ; 39. Q×P, P—B 6 ! and wins.

31. ......   P—B 6 ch
32. K—Kt 1   Q×R ch !

and mates next move.

GAME 37

RUY LOPEZ

Exhibition game played during the Cologne Tournament, June, 1911.

White :   *Black :*
A. ALEKHIN.   S. VON FREYMANN.

1. P—K 4   P—K 4
2. Kt—K B 3   Kt—Q B 3
3. B—Kt 5   Kt—B 3
4. Castles   P—Q 3
5. Kt—B 3   B—Q 2
6. P—Q 4   P×P

This capture is premature and should be preceded by 6. ....B—K 2 ; 7. R—K 1 !, etc. The inversion of moves affords White advantageous possibilities of development.

7. Kt×P   B—K 2
8 Kt×Kt

Also very strong would be 8. B×Kt, P×B; 9. Q—B 3! But the system adopted by White brings about a most promising position.

| 8. ...... | B×Kt |

After 8. ....P×Kt the best reply would be 9. B—R 4, as adopted successfully by Marco against Breyer in the Budapest Tournament of 1913.

9. Q—K 2!

White delays the exchange of Bishops at B 6 until he has ensured the means of weakening Black's strong Pawn-position at B 2, B 3 and Q 3 entailed by this exchange.

This is strategically a correct point of view.

9.	Castles
10. B—Kt 5	R—K 1
11. K R—K 1	

To parry the threatened 11. .... Kt×P.

| 11. ...... | P—K R 3 |

Apparently Black's object in playing this move is to follow it up with 12. ....Kt—R 2 in the event of 12. B—K R 4, so as to force an exchange of Bishops, which would ease his position. White consequently selects another flight-square for his Bishop, to avoid this line of play.

| 12. B—K B 4 | Kt—Q 2 |

If now 12. ....Kt—R 2, then 13. B—B 4, and Black can no longer exchange his K B (13. .... B—Kt 4; 14. B—K Kt 3, B—R 5; 15. Q—R 5).

After the text-move White can realize the plan he had in mind when playing 9. Q—K 2, namely, the weakening of the adverse Queen's wing after the exchange of Black's Q B.

| 13. B×B! | P×B |
| 14. Q—B 4 | B—Kt 4 |

An ingenious defence which does not, however, bring about the desired result. But White cannot play 15. B×B, Q×B; 16. Q×P? on account of 16. ....Kt—K 4 and 17. ....Kt—B 6 ch.

| 15. B—Kt 3 | P—Q B 4 |
| 16. Q R—Q 1 | |

Threatening P—K 5.

16.	B—B 3
17. P—Kt 3	Kt—K 4
18. Q—K 2	P—Kt 3

In order to retain the Bishop, which will act effectively on the opponent's Black squares. White must now manœuvre with the utmost precision in order to maintain his advantage.

| 19. Kt—Q 5 | B—Kt 2 |

Position after Black's 19th move.

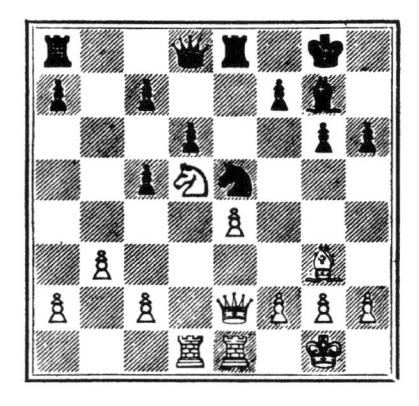

20. Q—R 6!

The most effective means of exploiting the weakness of Black's Queen-side. White now threatens to win a Pawn by 21. B×Kt and 22. Q—Kt 7. Black is consequently constrained to play P—Q B 3. It is interesting to note how this weakening move will impel Black to compromise his position more and more, until it finally becomes untenable.

20.	Q—B 1
21. Q—R 5	P—Q B 3
22. Kt—K 3	R—Q 1
23. B—R 4 !	

Forcing Black to play either 23. ....P—Kt 4 or 23. ....P—B 3, which is not much better; for 23. ....R—Q 2 is impossible because of 24. P—K B 4.

23.	P—Kt 4
24. B—Kt 3	Q—K 3
25. Kt—B 5	B—B 1
26. Q—B 3	

Now the threat of 27. P—B 4, Kt—Kt 3; 28. P×P, followed by 29. B×P, etc., forces Black to weaken his King-side still more.

| 26. ...... | P—B 3 |
| 27. P—B 4 | Kt—Kt 3 |

In answer to 27. ....Kt—B 2 White would bring his Queen to K R 5 via K B 3, with decisive effect. After the text-move he wins at least a Pawn.

28. Kt×P ch !	B×Kt
29. P—B 5	Q—K 2
30. P×Kt	B—B 1
31. Q—B 4 ch	K—Kt 2

If 31. ....K—R 1; 32. R—K B 1 followed by 33. Q—K 2 wins easily for White.

| 32. B×Q P ! | Black resigns |

GAME 38

SICILIAN DEFENCE

Winter-Tournament of the St. Petersburg Chess Society, March, 1912.

| *White :* | *Black :* |
| POTEMKIN. | A. ALEKHIN. |

| 1. P—K 4 | P—Q B 4 |
| 2. P—K Kt 3 | |

A good system of development against the Sicilian Defence, which was much favoured by Tchigorin. It has been adopted with success by Dr. Tarrasch in several Tournaments of recent years.

2.	P—K Kt 3
3. B—Kt 2	B—Kt 2
4. Kt—K 2	Kt—Q B 3
5. P—Q B 3	

But the advance of P—Q 4, prepared by this move, is not in the spirit of this system. White should simply have developed his pieces by 5. Q Kt—B 3; 6. P—Q 3; 7. Castles, etc.

| 5. ...... | Kt—B 3 |
| 6. Kt—R 3 | |

This illogical move allows Black to obtain at once the superior game. It would certainly have been better to play 6. P—Q 4, P×P; 7. P×P, P—Q 3; although in this case also the White centre Pawns would have become weak.

| 6. ...... | P—Q 4 |

Of course !

7. P×P	Kt×P
8. Kt—B 2	Castles
9. P—Q 4	

After this move the White Q P at once becomes weak. But 9. P—Q 3 was not much better.

9.	P×P
10. P×P	B—Kt 5
11. P—B 3	

The alternative 11. B—K 3 followed by Q—Q 2 and R—Q 1 was also unsatisfactory.

| 11. ...... | B—B 4 |

Threatening to win the Q P by B×Kt, etc.

| 12. Kt—K 3 | Q—R 4 ch |

This last move prevents Castling, for after 13. Q—Q 2 or 13. B—Q 2 the answer 13. ....Kt×Kt wins a piece.

13. K—B 2   Kt (Q 4)—Kt 5

Threatening amongst other things to win the Q P after B—Q 6.

14. Kt×B   Q×Kt
15. P—Kt 4   Kt—Q 6 ch
16. K—Kt 3

Position after White's 16th move.

16. ......   Kt×Q P !

Decisive.

17. P×Q

For if 17. Kt×Kt, Q—K 4 ch, etc., would give Black an easy win.

17. ......   Kt×P ch

and mates in two. If 18. K—Kt 4, P—R 4 ch and mate next move by the B or the Kt. If 18. K—R 3, Kt—B 7, a " pure mate."

GAME 39

QUEEN'S PAWN GAME

Winter Tournament of the St. Petersburg Chess Society, March, 1912.

White :   Black :
A. ALEKHIN.   H. LÖVENFISCH.

1. P—Q 4   P—Q B 4

The advance of this Pawn is rightly considered inferior even when prepared by 1..... Kt—K B 3; 2. Kt—K B 3. On the first move it constitutes in my opinion a grave positional error, for White at once obtains a great advantage in position by simply advancing the centre Pawns.

2. P—Q 5   Kt—K B 3
3. Kt—Q B 3   P—Q 3
4. P—K 4   P—K Kt 3

If instead of the text-move Black replies with 4. ....P—K 3 White's answer would be 5. B—Q B 4, etc., and the sequel would not be satisfactory for Black because of the weakness at his Q 3.

5. P—B 4

Already threatening P—K 5.

5. ......   Q Kt—Q 2
6. Kt—B 3

Position after White's 6th move.

If now 6. ....B—Kt 2 ; then 7. P—K 5, P×P ; 8. P×P, Kt—Kt 5 ; 9. P—K 6, Q Kt—K 4 ; 10. B—

Kt 5 ch, etc. This is why Black plays:

6.	P—Q R 3
7. P—K 5	P × P
8. P × P	Kt—Kt 5
9. P—K 6 !	

This demolishes Black's variation.

9.	Kt (Q 2)—K 4
10. B—K B 4	

Position after White's 10th move.

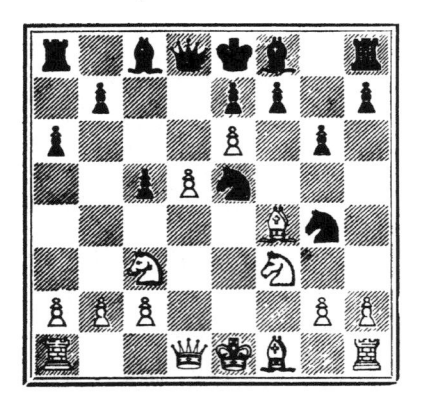

10.	Kt × Kt ch

Or 10. ....B—Kt 2; 11. Q—K 2, Kt × Kt ch; 12. P × Kt, Kt—B 3; 13. P × P ch, K × P; 14. Castles Q R, etc., with overwhelming advantage for White. After the text-move Black probably hopes for the reply 11. Q × Kt upon which he would obtain a playable game by 11. ....P × P!

11. P × Kt !	Kt—B 3
12. B—B 4 !	

This is preferable to the immediate capture of the K B P, a capture which the text-move renders much more threatening.

12.	P × P
13. P × P	Q—Kt 3

The alternative was: 13. ....Q × Q ch; 14. R × Q, B—Kt 2; 15. B—B 7, Castles; 16. B—Kt 6, and White wins a Pawn, at the same time maintaining the pressure. The move 13. ....Q—Kt 3, threatening two Pawns at the same time, is shown to be insufficient by an unexpected combination comprising a sacrifice by White.

14. Q—K 2 !

The initial move.

14.	Q × Kt P

At first sight there appears to be little danger in this capture, for K—Q 2 would be frustrated by 15. ....Kt—R 4; 16. B—K 5, B—R 3 ch; 17. K—Q 3, B × K P; 18. B × B, R—Q 1 ch, etc. But White had a different scheme in mind.

Position after Black's 14th move.

15. Kt—Kt 5 !

This attack by the Knight (which cannot be captured because of 15. ....P × Kt; 16. B × P ch, K—Q 1; 17. Q R—Q 1 ch) decides the issue in a few moves. Black has therefore nothing better than to accept the sacrifice and to capture both Rooks.

15.	Q × R ch
16. K—B 2	Q × R
17. Kt—B 7 ch	K—Q 1
18. Q—Q 2 ch	B—Q 2
19. P × B	

Threatening Kt—K 6 mate.

Black resigns.

For if 19. ....Kt×P ; 20. B—K 6 ; or if 19. ....P—K 4 then 20. Kt—K 6 ch, K—K 2 ; 21. P—Q 8 (Q) ch, R×Q ; 22. Q×R ch, K—B 2 ; 23. Kt×B dis. ch, K—Kt 2 ; 24. Q—K 7 mate.

GAME 40.

BISHOP'S GAMBIT

Second game of the match played at St. Petersburg, March, 1913.
(Result +7, =0, —3)

White :	Black :
A. ALEKHIN.	S. LEVITSKI.

1. P—K 4   P—K 4
2. P—K B 4   P×P
3. B—B 4   Kt—K B 3

This defence is now considered to be the best. The old line of play : 3. ....Q—R 5 ch ; 4. K—B 1, P—Q 4 ; 5. B×P, P—K Kt 4 is played less and less on account of Tchigorin's attack, 6. P—K Kt 3, P×P ; 7. Q—B 3 !, etc.

4. Kt—Q B 3   B—Kt 5

Black has now a "Ruy Lopez" with Schliemann's defence (P—K B 4) but with a move behind, evidently an important consideration. Very interesting, and probably better, is Bogoljuboff's move 4. ....P—B 3, as played by him successfully against Spielmann (Carlsbad, 1923).

5. K Kt—K 2

A new move which this game fails to refute. After 5. Kt—B 3, Castles ; 6. Castles, Kt × P ; White loses the initiative by 7. Kt×Kt, P—Q 4, etc., and therefore would have to sacrifice a Pawn permanently by playing 7. Kt—Q 5, with some attacking chances.

5. ......   P—Q 4

If 5. ....Kt×P White Castles and obtains a good attack for the sacrificed Pawn. With the text-move, Black in his turn intends a very audacious Pawn sacrifice, the soundness of which is, however, open to question.

6. P×P   P—B 6

Intending to compromise the White King's position ; but, as the sequel will show, the opening of the K Kt file is not without danger for Black and on the other hand White will momentarily have an extra Pawn.

7. P×P   Castles
8. P—Q 4

This move is inconsequent. After 8. Castles !, P—B 3 ; 9. P×P, Kt ×P ; 10. P—Q 4, B—K R 6 ; 11. R—B 2, R—B 1 ; etc., and Black's development is favourable, but the attack is insufficient to make up for the loss of a Pawn.

But after the text-move Black could and should have regained his Pawn by 8. ....Kt×P ; 9. Castles, B—K 3, etc., with a good game.

8. ......   B—K R 6

Position after Black's 8th move.

9. B—Kt 5 !

The plausible move was 9. Kt—B 4, protecting both Pawns and attacking the Bishop, but upon this Black had the following win in view: 9. ....R—K 1 ch; 10. K—B 2, Kt—Kt 5 ch! (seemingly inoffensive because of White's reply); 11. K—Kt 3, Kt—B 7 !!, etc. With the text-move White definitely assumes the initiative.

9.	B—Kt 7
10. R—K Kt 1	B × P
11. Q—Q 2	B—K 2

11. ....Kt—K 5 would be bad because of 12. B × Q, Kt × Q; 13. B—B 6, etc. On the other hand Black was threatened with 12. Q—B 4, and the variation 11. ....B × K Kt; 12. B × B, B × Kt; 13. Q × B, R—K 1 would be refuted by 14. Castles, R × B; 15. Q—B 3, etc.

12. Castles

Position after White's 12th move.

12.	B—R 4

Here again 12. ....Kt — K 5 would lose for Black, *e.g.*: 13. B × B, Kt × Q (if 13. ....Q × B; 14. Q—R 6!); 14. B × Q, Kt × B; 15. R × P ch!, K × R; 16. R—Kt 1 ch, K—R 3; 17. B—Kt 5 ch, K—Kt 3 (if K—R 4; 18. Kt—B 4 mate); 18. B—K 7 ch, followed by B × R, etc.

Now White has a comfortable attacking game.

13. Q R—K 1	Q Kt—Q 2
14. Kt—B 4	B—Kt 3
15. P—R 4 !	

Obviously threatening 16. P—R 5, etc.

15.	R—K 1
16. Q—Kt 2	

Now the threat is still more acute.

16.	B—B 1
17. P—R 5	B—K B 4

17. ....R × R ch first offered Black a more prolonged defence; but it is evident that in any event White's attack would have succeeded ultimately.

Position after Black's 17th move.

18. Kt—K 6 !

This irruption opens new lines of attack of a decisive nature for White. Black is forced to capture the Knight, as after 18. ....Q—B 1 White wins by 19. Q—B 3!

18.	P × Kt
19. P × P	K—R 1
20. P × Kt	R × R ch
21. R × R	B × Q P
22. P—R 6	

The winning move. Black must at the very least lose a piece at K B 3.

22.	B—B 3
23. P—Q 5	B—Q 2
24. R—B 1	P—Kt 4
25. B—Kt 3	Q—K 1
26. P—Q 6	

26. R × Kt was also sufficient.

26. ......   Kt—R 4

Or 26. ....B—B 3; 27. P—Q 7!, giving two variations:

I.—27. ....B × Q; 28. P × Q (Q), R × Q; 29. R × Kt!, etc.

II.—27. ....Q × P; 28. Q—B 2!, Kt—Kt 1; 29. Q × B! and wins.

It is with a view to the latter variation that White played 26. P—Q 6.

27. B—B 7   Black resigns

GAME 41

VIENNA GAME

Eighth game of the match at St. Petersburg, March, 1913.

White :	Black .
A. ALEKHIN.	S. LEVITSKI.
1. P—K 4	P—K 4
2. Kt—Q B 3	Kt—K B 3
3. B—B 4	Kt × P !

It is solely on account of this reply, which gives Black easily an equal game, that I have at the moment given up the Vienna opening.

4. Q—R 5

It is clear that after 4. Kt × Kt, P—Q 4!; or else 4. B × P ch, K × B ; 5. Kt × Kt, P—Q 4; Black emerges unscathed from the tribulations of the opening stages.

4.	Kt—Q 3
5. B—Kt 3	

Here White could have equalized by 5. Q × K P ch, Q—K 2 ; 6. Q × Q ch, B × Q, etc. But the sacrifice of a Pawn, which the text-move implies, is of doubtful value.

5. ......   Kt—B 3 !

The intention is to sacrifice the Exchange in the following variation : 6. Kt—Kt 5, P—K Kt 3 ; 7. Q—B 3. P—B 4 ; 8. Q—Q 5, Q—B 3 ; 9. Kt × P ch, K—Q 1 ; 10. Kt × R, P—Kt 3!; which ensures for Black a very strong and probably irresistible attack. The simple move 5. ....B—K 2 is also amply sufficient and would result, by a transposition of moves, in a position of the actual game.

6. P—Q 3   B—K 2

6. ....P—K Kt 3 followed by 7. ....B—Kt 2 was also to be considered. As can be seen Black, in this variation, has a wide choice of moves.

7. Kt—B 3   P—K Kt 3

This move, which was already played in the Paris Tournament of 1900 (Mieses—Marco) does not look natural, especially after B—K 2, and, indeed, is not the best. Black should simply have Castled, as the variation 8. Kt—K Kt 5, P—K R 3 ; 9. P—K R 4, Kt—Q 5! is not sufficient : after the move in the text Black will be unable to Castle.

8. Q—R 3	Kt—B 4
9. P—Kt 4	

This move has also been tried before, on several occasions, with varying continuations.

9.	Kt (B 4)—Q 5
10. B—R 6	Kt × B

An interesting idea aiming at a counter-attack, but at the same time premature, as Black is not yet sufficiently developed. The right move is 10. ....B—B 1 !, for after 11. B×B, R×B White is not in a position to regain the Pawn by 12. Kt×Kt, Kt×Kt ; 13. Q×P, because of the very strong reply 13. ....Q—Kt 4 !, preventing him from Castling on the Queen-side and leaving him with very doubtful prospects of attack.

11. R P×Kt   P—B 4

This move gives the clue to the preceding exchange, which would otherwise seem inexplicable. If now White were to play 12. P×P, Black would obtain a fine development by 12. ....P—Q 3, and 13. B×P.

12. B—Kt 7 !   P×P
13. Q—R 6 !

This sacrifice of a second Pawn promises White an attack both lasting and vigorous.

13. ......   B—B 1

Obviously forced.

14. B×B   R×B
15. Kt—K Kt 5   Kt—Q 5 !

This counter-attack offers on the whole the best chances. Quite insufficient would be 15. ....Q—B 3 ; because of 16. Castles K R !, etc.

16. Kt×P   R—K Kt 1

See Diagram.

17. Kt—Q 5 !

The only correct continuation of the attack, whose point will become evident on White's 23rd move. After the plausible move 17. Castles Q R, Black can disentangle himself by 17. ....Kt—B 4 ; 18. Q—Q 2, Q—R 5 ; etc., and White's attack can be repelled successfully.

17. ......   Kt×P ch

Position after Black's 16th move.

As the threatened 18. Kt—B 6 ch cannot be avoided, Black is compelled to seek compensation in the capture of the adverse Rook.

18. K—Q 2   Kt×R
19. R×Kt   P—B 3

Or if 19. ....P—Q 3 ; 20. Kt (R 7)—B 6 ch, K—B 2 ; 21. Kt× R, Q×Kt ; 22. Kt×P, followed by 23. Kt—Kt 5, etc., with a decisive attack.

20. Kt (R 7)—B 6 ch !
                    K—B 2
21. Kt×R   Q×Kt

If 21. ....P×Kt ; 22. Q—R 7 ch, K—B 1 ; 23. Q×Kt P, Q—K 1 ; 24. Q—Kt 5 !, Q—B 2 ; 25. Kt—B 6 !, P—Q 3 ; 26. P—R 3 !, P×P ; 27. R—K Kt 1, etc., with a winning attack.

22. Kt—Kt 6   R—Kt 1

See Diagram.

23. Kt—B 4 !

The winning move, for Black cannot prevent the opening of the King's file, which will prove decisive.

23. ......   P—Q 3

Position after Black's 22nd move.

If 23. ....K—K 3; 24. Kt×P, K×Kt; 25. Q—Kt 5 ch and White will win the Black Rook by a check at K 5 or K B 4.

24. Kt×Q P ch	K—K 2
25. Kt—B 4	B—B 4
26. R—K 1	Q—R 1
27. Q—K 3!	R—Q 1

After 27. ....K—Q 2 White wins by Q×R P, etc. The text-move allows of a still quicker termination.

28. Kt×P	K—B 3
29. Kt×P ch!	B×Kt
30. Q—K 5 ch	Black resigns

GAME 42

KING'S KNIGHT'S OPENING

Played in Paris, August, 1913.

White:	*Black:*
J. DE RODZYNSKI.	A. ALEKHIN.
1. P—K 4	P—K 4
2. Kt—K B 3	Kt—Q B 3
3. B—B 4	P—Q 3

Although seldom played this move is not inferior to 3. ...B—K 2, which constitutes the Hungarian Defence. The present game affords a typical example of the dangers to which White is exposed if he attempts to refute this move forthwith.

| 4. P—B 3 | B—Kt 5 |
| 5. Q—Kt 3 | Q—Q 2 |

Position after Black's 5th move.

6. Kt—Kt 5

Anticipating the gain of two Pawns.

If at once: 6. B×P ch, Q×B; 7. Q×P, K—Q 2!; 8. Q×R, B×Kt; 9. P×B, Q×B P; 10. R—Kt 1, Q×K P ch; 11. K—Q 1, Q—B 6 ch; and Black has at least a draw, as White cannot move his K to Q B 2, on account of Kt—Kt 5 ch, etc.

| 6. ...... | Kt—R 3 |
| 7. B×P ch | |

After 7. Q×P, R—Q Kt 1; 8. Q—R 6, R—Kt 3; 9. Q—R 4, B—K 2; followed by Castles, Black would obtain a sufficient compensation in development in exchange for the Pawn sacrificed.

7.	Kt×B
8. Kt×Kt	Q×Kt
9. Q×P	K—Q 2!

The sacrifice of the Exchange is entirely sound and yields Black a strong counter-attack.

10. Q×R   Q—Q B 5 !
11. P—B 3

Evidently forced.

Position after White's 11th move.

11. ......   B×P !

By this unexpected combination Black secures the advantage in any event. Incorrect would be, however, 10. ....Kt—Q 5 ; because of 11. P—Q 3, Q×Q P ; 12. P×Kt, B×P ; 13. Kt—B 3 !, etc.

12. P×B   Kt—Q 5 !
13. P—Q 3

This move loses at once. The only chance was perhaps : 13. P×Kt, with the following variation : 12. ....Q×B ch ; 13. K—K 2, Q×R ; 14. P—Q 5, Q×R P ch ; 15. K—Q 3, Q—Kt 8 ! ; 16. Q—B 6 ch, K—Q 1, etc., but Black's position is manifestly superior.

13. ......   Q×Q P
14. P×Kt   B—K 2 !

On this move White has the choice between the loss of the Queen or mate. He prefers the latter.

15. Q×R   B—R 5 mate.

GAME 43

QUEEN'S GAMBIT DECLINED

One of twenty simultaneous games played at Paris, September, 1913.

White :   *Black :*
A. ALEKHIN.   M. PRAT.

1. P—Q 4   P—Q 4
2. Kt—K B 3   Kt—Q B 3
3. P—B 4   P—K 3

Tchigorin's Defence is only playable if the Q B is developed at K Kt 5. The text-move which, on the contrary, obstructs this Bishop, can only create difficulties for Black.

4. Kt—B 3   P×P

A further renunciation. Black now abandons the centre, and it is not surprising that White, in a few moves, obtains an overpowering position.

5. P—K 3   Kt—B 3
6. B×P   B—Kt 5
7. Castles   B×Kt
8. P×B   Castles
9. Q—B 2   Kt—K 2
10. B—R 3   P—B 3
11. P—K 4   P—K R 3

Opposing the threat 12. P—K 5 followed by 13. Kt—Kt 5, but at the cost of a considerable weakening of the Castled position.

12. Q R—Q 1   B—Q 2
13. Kt—K 5   R—K 1

In order to liberate the Queen. A catastrophe at K B 7 is already in the air.

14. P—B 4   Q—B 2
15. P—B 5   Q R—Q 1

See Diagram.

16. Kt×B P !

This can hardly be termed a sacrifice, as White is in a position to

Position after Black's 15th move.

Position after Black's 21st move.

regain the piece with the superior position, but it is rather the initial move of the elegant final combination.

16. ......   K × Kt
17. P—K 5   Kt (K 2)—Kt 1
18. B—Q 6

Here White could have regained his piece by 18. P × Kt, P × P ! (if instead 18. ....Kt × P ; 19. P × P ch, B × P ; 20. R × Kt ch, etc.) ; 19. P × P ch, K—Kt 2 ! He quite rightly prefers to aim at the mate.

18. ......   Q—B 1
19. Q—K 2   P—Q Kt 4
20. B—Kt 3   P—Q R 4
21. Q R—K 1 !

The sequel clearly shows the object of this move.

21. ......   P—R 5

See Diagram.

Here White announced mate in 10 moves as follows : 22. Q—R 5 ch ! !, Kt × Q ; 23. P × P dbl ch, K—Kt 3 ; 24. B—B 2 ch, K—Kt 4 ; 25. R—B 5 ch, K—Kt 3 ! ; 26. R—B 6 dbl ch, K—Kt 4 ; 27. R—Kt 6 ch, K—R 5 ; 28. R—K 4 ch, Kt—B 5 ; 29. R × Kt ch, K—R 4 ; 30. P—Kt 3 !, any ; 31. R—R 4 mate.

GAME 44

VIENNA GAME

Exhibition game played at Paris, September, 1913.

White :	Black
A. ALEKHIN.	ED. LASKER.

1. P—K 4   P—K 4
2. Kt—Q B 3   Kt—K B 3
3. B—B 4   Kt—B 3
4. P—Q 3   B—B 4
5. B—K Kt 5

At the present time I should prefer 5. P—B 4, P—Q 3 ; 6. Kt—B 3, bringing about a position in the King's Gambit Declined favourable for White. The text-move, on the contrary, allows Black to equalize the game easily.

5. ......   P—Q 3
6. Kt—R 4

The continuation 6. Kt—Q 5; B—K 3 ; 7. Kt × Kt ch, P × Kt, 8. B × B, P × K B ; 9. Q—R 5 ch, K—Q 2, etc., leaves White with no advantage at all.

6. ......   B—Kt 3

In similar positions it is far more advantageous to play 6. ...B—K 3, with the intention of opening the centre files. However, the retreat of the B to Q Kt 3 is not wrong.

7. Kt×B	R P×Kt
8. Kt—K 2	B—K 3
9. Kt—B 3	

It is most important to maintain the command of the square at Q 5.

| 9. ...... | P—R 3 |
| 10. B—R 4 | Q—K 2 |

Position after Black's 10th move.

11. P—B 3 !

By this positional move, the result of exhaustive analysis, White, whilst reserving for himself full liberty of action on either wing, forces his opponent to decide on which side to Castle, in order to be able to elaborate his plan of attack accordingly.

Besides, the advance of the K B P is justified by the following considerations : the K B has a safe retreat should Black play P—K Kt 4, and there is an immediate attack by White's P—K Kt 4 should Black Castle on the King-side.

In the following variations Black would have had the advantage :

I.—11. Q—Q 2, B×B ; 12. P×B, Kt×P !

II.—11. Castles K R, P—K Kt 4 ; 12. B—K Kt 3, P—R 4.

| 11. ...... | Castles Q R |

As the sequel shows, White's attack, favoured by the imminent opening of the Q R file, will mature more quickly than Black's counter-attack on the King-side. Better therefore is 11. ....R—Q 1, although in this case White would secure an excellent game by 12. Kt —Q 5 !

12. Kt—Q 5

Forcing the exchange of several pieces, after which White will have a clear field and will be able to launch an attack against Black's Castled position by a general advance of his Pawns.

12.	B×Kt
13. B×B	P—K Kt 4
14. B—B 2	Kt×B
15. P×Kt	Kt—Kt 5

16. ....Kt—Kt 1 is somewhat better, though equally insufficient.

16. P—Q B 4

It is interesting to note that from this point until a decisive advantage is secured, White's plan of action comprises almost exclusively Pawn-moves.

In the handling of this game White is inspired by the example of the Grand-master of the eighteenth century, the immortal Philidor.

| 16. ...... | P—K B 4 |
| 17. Castles | P—R 4 |

17. ....Q R—Kt 1 would have saved a *tempo*. But Black's position was so compromised that the gain of one *tempo* would not have been sufficient to restore it.

18. P—Q R 4	Q R—Kt 1
19. P—R 5	P×P
20. R×P	

Threatening 21. R—R 8 ch and 22. Q—R 4 ch.

20.	Kt—R 3
21. P—Q Kt 4 !	K—Q 1
22. P—B 5	

Equally satisfactory was 22. P—Kt 5, Kt—B 4 (if 22. .... Kt—Kt 1 ; 23. R—R 7) ; 23. P—Q 4, but White intends to win a piece and consequently adopts the text-move.

22.	K—K 1
23. P—Q 4	K—B 2

This forced flight of the King shows clearly Black's mistake in Castling Q R.

24. P—Kt 5

Position after White's 24th move.

24. ......   Q P×P

Obviously the only chance, for 24. .... Kt—Kt 1 ; 25. Q P×P, P× K P ; 26. R—R 7 would have led to immediate disaster.

25. P×Kt	P—Kt 3
26. P—Q 6	

Interesting, and quite sufficient for victory. But 26. R—R 2, B P×P (or 26. .... K P×P ; 27. R—K 1, Q—Q 3 ; 28. Q R—K 2) ; 27. Q—Kt 3, K—Kt 2 ; 28. R—B 1 and 29. Q R—B 2 was still simpler.

26. ......   Q×P

If 26. .... P×P (Q 3), then 27. Q—Kt 3 ch and 28. Q×Kt P.

27. Q—Kt 3 ch	Q—K 3
28. P—Q 5	Q—Q 3
29. R—R 2	R—R 1
30. R—K 1	

The commencement of the decisive action against the weak Pawns on the adverse left wing.

30.	K R—Q 1
31. Q—Q 3	Q—K B 3

The only defence, for if 31. .... K—B 3 ; 32. P—B 4 ! and if 31. .... K—Kt 3 ; 32. P—Kt 4 ! and in both cases White wins easily.

Position after Black's 31st move.

32. P—Kt 4 !

In order to utilize the Q B against the Pawns on Black's K 4 and K Kt 4, after which Black's position will speedily become untenable.

32.	P—B 3
33. P×K B P	R×P

If 33. .... P×P ; 34. B—Kt 3, P—B 5 ; 35. Q—Q 1 and wins.

34. Q—K 4	P—R 5

Preventing 35. B—Kt 3.

35. Q—K Kt 4   Q—R 3
36. B—K 3   K—B 3
37. R—K Kt 2   R—K Kt 1
38. P—B 4!

The *coup de grâce*.

38. ......   K P × P
39. B × K B P!

Much stronger than 39. B—Q 4 ch, to which Black could still have replied by 39. ....K—B 2.

Black resigns.

GAME 45

SCOTCH GAME

Exhibition Game played at Moscow, March, 1914.

White: Black:
A. ALEKHIN.   DR. EM. LASKER.

1. P—K 4   P—K 4
2. Kt—K B 3   Kt—Q B 3
3. P—Q 4

In adopting in this my first encounter with the World's Champion, this comparatively little-played opening, my object was simply to avoid the well-trodden paths of the Ruy Lopez and the Queen's Gambit, both positional openings for which at the time I did not deem myself ripe enough.

3. ......   P × P
4. Kt × P   Kt—B 3
5. Kt—Q B 3   B—Kt 5
6. Kt × Kt   Kt P × Kt
7. B—Q 3   P—Q 4

These last moves constitute the best defence to the Scotch Game.

8. P × P   P × P
9. Castles   Castles
10. B—K Kt 5   B—K 3

The usual move, which offers Black the best chances, is here 10. ....P—B 3. After the text-move White could already play for a draw with 11. B × Kt, Q × B ; 12. Kt × P (not Q—R 5, P—K Kt 3 ; 13. Kt × P, Q—Q 1 ! and Black wins), B × Kt ; 13. Q—R 5, P—Kt 3 ; 14. Q × B, Q × P ; 15. Q R—Kt 1.

11. Q—B 3   B—K 2
12. K R—K 1

Preparing the combination which is to follow.

12. ......   P—K R 3

Position after Black's 12th move.

13. B × P!

With these little fireworks White forces the draw.

The fact that this combination, so closely connected with this opening, should never have occurred in master play nor have been pointed out in any analysis, is both curious and surprising.

This note was written before the game Romanovski—Capablanca, Moscow, 1925, was played, in which an analogous combination led to a draw.

13. ......   P × B
14. R × B!   P × R
15. Q—Kt 3 ch   K—R 1

Not 15. ....K—B 2, because of 16. Q—Kt 6 mate.

16. Q—Kt 6!

The point. Black cannot prevent the perpetual check by 17. Q×P ch and 18. Q—Kt 5 ch, etc. He can force it by playing *e.g.*: 16. .... Q—K 1. Therefore :

Drawn game.

GAME 46

QUEEN'S PAWN GAME

Moscow Championship Tournament,* 1916.

Brilliancy Prize

White :	Black :
A. ALEKHIN.	N. ZUBAREFF.
1. P—Q 4	Kt—K B 3
2. P—Q B 4	P—K 3
3. Kt—Q B 3	B—Kt 5
4. Q—B 2	P—Q Kt 3

In this position the fianchetto is hardly indicated, as White can obtain a very strong position in the centre. The right move was 4. .... P—B 4, hindering 5. P—K 4.

| 5. P—K 4! | B—Kt 2 |
| 6. B—Q 3 | B×Kt ch |

In order to secure at least some chances on account of White's doubled Pawn. After 6. ....P—Q 4; 7. B P×P, P×P; 8. P—K 5, Kt—K 5; 9. Kt—K 2, etc. White's game would remain superior.

7. P×B	P—Q 3
8. Kt—K 2	Q Kt—Q 2
9. Castles	Castles
10. P—B 4	

Already threatening to win a Pawn by 11. P—K 5.

10.	P—K R 3
11. Kt—Kt 3	Q—K 2
12. Q—K 2!	

Preparing 13. B—R 3, which, if played at once, would cause un-

* First prize without loss.

necessary complications after 12. ....Kt—Kt 5, threatening 13. .... Kt×P!

| 12. ...... | Q R—K 1 |

Black has completed his development very rapidly, but none of his pieces have any scope. It is easy to foresee that he will be unable to withstand the attack which his opponent is preparing in the centre.

13. B—R 3

With the strong threat 14. P—K 5, which compels Black to weaken his position still further.

| 13. ...... | P—B 4 |
| 14. Q R—K 1 | K—R 1 |

To make room for the Knight.

15. P—Q 5!

Taking advantage of the fact that Black cannot play 15. ....P×P, because of 16. Kt—B 5.

| 15. ...... | Kt—K Kt 1 |
| 16. P—K 5 | P—Kt 3 |

Preparing the capture of the Q P, still impossible at present for the above-mentioned reason.

17. Q—Q 2

Position after White's 17th move.

17. ...... K P×P

If here 17. ....Q P×P; 18. B P×P, P×P; 19. P—K 6!, B P×P; 20. B×Kt P, R×R ch; 21. Kt×R, R—K B 1; 22. P×P, and White's advantage is sufficient to win.

18. B P×P   P×P
19. P—B 4!

The opening of the long diagonal for the Q B decides the game in a few moves.

19. ......   K—R 2
20. B—Kt 2!   Kt (Kt 1)—B 3

If 20. ....P—B 3; 21. B×P ch, K×B; 22. Q—Q 3 ch, P—B 4; 23. Kt×P, R×Kt; 24. P×P, and White wins.

21. P×P   Kt—Kt 5
22. P—K 6   Q—R 5

The last hope. Evidently if 22. ....P×P; 23. B×P ch.

Position after Black's 22nd move.

23. R×P ch.

This combination forces the mate in a dozen moves.

23. ......   R×R
24. B×P ch!   K×B
25. Q—Q 3 ch   K—Kt 4
26. B—B 1 ch   Black resigns

For if 26. ....R—B 5; 27. Q—B 5 mate; or if 26. ....K—B 3; 27. Q—B 5 ch and mates in a few moves.

GAME 47

PHILIDOR'S DEFENCE

Exhibition Game at Kieff, May, 1916.

White:	*Black*:
A. EVENSSOHN.	A. ALEKHIN.

1. P—K 4   P—K 4
2. Kt—K B 3   P—Q 3
3. P—Q 4   Kt—K B 3

This move, introduced by Niemzovitch into Master play, is now thought stronger than 3. ....Kt—Q 2 (the Hanham variation, see Game No. 36).

4. Kt—B 3   Q Kt—Q 2
5. B—Q B 4   B—K 2

The usual move. In my opinion 5. ....P—K R 3 is more prudent.

Position after Black's 5th move.

6. Castles

For now White could have secured a slight advantage for the end-game by playing 6. P×P!, Q Kt×P! (not P×P, because of 7.

B×P ch, K×B ; 8. Kt—Kt 5 ch, K—Kt 1 ; 9. Kt—K 6, Q—K 1 ; 10. Kt×B P, followed by 11. Kt×R, and White has the advantage) ; 7. Kt×Kt, P×Kt ; 8. Q×Q ch, B×Q ; 9. B—Kt 5 followed by Castles Q R, and White, besides having the better development, has prospects of seizing the only open file.

The immediate sacrifice, however, would be unsound, e.g. : 6. B×P ch, K×B ; 7. Kt—Kt 5 ch, K—Kt 1 ; 8. Kt—K 6, Q—K 1 ; 9. Kt×B P, Q—Kt 3 ; 10. Kt×R, Q×P ! ; 11. R—B 1, P×P ! ; 12. Q×P, Kt—K 4, and Black has a winning attack.

6. ...... Castles
7. P×P

This exchange of Pawn only disengages Black's game. Better would be 7. Q—K 2, P—B 3 ; 8. P—Q R 4 ! and White has the advantage. (See game No. 9.)

7. ...... P×P
8. B—K Kt 5 P—B 3
9. P—Q R 4

This move is essential in this variation to prevent the possibility of a counter-attack eventually by ....P—Q.Kt 4.

9. ...... Q—B 2
10. Q—K 2 Kt—B 4

Now Black's game is preferable, for he has the prospect of occupying the squares Q 5 and K B 5, without giving his opponent counter-chances on the King-side or in the centre.

11. Kt—K 1

Without any necessity White assumes the defensive. 11. Q R—Q 1, followed by the doubling of Rooks on the Q file, was more likely to equalize the game.

Broadly speaking, the retreat of a Knight to the first rank, where it cuts the line of communication of the Rooks, is only admissible in very exceptional cases.

11. ...... Kt—K 3
12. B—K 3 Kt—Q 5 !
13. Q—Q 1

Or 13. B×Kt, P×B ; 14. Kt—Q 1, B—Q 3 ; 15. P—K Kt 3, B—K R 6 ; 16. Kt—Kt 2, Q R—K 1 ; with a marked advantage for Black.

13. ...... R—Q 1
14. Kt—Q 3 B—K 3
15. B×B

After the compulsory exchange of this Bishop, the development of which is the most serious difficulty of this variation, Black's game becomes far superior.

15. ...... Kt×B
16. Q—K 1

In view of the threat 16. ....P—B 4 ; and also to prepare the eventual advance of White's P—K B 4. But Black, quite rightly, ignores this counter-attack and simply increases the pressure in the centre.

16. ...... R—Q 2 !
17. P—B 3

For if now 17. P—B 4, then Kt—Kt 5 !, and White cannot play 18. P—B 5, because of R×Kt, followed by 19. ...Kt×B and 20. ...B—B 4.

17. ...... Q R—Q 1
18. B—B 2 Kt—R 4
19. Kt—K 2 P—Q B 4 !

This move prepares the following exchanges, the object of which is to weaken the Black squares in the adverse position.

20. P—Q Kt 3

If 20. Kt—B 3, P—B 5 ; 21. Kt—Q 5, Q—Q 3 ; 22. Kt—B 1, Kt (R 4)—B 5 ; and this last move will be even more powerful than in the actual game.

Position after White's 20th move.

20. ...... Kt (R 4)—B 5 !

Simple and decisive strategy. Black brings about the exchange of the two adverse minor pieces which might counteract his pressure on the Q file, leaving White with a Bishop only, the action of which is manifestly nil. The second phase of the game is a typical example of a regular blockade leading to the complete smothering of White's position.

21. Kt (K 2)×Kt   Kt×Kt
22. Kt×Kt   P×Kt
23. P—B 3

White was threatened with 23. ....P—B 5; 24. P—Q Kt 4, P—B 6; followed by R—Q 5.

23. ......   Q—K 4
24. R—R 2   R—Q 6
25. R—B 2   P—Q Kt 3
26. Q—B 1   Q—K 3

Freeing the square at K 4 with the intention of posting his Bishop there.

27. Q—Kt 1   B—B 3
28. P—Q Kt 4

A desperate bid for freedom. If Black takes the Pawn the White Rooks can occupy the Q B file.

28. ......   P—B 5

But Black opposes this plan.

29. Q—B 1   P—K Kt 4

Before assaulting the enemy's entrenchments it is essential to block the King-side completely and to secure the command of the diagonal Q R 2—K Kt 8.

30. P—R 3   B—K 4
31. Q—R 1

Another attempt to free himself, this time by opening the Q R file. Like the preceding one it is doomed to failure.

31. ......   P—K R 4
32. P—R 5   P—Kt 5
33. P×Q Kt P   P×Kt P

Position after Black's 33rd move.

34. B—R 4

If 34. R P×P, R P×P; 35. P×P, Q×P; 36. B×P, R—Q 7; 37. R×R, R×R; 38. B—B 2, P—B 6; and Black wins.

34. ......   P—B 3
35. B—K 1

Otherwise Black plays 35. .... P—Kt 6 and the White B would remain locked out for the rest of the game.

| 35. ...... | P—Kt 6 |
| 36. Q—R 7 | |

This skirmish momentarily retards the Pawn's advance to Q Kt 4, followed by the entry of the Queen at K 6 via Q Kt 3.

| 36. ...... | Q—B 3 ! |

Threatening 37. ....R—R 1.

37. Q—R 3	P—Kt 4
38. Q—Kt 2	Q—Kt 3 ch
39. K—R 1	R—Q 8
40. R—B 1	

Position after White's 40th move.

| 40. ...... | Q—K 6 ! |

Definitely maintaining one Rook at Q 8 after the exchange of the other, which settles the fate of White's Bishop and of the game.

41. R—R 1	R × R
42. Q × R	Q—K 7
43. R—Kt 1	R—Q 8 !

Winning at once, for there is no perpetual check.

44. Q—R 8 ch	K—Kt 2
45. Q—R 7 ch	K—Kt 3
46. Q—K 7	Q × B !
47. Q—K 8 ch	K—Kt 4
48. Q—Kt 8 ch	K—R 5

White resigns.

GAME 48

FRENCH DEFENCE

Played in a blindfold exhibition at the military hospital in Tarnopol, September, 1916.

| *White :* | *Black :* |
| A. ALEKHIN. | M. FELDT. |

1. P—K 4	P—K 3
2. P—Q 4	P—Q 4
3. Kt—Q B 3	Kt—K B 3
4. P × P	Kt × P
5. Kt—K 4	

More usual is 5. Kt—B 3, but the text-move, which aims at preventing 5. ....P—Q B 4, is equally to be recommended.

| 5. ...... | P—K B 4 |

A weakening of the centre which will ultimately prove fatal. The best move was 5. ....Kt—Q 2, with P—Q B 4 to follow eventually.

| 6. Kt—Kt 5 ! |

A good move. White intends to play his Knight to K 5, thereby taking immediate advantage of the weakness created by his opponent's previous move.

6.	B—K 2
7. Kt (Kt 5)—B 3	
	P—B 3

A lost *tempo*. Better is 7. ....Castles.

8. Kt—K 5	Castles
9. K Kt—B 3	P—Q Kt 3
10. B—Q 3	B—Kt 2
11. Castles	R—K 1

If here 11. ....Kt—Q 2, then 12. P—B 4, Kt (Q 4)—B 3 ; 13. Kt—Kt 5, etc.

12. P—B 4	Kt—B 3
13. B—B 4	Q Kt—Q 2
14. Q—K 2	P—B 4

Here 14. ....Kt—B 1 was essential. The text-move allows of a brilliant finish.

Position after Black's 14th move.

15. Kt—B 7 !

This threatens 16. Q×P, followed by the smothered mate, if the Black Queen moves.

15. ......   K×Kt
16. Q×P ch !

The point of the combination.

16. ......   K—Kt 3

Or if 16. ....K×Q ; 17. Kt—Kt 5, mate. Or if 16. ....K—B 1 ; 17. Kt—Kt 5, and White wins.

White announced mate in two by 17. P—K Kt 4 !, B—K 5 ; 19. Kt—R 4, mate.

GAME 49

Conclusion of an Odds Game, played at Petrograd, December, 1917.

White :   *Black :*
A. ALEKHIN. M. GOFMEISTER.

See Diagram.

Black in this position threatens on the one hand 1. ....Kt—K 5 and 2. ....B—B 2 ch ; and on the other hand perpetual check by 1. ....Kt—B 8 ch ; 2. K—R 1, Kt—Kt 6 ch.

Despite these two threats White succeeds in forcing the win as follows :

1. P—B 5 !

Threatening to open the Q B file with decisive effect, as the following variations prove :

I.—1. ....Kt—B 8 ch ; 2. K—R 1, Kt—Kt 6 ch ; 3. R×Kt, Q×R ; 4. P×P, Q×Q (or 4. ....R×R ; 5. Q×B ch, Q—Kt 1 ; 6. Q×R, P×P ; 7. Q×P and wins) ; 5. R×R ch, Q—Kt 1 ; 6. P—Kt 7 ch, R×P ; 7. P×R ch, K×P ; 8. R×Q ch, K×R ; 9. B—B 2, P—B 4 ; 10. P—Kt 3 and White has a won end-game with his extra Pawn.

II.—1. ....Kt—K 5 (B 4) ; 2. P×P, Kt×Q ; 3. P—Kt 7 ch, R×P ; 4. P×R ch, Kt×P ; 5. R×R mate.

To avoid these dangers Black is therefore compelled to play :

1. ......   P—Kt 4.

Black by this move keeps up his threats, which indeed appear still more formidable.

Initial Position.

Position after Black's 1st move.

Position after White's 4th move.

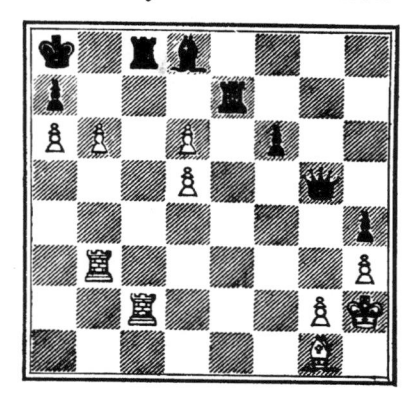

2. P×P !

A fresh surprise. As on the preceding move, the attempt at perpetual check proves abortive, e.g.:
2. ....Kt—B 8 ch; 3. K—R 1, Kt—Kt 6 ch; 4. R×Kt, Q×R; 5. P—Kt 6, Q×Q (or 5. ....P×P, 6. P×P !); 6. P×Q !, R×R; 7. P×R, B×K P; 8. P—Kt 7 ch, K—Kt 1; 9. B—R 2 ch, R—B 2; 10. B—B 4 !, B—B 4; 11. P—Kt 3, P×P; 12. P—R 4, B—Q 5; 13. B×R ch, K×B; 14. P—Q 6 ch, K—Kt 1; 15. P—Q 7, B—Kt 3; 16. P—R 5 and wins.

Black is therefore compelled to try out his counter-chances with his next move.

2. ......   Kt—K 5
3. P—Kt 6 ! Kt×Q

Already there is no longer any choice, for if 3. ....P×P; 4. P×P ! and wins.

4. P×Kt

A truly extraordinary position ! Black, with a whole Queen to the good, can no longer save the game !
See Diagram.

4. ......   R (K 2)—Q B 2

All other moves of Black would irretrievably have resulted in his defeat, e.g.:

I.—4. ....R×R; 5. P—Kt 7 ch, R×P; 6. P×R ch, K—Kt 1; 7. B×P ch, and mates in two.

II.—4. ....R—Kt 1; 5. P—Kt 7 ch and mates in three.

III.—4. ....P×P; 5. R×R ch, K—R 2; 6. P×R, B×P (6. ....Q—K 4 ch or Q—B 5 ch would only modify the inevitable result, seeing that the Queen, situated on a black square, would still be *en prise* after the discovered check); 7. B×P ch, K×P; 8. R—R 8 ch and wins with the discovered check from 9. B—K 3.

IV.—4. ....B—B 2 !; 5. P—Kt 7 ch, K—Kt 1; 6. P×B ch, R (K 2)×P [if 6. ....R (B 1)×P ?; 7. B×P ch !]; 7. R×R !, Q—B 5 ch (White's Rook cannot be captured by the Rook, on account of B×P ch, nor by the King, on account of R—B 3 ch ; if instead 7. ....R—Kt 1, then 8. R—B 2, threatening 9. K—R 1; 10. B—R 2 and wins); 8. K—R 1, Q×R; 9. B—R 2, Q×B ch; 10. K×Q and White easily wins the end-game.

5. P—Kt 7 ch K—Kt 1
6. P—Q 7 !

The *coup de grâce.*

| 6. ...... | Q—Kt 6 ch |
| 7. K—R 1 ! | Black resigns |

Final Position.

GAME 50

PETROFF'S DEFENCE

Masters' Triangular Tournament at Moscow, May, 1918.*

White :	Black :
A. ALEKHIN.	A. RABINOVITCH.
	(Vilna)
1. P—K 4	P—K 4
2. Kt—K B 3	Kt—K B 3
3. Kt × P	P—Q 3
4. Kt—K B 3	Kt × P
5. Kt—B 3	P—Q 4

This ingenious sacrifice of a Pawn is not quite sound, but not for the reasons adduced in the eighth edition of the *Handbuch* and other works. The variation adopted by White in the present game seems to be the only one which secures the advantage.

6. Q—K 2	B—K 2
7. Kt × Kt	P × Kt
8. Q × P	Castles
9. B—B 4	

* First prize, without loss.

Not 9. P—Q 4, to which Black can reply 9. ....R—K 1; which would now be useless because of 10. Kt—K 5.

| 9. ...... | B—Q 3 |

Position after Black's 9th move.

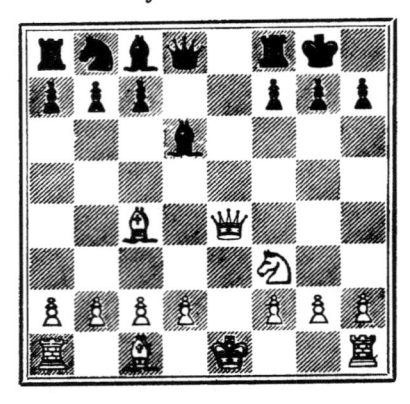

10. Castles

An innovation.

In the game Leonhardt—Schlechter (Barmen, 1905)—which according to the *Handbuch* refutes Black's fifth move—White continued 10. P—Q 4, R—K 1; 11. Kt—K 5, B × Kt; 12. P × B, Q—K 2 ?; 13. P—B 4, B—B 4; 14. Q × B, Q—Kt 5 ch; 15. B—Q 2, Q × B; 16. Q—Q 3, maintaining the Pawn with an excellent game. But by simply playing 12. .... Kt—B 3 (instead of 12. .... Q—K 2) Black could have obtained an even game, as the following main variation shows: 12. ....Kt—B 3; 13. B—B 4 (if 13. P—B 4, Q—R 5 ch; 14. P—Kt 3, Q—R 6; 15. B—B 1, Q—R 4, with a strong attack for Black), Q—R 5; 14. Castles Q R, R × P; 15. R—Q 8 ch, Q × R; 16. B × R, Q—K 2; 17. R—K 1, Kt × B; 18. Q × Kt, Q × Q; 19. R × Q, K—B 1.

LOCAL TOURNAMENTS, ETC.

10. ......   R—K 1
11. Q—Q 3   Kt—B 3

At first sight Black's prospects seem very promising, for his opponent has to contend with serious difficulties of development. But thanks to the manœuvre which follows, and which alone explains the tactics adopted hitherto, White not only surmounts all obstacles, but secures in addition a lasting initiative.

12. P—Q Kt 3 !   Q—B 3

Position after Black's 12th move.

13. B—Kt 2 !

An unexpected sacrifice which Black is compelled to accept, for after 13. ....Q—R 3 ; 14. K R—K 1, B—K Kt 5 ; 15. P—K R 3, he has no sort of compensation for the lost Pawn, *e.g.* : 15. ....B×P ; 16. P×B, Q×R P ; 17. B×P ch, etc.

13. ......   Q×B
14. Kt—Kt 5   B—K 3

The following alternative is hardly better : 14. ....P—K Kt 3 ; 15. B×P ch, K—Kt 2 (or 15. ....K—B 1 ; 16. B×R, K×B ; 17. Q R—K 1 ch, followed by 18. P—Q B 3 ! with a decisive attack for White) ; 16. B×R, Q—K 4 ;

17. Q—Q B 3, Kt—Kt 5 ; 18. P—B 4 !! and White maintains the gain of the Exchange.

15. B×B   P×B
16. Q×P ch   K—B 1

Position after Black's 16th move.

17. Q R—K 1

Immediately decisive would be 17. P—Q B 3 !, *e.g.* :

I.—17. P—Q B 3 !, Q×Q P ; 18. Q—R 8 ch, K—K 2 ; 19. Q×P ch, K—Q 1 ; 20. Q R—Q 1, Q—B 5 ; 21. P—K Kt 3 ! and Black's Queen is trapped, for if 21. ....Q—B 1 ; 22. Kt×P ch and wins ; or if 21. ....Q—B 4 ; 22. Kt—B 7 ch, K—B 1 ; 23. R×B ! and wins.

II.—17. P—Q B 3 !, B—K 4 ; 18. Q—R 5 !, K—Kt 1 ; 19. Q—B 7 ch, K—R 1 ; 20. P—K B 4, B—B 3 ; 21. R—B 3 !, Q×R ch ; 22. K—B 2, B×Kt ; 23. P×B and White wins.

The move in the text also leads to a win, but with somewhat greater difficulty.

17. ......   Q—B 3 !
18. Q—R 5

Insufficient would be here 18. Q—R 8 ch, K—K 2 ; 19. R×P ch, K—Q 2 !

18. ......   K—Kt 1
19. R—K 3 !

The strongest continuation of the attack, and at the same time setting a trap which takes Black unawares.

19. ......   B—B 5

Relatively better would be 19. ....Kt—Q 5 ; 20. R—R 3, P—K Kt 3 ; 21. Q—R 7 ch, K—B 1 ; 22. Q—Q 7 !, R—K 2 (the only move, for if 22. ....K—Kt 1 ; 23. R—R 8 ch ! and White wins) ; 23. Kt—R 7 ch, K—Kt 2 ; 24. Kt×Q, R×Q ; 25. Kt×R, R—Q 1 ; 26. R—Q 3, Kt—K 7 ch ; 27. K—R 1, R×Kt. (or 27. ....Kt—B 5 ; 28. Kt—K 5, etc.) ; 28. P—Kt 3, P—K 4 ; 29. P—Q B 3 and White has the advantage.

20. Q—R 7 ch   K—B 1
21. Q—R 8 ch   K—K 2
22. R×P ch   Q×R

Now compulsory, for if 22. .... K—Q 2 ; 23. R×Q, followed by 24. R×B. etc.

23. Q×P ch   K—Q 3
24. Kt×Q   R×Kt

Black's three pieces for the Queen are not a sufficient compensation, for in addition to White's extra Pawns, he has prospects of a direct attack on the adverse King.

25. P—Q 4   Q R—K 1
26. P—B 4   R (K 1)—K 2
27. Q—B 8   R—K 5

See Diagram.

28. Q—B 5 !

Winning at least another piece. The only possible defence is 28. .... R (K 2)—K 3 ; after which there follows 29. Q—B 5 ch, and 30. P—Q 5. But Black selects the shortest way.

28. ......   R×P
29. P—B 5 mate.

Position after Black's 27th move.

GAME 51

BISHOP'S OPENING
(*Berlin Defence*)

Played in a blindfold performance of six games at Odessa. December, 1918.

White :	*Black :*
W. Gonssiorovski.	A. Alekhin.

1. P—K 4   P—K 4
2. B—B 4   Kt—K B 3
3. P—Q 3   P—B 3 !

The most energetic line of play against the opening selected by White.

4. Q—K 2   B—K 2
5. P—B 4   P—Q 4 !
6. K P×P

If 6. B P×P, then 6. ....Kt×P.

6. ......   K P×P
7. B×P   Castles
8. Q Kt—Q 2

White, being already behind in his development, cannot afford to further that of his opponent by playing 8. P×P, Kt×P ; etc.

8. ......   P×P
9. B—Kt 3

Position after White's 9th move.

19. R×R ch	Q×R
20. Kt—K 4	Q×Kt !
21. B—Q 2	

Position after White's 21st move.

9.	P—Q R 4 !

In order to induce the weakening of White's Queen-side by compelling the reply 10. P—Q R 4.
Less strong is 9. ....R—K 1, because of 10. Castles.

10. P—B 3

This move leads to the loss of an important Pawn. Comparatively better is 10. P—Q R 4.

10.	P—R 5
11. B—B 2	P—R 6 !
12. P—Q Kt 3	R—K 1
13. Castles Q R	

There is nothing better.

13.	B—Q Kt 5
14. Q—B 2	B×P
15. B—Kt 5	Kt—B 3
16. Kt—B 3	P—Q 5 !
17. K R—K 1	

This plausible move causes an immediate catastrophe. But in any case the game was virtually lost.

17.	B—Kt 7 ch
18. K—Kt 1	Kt—Q 4 !

A disagreeable surprise. The threat of an immediate mate can only be parried with the loss of a piece.

21.	Q—K 6 !
22. R—K 1 !	

White returns the compliment by leaving his Queen *en prise*, as mate is threatened by R—K 8. But the danger is short-lived.

22.	B—B 4 !
23. R×Q	P×R
24. Q—B 1	

Black announced mate in three by 24. ....P × B ; 25. B—Q 1, Kt (B 3)—Kt 5 ! ; 26. any, Kt—B 6 mate.

GAME 52

DANISH GAMBIT

Moscow Championship,* October, 1919.

White :	*Black :*
A. ALEKHIN.	K. ISSAKOFF.
1. P—K 4	P—K 4
2. P—Q 4	P×P
3. P—Q B 3	P×P

First prize, without loss.

Declining the Gambit by 3. .... P—Q 4. or 3. .... Q—K 2 is, in my opinion, preferable.

4. Kt×P !

White, by giving up only one Pawn, secures as vigorous an attack as in the Danish Gambit, which has been completely neglected since Schlechter's discovery : 4. B–Q B 4, P×P ; 5. B×P, P—Q 4 ! ; 6. B×Q P, Kt—K B 3 !

4. ......   B—Kt 5

In a game Alekhin—Verlinski, played at Odessa in 1918, Black played 4. ....Kt—Q B 3. There followed : 5. B—Q B 4, P—Q 3 ; 6. Kt—B 3, Kt—B 3 ; 7. Q—Kt 3, Q—Q 2 ; 8. Kt—K Kt 5, Kt—K 4 (Kt—Q 1 is better) ; 9. B—Kt 5, P—B 3 ; 10. P—B 4 !, P×B ; 11. P×Kt, P×P ; 12. B—K 3 !, B—Q 3 ; 13. Kt×Kt P, Castles ; 14. R—Q 1, Kt—K 1 ; 15. Castles, Q—K 2 ; 16. Kt×B, Kt×Kt ; 17. Q—R 3 ! (not 17. Q—Kt 4, because of Kt—B 4), R—Q 1 ; 18. Kt×B P, B—Kt 5 ; 19. R×Kt, R—K 1 ; 20. B—Kt 5, Q—B 2 ; 21. Q—Q Kt 3, B—K 7 ; 22. Kt×P ch, K—R 1 ; 23. R—B 1, R—K B 1 !, an ingenious resource which very nearly saves the game.

See Diagram.

24. Q—Q 1 ! ! (the only move), Q—R 4 ; 25. Q×B, Q×Kt ; 26. R—Q 5, and Black resigns.

5. B—Q B 4   P—Q 3

Black need not fear 6. B×P ch, K×B ; 7. Q—Kt 3 ch, B—K 3 ; 8. Q×K B, Kt—Q B 3 ! ; 9. Q×P, Kt—Q 5 ; which, on the contrary, would give him a very strong attack.

6. Kt—B 3	B×Kt ch
7. P×B	Kt—Q B 3
8. Castles	Kt—B 3
9. B—R 3	

Position after Black's 23rd move, in sub-variation on Black's 4th move.

More in the spirit of the opening is at once 9. P—K 5, and if 9. .... P×P ; 10. Q—Kt 3, with prospects of a strong attack for White. After the text-move Black could have secured a satisfactory game by 9. ....B—Kt 5 ; 10. Q—Kt 3, Kt—Q R 4 ! ; 11. B×P ch, K—B 1 ; 12. Q—R 4, B×Kt ; 13. P×B, K×B ; 14. Q×Kt, R—K 1, etc.

| 9. ...... | Castles |
| 10. P—K 5 | Kt—K Kt 5 |

After 10. ....Kt—K 1 ; 11. P—K R 3 !, B—B 4 ; 12. R—K 1, etc. Black would have a very precarious game, the K R and K Kt being immobilized. He therefore prefers to give back the Pawn in order to complete his development.

11. P×P	P×P
12. B×P	R—K 1
13. R—K 1 !	

Preparing to sacrifice the K B eventually. It is clear that Black cannot play 13. ....R×R ch ; 14. Q×R, Q×B ; 15. Q—K 8 ch, Q—B 1 ; 16. B×P ch, K—R 1 ; 17. Q×Q mate.

| 13. ...... | B—B 4 |

Preferable, however, would be 13. ....R×R ch ; 14. Q×R, B—B 4 ; 15. R—Q 1, Q—K 1 ; 16. Kt—Q 4 !, and Black, although having slightly the inferior game, is safe from immediate disaster.

Position after Black's 13th move.

14. B×P ch !

A pretty combination. Its object is to keep the K Kt from K B 3 by forcing the Black King to occupy that square.

14. ......   K×B
15. Q—Q 5 ch   K—B 3

Evidently compulsory. If 15. ....B—K 3 ; 16. Kt—Kt 5 ch, etc., and if 15. ....K—Kt 3 ; 16. R×R, followed by 17. Kt—R 4 ch and White wins.

16. P—K R 3   B—K 3

Or if 16. ....Kt—R 3 ; 17. P—Kt 4, etc.

17. Q—Q 2 !   Kt—R 3
18. P—Kt 4

Regaining by force the piece he has sacrificed.

See Diagram.

18. ......   P—K Kt 3 !

The only resource.

Position after White's 18th move.

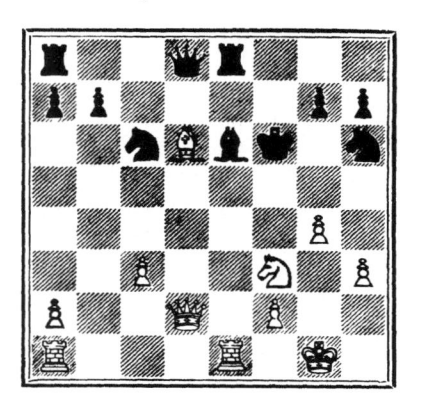

If 18. ....Kt—B 2 or K Kt 1, White wins with the following problem-like variation : 19. Q—B 4 ch, K—Kt 3 ; 20. B—K 7 ! !, Q×B ; 21. R×B ch and mates.

19. P—Kt 5 ch

Also very strong would be 19. Q×Kt, Q×B ; 20. P—Kt 5 ch, K—B 2 ! ; 21. Q×R P ch, K—B 1 ; 22. Q×K Kt P, with a winning attack.

After the text-move, which wins back the piece, the Black King contrives to escape danger temporarily.

19. ......   K—B 2
20. P×Kt   Q—B 3
21. Kt—Kt 5 ch K—Kt 1
22. P—K B 4   Q R—Q 1
23. Q R—Q 1   B—B 5

Black hopes to take advantage of the fact that White's Q B is pinned, in order to seize the open King's file, but White's reply destroys this last hope.

See Diagram.

24. B—K 7 !

The same move as in the variation referred to after Black's 18th move, but with an entirely different aim.

24. ......   R×Q

Position after Black's 23rd move.

Compulsory, for if 24. ... Kt × B ; 25. Q × R ; and if 24. .... Q × B ; 25. R × Q and White wins.

25. B × Q	R × R ch
26. R × R	B—B 2
27. Kt—K 4 !	

Winning at least the K R P and at the same time creating a mating position.

27.	R × P
28. B—Kt 7	B—Kt 6
29. Kt—B 6 ch	K—B 2
30. Kt × P	Black resigns.

PART TWO

CHAPTER XII

ALL-RUSSIAN MASTERS' TOURNAMENT AT MOSCOW, OCTOBER, 1920

GAME 53

QUEEN'S PAWN GAME

White : *Black :*
E. RABINOVITCH. A. ALEKHIN.
(St. Petersburg)

1. P—Q 4   Kt—K B 3
2. Kt—K B 3   P—Q Kt 3
3. P—B 4   P—K 3
4. Kt—B 3

Rubinstein's system, 4. P—K Kt 3 and 5. B—Kt 2 here, or on the next move, is considered better.

4. ......   B—Kt 2
5. P—K 3

This allows Black to occupy the square K 5 with effect, and thus to secure at least an equal game.

5. ......   B—Kt 5
6. Q—B 2   Kt—K 5
7. B—Q 3   P—K B 4

In this manner Black has brought about a position, favourable to himself, of the Dutch Defence.

8. Castles

White could here have selected another line of play : 8. B—Q 2, B×Kt ; 9. B×B, Castles ; 10. Castles Q R, after which Black seizes the initiative by 10. ....P—Q R 4! and 11. ....Kt—R 3 (Sämisch—Alekhin, Pistyan, 1922).

8. ......   B×Kt
9. P×B   Castles
10. Kt—Q 2

The only way to enforce the advance of the K P.

10. ......   Q—R 5 !

An important developing move to which White cannot reply by 11. P—Kt 3 without disadvantage, because of 11. ....Kt—Kt 4 ! and if 12. P—K 4 then 12. ....P×P ! and Black wins.

11. P—B 3   Kt×Kt
12. B×Kt   Kt—B 3

12. ....P—B 4 would not be so good, because of 13. P—Q 5 !

13. P—K 4   P×P
14. B×P

White appears to over-rate the strength of his position. More correct was 14 P×P, P—K 4 !; 15. P—Q 5 ; Kt—K 2 ; 16. P—B 5 !, Kt—Kt 3 (not 16. ....P×P, because of 17. P—Q 6 and

18. Q—Kt 3 ch); 17. P×P, R P×P, with about an equal game.

14. ...... Kt—R 4

Securing a slight advantage, should White choose the best variation, 15. B×B, Kt×B; 16. K R—K 1, by reason of White's doubled Pawns on the Q B file.

15. Q R—K 1

This plausible move leads to the loss of a Pawn.

15. ...... B×B!
16. R×B Q—R 4
17. Q—R 4

There was no satisfactory defence to the Q B P, *e.g.*: 17. R—K 5, R—B 4!; 18. R×R, Q×R; 19. Q×Q, P×Q, and Black has virtually a won end-game.

17. ...... Kt×P!

Now Black has every justification for anticipating victory, yet in spite of his advantage in material it is not easy to achieve it, for the adverse position shows no weak point.

18. R—K 2

Clearly, if 18. Q×Kt, P—Q 4; 19. Q—Kt 5, P—Q R 3 and Black wins.

18. ...... P—Q Kt 4
19. Q—Kt 3 Q—K B 4
20. K R—K 1 Q R—Kt 1
21. B—B 1 P—Q R 4
22. R—K 4 P—R 5
23. Q—Q 1 Q R—K 1

Having consolidated the dominating position of his Knight, Black now prepares an action in the centre which will enable him to shatter the hostile position, although allowing his opponent apparent compensations.

24. Q—K 2 P—B 4!

Although this temporarily increases the range of action of White's Q B, yet by this reason the Bishop later on becomes an object of attack.

This plan demanded an exhaustive examination of the tactical possibilities of the position, and was not undertaken until Black was perfectly convinced that it would ultimately result in his favour.

25. B—K 3 P×P
26. B×P

Position after White's 26th move.

26. ...... P—K 4!

The beginning of a series of extremely interesting complications. The Pawn cannot be captured by the Bishop, because of 27. ....P—Q 4!, and the variation 27. B—B 5, P—Q 4; 28. R×Kt, Kt P×R; 29. B×R, Q×B, would also be to Black's advantage.

27. P—B 4!

Undoubtedly the best chance. White intends to answer 27. .... P—Q 4 with 28. R×P, Kt×R; 29. B×Kt, which would give him quite a defendable game.

27. ...... P—Q 3

Sufficing for the protection of the Pawn, because of the mate in two moves after 28. P×P, P×P ; 29. B×P ?, Kt×B ; 30. R×Kt, R×R ; 31. Q×R, etc.

28. P—R 3

Again threatening Black's K P, which he will at once defend in an indirect manner.

28. ......   R—K 3 !
29. P×P   P×P
30. B—B 5 !

Not 30. B×P on account of 30. ....R (B 1)—K 1 ; 31. R—K B 1, Q—Kt 3 ; 32. R×Kt, R×B and wins.
The text-move appears full of promise, seeing that the Black Rook cannot leave the K B file, e.g. : 30. ....R—Q 1 ; 31. R—K B 1, Q—Kt 3 ; 32. R—Kt 4, Q—R 3 ; 33. Q—B 3 ! and wins.

30. ......   R—B 2 !

The initial move of a sacrificial combination intended to yield a decisive attack. As a mere defensive move, 30. ....K R—B 3 would be adequate, as White could not answer 31. R—Kt 1 because of 31. ....Kt—Q 7 !

31. R—Kt 1

Seemingly recovering his Pawn with a good game, for 31. ....Kt—Q 7 is now impossible on account of 32. Q×Kt, threatening Q—Q 8 ch, etc.

31. ......   P—R 3

This parries the threat of mate and compels the opponent to persevere on the perilous path on which he is proceeding.

32. R×Kt P   Kt—Q 7 !
33. R×R P

White has no longer any defence, for if 33. R—K Kt 4, Black would win in an analogous manner to that in the text.
If 33. R—K 3, then 33. ....R—K Kt 3 (this diversion was the special point of playing the K R to B 2 instead of B 3 on the 30th move) ; 34. R—Kt 8 ch, K—R 2 ; 35. R—Kt 2 (or 35. Q×Kt, Q—B 8 ch ; 36. K—R 2, R—B 7 and wins), Kt—B 6 ch ; 36. K—R 1, Q×P ch ! and mates next move.

Position after White's 33rd move.

33. ......   Q—B 7 .

After this move, which explains the foregoing sacrifice of two Pawns, White is lost, owing to inability to withdraw his Rooks to secure the defence of his first rank.

34. R—R 8 ch   K—R 2
35. K—R 1   R—B 8 ch
36. B—Kt 1   R×B ch !

A pretty final combination.

37. K×R   Q—B 8 ch
38. K—B 2   R—B 3 ch
39. K—K 3

If 39. K—Kt 3, Kt—B 8 ch. Now Black's next move wins the Queen or mates.

39. ......   Kt—Kt 8 ch !
White resigns.

CHAPTER XIII

INTERNATIONAL TOURNAMENT AT TRIBERG
JULY, 1921

GAME 54

QUEEN'S PAWN GAME

White: Black:
A. A. SELESNIEFF.   A. ALEKHIN.

1. P—Q 4   Kt—K B 3
2. Kt—K B 3   P—Q Kt 3

This move is possible before P—K 3, because White has played 2. Kt—K B 3, but after 2. P—Q B 4 it is not good on account of 3. Kt—Q B 3, B—Kt 2 ; 4. Q—B 2 ! (see Game No. 77)

     3. P—K Kt 3

In my opinion best, as White's Bishop on K Kt 2 is at least as strong as Black's on Q Kt 2.

3. ......   B—Kt 2
4. B—Kt 2   P—Q 3

This system of development was introduced by the author in one of his match-games against Teichmann at Berlin. 1921. Its only defect is that Black's Q B 3 may eventually become weak, a weakness, however, which does not present very great drawbacks.

     5. Castles

In the course of the same tournament a game Brinckmann—Alekhin was continued as follows: 5. P—Kt 3, Q Kt—Q 2 ; 6. B—Kt 2, P — K 4 ; 7. P × P, P × P ; 8. Castles, P—K 5 ! ; 9. Kt—K 5, B—Q 3 ; 10. Kt × Kt, Q × Kt ; 11. Kt—Q 2, Q—K 3 ; 12. P—K 3, P—K R 4 ! ; 13. Q—K 2, P—R 5 ; 14. Kt—B 4, B—B 4 ; 15. K R—Q 1, B—Q 4 ; 16. Kt—R 3, P × P ; 17. R P × P, P—R 3 ; 18. P—Q B 4, B—Kt 2 ; 19. Kt—B 2, Q—B 4 ; 20. B—R 3, B × B ; 21. Kt × B, Kt—Kt 5 ; 22. Kt—B 2, R—R 7 ; 23. Q—Q 2, K—K 2 ! ; 24. Kt—Kt 4, Q R—R 1 ; 25. Q—K 2, Q—B 6 ! ! ; 26. Resigns.

5. ......   Q Kt—Q 2
6. B—B 4

To prevent 6. .... P—K 4.

6. ......   P—K R 3

Threatening P—K Kt 4 in some combinative variations ; but the real intention is to make this advance only when Black is assured of an immediate and definite advantage.

     7. Kt—B 3

Allowing the following demonstration aimed at the Q P.

INTERNATIONAL TOURNAMENT AT TRIBERG

7.	P—B 4
8. P—Q 5	

After 8. P×P, Kt×P, Black would also have secured a very promising position.

| 8. ...... | P—Q Kt 4 ! |

Otherwise White by playing 9. P—Q R 4! would prevent Black from seizing the initiative on the Queen-side.

| 9. Kt—K 1 | |

White's Q·P is certainly more valuable than Black's Q Kt P.

9.	P—Q R 3
10. P—Q R 4	P—Kt 5
11. Kt—K 4	Kt×Kt
12. B×Kt	P—Kt 3

So as to develop the Bishop at K Kt 2, the object of the manœuvre commencing 7. ....P—B 4.

| 13. P—B 4 | P×P e. p. |

Absolutely essential to prevent White from blocking the Queen-side, which would have enabled him to undertake a strong attack by the advance of his centre Pawns, without fear of molestation.

14. P×P	B—Kt 2
15. R—Kt 1	R—Q Kt 1
16. P—B 4	Castles
17. Q—B 2	P—Q R 4

Preparing the following sacrifice of the Exchange.

18. Kt—B 3	Q—B 2
19. B—Q 2	B—R 3
20. B—Q 3	

See Diagram.

| 20. ...... | R—Kt 5 !! |

Absolutely correct. The strong passed Pawn thus resulting, supported by the Bishop on K Kt 2, and the possibilities of attack on White's Q B P are, on the whole, worth more than the Exchange.

Position after White's 20th move.

21. B×R	B P×B
22. Kt—Q 2	Kt—B 4

But this move is illogical. Black could have demonstrated the correctness of his sacrifice more clearly by 22. ....R—Q B 1, followed by 23. ....Kt—Kt 3 or also 23. ....Kt—K 4, and if necessary 23. ....B—B 6.

| 23. Kt—Kt 3 ! | |

Position after White's 23rd move.

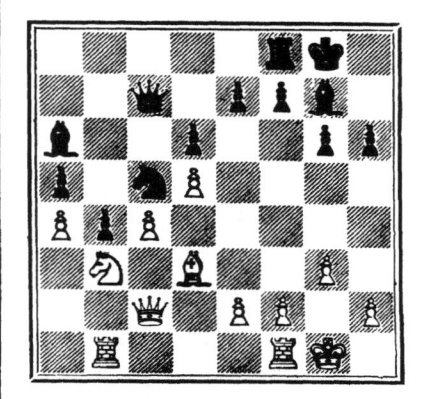

A strong move, the value of which was not appreciated in good time. If Black replies to it by 23. ....Kt×P, White could advantageously continue 24. R—R 1 !, Kt—B 4 ; 25.

Kt×P, B×R; 26. R×B, K—R 2 (else 27. B×P!); 27. Kt—B 6. Or if 23. ....R—B 1; 24. Kt×Kt, Q×Kt; 25. K R—B 1, B—B 6; 26. Q—Kt 3 (not 26. R—Kt 3, B×P; 27. R×B, P×R; 28. B×P, on account of 28. ....K—Kt 2!), Q—Q 5; 27. R×B, P×R; 28. R—Q B 1 and White cannot lose.

23. ......   Kt—Q 2

So Black must submit to this temporary retreat, while threatening 24. ....R—Q B 1. But White seizes the opportunity to eliminate his weak Q B P by a counter-sacrifice which opens new lines and affords at the same time excellent chances.

Position after Black's 23rd move.

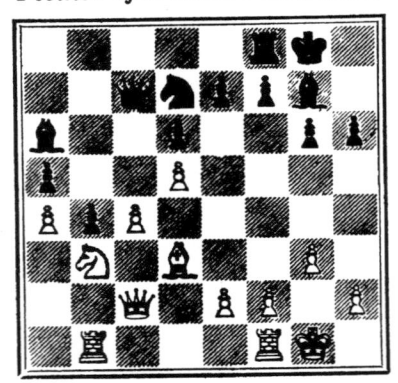

24. P—B 5!   B×B
25. P×B!

After 25. Q×B, P×P, Black's passed Pawns would soon decide the game. The text-move parries this danger, whilst opening the King's file for White. On the other hand there is the drawback, very slight though it may be, of weakening the King's position, and particularly K B 3, a weakness which Black will exploit later on.

25. ......   P×P
26. K R—K 1

Against the plausible move 26. Q—B 4, which was equally to be considered, Black would have retorted 26. ....Q—Q 3!; 27. Kt×R P, Kt—K 4; 28. Q—Kt 3, R—R 1, with excellent chances.

26. ......   Kt—K 4
27. R—K 3

The attempt to give back the Exchange, in his turn, would have been insufficient: 27. Q×P, Kt—B 6 ch; 28. K—B 1, Q×Q; 29. Kt×Q, Kt—Q 7 ch!; 30. K—K 2, Kt×R; 31. R×Kt, R—Q 1! and Black wins a Pawn.

27. ......   R—B 1
28. R—Q B 1   Q—Q 2!
29. P—Q 4   Kt—Kt 5
30. R—K 4

If 30. P×P, Kt×R; 31. P×Kt, Q×R P!, but not 31. ....Q×Q P.

30. ......   P—B 5!

Now Black's Queen-side Pawns become very threatening. The question is, how to maintain them! The game now enters upon its most critical phase.

31. Kt—B 5

If 31. Kt×P, obviously 31. ....Q×Q P and Black wins easily.

31. ......   Q—B 4!
32. Q—K 2!

White has defended himself excellently, and hopes to obtain a decisive advantage by the text-move, which threatens the Knight and the B P at the same time; but Black's reply gives him a disagreeable surprise.

See Diagram.

32. ......   P—Kt 6!!

Before deciding on this surprising move, Black had to visualize the following variations, apart from the continuation in the text.

Position after White's 32nd move.

I.—33. R—B 4, Q—R 4 ; 34. R×Kt, P—Kt 7 ; 35. R—Kt 1, Q 1 or K 1 (if 35. Q×Kt P, Q×R as in the game), B×P and Black's Pawns become overwhelming.

II.—33. Q×Kt, P—Kt 7 ; 34. R—Kt 1, Q×Q ; 35. R×Q, P—B 6 ; 36. Kt—Q 3, R—B 5 ; 37. Kt×P !, R—Kt 5 ! ; 38. R—K 4, K—B 1 with advantage to Black, for if 39. R—Q B 1, P—B 4 ! ; 40. Kt—Q 3, P×R ; 41. Kt×R, P×Kt ; 42. P—R 5, B×P ; 43. P—R 6, K—B 2 ! and wins.

33. R×Kt	P—Kt 7
34. Q×Kt P	Q×R
35. R×P	

Apparently White has chosen the simplest method of extricating himself from his difficulties, for he has eliminated the passed Pawns and remains a Pawn to the good. However, Black's next move creates new difficulties for him.

35. ...... P—K R 4 !

Profiting by the immobility of the hostile pieces to threaten a mating attack by P—R 5—R 6, followed by Q—B 6.

36. Q—B 2

The only resource for the defence, in fact, consists in playing the White Queen to Q 3.

36. ...... P—R 5

Naturally not B×P, on account of 37. K—Kt 2 !

37. Q—Q 3 R—Q 1 !

37. P—R 6 would be insufficient, as after 38. P—B 3, Q—R 4 (38. ....Q—Kt 4 ? ; 39. Kt—K 4 !) ; 39. Q—K 4, Q—R 3 ; 40. R—B 2, White could defend himself satisfactorily.

38. P—B 3 Q—R 4

Not 38. ....Q—R 6 on account of 39. P—Kt 4, R—Kt 1 ; 40. Kt—K 4, R—Kt 7 ; 41. R—B 8 ch !, B—B 1 ; 42. Kt—B 2 and White would win the Exchange.

39. Q—K 4	P×P
40. P×P	Q—Kt 4 !
41. K—Kt 2	Q—Q 7 ch

After 41. R×P White would have forced the exchange of Queens by 42. P—B 4, Q—R 4 ; 43. Q—B 3, and Black would have difficulty in securing the win.

42. K—R 3 B—B 3 !

In order to occupy the K R file with the Rook : the only means of securing the win.

43. R—B 2	Q—R 3 ch
44. K—Kt 2	K—Kt 2
45. P—Kt 4	

Otherwise this Pawn would be lost, without any compensation.

45. ...... R—K R 1
46. K—B 2 !

It will be admitted that White defends himself with remarkable coolness.

Position after White's 46th move.

46. ......   R—Q Kt 1 ! !

The point of the manœuvre initiated by 42. ....B—K B 3. Black's Rook was brought to the K R file solely in order to force the entry of the Queen into the hostile game by that means. Its mission accomplished, the Rook returns to the Queen-side and contributes to an attack against the key of the hostile positions (White's Pawn on Q 4), a manœuvre against which White is absolutely defenceless.

47. K—K 2	R—Kt 5
48. R—Q 2	Q—R 7 ch
49. K—K 3	

Or 49. K—Q 3, Q—Kt 8 !

| 49. ...... | Q—Kt 8 ch |
| 50. K—K 2 | B × P |

Now White could well have resigned, but, on the contrary, he tries a desperate move and by his tenacity he achieves a partial success.

51. Kt—Q 3   R—Kt 8

51. ....B—B 6 !; 52. Kt × R, Q—Kt 7 ch was immediately decisive.

52. Kt—B 1 !   B—B 6 !

With 52. ....R—Q Kt 5 ; 53. Kt—Q 3 (there is nothing better) Black could have brought about the same position as after White's 51st move ; but he prefers to accept the *fait accompli*, as the variation on the text appears to him to be sufficiently clear and satisfactory.

53. Q × R	Q—Kt 7 ch
54. K—Q 3	Q × R ch
55. K—B 4	Q—Q 5 ch
56. K—Kt 3	

Position after White's 56th move

56. ......   B—R 8 !

The continuation which Black had in view when playing 52. .... B—B 6. Now White will find it impossible to defend his Pawns.

For example, if 57. Kt—Q 3, Q × Q P ch ; 58. K—R 3, B—B 3 ; 59. Q—Q 1, P—Kt 4 ! ; 60. Q—K 2, Q—Q B 5 ! ; 61. Q—Q 1, Q—B 6 ch ; 62. K—R 2, P—K 3 ! and Black wins.

57. K—R 3	Q—B 4 ch
58. K—R 2	B—B 3
59. P—Kt 5	

Another desperate attempt. As the sequel will show, White follows a plan which promises him an illusory salvation.

59.	Q×P ch
60. Kt—Kt 3	Q×Kt P
61. Q—K 1	

Staking his last hope on the Q R P, but his opponent will soon destroy this last illusion, by sacrificing his B for the Q R P, after which the Black passed Pawns on the Kingside win very easily.

61.	Q—Kt 7 ch
62. Q—Q 2	Q×P !
63. Q×P	P—Kt 4
64. Q—K 1	Q—B 6
65. Q×Q	B×Q
66. P—R 5	B×P
67. Kt×B	P—Kt 5
68. Kt—B 4	P—Kt 6
69. Kt—Q 2	K—Kt 3
70. K—Kt 2	K—B 4
71. Kt—B 3	K—B 5
72. Kt—Kt 1	K—K 6
73. K—B 2	K—B 7
74. Kt—R 3 ch	K—B 8

White resigns.

A very difficult and interesting game in all its phases.

GAME 55

QUEEN'S PAWN OPENING

Brilliancy Prize

White :	Black :
A. ALEKHIN.	E. D. BOGOLJUBOFF.
1. P—Q 4	Kt—K B 3
2. Kt—K B 3	P—K 3
3. P—B 4	P—Q Kt 3

This variation, abandoned by Bogoljuboff in consequence of this game, has been played with success in recent tournaments by the masters Sämisch and Niemzovitch. Black's defeat in this game cannot therefore be attributed to this variation, but solely to his fifth move. (See note thereto.)

4. P—K Kt 3	B—Kt 2
5. B—Kt 2	P—B 4

This move gives White the choice of two replies. Besides 6. P×P as in the present game, White can also continue with 6. P—Q 5, P×P ; 7. Kt—R 4 (proposed by Rubinstein in the latest edition of Collijn's *Lärobok*), and it is difficult to see how Black is to free his game. (Compare, however, the game Alekhin—Capablanca from the New York Tournament, 1927.)

The correct move for Black is : 5. ....B—K 2 ; followed by 6. Castles, Castles ; 7. Kt—B 3, P—Q 4 ; 8. Kt—K 5 !, Q—B 1 ! (suggested by Sämisch), with a satisfactory game.

Less good, however, would be :

I.—8. ....Q Kt—Q 2 ; 9. P×P Kt×Kt (P×P is better) ; 10. P—Q 6 ! (Bogoljuboff—Niemzovitch, Carlsbad, 1923), or

II.—8. ....P—B 3 ; 9. P—K 4, Q Kt—Q 2 ; 10. Kt×Q B P !, B×Kt ; 11. K P×P, B—Kt 2 ; 12. P—Q 6 and White wins a Pawn (a variation suggested by the author).

6. P×P

As the sequel shows, White secures an advantage by this simple move, thanks to the pressure he will exert on the open Q file.

6.	B×P

The position of the Black Bishops is stronger in appearance than in fact, as White's castled position is perfectly secure.

7. Castles	Castles
8. Kt—B 3	P—Q 4

Giving White the opportunity of unmasking the K B with advantage. Relatively better is : 8. ....Kt—R 3, although in this case also the weakness of his Q P would have been a source of difficulty for Black.

9. Kt—Q 4 !

Not 9. Kt—K 5, because of the reply 9. ....Q—B 2; 10. B—B 4, Kt—R 4, etc.

| 9. ...... | B×Kt |

Perceiving the possibility of ridding himself of the troublesome Q P, Black allows his opponent the advantage of having two Bishops, which, in this position, implies a very marked superiority. On the other hand, it is true that the alternative: 9. ....Kt—B 3; 10. Kt ×Kt, B×Kt; 11. B—Kt 5, B—K 2; 12. R—B 1, is hardly more attractive.

| 10. Q×B | Kt—B 3 |
| 11. Q—R 4 | P×P |

Hoping to obtain an approximately equal game by Kt—K 4 or Kt—Q R 4, once White has recaptured the Q B P with the Queen. But White is careful to refrain from that course, and prefers to launch a direct attack on the King's position, which, despite appearances, is insufficiently defended.

| 12. R—Q 1! | Q—B 1 |

Forced. If 12. ....Q—K 2; 13. B—Kt 5, P—K R 3; 14. B×Kt, Q×B; 15. Q×Q, P×Q; 16. R—Q 7, winning Kt and B for the Rook.

| 13. B—Kt 5! | Kt—Q 4 |

Or 13. ....Kt—Q 2; 14. Kt—K 4, with a strong attack for White. With the text-move Black hopes to exchange one of the White Bishops by discovering his Q B on the 15th move.

| 14. Kt×Kt | P×Kt |
| 15. R×P! | |

This unexpected capture which, at first sight, seems to expose the Rook to an attack by Black's Q B, is fully justified by the sacrificial variations following upon White's next move.

| 15. ...... | Kt—Kt 5 |

It is clear that other replies would be no better.

Position after Black's 15th move.

16. B—K 4!!

Decisive, as is shown in the variations given farther on. The reader will clearly perceive a similarity with other games (which also gained brilliancy prizes) namely : *v.* Sterk at Budapest (Game No. 56), Rubinstein at Carlsbad (Game No. 80) and Selesnieff at Pistyan (Game No. 63).

The leading characteristic in these games is an unforeseen but immediately decisive attack.

The chief point in these attacks lies in the fact that none of them was prepared in the immediate vicinity of its objective. On the contrary, all the preliminary manœuvres which tended to divert the adverse pieces from the defence of their King took place in the centre or on the opposite wing. Furthermore, it is interesting to note that the deciding move, a real hammer-blow, is played by a Bishop and always involves sacrificial variations.

These repeated attacks in the same manner, in the course of games of widely different character, seem to me to constitute a very precise criterion of a player's style,

INTERNATIONAL TOURNAMENT AT TRIBERG

or at least, of the evolution of his style.

16. ......   P—B 4

Other variations would be no better, e.g.:

I.—16. ....P—K R 3 ; 17. B × P, P—B 4 ; 18. Q—Kt 5, Q—B 2 ; 19. B×Kt P, Q×B ; 20. Q×Q ch, K×Q ; 21. R—Q 7 ch, followed by B×B and White wins.

II.—16. ....P—Kt 3 ; 17. B—B 6, Kt×R ; 18. B×Kt and White wins. After the text-move Black loses the Queen against Rook and Bishop, and White's victory is only a question of time.

17. B×P !	R×B
18. R—Q 8 ch	Q×R
19. B×Q	R—Q B 1
20. R—Q 1	R—K B 2
21. Q—Kt 4	Kt—Q 6

An inoffensive manœuvre. Black is quite helpless, and can only hope for a miracle !

22. P×Kt	R×B
23. P×P	Q R—K B 1
24. P—B 4	R—K 2
25. K—B 2	P—K R 3
26. R—K 1	B—B 1
27. Q—B 3	R (K 2)—K B 2
28. Q—Q 5	P—K Kt 4
29. R—K 7	P×P
30. P×P	Black resigns

CHAPTER XIV

INTERNATIONAL TOURNAMENT AT BUDAPEST
SEPTEMBER, 1921

GAME 56

QUEEN'S GAMBIT DECLINED

Brilliancy Prize

White :	*Black :*
A. ALEKHIN.	K. STERK.

1. P—Q 4   P—Q 4
2. Kt—K B 3   Kt—K B 3
3. P—B 4   P—K 3
4. Kt—B 3   Q Kt—Q 2
5. P—K 3

After Black's last move, which is probably inferior to 4. ....B—K 2, White has the choice of several good continuations :

I.—5. B—Kt 5 (if 5. B—B 4 ?, P×P ; 6. P—K 3, Kt—Kt 3 !).

II.—5. P×P, P×P ; 6. B—B 4 ! (suggested by Sämisch). On the other hand, Soldetenkoff's ingenious move, 6. Q—Kt 3, proves insufficient, as the following variation shows : 6. ....P—B 3 ; 7. P—K 4, Kt×P ! ; 8. Kt×Kt, Q—K 2 !

III.—5. P—K 3, the text-move, less energetic perhaps, but affording White a slight advantage in development, if correctly followed up.

5. ......   B—Q 3

A risky move which White does not exploit in the most energetic manner. Black obtains a satisfactory game by the more solid variation 5. ....B—K 2 ; 6. B—Q 3, P×P ; 7. B×B P, P—B 4.

6. Kt—Q Kt 5.

With this reply, original but of doubtful value, White lets slip his chances. The retort 6. P—B 5, B—K 2 ; 7. P—Q Kt 4 followed by 8. B—Kt 2 was indicated, and would have enabled White to exercise pressure on the Queen's side before Black, by reason of his loss of time, could undertake a counter-demonstration in the centre. The text-move is intended to prevent 8...P—K 4, after 6. B—Q 3, P×P ; 7. B×B P, Castles ; 8. Castles, but the loss of time occasioned allows Black to equalize the game without difficulty.

6.	B—K 2
7. Q—B 2	P—B 3
8. Kt—B 3	Castles
9. B—Q 3	P×P
10. B×P	P—B 4 !

Black, as can easily be seen, has been fortunate enough to surmount all the difficulties of the opening.

11. P×P

After 11. Castles, Kt—Kt 3 ; 12. B—Q 3, P×P ; 13. P×P, B—Q 2 White would not have sufficient compensation for his isolated Q P.

11.	......	B×P
12.	Castles	P—Q Kt 3
13.	P—K 4	

White, after his careless treatment of the opening, seeks complications which are not without danger to himself.
13. P—Q Kt 3, B—Kt 2; 14. B—Kt 2, R—B 1; 15. Q—K 2 would suffice to equalize the game.

13.	......	B—Kt 2
14.	B—K Kt 5	

Not 14. P—K 5, Kt—Kt 5!; 15. Kt—K Kt 5, P—Kt 3; 16. Kt×R P, Q—R 5; 17. P—K R 3, Q—Kt 6, followed by mate.

14.	......	Q—B 1!

A very good move which puts an end to all the opponent's fond hopes. Not only is Black out of danger, but it is actually he who is going to undertake a counter-attack.

15. Q—K 2

Preventing the threatened 15. ....B×P ch. However, 15. B—Q 3 was preferable.

15.	......	B—Kt 5!

Position after Black's 15th move.

This move marks the critical phase. White, whose game is compromised, will make a serious effort to maintain equality. What is he to do? Neither 16. P—K 5, Kt—Kt 5; nor 16. Q R—B 1, B×Kt; 17. B—Q 3, Kt—B 4!; 18. R×B, B×P!; 19. B×Kt, B×B, threatening B×R, etc., would be sufficient. After a quarter of an hour's perplexity, White succeeded in resolving the difficulty.

16.	B—Q 3	B×Kt

Position after Black's 16th move.

17. K R—Q B 1!

The saving move, because if Black now plays 17. ....Kt—B 4, which is his best, the continuation would be 18. R×B, B×P; 19. B×Kt, B×B; 20. Q—K 3! Here is the difference from the preceding variation: Black's Q B no longer attacks White's Rook on K B 1. 20. ....P×B; 21. P—Q Kt 4, B—Kt 3; 22. P×Kt, P×P; 23. R×P, Q moves anywhere; 24. P—K R 4 and White will find his attacking possibilities adequate compensation for the Pawn thus sacrificed.

17.	......	Kt×P

Black attempts to win a Pawn without compromising the position of his King but does not sufficiently count the danger to which he exposes his Kt on B 4.

18. B×Kt   B×B
19. Q×B   Kt—B 4
20. Q—K 2 !

More energetic than 20. Q—Kt 1, suggested by some annotators, which would have yielded the win of only two minor pieces for a Rook, after 20. ....B—Kt 5; 21. P—Q R 3, Q—Kt 2, while allowing Black numerous defensive possibilities.

20. ......   B—R 4
21. Q R—Kt 1 Q—R 3
22. R—B 4   Kt—R 5

An ingenious resource, but inadequate. If 23. P—Q Kt 4, then 23. ....Kt—B 6!

However, Black has no longer any saving move. If, for example, 22. ....P—B 3, then 23. B—R 4 !, etc.

Position after Black's 22nd move.

23. B—B 6 !!

The initial move of a mating attack as elegant as it is unexpected, which leads to this end in a few moves. Black is threatened with 24. R—K Kt 4, Q×Q; 25. R×P ch and mate next move. If 23. ....P—R 4; 24. R—K Kt 4!, Q×Q; 25. R×P ch, K—R 1 ; 26, Kt—Kt 5 ! and Black has no defence against 27. R—R 7 ch, followed by 28. R—R 8 mate. If 23. ....P—R 3; 24. Kt—K 5 ! with the threat Q—Kt 4, and White wins.

23. ......   K R—Q B 1 !

The only move ! White replies to it by a new surprise.

24. Q—K 5 !

The necessary corollary to the preceding move.

Position after White's 24th move.

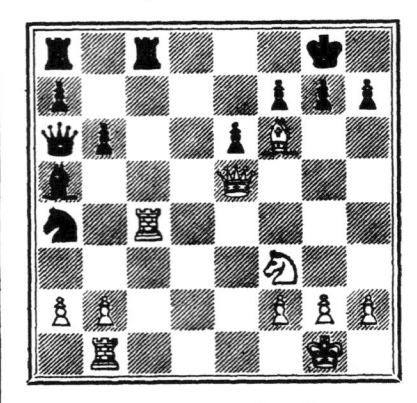

24. ......   R—B 4

The following variations are also insufficient :

I.—24. ...Q×R ; 25. Q—K Kt 5, K—B 1 ; 26. Q×P ch, K—K 1 ; 27. Q—Kt 8 ch, K—Q 2 ; 28. Kt—K 5 ch, K—B 2 ; 29. Q×P ch, followed by 30. Kt×Q.

II.—24. ...R×R ; 25. Q—K Kt 5, R—K Kt 5 ; 26. Q×R, P—Kt 3 ; 27. Q×Kt.

III.—24. ....P×B ; 25. R—Kt 4 ch and mate in two moves.

The text-move avoids the variation 25. R×R, P×B, etc., but White answers with a still stronger reply.

25. Q—Kt 3 !

Simple and decisive.

25.	......	P—Kt 3
26.	R×Kt	Q—Q 6
27.	R—K B 1	Q—B 4
28.	Q—B 4	Q—B 7
29.	Q—R 6	Black resigns.

GAME 57

QUEEN'S PAWN GAME

White :   *Black :*
A. ALEKHIN.   E. D. BOGOLJUBOFF.

1. P—Q 4	Kt—K B 3
2. P—Q B 4	P—K 3
3. Kt—K B 3	B—Kt 5 ch

3. ....P—Q 4 or 3. ....P—Q Kt 3 would be preferable.

| 4. B—Q 2 | B×B ch |

This exchange assists White's development. Black's K B in the Queen's Gambit is far too valuable a defensive piece to be exchanged at the commencement with loss of time.

5. Q×B	Castles
6. Kt—B 3	P—Q 4
7. P—K 3	Q Kt—Q 2
8. B—Q 3	P—B 3
9. Castles K R	

Allowing Black to free himself by an ingenious manœuvre. White could have frustrated this plan by 9. R—Q 1 !, and Black's position would have remained very cramped.

| 9. | ...... | P×P |
| 10. | B×P | P—K 4 ! |

Taking advantage of the exposed position of White's Queen, for if now 11. P×P, then 11. ....Kt×P !, and Black equalizes with ease.

Position after Black's 10th move.

11. B—Kt 3 !

By this move, which prevents Black from gaining time later on with Kt—Kt 3, White indirectly meets 11. ....P—K 5, which would now result merely in the loss of a Pawn after 12. Kt—Kt 5, and thus White still maintains a slight superiority.

The sacrifice 11. B×P ch would only lead to a draw, e.g. :—

I.—11. B×P ch, R×B ; 12. P×P, Kt—Kt 5 ; 13. P—K 6, R×Kt ! ; 14. P×Kt, B×P ; 15. P×R, Kt×R P ! (not 15. ....Q—R 5, because of 16. Q—Q 6) ; 16. K×Kt, Q—R 5 ch and draws by perpetual check.

II.—11. B×P ch, K×B ? ; 12. P×P, Kt—Kt 5 ; 13. Q R—Q 1 !, Q—K 2 ; 14. P—K 6 ch !, K×P ; 15. Q—Q 4, Kt (Kt 5)—K 4 ; 16. Kt×Kt, Kt×Kt ; 17. P—B 4 !, and White obtains a strong attack.

11. ......   Q—K 2

In his game against Johner (Pistyan, 1922), Grunfeld tried 11. ....P×P ; 12. Q×P (12.

P×P also deserves consideration), Q—Kt 3 and finally secured the draw. After the text-move the superiority of White's game is clear.

12. P—K 4 !   P×P
13. Kt×P   Kt—B 4

13. ....Kt×P is impossible, both now and on the next move, on account of Q—K 3, winning a piece.

14. B—B 2   R—Q 1
15. Q R—Q 1

Threatening 16. Kt×P, etc.

15. ......   B—Kt 5
16. P—B 3   Kt—K 3
17. Q—B 2   Kt×Kt
18. R×Kt   B—K 3
19. K R—Q 1

Black was compelled to abandon the only open file in order to develop his Q B. Furthermore, the White centre Pawns, thanks to their mobility, will be able to attack Black's Knight and Bishop successfully.

As against this, the notorious " majority of Pawns on the Queenside " is not, at the moment, of any value, for their advance, as is shown in the present game, will give rise to new weaknesses, which the opponent will turn to advantage. The game is already virtually decided.

19. ......   P—Q Kt 3

Defending his Q R P, which is indirectly attacked.

20. P—K R 3 !

Preparing the advance of the B P.

20. ......   P—B 4

This move leads to nothing, seeing that it does not compel the exchange of Rooks. It would have been rather better (now or on the 22nd move) to take measures against the advance of White's K P and K B P, by playing, for example, ...Kt—K 1 followed by ....P—B 3.

21. R (Q 4)—Q 2   R×R
22. Q×R   P—B 5
23. P—B 4   P—Kt 3

If 23. ....Q—B 4 ch, simply 24. Q—Q 4 ! and Black's position after the exchange of Queens would be untenable, despite his majority on the Queen's side.

24. Q—Q 4

Threatening to win a Pawn by 25. P—B 5.

24. ......   R—Q B 1

Position after Black's 24th move.

25. P—K Kt 4 !

Decisive ! Black has no longer any adequate defence against the threats 26. P—B 5, or 26. P—K 5, followed by 27. P—B 5.

25. ......   B×P

A desperate sacrifice which cannot defer the imminent catastrophe any more than other attempts.

26. P×B   Kt×Kt P
27. K—Kt 2 !   P—K R 4
28. Kt—Q 5   Q—R 5
29. R—K R 1   Q—Q 1
30. B—Q 1 !   Black resigns.

An instructive game from the strategic point of view.

GAME 58

ALEKHIN'S DEFENCE

White : *Black :*
A. STEINER. A. ALEKHIN.

1. P—K 4   Kt—K B 3

This new defence was played for the first time by myself in a consultation game at Zurich (August, 1921), and was introduced into master practice shortly afterwards at the Budapest Tournament in September of the same year. Its correctness now seems perfectly established. One of the most searching proofs of its vitality lies in the fact that Dr. Emmanuel Lasker, ex-champion of the world, although openly opposed to this defence, successfully adopted it against Maroczy at the New York Tournament (March–April, 1924), after having tried in vain to demolish it.

In the course of an encounter between Dr. Lasker and Dr. Tarrasch, Black obtained a clearly superior, if not a winning, game in the following way : 1. P—K 4, Kt—K B 3 ; 2. P—K 5, Kt—Q 4 ; 3. P—Q 4, P—Q 3 ; 4. P—Q B 4, Kt—Kt 3 ; 5. P—B 4, P×P ; 6. B P×P, Kt—B 3 ; 7. B—K 3, B—K B 4 ; 8. Kt—Q B 3, P—K 3 ; 9. Kt—B 3, B—Q Kt 5 ; 10. B—Q 3, B—Kt 5 ! ; 11. B—K 2, B×Kt ; 12. P×B, Q—R 5 ch ; 13. B—B 2, Q—B 5 !

2. P—K 5

In a game Bogoljuboff—Alekhin (Carlsbad, 1923), White tried 2. Kt—Q B 3, upon which Black replied by 2. ....P—Q 4 (2. ....P—K 4, transposing into the Vienna Game, is also to be considered), leading to the continuation 3. P—K 5, K Kt—Q 2 ! ; 4. P—Q 4, P—Q B 4 ! ; 5. B—Q Kt 5, Kt—Q B 3 ; 6. Kt—B 3, and Black could have led into a very advantageous variation of the French Defence by 6. ....P—K 3, in place of the risky line 6. ....P—Q R 3 ; 7. B×Kt ch, P×B ; 8. P—K 6 !

2. ......   Kt—Q 4
3. P—Q 4

In a game Sämisch—Alekhin from the same tournament, White continued by 3. Kt—Q B 3, P—K 3 ! ; 4. Kt×Kt, P×Kt ; 5. P—Q 4, P—Q 3 ; 6. Kt—B 3, Kt—B 3 ; 7. B—K 2, B—K 2 ; 8. B—K B 4, Castles ; 9. Castles, P—B 3 ; 10. P×B P, B×P and Black has a slightly superior game.

3. ......   P—Q 3
4. B—Kt 5

After this move, whose object is to hinder the advance of the hostile K P, White loses his advantage, because of the difficulties he will experience in defending his K P. The most dangerous line of play for Black is undoubtedly 4. P—Q B 4 followed by 5. P—B 4.

4. ......   P×P
5. P×P   Kt—Q B 3
6. B—Kt 5   B—K B 4 !

Black is not concerned about the possibility of doubled Pawns. If 7. B×Kt ch, the possession of his two Bishops, the open Q Kt file and his better development would constitute a great compensation for the slight weakness on Q B 3.

7. Kt—K B 3   K Kt—Kt 5 !

The win of a Pawn by this last move required a minute examination of all its consequences.

8. Kt—R 3   Q×Q ch
9. R×Q !

The best reply, for if 9. K×Q, Castles ch; 10 K—B 1, P—B 3, Black's game would be distinctly superior.

9.	Kt×P ch
10. Kt×Kt	B×Kt
11. R—Q B 1	B—K 5
12. Kt—Q 4	

If 12. P—K 6, Black would have answered simply 12. ....P—B 3! followed by 13. ....Castles.

12.	B×P
13. R—K Kt 1	

Position after White's 13th move.

13. ...... Castles

The point of the manœuvre initiated on the 7th move. Nevertheless, the material advantage of a Pawn which Black has succeeded in securing seems very difficult to utilize, because of his backward development.

14. Kt×Kt	B×Kt
15. B×B	P×B
16. R×P	R—Q 4
17. B—B 4	P—K 3
18. K—K 2	

See Diagram.

How ought Black to strengthen his position now? For example,

Position after White's 18th move.

here are two plausible suggestions which give no satisfactory result against a correct defence:

I.—18. ....P—Kt 3; 19. R (Kt 1) —Q B 1, R—Q 2; 20. B—K 3, K—Kt 2; 21. R (B 6)—B 3, B—Kt 2; 22. R—Kt 3 ch, K—R 1; 23. B×P!, B×P; 24. R—B 4 with the better game for White.

II.—18. ....P—K Kt 4; 19. R×Kt P!, B—R 3; 20. R—Kt 4, B×B; 21. R×B, R×P ch; 22. K—B 1, K—Kt 2; 23. R—Q B 3, and Black has no chance of winning.

18. ...... B—B 4!

....whereas this move, which at first sight does not seem better than the preceding moves, is the only one enabling Black to maintain his advantage.

19. P—Q Kt 4!

The right reply, permitting White to force a favourable exchange. It is clear that Black's Kt P cannot be taken at once, owing to 19. ...K—Kt 2.

19.	B×Kt P
20. R×Kt P	R—Q 2
21. B—K 3	

Position after White's 21st move.

Black is once again faced with a very difficult problem. How is he to secure the defence of his weak Pawns on both wings? His lone Bishop is insufficient for this task, since if it be brought to Q Kt 3 via Q R 4, thereby adequately protecting his right wing, White would transfer his attack to the opposite wing and would eventually win at least a Pawn by R—B 4 followed by R—K R 4.

On the other hand, if Black withdraws his Bishop to K B 1, in order to secure the protection of his left wing, White would take the Queenside as his objective and would obtain a strong attack by R—Kt 4 followed by R—Q R 4.

Black must therefore provisionally avoid the displacement of his Bishop, in order to be able to utilize it for the defence of whichever wing is threatened.

His following moves are dictated by the above considerations.

21.	......	P—Q R 4 !
22.	R—B 4	P—R 4
23.	R—R 4	B—B 6 !
24.	R—Kt 5	R—Q 4
25.	P—B 4	P—K B 3 !

Definitely maintaining his material advantage, which he is enabled to exploit by the following exchanges.

26.	R (Kt 5) × P	R × R
27.	R × R	P × P
28.	P × P	B × P
29.	R—R 7	

29. P—K R 4 would leave White some hope of a draw, but after the text-move Black forces the exchange of this dangerous Pawn.

29.	......	R—Kt 4 !
30.	K—B 3	R—Kt 7
31.	R—R 5	

Forced, since after 31. P—K R 4, R × P, Black's passed Q R P would be at least as dangerous as White's passed K R P.

| 31. | ..... | B × P |
| 32. | R × P | B—Q 3 |

The ensuing end-game, although won for Black, nevertheless offers several technical difficulties, and is not devoid of interest.

| 33. | K—K 4 | K—Q 2 |
| 34. | B—Q 4 | |

Temporarily preventing 34. .... P—K 4, which Black now prepares by the following Rook-manœuvre.

| 34. | ...... | R—Q 7 ! |

Hindering K—Q 3—B 4, etc.

35.	B—K 3	R—K 7
36.	K—Q 3	R—K 8 !
37.	B—Q 4	R—Q B 8

37. ....P—K 4 would still be premature, on account of 38. B—B 3.

38.	B—K 3	R—Q 8 ch
39.	K—K 4	R—K 8
40.	K—Q 3	P—K 4

At last it is playable !

148 MY BEST GAMES OF CHESS

41. B—B 2	R—K B 8
42. B—K 3	K—K 3
43. K—K 4	R—K R 8
44. B—B 2	R—R 7
45. B—K 3	R—R 5 ch
46. K—Q 3	B—Kt 5 !

Thereby securing for his King access to the square Q 4, which is clearly of great importance.

47. R—R 7

Or 47. R—R 4, K—Q 4 ; 48. P—Q R 3, P—K 5 ch ; 49. K—B 2, B—Q 3.

47.	P—B 4
48. P—R 3	P—B 5 ch
49. K—K 2	B—Q 3
50. R—R 8	

In order to pin the adverse Bishop by R—Q 8, after .... K—Q 4.

50.	R—R 7 ch
51. K—Q 1	R—R 6 !
52. K—Q 2	K—Q 4
53. R—Q 8	

Position after White's 53rd move.

| 53. ...... | P—B 6 ch ! |

The *coup-de-grâce*.

54. K—K 2

If 54. K—Q 3, Black had foreseen the following pretty finish : 54. ....P—B 7 ; 55. R—Q B 8, B—K2 ! ; 56. R×P, B—Kt 4 ; 57. R—K 2, P—K 5 ch ; 58. K—Q 2, R×B ; 59. R×R, K—Q 5, and wins.

54.	K—K 5 !
55. R×B	R×B ch
56. K—B 2	R—Q 6
57. R—Q B 6	R—Q 7 ch
58. K—K 1	K—Q 6
59. R—Q 6 ch	K—B 7
60. R—K 6	R—Q 4
61. K—K 2	K—Kt 6
62. R—Q B 6	P—B 7

White resigns.

GAME 59

QUEEN'S PAWN GAME

| *White :* | *Black :* |
| A. ALEKHIN. | Z. V. BALLA. |

1. P—Q 4	P—Q 4
2. Kt—K B 3	P—K 3
3. B—B 4	P—Q B 4
4. P—K 3	Kt—Q B 3
5. P—B 4	

5. P—B 3 would be more in accordance with the system springing from B—B 4. The main object of the text-move is to avoid the beaten track.

| 5. ...... | Kt—B 3 |

If 5. ....Q—Kt 3 White could have answered 6. Kt—B 3 !, and if Q×Kt P ; 7. Kt—Q Kt 5, etc.

| 6. Kt—B 3 | B P×P |
| 7. K P×P | Kt—K 5 |

This demonstration is clearly premature, White being better developed. 7. ....Q—Kt 3 was also unfavourable for Black, on account of 8. P—B 5 !, Q×Kt P ; 9. Kt—Q Kt 5, etc. On the other hand, he could have obtained a fairly satisfactory game by 7. .... B—Kt 5 ; 8. B—Q 3, P×P ; 9. B×B P, Castles.

INTERNATIONAL TOURNAMENT AT BUDAPEST

8. B—Q 3	B—Kt 5
9. R—Q B 1	Q—R 4
10. Q—Kt 3	P×P
11. B×P	P—K Kt 4

Having embarked on a dangerous voyage, Black is compelled to persevere at all costs. This advance makes it unsafe to Castle King-side, without inconveniencing White in any way.

Better was 11. ....Castles ; 12. Castles, Kt×Kt ; 13. P×Kt, B—K 2 ; 14. K R—K 1 !, and if 14. ....P—Q Kt 3 ; 15. P—Q 5, etc., although in this case also White's superiority in position is manifest.

| 12. B—K 3 | P—Kt 5 |
| 13. Kt—K 5 ! | |

If this Knight had been compelled to retire, perhaps to Kt 1 or Q 2, Black's preceding manœuvre would have had some measure of justification.

13.	Kt×K Kt
14. P×Kt	B×Kt ch
15. P×B	P—Kt 3

If 15. ....Q×K P ; 16. B—Q 4, Q—B 5 ; 17. B—Kt 5 ch, followed by 18. Castles, with a winning attack.

16. Castles

Intending the following sacrifice. But owing to the complications to which it gives rise, I would prefer now-a-days the simpler variation, 16. B—Kt 5 ch, B—Q 2 ; 17. B×B ch, K×B ; 18. Castles, as now the Black King is left in the centre, and White obtains a strong attack (18. ....K—B 2 ; 19. Q—Kt 4 !). But White hoped for a still better result with the text-move. and his opponent lends himself to it by accepting the sacrifice.

| 16. ...... | B—Q 2 ! |

16. Castles (K R) would clearly be equivalent to suicide.

Position after Black's 16th move.

17. K R—Q 1 !

The most energetic way of taking advantage of Black's compromised position ; in reply to this move Black should decide upon : 17. ....Castles (Q R) ! ; 18. Q—Kt 4 !, Q×Q ; 19. P×Q, K—Kt 2 ; 20. B—K 2 !, threatening P—B 3, after which Black would have lost a Pawn, with a long end-game in view. But he cannot resist the bait of the Rook, and this indiscretion costs him the game.

| 17. ...... | B—R 5 |
| 18. Q—Kt 1 | Kt×Q B P |

If 18. ....B×R ; 19. B—Kt 5 ch ! [not 19. Q×Kt, Castles (Q R)!], K—K 2 ; 20. Q×Kt, with a winning attack.

| 19. R×Kt | Q×R |

19. ....B×R would evidently be equally disastrous.

20. B—Kt 5 ch	B×B
21. Q×B ch	K—B 1
22. B—R 6 ch	K—Kt 1
23. Q—Q 7 !	

If now 23. ....Q—B 1, then 24. Q—K 7 followed by mate in two moves.

Black resigns.

CHAPTER XV

INTERNATIONAL TOURNAMENT AT THE HAGUE, NOVEMBER, 1921

GAME 60

SICILIAN DEFENCE

White :   *Black :*
F. D. YATES.   A. ALEKHIN.

1. P—K 4   P—Q B 4
2. Kt—K B 3   P—K 3
3. P—Q 4

This move has the disadvantage of allowing Black to choose the following equalizing variation. On this account it is preferable to play first 3. B—K 2 (see game No. 97).

3. ......   P × P
4. Kt × P   Kt—K B 3
5. Kt—Q B 3

Concerning 5. B—Q 3 see Game No. 93.

5. ......   B—Kt 5
6. B—Q 3   P—K 4 !

6. ....P—Q 4 would be inferior, on account of 7. P—K 5, K Kt—Q 2; 8. Q—Kt 4 ! The text-move was introduced into master practice by Jaffe at the Carlsbad Tournament of 1911.

7. Kt—K 2

If 7. Kt—B 5, Castles ; 8. B—K Kt 5, P—Q 4 ! and Black has the better game, since if 9. P × P, P—K 5 !; 10. B × P, R—K 1; 11. Kt—Kt 3, Kt × B, winning a piece.

7. ......   P—Q 4
8. P × P   Kt × P
9. Castles   Kt—Q B 3

Black has achieved a satisfactory development. There is room for improvement in one respect, the impossibility of Castling immediately, on account of Kt × Kt, followed by B × P ch winning the Queen.

10. Kt × Kt   Q × Kt
11. P—Q R 3 !

Preparing the advance of the Queen-side Pawns, which can be utilized for the end-game, and also seeking to keep the Black King in the centre as long as possible by the tactical threats which are made possible by the momentarily exposed position of Black's pieces.

11. ......   B—R 4

Not 11. ...B—K 2 ; 12. Kt—B 3, Q—K 3 (or 12. ....Q—Q 1; 13. Q—R 5) ; 13. Kt—Kt 5, with the better game.

INTERNATIONAL TOURNAMENT AT THE HAGUE

12. P—Q Kt 4   B—B 2
13. R—K 1

Now 13. Kt—B 3 would be ineffectual after 13. ....Q—K 3; 14. Kt—Kt 5, B—Kt 1, or 14. Q—R 5, Q—Kt 5!

Position after White's 13th move.

13. ......   P—B 4

A risky move whose chief object is to reserve a good square of retreat for the Black Queen on K B 2. 13. ....B—K 3 was more prudent and sufficient for equality. A game Euwe—Alekhin (Pistyan, 1922), continued as follows: 14. Kt—B 3, Q—Q 2; 15. Kt—K 4, B—K Kt 5; 16. Kt—B 5, Q—B 1; 17. Q—Q 2, Castles; 18. B—K 4!, B—Kt 3; 19. Q—B 3, B×Kt; 20. Q×B, B—B 4; 21. B×Kt, Q×B; 22. Q×Q, P×Q. Drawn game.

14. P—Q B 4

This colourless line of play allows Black at last to bring his King into safety and thus obtain the better game.
More energetic was 14. Kt—B 4, Q—B 2; 15. P—Kt 5!, Kt—K 2; 16. P—Kt 6!, P×P; 17. B—Kt 5 ch, Kt—B 3; 18. Q—Q 3!, definitely fixing the hostile King, with excellent chances of attack.

14. ......   Q—B 2
15. Kt—B 3   Castles
16. Kt—Q 5

This Knight, as will be seen in the sequel, cannot be maintained in this position and will soon be exchanged against a Black piece inactive until now.
This simple fact sufficiently demonstrates White's faulty strategy initiated by 14. P—Q B 4.

16. ......   B—K 3

Position after Black's 16th move.

17. B—Kt 2

A little trap. If now 17. ....B×Kt; 18. P×B, Q×P; then 19. B×B P, Q×Q; 20. B—K 6 ch, regaining his Pawn with a very good game.

17. ......   P—K 5
18. Kt×B

If at once 18. B—K B 1, then 18. ....B—K 4, with a manifest superiority of position.

18. ......   Q×Kt
19. B—K B 1   Kt—K 4!
20. B×Kt

Relatively best, for if 20. P—B 5, then 20. ....Kt—Kt 5, provoking the weakening of White's King's position, the consequences of which might have been disastrous for him very quickly.

20.	Q×B
21. Q—B 2	Q R—Q 1
22. Q R—Q 1	R×R !

By this unexpected exchange (unexpected, because it temporarily yields to the adversary the only open file) Black forces either (1) the advance of his P to B 5, whereby, sooner or later, in addition to good prospects of direct attack, he can secure a strong passed Pawn on the King's file, or (2) as in the actual game, the exchange of Queens, which secures for him a superior end-game.

23. Q×R

If 23. R×R, then 23. .... P—B 5 !

Position after White's 23rd move.

| 23. ...... | Q—B 6 ! |

Against this move White has nothing better than to offer an exchange of Queens, because after 24. R—K 3 Black would gain the necessary time by 24. .... Q—B 3, to occupy the Queen-file, which would be decisive.

The ensuing end-game, which offers some analogy with that which I played against Teichmann (see Game No. 91), admits of a majority of Pawns on the Queen-side for White, but this advantage is here somewhat illusory. On this subject I am anxious to state that one of the most notorious prejudices of modern theory lies in the fact that this majority is *in itself* considered an advantage, without any reference to whatever Pawns or, more especially, pieces are concerned.

In the present game Black has very evident compensations : (1) the greater mobility of the Black King, the adverse King being hampered by his own Pawns. (2) the dominating position of the Black Rook on the only open file. With correct play, these points should ensure a win.

24. Q—B 1	Q×Q
25. R×Q	R—Q 1
26. P—K Kt 3	

This and the next two moves aim at the exchange of Bishops, since the Rook ending would yield White an almost certain draw.

| 26. ...... | K—B 2 |
| 27. P—B 5 | K—B 3 |

Avoiding exchanges, on the above grounds.

28. B—B 4	B—B 1 !
29. P—Q R 4	P—K Kt 4
30. P—Kt 5	P—B 5
31. K—B 1	

With the object of opposing his Rook to that of Black, after 32. K—K 1, but the latter voluntarily abandons the command of the Queen-file in order to occupy the seventh rank with his Rook, thus facilitating the decisive advance of his Pawns.

31.	R—Q 7 !
32. K—K 1	R—Kt 7
33. P×P	P×P
34. B—K 2	

White was threatened, if 34. R—Q 1, with 34. ....B—Kt 5; 35. R—Q 6 ch, K—K 2; 36. R—Q 4, B—B 6, followed by P—K 6, winning.

| 34. ...... | K—K 4! |
| 35. P—B 6 | P × P |

Position after Black's 35th move.

36. R × P

If 36. P × P, P—B 6; 37. B—Q 1, P—K 6; 38. B × P, P × P ch; 39. K—B 1, B—R 3 ch; or 37. B—B 1, P—K 6; 38. P × P, P—B 7 ch; 39. K—Q 1, B—Kt 5 ch and mates next move.

| 36. ...... | B—K 3 |
| 37. B—Q 1 | R—Kt 8 |

With the double threat 38. .... B—Kt 6 and 38. ....B—Kt 5, against which White cannot defend himself by 38. K—Q 2 on account of 38. ....P—K 6 ch; 39. P × P, P × P ch; 40. K—B 2, B—B 4 ch.

38. R—B 5 ch	K—Q 5
39. R—B 2	P—K 6
40. P × P ch	P × P
41. R—B 6	B—Kt 5
42. R—Q 6 ch	K—B 4
43. P—R 3	B—R 4

Now the threat of 44. ....P—K 7 wins both the Rook and the Bishop.

White resigns.

GAME 61

QUEEN'S GAMBIT DECLINED

White: *Black:*
A. ALEKHIN.   A. RUBINSTEIN.

1. P—Q 4	P—Q 4
2. Kt—K B 3	P—K 3
3. P—B 4	P—Q R 3

A move of Janowski's, quite frequently played by Rubinstein in recent tournaments, but without appreciable success. Necessary in the greater number of the variations of the Queen's Gambit Accepted. 3. ....P—Q R 3 is here merely a loss of time, and in addition creates weaknesses on the Queen-side when White continues by 4. P × P, or even 4. P—B 5, as in the present game.

4. P—B 5

4. P × P is quite sufficient to secure a slight superiority of position, as was shown by the games Johner—Rubinstein and Kostich—Rubinstein in the Teplitz-Schönau Tournament of 1922 among others. The former game continued 4. P × P, P × P; 5. Kt—B 3, Kt—K B 3; 6. B—Kt 5, B—K 2; 7. P—K 3, Castles; 8. B—Q 3, P—Q Kt 3 (a little better, but also insufficient to equalize the game, was 8. ....Q Kt—Q 2; 9. Q—B 2!); 9. B × Kt!, B × B; 10. Q—B 2, P—K R 3, and Johner could have obtained a very strong attack against Black's weakened Castled position by 11. P—K R 3, followed by 12. Castles Q R and P—K Kt 4.

In his game against Kostich Rubinstein tried 5. ....B—K 2 in place of 5. ....Kt—K B 3, and the continuation was 6. B—B 4, Kt—K B 3; 7. P—K 3, Castles; 8. B—Q 3, Q Kt—Q 2; 9. Castles, R—K 1; 10. R—B 1, P—Q Kt 3, after which White could have obtained a distinctly superior game by

11. P—K R 3 (in order to conserve his Q B against the threat of exchange by Kt—R 4).

In the present game, the first which I played against Rubinstein after a seven-year interval, I voluntarily adopted a new line of play in order to avoid the variations resulting from 4. P×P (because I rightly thought them very familiar to Rubinstein), resolved that I would do or die!

4. ......   Kt—Q B 3

Wishing to play 5. ....P—K 4, which White must oppose by every means at his disposal.

5. B—B 4   K Kt—K 2
6. Kt—B 3   Kt—Kt 3

Position after Black's 6th move.

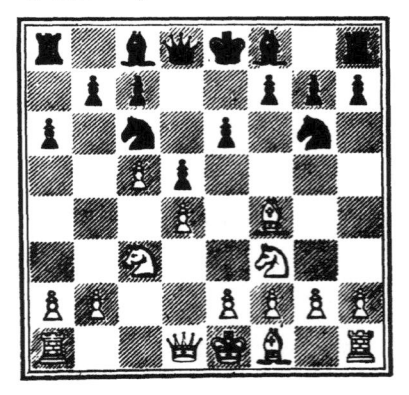

7. B—K 3!

A move rather out of the common! White, while preventing 7. ....P—K 4, avoids the exchange of his Q B.

I learnt, some time after the game ended, that Rubinstein in Collijn's *Lārobok* only examined 7. P—K 3, a variation leading to equality.

7. ......   P—Kt 3

Black, giving up hope of breaking through in the centre, at least eliminates the cramping adverse Q B P, and reckons to secure an advantage in development, by reason of the unusual position of White's Q B at K 3.

8. P×P   P×P
9. P—K R 4!

The only means of weakening the black squares of the enemy's position, and thus obtaining a future for his Q B.

9. ......   B—Q 3

If 9. ....P—K R 4, then 10. B—K Kt 5, P—B 3; 11. Q—B 2 followed by 12. B—Q 2, P—K 3, P—Q R 3 and B—Q 3, with the better game for White.

10. P—R 5   K Kt—K 2

Not 10. ....Kt—B 5?; 11. P—K Kt 3.

11. P—R 6!

The point! If Black captures the R P, he weakens his own R P without the slightest compensation. In the other case White's Q B will occupy the diagonal K R 4—Q 8, where it exercises a very embarrassing pressure.

11. ......   P—Kt 3
12. B—Kt 5   Castles

More prudent was 12. ....P—B 4 first, after which Black would not have had to fear the threat of mate at K Kt 2, although in any case White's game would have already been preferable.

13. B—B 6!

See Diagram.

An extraordinary position after the 13th move of a Queen's Gambit! During the first thirteen moves White has played his Q B P thrice, his K R P thrice and his Q B four

Position after White's 13th move.

times, after which he has obtained a position in sight of a win, if not actually a winning one.

It is especially with respect to the original opening of this game that people often speak of a "hyper-modern technique," a "neo-romantic school," etc.

The question is in reality much simpler. Black has given himself over to several eccentricities in the opening (3. .... P—Q R 3 ; 5. .... K Kt—K 2 ; 6. ....Kt—Kt 3) which, without the reaction of his opponent (for example, 7. P—K 3 instead of 7. B—K 3 or 9. P—K Kt 3 instead of 9. P—K R 4) would in the end give him a good game.

It is, therefore, as a necessity, and not with a preconceived idea, that I decided upon the advance of the K R P, preventing Black from securing an advantage in the centre. But, as a rule, in the opening stages of a game such eccentricities are in accordance neither with my temperament nor my style, as the reader can see from the perusal of this book.

13.	......	P—Q Kt 4
14.	P—K 3	B—Q 2
15.	B—Q 3	R—B 1

Black dreams only of the possibility of an immediate attack by White (commencing by Kt—K Kt 5, or Kt—K 5 followed by Q—B 3), which he hopes to thwart by a demonstration on the Queen-side (Q—R 4, B—Kt 5).

With this idea, the preparatory move 15. ....R—B 1 would have been very useful. But as White is not compelled to bestir himself as long as the opponent does not trouble him seriously, it would have been better for Black to play at once 15. ....Kt—R 4, followed by 16. ....B—Kt 5, and thus compel White, by this semblance of a counter-attack, to take some defensive measures.

16. P—R 4 !

Whereas it is now White who seizes the initiative on the left flank, forcing Black to block this side, which allows him to post his Q Kt in a dominating position, without loss of time.

16.	......	P—Kt 5
17.	Kt—K 2	Q—Kt 3
18.	Kt—B 1 !	

Preventing 18. ....P—Kt 6.

| 18. | ...... | R—B 2 |
| 19. | Kt—Kt 3 | Kt—R 4 |

Too late !

Position after Black's 19th move.

20. Kt—B 5!

By this manœuvre White transforms his positional advantage into a gain of material, Black being unable to capture the Knight, e.g.:
20. ....B×Kt; 21. P×B, Q×P; 22. B—Q 4, Q—B 3; 23. Kt—K 5, Q—Kt 2; 24. Kt—K Kt 4, etc., winning the Exchange. If 20. .... B—B 1, then 21. Kt—K 5, with similar variations.

| 20. ...... | Kt—B 5 |

This move is not a whit better than those which precede it. It allows White the choice between two very good variations, but it happens that White chose the less decisive one.

| 21. B×Kt | P×B |
| 22. Kt—K 5 | |

22. Kt—K 4 would force the win of the Exchange, and also maintain the attack, in view of the double threat 23. Kt×B followed by 24. B—K 5; and 23. B—Kt 7, followed by 24. Kt—B 6 mate.

| 22. ...... | B×Kt (K 4) |
| 23. B×Kt! | |

Position after White's 23rd move.

| 23. ...... | B—Q 3! |

With his clear judgment of position, Rubinstein at once recognizes that the sacrifice of the Exchange still offers him the best chance.

Indeed, after 23. ....R—K 1; 24. P×B, R×B; 25. Kt—K 4! (not 25. Q—B 3, P—B 4; 26. P×P e. p., R—B 2 with defensive chances), Black would have lost more speedily than in the actual game, e.g.:

I.—25. ....P—B 4; 26. Q—Q 6, B—B 3; 27. Kt—B 6 ch, K—B 2; 28. Q—Q 8!, B—K 1; 29. Kt×P and wins.

II.—25. ....B—K 1; 26. Kt—B 6 ch, K—R 1; 27. Q—Q 8, R—Kt 2; 28. R—Q 1, Q—B 3; 29. Castles, and White wins.

24. B×R	B×B
25. Kt×B	R×Kt
26. P—R 5!	

Preventing the consolidation of Black's Pawn-position by 26. .... P—R 4.

26.	Q—B 3
27. Q—B 3	R—Q 4
28. R—Q B 1!	

This move, which forces the advance of the Q B P, is intended to clear up the position on the Queen's side, in order to place his pieces in the most favourable way.

28.	Q—B 2
29. Q—K 2	P—B 6
30. P×P	P×P
31. Q×P	R×R P
32. Q—Q 3	B—R 6

If 32. ....R—R 6, White would have continued 33. K—K 2, followed by 34. R—R 1.

| 33. R—B 2 | B—Kt 7 |
| 34. K—K 2! | |

Not 34. Castles, on account of 34. ....R—R 4, winning the K R P, with good drawing chances.

INTERNATIONAL TOURNAMENT AT THE HAGUE

34.	......	Q—B 3
35.	P—B 3	P—B 4
36.	R—Q Kt 1	Q—Q 3

If 36. ....Q—Q 4, then 37. K—B 2, threatening 38. R×P, B×R; 39. Q×B, R—R 1; 40. Q—B 7 and wins.

37.	Q—B 4	K—B 2
38.	Q—B 8	Q—R 3 ch

The exchange of Queens is forced, as White threatens 39. Q—K R 8.

39.	Q×Q	R×Q
40.	P—K 4	P—Kt 4
41.	K—Q 3	K—Kt 3

Position after Black's 41st move.

42. P—Q 5 !

Thus obtaining a passed Pawn, which decides the game in a few moves. Black's desperate attempts to obtain a last chance on the King's side merely succeed in leading his King into a *cul-de-sac*.

42.	......	P×P ch
43.	P×P	P×P
44.	P×P	R—R 5
45.	R—Q 1 !	

Indirectly securing the advance of the Q P.

45.	......	K×P
46.	P—Q 6	K—R 4
47.	P—Q 7	R—R 1
48.	K—K 4	R—Q 1
49.	K—B 5	K—R 5
50.	R—R 1 ch	K—Kt 6
51.	R—R 3 mate.	

CHAPTER XVI

INTERNATIONAL TOURNAMENT AT PISTYAN
APRIL, 1922

GAME 62

QUEEN'S PAWN GAME

Brilliancy Prize

White :	Black :
Dr. S. Tarrasch.	A Alekhin.
1. P—Q 4	Kt—K B 3
2. Kt—K B 3	P—K 3
3. P—B 4	P—B 4

With the intention of investigating, on the next move, the gambit discovered by the Moscow amateur, Blumenfeld. Since then it has been shown that this Gambit is not favourable for Black if White should decline it.

4. P—Q 5	P—Q Kt 4
5. P×K P	

The acceptance of the gambit yields Black a formidable position in the centre. The right move was 5. B—Kt 5 ! Equally possible, although less strong, is 5. P—K 4, played by Rubinstein against Tartakover at Teplitz—Schönau, 1922.

An instructive game, Grünfeld—Bogoljuboff, from the Vienna Tournament of 1922, was continued as follows : 5. B—Kt 5, P—K R 3 ; 6. B×Kt, Q×B ; 7. Kt—B 3, P—Kt 5 ; 8. Kt—Q Kt 5, Kt—R 3 ; 9. P—K 4 !, Q×P ; 10. B—Q 3 !, Q—B 3 ; 11. P—K 5, Q—Q 1 ; 12. P×P, Q P×P ; 13. B—K 4 !, Q× Q ch ; 14. R×Q, R—Q Kt 1 ; 15. B—B 6 ch, K—K 2 ; 16. Kt×P, P—Kt 4 ; 17. B—Kt 5, B—K Kt 2 ; 18. Kt—B 6 ch and mates next move.

5.	B P×P
6. P×P	P—Q 4
7. P—K 3	

Black threatened to regain his Pawn with the better game by 7. ....Q—R 4 ch. However, 7. Q Kt —Q 2 followed by P—Q Kt 3 and B—Kt 2 offered White better defensive chances.

7.	B—Q 3
8. Kt—B 3	Castles
9. B—K 2	B—Kt 2
10. P—Q Kt 3	Q Kt—Q 2
11. B—Kt 2	Q—K 2

Black has completed his development, and prepares in perfect safety the advance of his K P, which, encompassing still more the adverse game, secures him a very strong attack against White's King.

12. Castles	Q R—Q 1

Black has no need to hasten the advance of his K P, his opponent at present being able to attempt absolutely nothing.

INTERNATIONAL TOURNAMENT AT PISTYAN

13. Q—B 2   P—K 4
14. K R—K 1

In order to defend the square K R 2, by bringing his K Kt via Q 2 to K B 1.
From now on White defends himself in the most skilful way, but his game is already too far compromised by the strategic error of the opening, ceding the centre to his opponent in exchange for a Pawn of little value.

14. ......   P—K 5
15. Kt—Q 2   Kt—K 4
16. Kt—Q 1   Kt (B 3)—Kt 5
17. B × Kt (Kt 4)

This exchange is forced, for if 17. Kt—B 1, then 17. ....Kt—B 6 ch !

17. ......   Kt × B
18. Kt—B 1

Position after White's 18th move.

18. ......   Q—Kt 4 !

The correct continuation of the attack. White has adequately defended the squares K B 2 and K R 2, but the point K Kt 2 is still vulnerable. So it is against this point that Black intends to undertake a double attack, bringing the Knight to K R 5 via K R 3 and K B 4.

To parry this threat White will be compelled to weaken his position afresh by playing P—K R 3 which, as we shall see by the sequel, will allow the decisive advance of Black's Q P.

19. P—K R 3   Kt—R 3
20. K—R 1   Kt—B 4
21. Kt—R 2

It is clear that White's three last moves were the only ones possible to secure the defence of the threatened point by R—K Kt 1.

21. ......   P—Q 5 !

This Pawn becomes a new and formidable means of continuing the attack. White cannot capture it, *e.g.*: 22. P × P, P—K 6 ! ; 23. Kt × P (or 23. R—K Kt 1, Q—Kt 6 ! and wins), Kt × Kt ; 24. P × Kt, Q—Kt 6 ! and wins.

22. B—B 1   P—Q 6
23. Q—B 4 ch   K—R 1
24. B—Kt 2

Position after White's 24th move.

24. ......   Kt—Kt 6 ch

The beginning of the final manœuvre. It is clear that the Knight cannot be taken, on account of 25. ....Q × Kt P, forcing mate. After the following move Black could have won the exchange by 25. ....P—Q 7, but he preferred to wind up the game by a forced combination.

25. K—Kt 1   B—Q 4
26. Q—R 4

If 26. Q—B 3 or 26. Q—B 1; Kt—K 7 ch, winning easily.

26. ......   Kt—K 7 ch
27. K—R 1   R—B 2 !

There was no reason to complicate the game by the sacrifice of the Q R P.

28. Q—R 6   P—R 4 !

As we shall see by the continuation, this was necessary to prepare the sacrifice of the Bishop on the 34th move.

29. P—Kt 6   Kt—Kt 6 ch

Not 29. ....P×P on account of 30. R×Kt, P×R ; 31. Q×K P, giving White possibilities of defence.

30. K—Kt 1   P×P
31. Q×Kt P   P—Q 7 !

Now this advance of the Q P is absolutely decisive.

32. R—K B 1   Kt×R
33. Kt×Kt

Position after White's 33rd move.

33. ......   B—K 3 !!

After this move White can no longer defend himself against the ensuing mating attack. For example, if he had attempted to protect the square K Kt 2 by 34. Q—B 6 followed by 35. Q×K P, the game would have terminated as follows: 34. Q—B 6, R—B 6!; 35. Q×K P, B—Q 4 ; 36. Q—Q R 4, Q×P ch!!; 37. K×Q, R—Kt 6 ch ; 38. K—R 2, R—Kt 7 ch ; 39. K—R 1, R—R 7 ch ; 40. K—Kt 1, R—R 8 mate. Against the plausible move 34. K—R 1 the sacrifice of the Q B wins at once.

34. K—R 1   B×P !
35. P×B   R—B 6
36. Kt—Kt 3   P—R 5 !

The object of 28. ....P—K R 4 ! is now shown.

37. B—B 6

Ingenious but doomed to failure, like all other attempts.

37. ......   Q×B
38. Kt×P   R×P ch

If now 39. K—Kt 1, B—R 7 ch and Black wins the Queen ; and if 39. K—Kt 2, Q—B 6 ch and mates next move.

White resigns.

GAME 63

QUEEN'S GAMBIT DECLINED

White :	*Black* :
A. ALEKHIN.	A. SELESNIEFF.

1. P—Q 4   P—Q 4
2. Kt—K B 3   Kt—K B 3
3. P—B 4   P—K 3
4. Kt—B 3   B—K 2
5. B—Kt 5   Q Kt—Q 2
6. P—K 3   Castles
7. R—B 1   P—B 3
8. B—Q 3

I consider this old move at least as good as the modern move 8. Q—B 2, because the White Queen must lose a *tempo* in order to occupy K 2, *its natural square in the Queen's Gambit Declined.*

8. ......   P × P

The best reply, beyond doubt. It is essential for Black to capture the B P, and to play 9. ....Kt—Q 4, *before White has Castled*, because otherwise the latter can prevent the exchange of his Knight on Q B 3 by playing Kt—K 4! with a far superior game (see Game No. 88); whereas before Castling the move is not without danger and leads to variations of great complexity.

9. B × P   Kt—Q 4
10. B—B 4

In order to avoid the dull equalizing variation, 10. B × B, Q × B ; 11. Castles, Kt × Kt ; 12. R × Kt, P—K 4.
But this move is venturesome, as Black's energetic play in the present game shows.
It is more playable in the variation arising from 8. Q—B 2, which, against Black's Kt—Kt 3, allows of the withdrawal of the K B to Q 3 without loss of time, owing to the threat on the hostile K R P.

10. ......   Kt × B
11. P × Kt   Kt—Kt 3
12. B—Kt 3   Kt—Q 4
13. Q—Q 2

Again best. If 13. P—K Kt 3, Kt × Kt ; 14. P × Kt, P—Q B 4, followed by 15. ....P—Q Kt 3 and 16. ....B—Kt 2, and the security of White's King will be compromised in view of the weakness of the white squares.

13. ......   Q—Q 3
14. Kt—K 5

Avoiding P—K Kt 3 for the above reason.

14. ......   Kt × Kt !

Simple and strong ! Black, in addition to his two Bishops, has chances of undertaking a counter-attack on the Queen's side.

15. P × Kt   P—Q B 4
16. Castles   P—Q Kt 4 !

Black's game seems at present preferable, and White must manœuvre with circumspection to preserve equality.

17. B—B 2 !

An important move with the double threat 18. Q—Q 3, followed by Q × Kt P; and 18. B—K 4, followed by Kt—B 6, and on this account preventing Black from completing his development by 17. ....B—Kt 2.

17. ......   B—R 3
18. K R—K 1   Q R—Q 1
19. Q R—Q 1   P × P

By playing 19. ....P—Kt 3 immediately, Black would have maintained an excellent position, with good chances on the Queen's side. On the contrary, the text-move, which frees the position in the centre, is distinctly advantageous to White, and the latter succeeds in taking advantage of it by undertaking an attack as lively as it is interesting.

20. P × P   P—Kt 3

Inevitable, sooner or later.

See Diagram.

21. B—Kt 3 !

This move first threatens 22. Kt × B P ! and secondly prevents the manœuvre 21. ....B—Kt 2 and 22. ....B—Q 4, on account of the following variation : 21.....B—Kt 2;

Position after Black's 20th move.

Position after Black's 25th move.

22. Q—Q 3, P—Q R 3 (or P—Kt 5); 23. Kt×Kt P!!, R P× Kt; 24. R×P!, P×R (if 24. .... Q moves anywhere; 25. R×P ch); 25. Q×P ch, K—R 1; 26. B—B 2 and mates in a few moves.

21. ......   B—B 1

Preventing the threatened sacrifice.

22. Q—K 2!   P—Q R 3
23. P—Q 5   Q—Kt 3

If 23. ....P×P; 24. B×P followed by 25. Kt×B P.

24. Kt—B 6   Q R—K 1
25. Kt×B ch   R×Kt

See Diagram.

26. P—B 5!

If Black accepts the sacrifice, White wins as follows: 26. Kt P× P; 27. P—Q 6!, R—Kt 2 (or A); 28. Q—K 5, P—R 3; 29. Q—B 6, K—R 2; 30. B×P.

(A).—27. ....R—Q 2; 28. Q—Q 2!, K R—Q 1; 29. Q—Kt 5 ch, K—B 1; 30. Q—R 6 ch, K—K 1 (if 30. ....K—Kt 1; 31. R—Q 3!); 31. R×P ch and mates in three moves.

26. ......   R—Kt 2

In this way Black loses a Pawn without weakening White's attack. Black's game rapidly becomes hopeless.

27. B P×K P   P×P
28. P×P   R—K 2
29. R—Q 7!   K R—K 1

The Rook cannot be taken, for if 29. ....B×R; 30. P×B (dis. ch), K—R 1, White would not continue 31. Q×R?, but would first play 31. P—Q 8=Q!

30. Q—B 3   Q—B 4
31. Q—B 7 ch!   K—R 1
32. Q—B 6 ch   K—Kt 1
33. P—K R 4!

If now 33. ....R—K B 1, then clearly 34. Q×R (K 7), Q×P ch; 35. K—R 2, Q—B 5 ch; 36. K—R 1 and wins.

Black resigns.

GAME 64

QUEEN'S PAWN GAME

White:	*Black:*
P. JOHNER.	A. ALEKHIN.

1. P—Q 4   Kt—K B 3
2. Kt—K B 3   P—K 3
3. P—B 4   P—B 4

It has been shown subsequently that this move is not quite correct (see Game No. 62). The right move here was 3. ....P—Q 4, or 3. ....P—Q Kt 3.

4. Kt—B 3

This answer is insufficient to secure White an advantage. He must play 4. P—Q 5, and if 4. ....P—Q Kt 4 ; 5. B—Kt 5 !, with the better game.

But my opponent had still fresh in his memory my game against Dr. Tarrasch, played in the first round of the same tournament (see Game No. 62), in which White, having adopted the continuation 4. P—Q 5, sustained a classic defeat; and he therefore preferred the move in the text, apparently more conservative, but also duller.

4. ......   P × P
5. Kt × P   P—Q 4

This move allows White, should he so desire, to simplify the position, with an almost certain draw in view. 5. ....B—Kt 5 was more energetic, leading to a complicated game not without chances for Black.

6. P × P   Kt × P
7. Kt (Q 4)—Kt 5 !

Threatening 8. Kt × Kt, P × Kt ; 9. Q × P !

7. ......   B—Q 2

In order to answer 8. Kt × Kt with 8. ....B × Kt.

8. P—K 4   Kt × Kt
9. P × Kt !

Much better than 9. Kt × Kt, after which Black could have obtained a slight advantage in position by 9. ....B—B 4.

9. ......   Q—R 4
10. R—Q Kt 1 !

More energetic than the defensive move 10. Q—Kt 3. For the sacrificed Q R P White, thanks to his two Bishops, obtains a position full of promise, and Black in the sequel will be compelled to return the Pawn, in order to complete his development.

10. ......   P—Q R 3

If any other move, White would defend his Pawn by R—Kt 3 ; or he could play 11. Kt—Q 6 ch in spite of it.

11. Kt—Q 6 ch   B × Kt
12. Q × B   Q × P ch
13. B—Q 2   Q—Q B 3
14. Q—B 4

White over-estimates his prospects of attack, forgetting that his own King is not in safety. He ought to have been content to regain his Pawn, with a good game, by 14. Q—Kt 4, P—Q R 4 ! ; 15. Q × Kt P, Castles ! The text-move, on the contrary, speedily allows Black to seize the initiative.

14. ......   Castles
15. B—Q 3

Position after White's 15th move.

15. .....   P—K 4 !

By this sacrifice Black opens up new lines for his pieces, and taking advantage of the fact that White has still not Castled, undertakes a direct attack against the position of the hostile King.

Against any other move White would himself have obtained a powerful attack by 16. P—K 5!

16. Q×K P   R—K 1
17. Q—Q 4

If 17. Q—Kt 3, R×P ch; and if 17. Q—B 4, B—K 3 followed by 18. ....Kt—Q 2 and 19. ....Kt—B 4, both with advantage to Black.

17. ......   Q—K Kt 3!

Position after Black's 17th move.

18. P—B 3

White already finds himself in a very difficult position, since he cannot Castle on account of 18. ....B—R 6, winning the Exchange. On the other hand, if 18. P—B 4 Black would have avoided the dangerous variation resulting from 18. ....Q×Kt P; 19. R—Kt 1, Kt—B 3; 20. Q—K 3, Q×R P; 21. B—B 3, and would have made certain of an advantage by 18. ....Kt—B 3!; 19. Q—B 2 (or 19. Q×B, Q×P; 20. R—K B 1, Q R—Q 1), B—B 4!

18. ......   Q×P!

This move, at first sight hazardous, was the result of a long and minute calculation.

19. R—K Kt 1   Kt—B 3
20. Q—K 3   Q×R P
21. B—B 3   P—K Kt 3!

Not 21. ....Kt—K 4 on account of 22. R×P ch!, K×R; 23. Q—Kt 5 ch, K—R 1 (if 23. ....K—B 1?; 24. B—Kt 4 ch!); 24. P—B 4! and Black would have been compelled to satisfy himself with a draw.

22. R×P   Q R—Q 1!

The preparation for the final action.

23. B—B 6

It is manifest that with a Pawn less and in view of the exposed position of his King, other moves would not save White. That chosen allows Black to conclude energetically and rapidly.

23. ......   Kt—K 4!

Threatening 24. ....Kt×P ch.

24. B—K 2

Position after White's 24th move.

24. ......   B—Kt 4!

Practically ending the game, for if 25. B×R, then 25. ....B×B wins at once, on account of the threat 26. ....Kt×P ch. White is therefore forced into a general liquidation, after which his position remains absolutely without the slightest hope.

25. B×Kt   R×B
26. B×B   R×B
27. R×R   P×R

Threatening to lead into a winning Pawn-ending by 28. R—Q 7!, etc. If 28. R—B 1, then 28. ....Q—Q B 7 and wins.

White resigns.

GAME 65

QUEEN'S GAMBIT DECLINED

Brilliancy Prize

White :   *Black :*
A. ALEKHIN.   H. WOLF.

1. P—Q 4   P—Q 4
2. Kt—K B 3   P—Q B 4
3. P—B 4   B P×P

The usual move is 3. ....P—K 3, transposing into the Tarrasch Defence. After the exchange of Pawns in the centre we reach a symmetrical position in which the advantage of the move always secures for White a slight advantage in position.

If in this game he obtains a better result, that is solely due to the fact that his opponent allows himself to go in for an innovation especially risky when his development is already behindhand.

4. P×P   Kt—K B 3
5. Kt×P   P—Q R 3

Black wished to avoid the variation 5. ....Kt×P; 6. P—K 4, Kt—K B 3; 7. B—Kt 5 ch, B—Q 2; 8. P—K 5!, B×B; 9. Kt×B, Q×Q ch; 10. K×Q, Kt—Q 4; 11. Kt (Kt 1)—B 3, to the advantage of White, mentioned in the latest edition of Collijn's *Lärobok*. But this variation, like many others indicated in that work, which are indeed interesting but scarcely accurate, can be improved by 6. ....Kt—Kt 5! in place of 6. ....Kt—K B 3, after which White's advantage would be difficult to demonstrate.

The text-move does not seem risky, Black intending to capture the Q P on the next move. Its refutation is therefore only the more instructive.

Position after Black's 5th move.

6. P—K 4!!

Sacrificing the K P to retain the Q P which, as will be seen in the sequel, exercises a very strong pressure on the opponent's game.

6. ......   Kt×K P
7. Q—R 4 ch !

In order to provoke the obstruction of the Queen's file by a Black piece, which cuts off the attack of Black's Queen on his Q P.

7. ......   B—Q 2

Not 7. ....Q—Q 2 on account of 8. B—Q Kt 5.

8. Q—Kt 3   Kt—B 4

This square is hardly indicated for the Knight, but on the other hand he must secure the defence of his Q Kt P; and 8. ....Q—B 2 or 8. ....B—B 1 is scarcely any better, seeing that Black's Queen would soon be dislodged from this file by White's Rook.

9. Q—K 3!

Much stronger than the plausible move 9. Q—K B 3, on which Black could have freed himself by 9. .... P—K 4, for if 10. P × P e. p., Kt × P; 11. Kt × Kt, B × Kt!; 12. Q × P?, B—Q 4! and Black must win. Whereas, after the text-move, the advance of Black's K P would give White the opportunity of exercising strong pressure on the King-file.

Black therefore resigns himself to the development of his K B in fianchetto, but equally without success.

9. ......   P—K Kt 3

Position after Black's 9th move.

10. Kt—K B 3!

This gain of time allows White to prevent 10. ....B—Kt 2, followed by 11. ....Castles. Black's King being kept in the centre, White's attack will be facilitated, thanks to his superior development.

The opening of this game offers some analogies with that of Game No. 61, played at The Hague against Rubinstein.

In the one, as in the other, the advantage won results from repeated movements of the same pieces (here the first eleven moves contain four displacements of the Queen and three of the King's Knight).

But the possibility of like manœuvres in the opening phase is *solely* attributable, I must reiterate, to the fact that the opponent has adopted faulty tactics, which must from the first be refuted by an energetic demonstration. It is clear, on the contrary, that in face of correct development, similar anomalous treatment would be disastrous.

It cannot therefore be any question of a " Modern System," but just simply of exploiting in a rational manner the opponent's mistakes.

I cannot conceive why there is such an ardent desire to discover in a game of chess anything more subtle than it has to offer, for I am of opinion that the real beauty which it possesses should be more than sufficient for all possible demands.

10. ......   Q—B 2
11. Q—B 3   R—K Kt 1
12. B—K 3   P—Kt 3
13. Q Kt—Q 2

13. P—Q Kt 4 would be an error of judgment, because Black would have saved his piece by 13. .... B—Kt 2; 14. Kt—Q 4, Q—R 2! White therefore prefers to complete his development before undertaking decisive action.

13. ......   B—Kt 2
14. B—Q 4   B × B
15. Q × B

White, having rid himself of Black's K B, the only piece which could inconvenience him, the position of the opponent will very soon become desperate.

15. ......   B—Kt 4

It would be difficult to suggest another means of developing his Queen-side. After 15. ....B—B 4; 16. B—K 2, Q Kt—Q 2 would be impossible, on account of 17. P—K Kt 4, B—B 7; 18. R—Q B 1.

16. B×B ch   P×B
17. Castles (K R) R—R 5

This skirmish comes to nothing. To tell the truth, it is difficult to point out here a rational move.

18. P—Q Kt 4   Q—Q 1
19. P—Q R 3!

White has no reason to hurry himself, considering the lack of resource of the adverse position.

19. ......   Q Kt—Q 2
20. K R—K 1   K—B 1
21. P—Q 6!

A preparation for the following sacrifice. If Black reply to this move with 21. ....P—K 3, the continuation would be 22. Q—K 3, Kt—Kt 2; 23. Q—Q 3, R—R 1; 24. Kt—K 4, winning the Q Kt P to start with.

21. ......   Kt—K 3

Position after Black's 21st move.

22. R×Kt!

By this combination, based on a precise calculation of all its possibilities, White demolishes the last defences of the enemy. He regains the Exchange sacrificed in a few moves, with a mating-attack.

22. ......   P×R
23. Kt—Kt 5   Q—Kt 1

Or 23. ....P—K 4; 24. Q—Q 5, Q—K 1; 25. Kt—K 6 ch, K—B 2; 26. Kt—B 7 ch, P—K 3; 27. Q—B 3 ch and wins.

24. Kt×K P ch   K—B 2

If 24. ....K—K 1; 25. Kt—K 4!

25. Kt—Kt 5 ch   K—B 1

If now 25. ....K—K 1; 26. R—K 1!

26. Q—Q 5!   R—Kt 2

Clearly forced.

27. Kt—K 6 ch   K—Kt 1
28. Kt×R ch   K×Kt
29. P×P   Kt—B 3
30. Q×P   R—R 2
31. R—K 1   Q—Q 3
32. P—K 8 (Kt) ch

The simplest method of securing the win.

32. ......   Kt×Kt
33. Q×Kt   Q×Kt
34. Q—K 5 ch   K—B 2
35. P—K R 4   R×P

This desperate capture conceals a last trap.

36. Q—K 8 ch   K—Kt 2
37. R—K 7 ch   K—R 3
38. Q—B 8 ch   K—R 4
39. R—K 5 ch   K—Kt 5
40. R—Kt 5 ch!

Avoiding the trap. If now 40. P—B 3 ch, K—Kt 6; 41. R—Kt 5 ch, Q×R!; 42. P×Q, R—R 8 mate!

Black resigns.

GAME 66

RUY LOPEZ

White :   *Black :*
Dr. K. Treybal.   A. Alekhin.

1.	P—K 4	P—K 4
2.	Kt—K B 3	Kt—Q B 3
3.	B—Kt 5	P—Q R 3
4.	B—R 4	Kt—B 3
5.	Kt—B 3	B—K 2
6.	Castles	P—Q Kt 4
7.	B—Kt 3	P—Q 3
8.	P—Q R 4	R—Q Kt 1

This move, although recommended by Collijn's *Lärobok*, is distinctly inferior to 8. ....P—Kt 5, for it abandons the Q R file to White without any compensation.

9.	P×P	P×P
10.	P—K R 3	Castles
11.	Q—K 2	B—Q 2

Indirectly defending the Pawn attacked, for if 12. Kt×Kt P, Kt×P; 13. Kt×B P, Kt×Q P (or Kt—B 4); 14. B×Kt, Q×Kt and Black has an excellent game.

12. P—Q 3

Position after White's 12th move.

12. ......   Q—B 1

Insufficient would be 12. .... Kt—Q 5; 13. Kt×Kt, P×Kt; 14. Kt—Q 5, Kt×Kt; 15. B×Kt, P—Q B 3; 16. B—Kt 3, B—K 3; 17. B×B, P×B; 18. R—R 7, R—R 1; 19. R×R, Q×R; 20. Q—Kt 4, Q—B 1; 21. B—R 6, R—B 2; 22. R—R 1 with advantage to White.

The text-move prepares the following series of exchanges, and allows Black to adopt a more complicated line of play, commencing 13. ....Kt—Q 1, and 14. ....P—Q B 4 should White choose to prevent 13. ....Kt—Q 5 by 13. B—K 3.

13. K—R 2

Preventing a subsequent sacrifice of Black's Q B at K R 3. But as the danger was not imminent White would have done better to continue his development by 13. B—K 3.

After the text-move Black has at least an equal game.

13.	......	Kt—Q 5
14.	Kt×Kt	P×Kt
15.	Kt—Q 5	Kt×Kt
16.	B×Kt	P—B 3
17.	B—Kt 3	B—K 3 !
18.	P—K B 4	

The variation 18. B×B, Q×B; 19. P—K B 4, P—K B 4 would not yield White any advantage.

The text-move is the prelude to a hazardous King-side attack, since Black will get in first with an energetic counter-attack in the centre.

18.	......	B×B
19.	P×B	R—R 1 !

Not 19. ....Q—K 3 because of 20. P—B 5, Q×Kt P; 21. R—R 3, Q—Kt 5; 22. P—B 6 !, B×P; 23. R×B, P×R; 24. B—R 6, K—R 1; 25. Q—B 3, P—K B 4; 26. Q×P, P—B 3 ; 27. R—R 7 and wins.

INTERNATIONAL TOURNAMENT AT PISTYAN

20. R×R

If 20. R—Kt 1, then 20. .... Q—K 3, etc.

20.	Q×R
21. P—B 5	P—B 3 !

Much better than 21. .... B—B 3, upon which White would have obtained a very fine game by 22. B—B 4, R—Q 1; 23. Q—K 1! followed by Q—Q R 1 or Q—Kt 3.

The move chosen prepares the advance of the centre Pawns.

22. P—K Kt 4

Having embarked on a perilous journey, White has no option but to persevere, for, were he to adopt a purely defensive plan, Black would have a still more easy game than in the text, e.g.: 22. P—Q Kt 4, P—B 4; 23. Q—Q B 2, Q—B 3 followed by 24. .... R—R 1.

22.	P—B 4
23. P—R 4	P—Q 4 !

Position after Black's 23rd move.

24. P—Kt 5

White has nothing better, *e.g.* :

I.—24. P×P, B—Q 3 ch; 25. B—B 4, R—K 1; 26. Q—Kt 2, B×B ch; 27. R×B, Q—Kt 1;
28. Q—K B 2, Q—K 4 ! and Black has the better game.

II.—24. P—K 5, Q—Kt 1 ! (not however 24. .... P×P; 25. Q×P, B×P because of 26. P—Kt 5 !, R—K 1; 27. Q—B 4, B—K 8; 28. P—B 6 with a strong attack for White); 25. B—B 4, P×P; 26. B×P, B—Q 3 with advantage to Black.

24.	Q P×P
25. Q P×P	Q—B 3
26. K—R 3	

Preparing 27. P—K 5. If 26. P—Kt 6, P—R 3; 27. Q—R 5, Q×P; 28. B×P, P×B; 29. Q×P, Q—K 7 ch, followed by 30...Q—K 6 ch, wins for Black.

26.	P—B 5
27. P—K 5	

White attempts the impossible to obtain the semblance of an attack, but in vain, for Black gets there first.

27.	P—Q 6
28. Q—K 1 !	

The only move. If 28. Q—K 3, P×K Kt P !; 29. R P×P, R×P !; 30. R×R, Q—K 3; 31. Q—K 4, P—Kt 3; 32. K—Kt 4 (or 32. Q—R 8 ch, K—Kt 2), P×R ch; 33. Q×P, Q×Q ch; 34. K×Q, B—R 6!! and wins.

28.	P×K P

If now 28. .... P×K Kt P White would have replied 29. B×P.

29. Q×P	B—Kt 5 !
30. P×P	P×P
31. Q—Q 4 !	

Threatening to break up the hostile Pawn formation by 32. P—Kt 3.

See Diagram.

31.	Q—Kt 4 !

The only move to win. It threatens both 32. .... R×P and

Position after White's 31st move.

32. ....P—Q 7! followed by 33. ....P—B 6. If White plays 32. K—Kt 2, then 32. ....B—R 4! and 33. ....R—Q 1 would also win without difficulty.

32. P—B 6	P—Q 7!
33. Q—B 4!	

Position after White's 33rd move.

Anticipating the continuation 33. ....P×B=Q; 34. R×Q, R—B 1; 35. Q—Kt 4! with drawing chances, since Black's K R 8 is not of the same colour as his Bishop.

By the ensuing combination, *the longest which I have ever undertaken*, Black avoids this doubtful variation and secures a winning Pawn-ending.

33.	Q—Q 2 ch!
34. K—Kt 2	P—Q 8=Q!
35. R×Q	Q×R
36. Q×P ch	R—B 2
37. Q×B	Q×B
38. Q—Kt 8 ch	R—B 1
39. P—B 7 ch!	

The key-move of a variation enabling White to recover his Rook. As we shall see shortly, Black's winning manœuvre initiated by 33. ....Q—Q 2 ch! comprises no less than 20 moves!

| 39. ...... | K×P |

Position after Black's 39th move.

40. Q—Kt 3 ch?

It is astonishing that a master of the strength of Dr. Treybal, so conspicuously endowed with the imaginative sense, should not have perceived 40. P—Kt 6 ch!, the only logical continuation.

Black could not have answered it by 40. ....K—Kt 1, on account of 41. P×P ch; nor by 40. ....P×P for in that case White would have forced a draw by perpetual check, *e.g.*: 41. Q—Kt 3 ch, K—B 3; 42. Q—K B 3 ch, K—K 2; 43. Q—R 3 ch, K—K 1; 44. Q—R 4 ch!, K—Q 1; 45. Q—R 8 ch, K—K 2; 46. Q—R 3 ch, K—B 2; 47. Q—Kt 3 ch, etc.

The only move to win was consequently 40. ....K×P !, leading to the forced continuation:
41. Q×R, Q×P ch ; 42. K—B 3, Q—B 6 ch ; 43. K—Kt 2, Q—Q 7 ch ; 44. K—Kt 3, Q—K 6 ch ; 45. K—Kt 2, Q—K 5 ch ; 46. K—Kt 3, Q—K 4 ch ; 47. K—Kt 2, K—R 4 ! ; 48. Q—B 3 ch, K×P ; 49. Q—R 3 ch, K—Kt 4 ; 50. Q×P, Q—K 7 ch ; 51. K—Kt 3 or K—Kt 1, Q—Kt 5 ch ; 52. any, Q—B 4 ch or Q—R 4 ch, and Black wins by forcing exchange of Queens next move.

40. ......   K—Kt 3 !

And White can only give a few harmless checks, e.g.: 41. Q—K 6 ch, K—R 4 ; 42. Q—K 2 ch, K×P ! and wins.

White resigns.

GAME 67

QUEEN'S GAMBIT DECLINED

| White : | Black : |
| A. ALEKHIN. | K. HROMADKA. |

1. P—Q 4	P—Q 4
2. Kt—K B 3	Kt—K B 3
3. P—B 4	P—B 3
4. Kt—B 3	Q—Kt 3

Played for the first time by Süchting against Schlechter at the Carlsbad Tournament, 1911. The best reply to this move seems to be 5. P—B 5, Q—B 2 ; 6. P—K Kt 3 !, followed by 7. B—B 4. The line of play which still gives Black the most chances is in my opinion 4. ....P×P, followed by 5. .... P—Q Kt 4 and, if needed, P—Kt 5 etc. (See Game No. 71).

5. P—K 3

Solid, but without vigour. As we shall see later, Black could have equalised the game at a certain stage.

5.	B—Kt 5
6. P×P	P×P
7. Q—R 4 ch	B—Q 2

Best. If 7. ....Kt—B 3 ; 8. Kt—K 5, B—Q 2 ; 9. B—Kt 5, P—K 3 ; 10. Kt×B, Kt×Kt ; 11. P—K 4 ! with an attack similar to that in the present game, after White's 13th move.

8. B—Kt 5	P—Q R 3
9. B×B ch	Q Kt×B
10. Castles	P—K 3
11. Kt—K 5	

White has not secured an advantage of development sufficient to be able to exploit the pinning of Black's Q Kt, especially against a correct defence.

11. ......   Q—R 2

It is solely owing to this loss of time that White succeeds in getting up an attack. The right move was 11. ....Q—Kt 5 ! provoking the exchange of Queens and unpinning the Knight, after which Black would have had nothing to fear. Whereas now, for want of being able to Castle, his position in the centre will be completely demolished.

12. Kt×Kt !   Kt×Kt

Position after Black's 12th move.

13. P—K 4 !

The commencement of a dangerous offensive whose result will be the formation of a strong passed Pawn in the centre.

The following moves of Black are practically forced, because he must necessarily and at all costs prevent the opening of the King's file.

13.	P—Q Kt 4
14. Q—B 2	P × P
15. P—Q 5 !	P—K 4
16. P—Q R 4 !	

Before recapturing the Pawn, it is not unnecessary to provoke a new weakness in the adverse Queen-side.

16.	P—Kt 5
17. Kt × P	Q—Kt 2

If 17. .... B—B 4 ; 18. B—K 3 !, B × B ; 19. Kt—Q 6 ch, K—K 2 ; 20. Kt—B 5 ch followed by 21. P × B, with a very strong attack.

18. R—Q 1	R—B 1
19. Q—K 2	B—K 2

Black vainly hopes to bring his King under cover.

20. Q—Kt 4	P—Kt 3

Forced, for if 20. .... Castles ; 21. B—R 6.

Position after Black's 20th move.

21. B—Kt 5 !

Definitely fixing the Black King in the centre, which, in conjunction with the numerous weaknesses in his position, ends in a rapid collapse by Black. Indeed, he can play without disadvantage neither 21. .... P—B 3, on account of 22. Q—K 6, nor 21. .... P—B 4, on account of 22. Q—R 4 !, and has nothing better than the exchange of Bishops, which deprives him of Castling.

21.	P—R 3
22. B × B	K × B
23. Q—R 4 ch	

In order to provoke a new weakness in the position of the adverse Pawns.

23.	P—Kt 4

If 23. .... P—B 3 ; 24. P—B 4 ! with a very strong attack.

24. Q—Kt 4	R—B 5
25. Q—B 5	

Among other things, threatening 26. Q × P ch followed by 27. Kt—Q 6 ch.

25.	R—K B 1
26. P—Kt 3 !	

26. Kt—B 6 would be premature, on account of 26. .... R—B 5.

26.	R (B 5)—B 1
27. Kt—B 6 !	

The decisive move. If 27. .... Kt × Kt ; 28. P—Q 6 ch !

27.	R—B 4
28. Kt × Kt	Q—B 1

If 28. .... Q × Kt ; 29. Q × K P ch, K—Q 1 ; 30. Q R—B 1, R × R ; 31. R × R and White wins.

29. P—Q 6 ch

Winning a Rook after 29. .... K—Q 1 ; 30. Q—B 6 ch, K × Kt ; 31. Q—K 7 ch, K—B 3 ; 32. P—Q 7 !

Black resigns.

CHAPTER XVII

INTERNATIONAL TOURNAMENT AT LONDON
AUGUST, 1922

GAME 68

QUEEN'S PAWN GAME

White :   *Black :*
A. ALEKHIN.   M. EUWE.

1. P—Q 4   Kt—K B 3
2. Kt—K B 3   P—K Kt 3

This variation, introduced into master-practice by Grünfeld, rests upon the following ideas :—The development of the K B in fianchetto, and the withholding of P—Q 4 until White has developed his Kt at Q B 3. By this means Black, after 3 P—B 4, B—Kt 2 ; 4. Kt—Q B 3, P—Q 4 ; 5. P×P, Kt×P ; 6. P—K 4, Kt×Kt ; 7. P×Kt reserves the possibility of attacking the hostile centre by P—Q B 4, opening up good prospects for his Bishop on K Kt 2.

Consequently, the best line of play for White consists in moving the Q Kt only after having augmented the pressure on the square Q 5 by P—K Kt 3 and B—Kt 2, which seems to secure him a slight advantage, as shown among others by the games Alekhin—Muller (Margate, 1923), Sämisch—Grünfeld (Carlsbad, 1923) and Alekhin—Réti (New York, 1924).

3. B—B 4

Trying a new system which occasions Black less difficulty than the line of play quoted above. Compare also the games Capablanca—Réti and Rubinstein—Euwe from the same Tournament.

3. ......   B—Kt 2
4. Q Kt—Q 2   P—B 4 !

A good move.

5. P—K 3

If 5. P×P, Black regains the Pawn with advantage by 5. .... Kt—R 3 !

5. ......   P—Q 3
6. P—B 3   Kt—B 3
7. P—K R 3

This move is essential to reserve a square of retreat for the Q B in case of Kt—K R 4.

7. ......   Castles
8. B—B 4 !

The best square for this Bishop. The reply 8. ....P—Q 4 is clearly not to be feared, as it would merely enhance the prospects of the opposing Q B.

8. ......   R—K 1

Preparing P—K 4, which will, however, have the disadvantage of weakening the square Q 3.

9. Castles	P—K 4
10. P×KP	Q Kt×P

The capture with the Knight yields White at once a very perceptible, if not decisive, advantage in position. Black would do better by 10. ...P×P; 11. B—R 2, B—K 3; 12. B×B, R×B; 13. Kt—B 4, after which White's advantage, undeniable as it is, would be very difficult to take advantage of.

11. B×Kt !	P×B

Position after Black's 11th move.

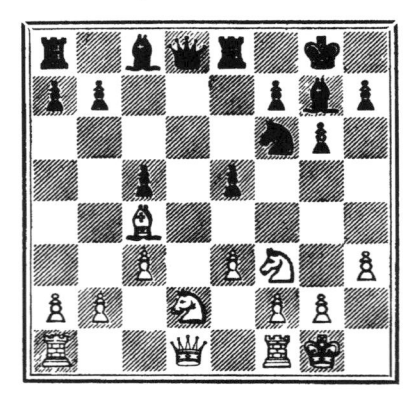

12. Kt—K Kt 5 !	

This simple move, as seen later on, assures White the possession of the only open file.

12.	B—K 3

An heroic resolution, because after the doubling of the Pawns, Black's K B is left quite without action. Somewhat better was 12. ....R—B 1; 13. Kt (Q 2)—K 4 !, Q×Q (if 13. ....Kt×Kt ?; 14. B×P ch !); 14. K R×Q, Kt×Kt ; 15. Kt×Kt, P—Kt 3, although, in this case also, White would have secured excellent winning chances.

13. B×B	P×B
14. Kt (Q 2)—K 4	Kt×Kt
15. Q×Q	K R×Q
16. Kt×Kt	P—Kt 3
17. K R—Q 1	K—B 1
18. K—B 1 !	

White could have won a Pawn by 18. Kt—Kt 5, but that would have allowed Black to force exchange of Bishop against Knight, by 18. ....K—K 2 ; 19. Kt×R P, B—R 3 ; 20. P—K R 4, R—R 1, with good drawing chances.

18.	K—K 2

If 18. P—B 5, then 19. Kt—Q 6 ! But now Black threatens, by means of 19. ....P—B 5, to occupy Q 4 and later Q 6 with his Rook.

19. P—Q B 4 !	

Preventing the above threat, and at the same time making the third rank free for the Rook, which is very important, as shown later.

19.	P—K R 3
20. K—K 2	R×R
21. R×R	R—Q Kt 1

Black is compelled to avoid the exchange of Rooks, which would enable White to force the win in the following way : 21. ....R—Q 1 ; 22. R×R, K×R.

Position after Black's 22nd move in sub-variation.

1st phase.—23. P—K R 4! followed by P—K Kt 4 and P—Kt 5 on which Black will have nothing better than P—K R 4, seeing that the exchange of Pawns abandons the square K R 4 to White's Knight.

2nd phase.—P—Q Kt 3, followed by K—Q 3, Kt—B 3 and K—K 4.

3rd phase.—The manœuvring of the White Knight to Q 3, after which Black must immobilize his King on Q 3 in order to be able to defend the doubly attacked K P.

4th phase.—And lastly P—B 4! forcing the win of the K P or the K Kt P, after which the advantage secured will be decisive.

By avoiding the exchange of Rooks, Black will make the task of his opponent more difficult.

22. R—Q 3   B—R 1

Position after Black's 22nd move.

23. P—Q R 4!

The only means of forcing the decisive entry of the White Rook into the enemy's game. White takes advantage of the fact that Black cannot reply by 23. ....P—Q R 4, on account of 24. R—Kt 3! winning the Q B P or the Q Kt P.

23. ......   R—Q B 1
24. R—Kt 3   K—Q 2
25. P—R 5!   K—B 3

It is obvious that it is better to abstain from capturing White's Q R P, because of 26. R—Kt 5.

26. P×P   P×P
27. R—R 3   B—Kt 2
28. R—R 7   R—B 2

Black reconciles himself to the exchange of Rooks, but White now considers that by avoiding it he will attain the victory still more speedily.

29. R—R 8!   R—K 2
30. R—B 8 ch K—Q 2
31. R—K Kt 8! K—B 3
32. P—R 4

In order to block in the Bishop completely before undertaking the decisive manœuvre with his Knight.

32. ......   K—B 2
33. P—K Kt 4 K—B 3
34. K—Q 3

This was not quite necessary, seeing that White's King will be compelled to return to its starting point. By 34. P—Kt 3 White could have shortened the game by several moves.

34. ......   R—Q 2 ch
35. K—B 3   R—K B 2
36. P—Kt 3   K—B 2
37. K—Q 3   R—Q 2 ch
38. K—K 2   R—B 2
39. Kt—B 3!

In order to post this Knight on Q Kt 5, where its action will be still more powerful than on K 4.

39. ......   R—K 2
40. P—Kt 5   P×P
41. P×P   K—B 3
42. K—Q 3

White has at his command another winning line also, based upon the manœuvre Kt—K 4—Q 2—B 3—R 4 winning the K Kt P, but he prefers to follow the path which he has traced out for himself.

42.	R—Q 2 ch
43. K—K 4	R—Kt 2
44. Kt—Kt 5	R—K 2

If 44. ....R—K B 2, then 45. R—B 8 ch followed by Kt—Q 6 ch, winning the Rook.

| 45. P—B 3 | K—Q 2 |

The only move. If 45. ....K—Kt 2, then 46. Kt—Q 6 ch followed by Kt—K 8, winning the Bishop.

| 46. R—Q Kt 8 | K—B 3 |
| 47. R—B 8 ch | K—Q 2 |

Or 47. ....K—Kt 2 ; 48. Kt—Q 6 ch, K—R 2 ; 49. R—K Kt 8 and wins.

| 48. R—B 7 ch | K—Q 1 |
| 49. R—B 6 ! | |

Forcing the first gain of material, but also immediately decisive.

| 49. ...... | R—Kt 2 |
| 50. R×K P | Black resigns. |

GAME 69

QUEEN'S GAMBIT DECLINED

White :	Black :
A. ALEKHIN.	F. D. YATES.
1. P—Q 4	Kt—K B 3
2. P—Q B 4	P—K 3
3. Kt—K B 3	P—Q 4
4. Kt—B 3	B—K 2
5. B—Kt 5	Castles
6. P—K 3	Q Kt—Q 2
7. R—B 1	P—B 3
8. Q—B 2	R—K 1

This move is inferior to 8. ....P—Q R 3, because after 9. B—Q 3 ! Black can no longer transpose into the system of defence which still offers him the best chances.

| 9. B—Q 3 | P×P |

Reverting to Capablanca's defence (see Game No. 79) with the sole difference that his K R is at K 1 instead of K B 1, which is not of much importance. If 9. ....P—Q R 3 White could now advantageously reply 10. P×P !, taking advantage of the fact that Black cannot at this point recapture the Pawn with his Knight.

On the other hand, after 9. ....P—K R 3 ; 10. B—B 4 ! (see Game No. 80, note to Black's 8th move), P—R 3, the exchange at Q 5 would be entirely to White's advantage, e.g. :

11. P×P ! (but not 11. P—B 5, B×P ! ; 12. P×B, P—K 4, threatening 13. ....P—K 5, thus regaining the piece with a very fine game—compare the game Euwe—Spielmann, Mährisch-Ostrau, 1923), Kt×P ; 12. Kt×Kt, K P×Kt ; 13. Castles, Kt—B 3 ; 14. P—K R 3, etc., and White will be able to undertake an attack on the Queenside by R—Kt 1, P—Q Kt 4, P—Q R 4 and P—Kt 5, leaving his opponent without appreciable counter-chances.

| 10. B×P | ·Kt—Q 4 |
| 11. Kt—K 4 | |

The right move here was 11. B×B. Regarding the inadequacy of 11. Kt—K 4, compare Game No. 79. It should be noticed that in the variation 11. ....Q—R 4 ch, etc., the position of the Rook at K 1 is rather an advantage for Black.

| 11. ...... | P—K B 4 |

Among the various replies to be considered by Black this is undoubtedly the least worthy of commendation. Apart from the fact that it in no wise incommodes White's Castling, it yields the splendid square at K 5 to the adverse Knight without the slightest compensation.

From this point Black's game may be considered strategically lost, which is not to say that the realization of victory will be an easy matter.

12. B×B	Q×B
13. Q Kt—Q 2	P—Q Kt 4

This move, which aims at the liberation of the useless Q B, is worse than the disadvantage which it seeks to mitigate, for White will now seize control of the Q B file and especially the square Q B 5, which Black has just given up by the text-move.

Black would have done better to occupy the opponent with the following diversion : 13. ....Kt (Q 4)—Kt 3 ; 14. B—Q 3, P—K Kt 3, preparing P—K 4 ; or 14. B—Kt 3, P—Q R 4 ; 15. P—Q R 4, Kt—Q 4 and Kt—Kt 5, although in these cases also his prospects were doubtful.

14. B×Kt	B P×B

Position after Black's 14th move.

15. Castles

White's next moves are based upon simple but indisputable logic. By the occupation of the square Q B 5 by one of his Knights, he will force its exchange against the opposing Q Kt, after which he will be able to settle his second Knight on the same square without fear of molestation.

15.	P—Q R 4
16. Kt—Kt 3	P—R 5
17. Kt—B 5	Kt×Kt
18. Q×Kt !	Q×Q

The exchange of Queens would ultimately have become inevitable.

And now Black is entirely at the mercy of his opponent, who will be free to choose the best road to victory.

19. R×Q	P—Kt 5
20. K R—B 1	B—R 3
21. Kt—K 5 !	

The Knight arrives at the right moment to prevent Black opposing his Rooks on the Q B file, *e.g.* : 21. ....K R—Q B 1 ; 22. R×R ch, R×R ; 23. R×R ch, B×R ; 24. Kt—B 6, with the double threat 25. Kt—K 7 ch and 25. Kt×Kt P, which would make the win certain for White.

21.	K R—Kt 1
22. P—B 3 !	

Preparing the decisive advance of the White King.

22.	P—Kt 6
23. P—Q R 3	P—R 3

Position after Black's 23rd move.

24. K—B 2 !

The starting-point of a mating-manœuvre based on the following considerations: as Black must avoid the exchange of Rooks and as his pieces are kept on the Queenside, to secure the defence of his Pawns, the Black King must sooner or later succumb to the combined assault of the four White pieces, including the King.

24. ......   K—R 2
25. P—R 4!

Hindering ....P—Kt 4, after ....K—Kt 3 and ....K—R 4.

25. ......   R—K B 1
26. K—Kt 3   R (B 1)—Q Kt 1

Black has to resign himself to complete inactivity.

27. R—B 7

Threatening among other things 28. Kt—Q 7 and 29. Kt—B 5 or 29. Kt—Kt 6.

27. ......   B—Kt 4
28. R (B 1)—B 5!

In order to double Rooks on the 7th rank by 29. R—K 7!, R—K 1; 30. R (K 7)—K B 7 and 31. R (B 5)—B 7.

28. ......   B—R 3
29. R (B 5)—B 6 R—K 1
30. K—B 4

The doubling of the Rooks on the 7th rank by R—K B 7 being now assured, White brings his King to the centre.

30. ......   K—Kt 1
31. P—R 5!

Foreseeing the final manœuvre, for whose success it is essential to prevent Black's King from emerging at K Kt 3 after 35. Kt—Q 7!

31. ......   B—B 8

It is curious to observe that the Q B, although having full liberty of action, cannot take any part in the defence.

32. P—Kt 3

A waiting-move. 32. R—B 7 would now be premature, because of 32. ....Q R—B 1.

32. ......   B—R 3

If 32. ....B—K 7 White would have continued his attack by 33. Kt—Kt 6 followed by 34. Kt—R 4 and 35. K—K 5.

33. R—B 7   K—R 2

Black is quite unable to forestall the mating attack by 33. ....R—K B 1, since White would have very speedily concluded the game after capturing the K P.

34. R (B 6)—B 7 R—K Kt 1
35. Kt—Q 7!

This threat to win the Exchange forces the following reply.

35. ......   K—R 1
36. Kt—B 6!   R (Kt 1)—K B 1

In the hope of bringing about the exchange of one Rook at least.

37. R × P!

This sacrificial combination forces mate in at most seven moves.

37. ......   R × Kt

See Diagram.

38. K—K 5!

The point of the combination! The Black Rook can neither retire, nor can it be defended by the other Rook, without allowing a mate in two moves. But even after its capture by the White King, mate can only be delayed by problem moves.

Black resigns.

Position after Black's 37th move.

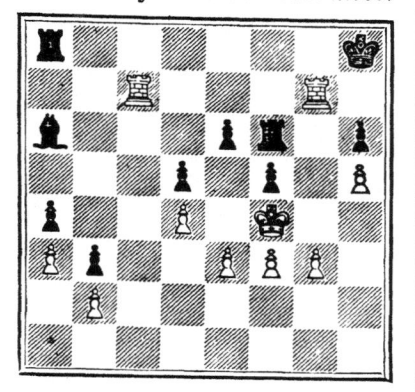

GAME 70

QUEEN'S GAMBIT DECLINED

White:	Black:
A. RUBINSTEIN.	A. ALEKHIN.

1.	Kt—K B 3	P—Q 4
2.	P—Q 4	Kt—K B 3
3.	P—B 4	P—B 3
4.	Kt—B 3	P×P

The acceptance of the Gambit at this stage of the game was made the object of an analysis by Alapin about fifteen years ago, but his attempts to popularize it did not fructify.

His analysis mentioned, after 5. P—K 3, P—Q Kt 4; 6. P—Q R 4, the moves Kt—Q 4 and Q—Kt 3. Not until the London Tournament of 1922, where my innovation 6. ....P—Kt 5! was disclosed, did the variation receive a new lease of life.

5. P—Q R 4

Rubinstein, who was already familiar with my analysis, followed religiously the line of play adopted against me by Bogoljuboff some rounds previously in the same tournament, but Black gets out of all his difficulties by the development of his Q B.

5.	......	B—B 4 !
6.	P—K 3	P—K 3
7.	B×P	B—Q Kt 5 !

This is played not to exchange the K B against the Q Kt, but solely to post the Bishop in the most effective manner in this position.

| 8. | Castles | Castles |
| 9. | Kt—K 2 | |

This manœuvre, which aims at the exchange of Black's Q B, requires too much time and is the chief cause of all White's subsequent difficulties. The simple developing move B—Q 2, here or on the next move, would have most easily secured equality, for he could not hope for more in the present circumstances.

9.	......	Q Kt—Q 2
10.	Kt—Kt 3	B—Kt 3
11.	Kt—R 4	P—B 4 !

Black takes advantage of the time given him by his opponent to complete his development by undertaking an action in the centre.

12. Kt×B

Bogoljuboff in the above-mentioned game here continued with the hazardous move 12. P—B 4, Kt—Kt 3; 13 B—R 2, P×P; 14. P×P, Kt (B 3)—Q 4; 15. Kt—B 3, Q R—B 1; 16. Kt—K 5, B—B 7!; 17. Q—B 3, P—B 4!, with a great superiority in position for Black.

The exchange in the text, although more prudent, also leaves White struggling to develop his inactive Q B.

12.	......	R P×Kt
13.	P×P	Kt×P
14.	Q—K 2	

Threatening the advance of the K P, which Black will at once prevent.

14.	Kt (B 3)—K 5 !
15. Kt × Kt	Kt × Kt
16. Q—Kt 4	

The combination 16. B × P, P × B ; 17. Q—B 4, Q—Q 4 ! ; 18. Q × B, Kt × B P ! turns to Black's advantage. The text-move is preferable to 16. Q—B 3, against which Black could have replied 16. ....Kt—Q 3, a move at present impossible because of 17. B × P, etc.

16.	Kt—B 3
17. Q—B 3	

A fresh attempt to enforce P—K 4.

17.	Q—B 2

Gaining the necessary time to prevent once and for all the advance of the K P.

18. P—Q Kt 3	Q—K 4
19. R—R 2	Kt—K 5
20. P—R 5	

Simpler was 20. B—Kt 2. The continuation of the game shows that the text-move offers Black a chance of victory, by allowing him to support his Kt at Q B 6 by P—Kt 5 on his 29th move.

20.	K R—Q 1
21. B—Kt 2	B—B 6
22. B × B	

It is obvious that White cannot keep his two Bishops.

22.	Kt × B
23. R—B 2	P—Q Kt 4 !
24. P × P e. p.	P × P

The opening of the Q R, due to White's incautious 20th move, is an evident advantage for Black.

25. K R—B 1	Kt—R 7

To gain the time to advance his Q Kt P.

26. R—K 1	P—Q Kt 4
27. B—B 1	Kt—B 6
28. Q—B 4 !	

The exchange of Queens still affords White the best chance of escaping, seeing that it leads to the opening of the King's file for his Rooks, the other files being in his opponent's possession.

But the ensuing end-game is not a little in Black's favour.

28.	Q × Q
29. P × Q	P—Kt 5
30. P—Kt 3	

Position after White's 30th move.

30	R—R 6

However, this thoughtless move, which involves an important loss of time, deprives Black of most of his chances, for there was no reason to persuade White to post his Bishop at B 4, where it would have to go in any event.

It would have been far wiser to bring his King quickly to the centre by K—B 1, K—K 2, R—Q 5 and K—Q 3, after which Black could have contemplated the exchange of one Rook and the investment of the Q Kt P by the three remaining pieces.

After the text-move he lacks precisely one *tempo* to execute this manœuvre.

31. B—B 4	K—B 1
32. K—Kt 2	K—K 2
33. R—K 5 !	

INTERNATIONAL TOURNAMENT AT LONDON 181

It is just this reply which Black did not sufficiently appreciate when playing his 30th move. Now he has no time to play 33. ....R—Q 5, for White is threatening to enter into the hostile game via Q B 5 and Q B 8. Being compelled to defend himself, Black must temporarily forego the victory.

33. ......   R—Q B 1
34. P—R 4

This demonstration, which has no real point, would have been without effect had Black simply answered it by 34. ....R—B 3, whereas his actual reply allows White to introduce fresh complications.

34. ......   Kt—Q 4
35. R (B 2)—K 2 !

A good move which meets the threat 35. ....Kt—Kt 3 on account of 36. B×P !, and thus gains an important *tempo*.

35. ......   Kt—B 6
36. R—Q 2   R—B 3

Position after Black's 36th move.

37. P—R 5 !

This ingenious Pawn-sacrifice, which would have had no object if White's Rook were still on Q B 2, requires the greatest circumspection on Black's part, without impairing White's game.

The present game, more than any other, marks the evolution of Rubinstein's style: the deep strategist has become transformed into a clever tactician, whose every move conceals a hidden bolt, or prepares a fresh combination.

This opinion is confirmed, moreover, by the number of Brilliancy Prizes which he has carried off in recent tournaments, alongside such specialists in that art as Mieses and Spielmann.

37. ......   P—B 3
38. R—K 3   P×P
39. P—B 5   P—K 4
40. R (K 3)—Q 3

Threatening mate in three. Now we perceive the strong attacking position secured by White with his sacrifice.

40. ......   R—R 2
41. R—Q 8

This continuation of the attack, although deeply conceived, is finally shown to be inadequate because of a hidden defensive manœuvre, which, however, is the sole means of saving Black's game.

Whereas by 41. P—B 3, preventing 41. ....Kt—K 5, White could have forced the draw at once : 41. ....Kt—Kt 8 ; 42. R—Q 1, Kt—B 6 ; 43. R (Q 1)—Q 2, Kt—Kt 8, etc.

41. ......   Kt—K 5

The only way to prevent the threatened 42. R—K Kt 8.

42. R (Q 2)—Q 5 !

Black cannot answer this by the plausible move 42. ....Kt—Q 3, because of 43. R—K Kt 8, Kt×P (or 43. ....Kt×B ; 44. R×Kt P ch, etc.); 44. R (Q 5)—Q 8, Kt—Q 3; 45. R—Q Kt 8! and White wins.

42. ......   R—Q 3!
43. R—K Kt 8!

This appears at first sight decisive, as Black cannot continue 43. ....R×R without losing the Exchange by force after 44. B×R, but Black in his turn prepares a surprise for his opponent.

Position after White's 43rd move.

43. ......   R—R 7!

The saving move! Black is now protected from the threatened mate in a few moves commencing with 44. R—Kt 5, for he himself is menacing a mate in three moves by 44. ....R×P ch. White's next moves are therefore forced.

44. R×P ch   K—B 1
45. R—Kt 8 ch   K×R
46. R—Q 2 dis ch K—Kt 2
47. R×R (R 2)   R—Q 7!

The point of the whole combination—Black forces the exchange of the second Rook and leads into an ending which is clearly favourable for him, by reason of the weakness of White's Q Kt P and the limited range of action of White's King.

48. R×R   Kt×R
49. B—Q 5   P—K 5

Opposing 50. P—B 3 and by that fact hindering the approach of the White King to the Knight.

50. P—B 4 ?

This makes White's game indefensible, owing to his inability after to dislodge the 50. ....P—K 6, Knight, and thus oppose the march of Black's King to the Queen's wing. Rather better was 50. P—Kt 4!, P—R 5; 51. K—R 3, Kt—B 6; 52. P—Kt 5!, and the sacrifice of the Pawn would afford White some drawing chances owing to the reduced material left on the board.

The last phase of the game is instructive.

50. ......   P—K 6!

Now Black's King can proceed without hindrance to annex White's Q Kt P.

51. K—Kt 1   K—B 1
52. K—Kt 2   K—K 2
53. B—Kt 8   K—Q 3
54. B—B 7   K—B 4
55. B×P   Kt×P
56. K—B 3

White could have prolonged his resistance by 56. P—Kt 4, in which case the continuation would have been 56. ....Kt—Q 5; 57. P—Kt 5!, P×P (if 57. ....P—Kt 6?; 58. P×P!); 58. P×P, Kt×P; 59. B—B 7, K—Q 5; 60. K—B 1, K—Q 6; 61. K—K 1, Kt—R 5; 62. B—Q 5, P—Kt 6! and wins.

56. ......   K—Q 5
57. B—B 7

Now 57. P—K Kt 4 would yield White no chance after 57. ....K—Q 6, etc.

57. ......   K—Q 6!

The simplest.

58. B×Kt   K—Q 7!
59. B—B 4   P—Kt 6
60. B×P   P—K 7

White resigns.

CHAPTER XVIII

INTERNATIONAL TOURNAMENT AT HASTINGS
SEPTEMBER, 1922

GAME 71

QUEEN'S GAMBIT DECLINED

White: Black:
A. ALEKHIN.   DR. S. TARRASCH.

1. P—Q 4   P—Q 4
2. P—Q B 4   P—Q B 3
3. Kt—K B 3

The system of play introduced by Rubinstein against Bogoljuboff in this same tournament, namely 3. Kt—Q B 3, Kt—B 3 ; 4. P—K 3, B—B 4 ; 5. P×P, Kt×P ; 6. B—B 4 followed by 7. K Kt—K 2 ! is very interesting.

3. ......   Kt—B 3
4. Kt—B 3

During the London Tournament a few weeks previously I had introduced against this line of play a system of defence which I consider perfectly correct : 4. ....P×P, followed by 5. ....P—Q Kt 4 and 6. ....P—Kt 5.

Desiring to test its value when playing against it myself, I wished to give my opponent the opportunity here, presuming that Dr. Tarrasch, always on the watch for theoretical novelties, would be tempted to employ it in the present game.

Although the struggle turned in my favour, the result does not impair the value of the variation in question.

Indeed, there is reason to think that my opponent was not sufficiently versed in the particularly delicate subtleties of this defence.

The system has been subsequently adopted by masters of unquestionable authority, such as Dr. Em. Lasker against Réti at Mährisch-Ostrau, 1923 ; and Grünfeld against Bogoljuboff at Carlsbad, 1923.

4. ......   P×P
5. P—K 3

5. P—Q R 4 does not occasion Black any difficulties (See Game No. 70).

5. ......   P—Q Kt 4
6. P—Q R 4   P—Kt 5 !

6. ....Kt—Q 4, suggested by Alapin, has fallen into disuse as a result of his game against Rubinstein in the Pistyan Tournament of 1912.

7. Kt—R 2

If 7. Kt—Q Kt 1, Black can temporarily maintain his Pawn, free to give it back at a more propitious moment, e.g.: 7. Kt—Q Kt 1, B—R 3; 8. Kt—K 5, Q—Q 4!; 9. P—B 3, P—B 4!

7. ......   P—K 3
8. B×P

White has thus regained his Pawn, but his Q Kt is very badly placed. On the other hand, Black is slightly behind in his development and his Q B P, if he does not advance it in good time, runs the risk of becoming weak.

8. ......   B—K 2

Grünfeld played here 8. ....B—Kt 2 followed by 9. ....Q Kt—Q 2 and 10. ....P—B 4, which, in my opinion, is the only logical continuation. By delaying this manœuvre Black enables his opponent to forestall it.

9. Castles   Castles
10. Q—K 2   B—Kt 2

10. ....P—B 4 would now be dangerous, e.g.: 10. ....P—B 4; 11. P×P. B×P; 12. P—K 4, B—Kt 2; 13. B—K Kt 5 and 14. K R—Q 1 with advantage to White.

11. R—Q 1   Q Kt—Q 2
12. P—K 4

Now White's game is clearly preferable, owing to his strong position in the centre.

It is astonishing that in an identical position, Réti continued here against Lasker with 12. P—Q Kt 3 and 13. B—Kt 2, which dangerously weakens the square Q B 3.

But in this variation the square Q Kt 3 should be reserved for the Q Kt.

12. ......   P—Q R 4

The Q R P may become very weak, but if Black does not make this move White, after the manœuvre Kt—B 1 and Kt—Kt 3, threatens the advance of his own Q R P to Q R 6.

13. B—Kt 5   R—K 1

Black assures the subsequent protection of his K B by this Rook, thus freeing the Queen, which can escape from the uncomfortable opposition of White's Rook.

14. Kt—B 1   Q—Kt 3

Position after Black's 14th move.

15. Kt—Kt 3!

This posting of the Q Kt is particularly strong in similar positions, as I have already found in my two games against Maróczy and Rubinstein in the Hague Tournament of 1921.

Now White plays for the effective blockade of the adverse Q B P.

15. ......   P—R 3
16. B—K 3   B—R 3

Hindering 17. P—Q 5, to which he would now reply 17. ....B×B; 18. Q×B, K P×P; 19. P×P, freeing his game.

17. K Kt—Q 2! B×B
18. Kt×B   Q—B 2
19. Q—B 3

Defending his K P, and preparing P—Q 5 should Black later play P—B 4.

19. ......   P—B 4
20. B—B 4

20. P—Q 5 at once would give Black some chances after 20. .... P×P; 21. P×P, B—Q 3.

20. ......   Q—Kt 2
21. P—Q 5   P×P
22. P×P   Q—R 3!

An ingenious defence of the threatened Pawn, but of merely temporary efficacy.

Position after Black's 22nd move.

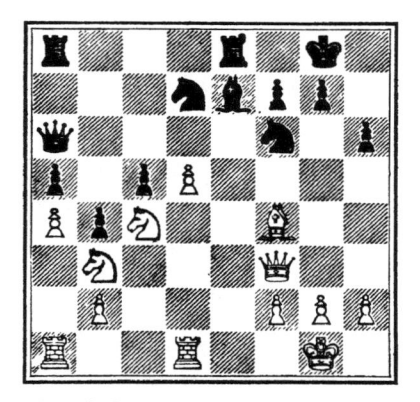

23. Q R—B 1

Black's Q R P could not be captured by the Kt on Kt 3, because of 23. ....B—Q 1!, nor by the Kt on B 4, because of 23. ....P—B 5!
But after the text-move this Pawn is defenceless. Upon 23. .... B—Q 1 there were several winning lines open to White, the simplest being probably 24. B—K 3!, Kt—K 5; 25. P—Q 6! threatening 26. B×R P, etc.

23. ......   B—B 1
24. Kt (Kt 3)×P   Kt—K 5
25. Kt—B 6!

Simplest, for if now 25. ....Q×P; 26. B×P!, P×B; 27. Q—Kt 4 ch and 28. Q×Kt (Q 7).

25. ......   P—K Kt 4

A despairing move!

26. B—K 5!   Kt×B
27. Kt (B 6)×Kt   P—B 3

Obviously the only possible reply.

28. Q×Kt   P×Kt
29. P—Q 6!   B—Kt 2
30. Q—Q 5 ch   K—R 1
31. Q×B P   Black resigns.

GAME 72

QUEEN'S GAMBIT DECLINED

White :   *Black :*
A. ALEKHIN.   E. D. BOGOLJUBOFF.

1. P—Q 4   Kt—K B 3
2. Kt—K B 3   P—K 3
3. P—B 4   P—Q 4
4. Kt—B 3   Q Kt—Q 2
5. B—Kt 5   B—K 2
6. P—K 3   Castles
7. R—B 1   P—Q R 3

This move is rightly held to be inferior, as White retains the option of blocking the opponent's game.
Somewhat better was 7. .... P—B 3.

8. P—B 5!   P—B 3
9. P—Q Kt 4   Kt—K 5
10. B—K B 4

Best, for each exchange of pieces would merely free Black's position.

10. ......   P—Kt 4

Energetic, but hazardous, quite in Bogoljuboff's style. Black wishes at all costs to free himself of White's dangerous Q B.

11. B—Kt 3   Kt×B
12. R P×Kt   P—B 4

Now it is Black in his turn who threatens to block White's position and thus repel the latter's attack, *e.g.*: 13. Kt—K 5, Kt×Kt; 14. Q—R 5, R—B 2; 15. P×Kt, P—Kt 5, and Black's position is still defendable. White's next move is intended to foil this plan.

Position after Black's 12th move.

13. P—Kt 4!

The only way to keep the initiative. White must already have foreseen the possibilities afforded him by the position arising from the exchange of Queens on the 18th move, despite his material inferiority.

13.	P×P
14. Kt—K 5	Kt×Kt
15. P×Kt	Q—B 2
16. Q—Q 4	R—B 4

The only logical answer; against any other developing or waiting move White would have secured a marked advantage by B—K 2 followed by B×P and P—B 4.

| 17. B—Q 3! | Q×P |
| 18. Q×Q! | |

Black, of course, hoped for 18. B×R, Q×B, with two Pawns for the Exchange and splendid attacking chances, but the text-move is a great disillusion for him.

| 18. . . . . . . | R×Q |
| 19. R×P | |

Black is temporarily a **Pawn** ahead, but his pieces are all so badly developed or situated that he will be compelled to submit to substantial loss of material.

| 19. . . . . . . | B—B 3 |

The only move. If 19. . . . . B—B 1?; 20. R—Q B 7, with 21. Kt—R 4 and 22. Kt—Kt 6 to follow.

It is interesting to observe that were it not for the unfortunate advance of the Q R P (6. . . . . P—Q R 3), which now allows of this Knight manœuvre, Black would have nothing to fear.

| 20. K—Q 2! | B—Kt 2 |
| 21. Q R—K R 1 | |

Preventing the development of Black's Q B, for if 21. . . . . B—Q 2 it is evident that White would win by 22. R×B ch and 23. R—R 7 ch.

| 21. . . . . . . | R—Kt 1 |
| 22. Kt—R 4! | |

Position after White's 22nd move.

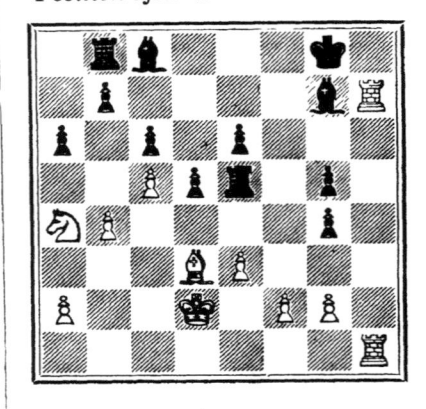

| 22. . . . . . . | R—B 4 |

The only means of developing the Queen-side. In spite of the gain of the Exchange White will experience some difficulty in improving upon his advantage.

23. B×R	P×B
24. R (R 7)—R 5!	B—K 3

Black is compelled to abandon the K Kt P, for if, *e.g.* : 24. .... B—B 3 ; 25. R—R 6, B—Kt 2 (or 25. .... K—Kt 2 ; 26. R×B, K×R ; 27. R—R 8 and 28. Kt—Kt 6 wins for White) ; 26. R—Kt 6, etc.

25. R×P	P—Q 5 !

Once again Black's best chance ; he thereby opens important diagonals for his Bishops and seizes the initiative for a time.

26. P×P	R—Q 1
27. K—B 3 !	

Not 27. K—K 3 because of 27. .... P—B 5 ch, etc.

27.	K—B 1

If 27. .... K—B 2 at once, then 28. R—R 7.

28. R—Q 1	K—B 2
29. Kt—Kt 6 !	

White plans to give back the Exchange on his next move, remaining a Pawn ahead in an evidently superior end-game.

29.	R—K R 1

Threatening 30. .... B—B 3.

30. R×B ch !	K×R
31. P—R 4	R—R 7
32. R—K Kt 1	P—B 5

See Diagram.

33. P—Q 5 !

White by this move, which could not be prevented by his opponent, secures a passed Pawn on the left wing, which will shortly cost Black

Position after Black's 32nd move.

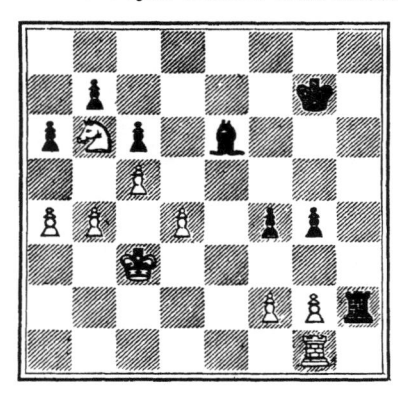

a piece. The remainder is merely a question of technique.

33.	P×P
34. K—Q 4	P—Kt 6
35. P—B 3	K—B 3
36. P—Kt 5	P×P
37. P×P	R—R 4
38. P—B 6	P×P
39. P×P	K—K 2
40. P—B 7	K—Q 3

There is nothing to be done, *e.g.* : 40. .... R—R 1 ; 41. R—Q B 1, B—B 1 ; 42. Kt×B ch, R×Kt ; 43. K×P and wins.

41. P—B 8=Q	B×Q
42. Kt×B ch	K—Q 2
43. R—B 1	R—R 7
44. R—B 2	Black resigns.

GAME 73

DUTCH DEFENCE

White :   *Black :*
E. D. BOGOLJUBOFF.   A. ALEKHIN.

1. P—Q 4	P—K B 4

A risky defence which up to the present I have adopted only very infrequently in serious games.

But in the present game I had positively to play for a win in order to make sure of first prize, whereas a draw was sufficient for my opponent to secure third prize, and hence I found myself forced to run some risks which were, after all, justified by the result.

2. P—Q B 4	Kt—K B 3
3. P—K Kt 3	

It is better to prepare the flank development of the K B in the Dutch Defence before playing P—Q B 4, because now Black can advantageously exchange his K B, which has only a very limited range of action in this opening.

3.	P—K 3
4. B—Kt 2	B—Kt 5 ch
5. B—Q 2	B×B ch
6. Kt×B	

The recapture with the Queen, followed by 7. Kt—Q B 3, is a little better.

6.	Kt—B 3
7. K Kt—B 3	Castles
8. Castles	P—Q 3
9. Q—Kt 3	

This manœuvre does not prevent Black from realizing his plan, but it is already difficult to suggest a satisfactory line of play for White.

9.	K—R 1
10. Q—B 3	P—K 4 !
11. P—K 3	

If 11. P×P, P×P ; 12. Kt×P ?, Kt×Kt ; 13. Q×Kt, White's Q Kt would be *en prise* to Black's Queen.

11.	P—Q R 4 !

It was very important to prevent P—Q Kt 4 temporarily, as will be seen later.

12. P—Kt 3

Not 12. P—Q R 3 on account of 12. ....P—R 5.

12.	Q—K 1 !
13. P—Q R 3	

Position after White's 13th move.

13.	Q—R 4 !

Now Black has secured an attacking position, for White cannot answer 14. P×P, P×P ; 15. Kt×P, Kt×Kt ; 16. Q×Kt on account of 16. ....Kt—Kt 5, winning outright ; nor can he play 14. P—Q Kt 4 ?, P—K 5 ; 15. Kt—K 1, P×P.

14. P—K R 4

A good defensive move, which secures new squares for his K Kt and revives the threat 15. P×P.

14.	Kt—K Kt 5
15. Kt—Kt 5	

White seeks to dislodge Black's Knight at once by 16. P—B 3, which, however, weakens his Pawn position still further. Possibly 15. P—Q Kt 4 would now be preferable.

15.	B—Q 2
16. P—B 3	

If 16. B×Kt, B×B ; 17. P—B 3, P×P ! ; 18. P×Kt, P×Q ; 19. P×Q, P×Kt, with the better endgame for Black.

INTERNATIONAL TOURNAMENT AT HASTINGS

16.	Kt—B 3
17. P—B 4	

Already compulsory, in view of the threatened 16. ....P—B 5 !

17.	P—K 5
18. K R—Q 1	

In order to protect the K Kt P (which was threatened by 18. .... Q—Kt 5 and 19. ....Kt—R 4) by Kt—B 1. However, the preliminary advance 18. P—Q 5 !, preventing Black from forming a centre, would have yielded White more chances of a successful defence.

18.	P—R 3
19. Kt—R 3	

Position after White's 19th move.

19.	P—Q 4 !

By this move Black completely wrecks his opponent's hopes in the centre, and shortly seizes the initiative on the Queen-side in quite unexpected fashion.

20. Kt—B 1	Kt—K 2

Preparing 21. ....P—R 5 !

21. P—R 4	Kt—B 3 !

Now this Knight can penetrate into the hostile camp via Q Kt 5 and Q 6.

22. R—Q 2	Kt—Q Kt 5
23. B—R 1	

The fact that White had to conjure up this complicated manœuvre in order to create faint chances on the King-side shows clearly the inferiority of his position.

Position after White's 23rd move.

23.	Q—K 1 !

This very strong move yields Black a new advantage in every case : either control of the square Q 4 after 24. P × P, or the opening of a file on the Queen-side after 24. P—B 5, P—Q Kt 4 !, or lastly, as in the actual game, the win of a Pawn.

24. R—K Kt 2	

White is still trying for 25. P—K Kt 4, but even this weak counter-chance will not be vouchsafed him.

24.	P × P
25. P × P	B × P
26. Kt—B 2	B—Q 2
27. Kt—Q 2	P—Q Kt 4 !

The renewal of the struggle for the centre squares, a struggle whose vicissitudes will culminate in a stirring and original finish.

28. Kt—Q 1 Kt—Q 6 !

Preparing the ensuing combination. 28. ....P × P would have been weak, for White's Knight would later have secured a good square at K 5.

29. R × P

If 29. P × P, B × P ; 30. R × P, Kt—Q 4 ; 31. Q—R 3, R × R ; 32. Q × R, Q—B 3 and Black has a winning attack.

29. ...... P—Kt 5 !
30. R × R

If 30. Q—R 1, R × R ; 31. Q × R, Q—R 1 ! ; 32. Q × Q, R × Q, and Black's Rook makes an inroad into White's game with decisive effect.

30. ...... P × Q !

As will be seen, this continuation is much stronger than 30. .... Q × R ; 31. Q—Kt 3, B—R 5 ; 32. Q—Kt 1, after which White could still defend himself.

31. R × Q

Position after White's 31st move.

31. ...... P—B 7 ! !

The point ! White cannot prevent this Pawn from Queening.

32. R × R ch K—R 2
33. Kt—B 2

It is clear that this is the only possible move.

33. ...... P—B 8 = Q ch
34. Kt—B 1

Position after White's 34th move.

34. ...... Kt—K 8 !

Threatening an unexpected and original " Smothered Mate."

35. R—R 2 Q × B P

A new threat of mate in a few moves, commencing with 36. .... B—Kt 4, which compels White to sacrifice the Exchange.

36. R—Q Kt 8 B—Kt 4
37. R × B Q × R
38. P—Kt 4

The only chance for White to prolong his resistance ; but Black retorts with a fresh surprise-move.

38. ...... Kt—B 6 ch !
39. B × Kt P × B
40. P × P

Forced, for if 40. P—Kt 5 Black would have obtained two united passed Pawns after 40. ....Kt—Kt 5.

Position after White's 40th move.

40. ......   Q—K 7!!

This move leads to a problem-like position, wherein White cannot move any piece without exposing himself to immediate loss, for example 41. Kt—R 3 or Kt 4, Kt—Kt 5! or Kt×Kt; or 41. R—R 3 or R 1, Kt—Kt 5 and wins.

Hence, after two unimportant moves, he must play P—K 4, which leads to an immediate liquidation, with a won end-game for Black.

41. P—Q 5   K—Kt 1!

Not, however, the plausible 41. ....P—R 4, upon which White could have saved himself by 42. Kt—R 3, followed by 43. Kt—Kt 5 ch.

42. P—R 5   K—R 2
43. P—K 4   Kt×K P
44. Kt×Kt   Q×Kt
45. P—Q 6

Being unable to defend his Pawns White endeavours to dislocate those of his opponent, but his game is hopelessly lost.

45. ......   P×P
46. P—B 6   P×P
47. R—Q 2

Position after White's 47th move.

47. ......   Q—K 7!

A pretty finish, worthy of this fine game. Black forces a winning Pawn end-game.

48. R×Q   P×R
49. K—B 2   P×Kt=Q ch
50. K×Q   K—Kt 2
51. K—B 2   K—B 2
52. K—K 3   K—K 3
53. K—K 4   P—Q 4 ch
White resigns.

CHAPTER XIX

INTERNATIONAL TOURNAMENT AT VIENNA
NOVEMBER, 1922

GAME 74

RUY LOPEZ

White:	Black:
A. ALEKHIN.	R. RÉTI.
1. P—K 4	P—K 4
2. Kt—K B 3	Kt—Q B 3
3. B—Kt 5	P—Q R 3
4. B—R 4	Kt—B 3
5. Kt—B 3	P—Q Kt 4
6. B—Kt 3	B—B 4

If it was Black's intention to develop his B at Q B 4, he should have done so before playing P—Q Kt 4, for after 5. ....P—Q Kt 4 he has nothing better than 6. ....B—K 2, which, however, gives him a satisfactory game.

The text-move, on the contrary, needlessly exposes him to grave perils.

7. Kt × P !

The correct reply, yielding White in every variation an extremely dangerous attack.

7.	Kt × Kt
8. P—Q 4	B—Q 3
9. P × Kt	B × P
10. P—B 4 !	

This move, which would be bad if Black's Q Kt P were still at Kt 2 and White's K B at Q R 4, because of 10. ....B × Kt ch and 11. ....Kt × P, shows the error of Black's 6th move.

10.	B × Kt ch
11. P × B	Castles

Forced now, for if 11. ....Kt × P; 12. B—Q 5.

12. P—K 5

If now 12. ....Kt—K 1; 13. Castles, P—Q 3; 14. P—B 5 with an irresistible attack for White.

White appears to have secured a decisive positional advantage, for the withdrawal of the Knight to K 1 is compulsory (12. ....Kt—K 5; 13. Q—Q 5 ! and wins): but my ingenious opponent succeeds in finding the only move to give him defensive chances, and in the sequel he shows in exemplary manner how to make the most of them.

12.	P—B 4 !

See Diagram.

The text-move threatens, should White capture the Knight, to shut off the hostile K B by 13. ....P—B 5, thereby leading into an end-game with Bishops of opposite colours.

INTERNATIONAL TOURNAMENT AT VIENNA

Position after Black's 12th move.

What is White to play to keep his advantage? The following variations, considered during the actual game, seemed to him quite inadequate:

I.—13. P×Kt, R—K 1 ch; 14. K—B 1, P—B 5.

II.—13. P—B 4, P—Q 4!; 14. P×Kt, R—K 1 ch; 15. K—B 1, Q×P! and 16. ....Q P×P.

III.—13. Castles, P—B 5; 14. P×Kt, Q×P; 15. Q—Q 5, Q—Kt 3 ch and 16. ....B—Kt 2.

IV.—13. B—Q 5, Kt×B; 14. Q×Kt, Q—Kt 3!; 15. B—K 3, B—Kt 2; 16. Q×B P, Q—Kt 3!, or:

V.—13. B—Q 5, Kt×B; 14. Q×Kt, Q—Kt 3!; 15. B—K 3, B—Kt 2; 16. B×P, B×Q; 17. B×Q, B×Kt P; 18. R—K Kt 1, B—K 5.

Black has the better game in the first four variations and has equality in the fifth.

13. B—R 3!!

The key-move of a deep combination whose principal variation consists of some ten moves and which results in the gain of a Pawn in a superior position.

It was evidently quite impossible to foresee, at this stage of the game, that this material advantage, in conjunction with the position, would prove insufficient for victory against the impeccable defence set up by Black.

13. ......   Q—R 4!

The best reply. Black indirectly defends his Q B P whilst attacking the hostile Q B, but White's manœuvre initiated by 13. B—R 3! is based upon the temporary removal of the Black Queen from the centre.

14. Castles   Q×B
15. P×Kt   P—B 5

Black is not excessively uneasy concerning the reply 16. Q—Q 5 (with the double threat 17. Q—Kt 5 and 17. Q×R), being convinced that he will save the situation by 16. ....Q—R 4 followed by the capture of the K B, which is cut off.

But, as the sequel shows, this calculation is only partly correct.

16. Q—Q 5!   Q—R 4!

Position after Black's 16th move.

17. P×P

Not 17. Q×R because of 17. .....Q—Kt 3 ch and 18. ....B—Kt 2, winning for Black.

| 17. ...... | Q—Kt 3 ch |
| 18. K—R 1 | K×P ! |

Once again the only move. If 18. ....R—Q 1; 19. B×P!, P×B (forced); 20. Q×R, B—Kt 2; 21. Q R—Kt 1 and White wins the Exchange.

Position after Black's 18th move.

19. B×P !

The point of the whole combination ! This Bishop, which appeared hopelessly doomed, gains a fresh lease of life, for if 19. ....P×B, then 20. Q×R and 21. Q R—Kt 1, as in the preceding note.

White, with his Pawn plus and considering the exposed position of Black's King, seems to have a comparatively easy win, but this is only a will-o'-the-wisp.

| 19. ...... | B—Kt 2 ! |
| 20. Q—K 5 ch | |

Equally after 20. Q—Kt 5 ch, Q—Kt 3, 21. B—Q 3, P—B 4 ! Black would have sufficient resources available.

| 20. ...... | Q—B 3 |
| 21. B—Q 3 | |

Position after White's 21st move.

| 21. ...... | K R—K 1 ! |

An excellent defensive move by which Black sacrifices a second Pawn in order to occupy the central files with his Rooks.

After 21. ....Q×Q; 22. P×Q, Q R—B 1; 23. R—B 4, R×P; 24. R—Kt 4 ch, K—R 1; 25. R—R 4, etc. Black probably could not save the game.

22. Q—R 5	P—R 3
23. Q—Kt 4 ch	K—R 1
24. Q×P	R—K 2
25. Q—Q 4	Q×Q !
26. P×Q	Q R—Q 1

Taking advantage of the fact that White's Q P cannot readily be defended, *e.g.*: 27. P—B 3, P—Kt 5 !; 28. P×P, R×P, followed by 29. ....R×Kt P, etc.

27. P—B 5 !

In order to secure an outpost by 28. P—B 6 after 27. ....R×P, with good attacking chances against the position of the hostile King, but Black prefers to temporize and to postpone the capture of the Q P until later, first taking a precautionary measure.

| 27. ...... | P—B 3 ! |

Position after Black's 27th move.

28. Q R—K 1

Reconciling himself to giving back one Pawn in order to exchange the formidable Black Bishop.
28. R—B 4, although temporarily preserving the advantage of two Pawns, would be insufficient for success, *e.g.:* 28. ....R—Kt 2; 29. B—B 1, R—Q B 1!; 30. R—B 2 or R—B 1, R—B 6 followed by 31. ....B—Q 4 or R—R 6, and White cannot possibly defend all his Pawns.

28. ......   R—Kt 2!

Of course not 28. ....R×R; 29. R×R, R×P because of 30. R—K 8 ch, K moves; 31. R—K 7 ch and White wins.

29. B—K 4   R×Q P
30. B×B   R×B
31. R—K 6

Winning a Pawn once again, but only momentarily.

31. ......   K—Kt 2!
32. R×R P   R—Q B 5

Still more exact was 32. ....R—Q R 5!, although the text-move is also adequate.

33. R—B 3

Obviously if 33. R—B 2, then 33. ....R (Kt 2)—B 2, and the Q B P could not be defended.

33. ......   R×P
34. P—R 3   K—B 2!

Forestalling the threatened 35. R—Kt 3 ch and 36. R—Kt 6.

35. R—K Kt 3   R—B 7
36. R—K Kt 6   R×P
37. R×P   K—Kt 2
38. R—K R 4   P—Kt 5!

After this move, which creates a permanent threat to dissolve the Queen-side Pawns, White's winning chances are reduced to vanishing point.

39. R—Kt 4 ch   K—B 2
40. R—Kt 3   R (B 4)—
                      Q Kt 4
41. R—Kt 3   K—Kt 3
42. K—R 2   R—Q B 4
43. R—R 4   R (B 4)—
                      Q Kt 4
44. P—R 4   R (Kt 4)—Kt 3
45. K—R 3   R (Kt 2)—Kt 1
46. P—Kt 3   P—B 4!
47. R—R 5   R—Q B 1
48. R—K B 3   R—K B 3
49. K—Kt 2   R—B 6!
50. R—R 8   R×R
51. K×R   R—B 3
52. R—Kt 8   R—B 5
53. R—Kt 6 ch   K—Kt 2
54. P—R 5   R—Q 5
55. R—Q B 6!   R—K 5
56. R—Kt 6 ch   K—B 2
57. P—Kt 4

The supreme effort!
See Diagram.

57. ......   R×P!

At once forcing the draw.

58. R×R   P×R ch
59. K×P   K—Kt 2!

Drawn game.

Black's King arrives just in time to stop White's Q R P, *e.g.:*

Position after White's 57th move

60. K—B 4, K—R 3; 61. K—K 4, K×P; 62. K—Q 4, K—Kt 4; 63. K—B 4, K—B 4; 64. K×P, K—K 3; 65. K—Kt 5, K—Q 2; 66. K—Kt 6, K—B 1, etc.

A splendid example of Réti's careful defence.

GAME 75

QUEEN'S GAMBIT DECLINED

White :	Black :
H. KMOCH.	A. ALEKHIN.

1. P—Q 4	Kt—K B 3
2. Kt—K B 3	P—Q 4
3. P—B 4	P—B 3
4. P—K 3	

If 4. Kt—B 3, the reply would be 4. ....P×P (see Games Nos. 70 and 71).

4.	B—B 4
5. Q Kt—Q 2	

This system of development, involving the advance of the Queenside Pawns, was successfully adopted by Réti against Spielmann in the Tournament at Teplitz-Schönau, which took place a few weeks before the Vienna Tournament, where the present game was played.

Doubtless this is the reason why my opponent, hypnotized solely by the result, adopted this system in preference to the usual moves 6. Q—Kt 3 or 6. P×P, without sufficiently fathoming the depths of this novelty.

5.	P—K 3
6. B—K 2	Q Kt—Q 2
7. Castles	B—Q 3
8. P—B 5	B—B 2
9. P—Q Kt 4	Kt—K 5
10. Kt×Kt	P×Kt !

Far better than the recapture with the Bishop, which Spielmann played in an analogous position in his game with Réti, for in this case Black, after 10. Kt—Q 2, P—B 4; 11. Kt×B, etc., cannot obtain sufficient attack to compensate for White's advantage on the Queenside.

11. Kt—Q 2   P—K R 4 !

The signal for the attack. As White will in any case be compelled to play P—B 4, there is no reason for Black to provoke it by Q—R 5. He therefore utilizes the time thus saved to strengthen his attacking position by a move which will enhance his prospects.

12. P—B 4

Black was threatening the sacrifice B×P ch, followed by Q—R 5 ch and Kt—B 3, yielding him a very powerful attack.

12. ......   P—K Kt 4
13. P—Kt 3

After this timid defensive move, which anticipates the desire of White's opponent, Black's attack becomes irresistible.

It would have been better to continue 13. Kt—B 4, Kt—B 3; 14. Kt—K 5, P×P; 15. P×P, P—R 3, although in this case also Black would remain with the better position on account of the weakness of the adverse Q P.

13. ...... Kt—B 3 !

Preparing the advance of the K R P, which would at this juncture be insufficient, because of 14. P—K Kt 4.
Obviously, if 14. P×P, Black would reply 14. ....Kt—Kt 5.

14. B—Kt 2   P×P
15. K P.×P

Or 15. Kt P×P, Kt—Kt 5, etc.

15. ......   P—R 5
16. Q—Kt 3

If 16. P—Kt 4, R—K Kt 1 ; 17. P—K R 3, Kt—Q 4 and White's K B P could not be saved.

16. ......   P×P
17. P×P   Kt—Q 4
18. Kt—B 4

White is already defenceless against the threatened sacrifice at his K B 4.

Position after White's 18th move.

18. ......   Kt×B P !

Decisive, for if 19. P × Kt, Q—R 5 ! winning ; and if 19. R × Kt, B × R ; 20. P × B, Q—R 5 ! and Black wins.

19. Q R—K 1   Q—Kt 4
20. P—Q 5   Kt—Q 6

....forcing mate in a few moves.

White resigns.

This short game shows once again the risks run by young players when blindly adopting certain innovations of the masters, without having carefully calculated all their consequences.

GAME 76

SICILIAN DEFENCE

White :   *Black* :
A. ALEKHIN.   F. SÄMISCH.

1. P—K 4   P—Q B 4
2. Kt—K B 3

With this move White secures the option sooner or later of advancing his Pawn to Q 4.
2. Kt—Q B 3, followed by P—K Kt 3, B—Kt 2, P—Q 3, K Kt—K 2, etc., has been successfully adopted on several occasions by Dr. Tarrasch.

2. ......   Kt—Q B 3

Giving up the idea of playing the Paulsen variation (P—K 3 followed by P—Q R 3 and Q—B 2, etc.), in which Black's Q Kt has no place at Q B 3.
If 2. ....P—K 3, White would still have delayed P—Q 4, and would have played 3. B—K 2, in order to answer 3. ....Q—B 2 with 4. P—Q 4, P×P ; 5. Kt×P, P—Q R 3 ; 6. P—Q B 4 !, thus obtaining a very fine game.

3. P—Q 4   P×P
4. Kt×P   P—K Kt 3
5. P—Q B 4

This system, which is aimed at contesting Black's fianchetto in the

Sicilian, was introduced about fifteen years ago by Maróczy, with the continuation:

5. ....B—Kt 2; 6. B—K 3, Kt—B 3; 7. Kt—Q B 3, P—Q 3; 8. B—K 2, upon which Black can secure a satisfactory game by 8. ....Kt—K Kt 5 !, as was shown by Breyer.

5.	B—Kt 2
6. Kt—Kt 3	

An innovation which seems to yield White a very good game; its main object is to suppress at once the pressure exerted by Black on the square Q 4.

With the same idea 6. Kt—B 2, followed by Kt—K 3, was also worthy of consideration.

6.	Kt—B 3
7. Kt—B 3	P—Q 3
8. B—K 2	B—K 3

The Q B is very badly posted on K 3, as White can discount the attack on his Q B P by the advance of this Pawn.

However, even after 8. .... Castles ; 9. Castles, B—Q 2 ; 10. B—K 3 followed by 11. P—B 3 and 12. Kt—Q 5 White's game would also have been superior.

9. Castles	P—K R 4

Position after Black's 9th move.

Ingenious, but hardly sound. Black intends to answer 10. P—B 4 with 10. ....Q—Kt 3 ch followed by 11. ....Kt—K Kt 5 ; and if 10. P—B 3 then 10. ....P—R 5 followed by 11. ....Kt—K R 4 (another of Breyer's manœuvres). But White, by playing simply 10. B—Kt 5 !, threatening 11. P—B 5, could have maintained the superiority in position which he had gained in the opening.

10. P—B 5

But this move is premature, for Black could obtain a satisfactory game by 10. ....P—Q 4 !, e.g.: 11. Kt—Q 4, Kt×Kt ; 12. Q×Kt, P×P ; 13. Q—Kt 4 !, Q—B 1 ; 14. Kt×P, Kt×Kt ; 15. Q×Kt, Castles, after which White's majority of Pawns on the Queen-side would have been largely compensated by the dominating position of the Black Bishops.

10.	P×P

A decisive strategic error. Despite the exchange of Queens Black will be unable to ward off the direct attack against his King, which is fixed in the centre.

11. Kt×P	B—Q B 1

If Black avoids the exchange of Queens by 11. ....Q—B 1, White would secure a positional advantage sufficient for victory by 12. Kt—Q 5, Castles ; 13. Kt×B, P×Kt (not 13. ....Q×Kt ; 14. Kt—B 7) ; 14. Kt—B 4, etc.

12. Q×Q ch	K×Q

Black would equally lose by 12. ....Kt×Q ; 13. Kt—Kt 5, Castles ; 14. Kt—B 7, R—Kt 1 ; 15. B—K B 4.

13. R—Q 1 ch	Kt—Q 2

He relies on being able to repulse the attack by 14. ....B×Kt followed by 15. ....K—B 2, or also by 14. ....Kt—Q 5, but White's next move shatters this hope.

14. B—Q B 4!

Decisive, for Black cannot defend his K B P, *e.g.*: 14. ....R—B 1; 15. Kt—Q Kt 5!, P—Q R 3 (or 15. ....P—Q Kt 3; 16. B—Q 5!, P×Kt; 17. B×Kt, R—Q Kt 1; 18. B—Q 2! and wins); 16. B×P!, R×B; 17. Kt—K 6 ch, K—K 1; 18. Kt (Kt 5)—B 7, mate.

| 14. ...... | B×Kt |

All other moves would likewise be inadequate.

Position after Black's 14th move.

15. B×P!

Not only winning a Pawn, but also completely demolishing the hostile position.

| 15. ...... | K—B 2 |

If 15. ....Kt—Q 5 White would continue 16. R×Kt and 17. Kt—K 6 mate.

16. Kt—K 6 ch	K—Kt 1
17. P×B	Kt (Q 2)—K 4
18. B—B 4	B×Kt
19. B×B	R—K B 1
20. B—Kt 3	

Threatening 21. R—Q 5. Black therefore loses another Pawn after 20. ....P—R 5; or else the Exchange by 20. ....R—B 3; 21. B×Kt ch and 22. R—Q 8 ch.

Black resigns.

GAME 77

QUEEN'S PAWN GAME

White: *Black:*
A. ALEKHIN.   E. KÖNIG.

| 1. P—Q 4 | Kt—K B 3 |
| 2. P—Q B 4 | P—Q Kt 3 |

This move is not good after 2. P—Q B 4, as the present game shows. 2. ....P—K 3 is more correct, in order to reply to 3. Kt—Q B 3 by 3. ....B—Kt 5!, and 3. Kt—K B 3 by 3. ....P—Q Kt 3!

| 3. Kt—Q B 3 | B—Kt 2 |
| 4. Q—B 2! | |

The right move. It was played for the first time by Teichmann against myself in our match at Berlin, 1921.

Now Black can no longer prevent his opponent from securing a strong position in the centre by P—K 4.

| 4 ...... | P—Q 4 |

Adopting the continuation of the game Euwe—Alekhin, Budapest, 1921, which ran 5. P×P, Kt×P; 6. P—K 4 (the correct move, introduced in the present game, is 6. Kt—B 3!), Kt×Kt; 7. P×Kt, P—K 4!; 8. P×P, Q—R 5!; 9. B—Kt 5 ch, Kt—Q 2; 10. Kt—B 3, Q×P ch; 11. Q×Q, B×Q, and ultimately resulted in a draw.

4. ....Kt—B 3, played in the above-mentioned match-game Teichmann—Alekhin, is equally inadequate, because of 5. Kt—B 3, P—K 3; 6. P—K 4, P—K 4;

7. P×P, Kt—K Kt 5; 8. B—B 4, B—B 4; 9. B—Kt 3, Q—K 2; 16. Castles.

5. P×P   Kt×P
6. Kt—B 3

Preventing the counter-attack 6. ....P—K 4, which alone could give Black equalizing chances.

6. ......   P—K 3
7. P—K 4   Kt×Kt
8. P×Kt   B—K 2
9. B—Kt 5 ch   P—B 3
10. B—Q 3   Castles

It was more prudent to delay this move, by playing first 10. .... Kt—Q 2, for now White will utilise his great advantage in development to undertake a strong attack against the inadequately defended position of the Black King.

11. P—K 5   P—K R 3

Comparatively best.

Position after Black's 11th move.

12. P—K R 4!

The initial move of the decisive attack. Apart from the manœuvre of the Rook via R 3, White threatens 13. Kt—Kt 5, followed by 14. B—R 7 ch and 15. B—Kt 8!

12. ......   P—Q B 4

To meet the latter threat, 13. Kt—Kt 5, by 13. ....P×P!; 14. B—R 7 ch, K—R 1; 15. B—Kt 8, P—Q 6!, but the entry of White's Rook decides the game in a few moves.

13. R—R 3!   K—R 1

This is not an adequate defence against the threatened 14. B×P. But equally after 13. ....P—B 4; 14. P×P e. p., B×P; 15. Kt—Kt 5, White wins easily.

14. B×P!   P—B 4

If 14. ....P×B, then of course 15. Q—Q 2 wins off-hand.

15. P×P e. p.   B×P
16. B—K Kt 5   P×P
17. Kt—K 5!   Kt—B 3
18. Q—K 2!   P—Kt 3

If 18. ....Kt×Kt, White mates in four moves.

19. B×P   K—Kt 2
20. B—R 6 ch   K—Kt 1

Or 20. ....K×B; 21. Q—R 5 ch and mates next move.

21. Kt×Kt

Since mate cannot be forced, White proceeds to a general liquidation which will leave him a Rook ahead.

21. ......   B×Kt
22. Q×P ch   K—R 1
23. B×R   Q×B
24. Q×B   Black resigns.

GAME 78

FRENCH DEFENCE

White :   *Black :*
A. ALEKHIN.   DR. S. TARTAKOVER.

1. P—K 4   P—K 3
2. P—Q 4   P—Q 4
3. Kt—Q B 3   Kt—K B 3
4. B—Kt 5   P×P

INTERNATIONAL TOURNAMENT AT VIENNA

A good move which seems to yield a perfectly satisfactory defence, especially in the variation adopted here by White.

5. B×Kt

Slightly preferable, although equally insufficient to yield White an advantage, is 5. Kt×P, B—K 2; 6. B×Kt, B×B; 7. Kt—K B 3.

5.	P×B
6. Kt×P	P—K B 4
7. Kt—Q B 3	

The withdrawal of this Knight to K Kt 3 offered still less prospect, because of the reply 7. ....P—B 4!

7.	B—Kt 2
8. Kt—B 3	Castles
9. Q—Q 2	

If 9. B—B 4, P—B 4!; 10. P—Q 5, P—Kt 4; 11. B×P, Q—R 4; 12. B—K 2, B×Kt ch; 13. P×B, Q×P ch, followed by 14. ....P×P with advantage to Black.

| 9. ...... | P—B 4! |

This move increases the action of Black's K B, and compels White to play very prudently to maintain equality.

| 10. P×P | Q—R 4 |
| 11. Kt—Q Kt 5! | |

The exchange of Queens resulting from this move avoids all danger of an attack directed against the White King. This attack might have become very dangerous with the aid of the two Black Bishops.

| 11. ...... | Q×Q ch |
| 12. Kt×Q | Kt—R 3 |

Not 12. ....B×P on account of 13. R—Q Kt 1, B—K 4; 14. Kt—B 4, with the better game for White.

| 13. P—Q B 3 | Kt×P |
| 14. Kt—Kt 3! | Kt×Kt |

Black's Knight had no good square; however, the resulting opening of the Q R file will allow White to exert pressure on his opponent's weakened Queen-side.

15. P×Kt	P—Q R 3
16. Kt—Q 6	R—Kt 1
17. P—Q Kt 4	

Preparing to undouble his Pawns by P—Kt 5.

| 17. ...... | R—Q 1 |
| 18. Castles | |

It would have been more prudent to capture the Q B at once with the Knight (with an end-game analogous to that in the game), for after the text-move Black could have provoked complications by 18. .... B—Q 2 and if 19. P—Kt 5, B—K 4!, the outcome of which would have been difficult to foresee.

18.	B—K 4
19. Kt×B	R×R ch
20. K×R	R×Kt

Position after Black's 20th move.

The ensuing end-game is clearly in White's favour:

(1) He has the majority of Pawns on the Queen-side.

(2) The position of his King, which is already in the centre of the board, is very promising for utilizing this advantage.

(3) All Black's Pawns are temporarily situated on squares of the same colour as the adverse Bishop, and those on the Queen-side can only be moved with difficulty.

(4) Black's K R P is isolated and therefore weak.

(5) Lastly, White will have a base for operations in the Q R file, possession of which cannot be disputed.

But the neutralizing force of the Bishops of opposite colour is such that, despite all these advantages, it is not certain that White could have succeeded in winning, if his opponent had not allowed him to occupy the fifth rank with his Rook (see Black's 24th move).

21. B—K 2	K—B 1
22. K—B 2	R—B 2
23. R—R 1	K—K 2
24. P—R 3	P—B 5

This attempt at counter-attack, which aims principally at playing B—Q 3 followed by P—K 4 and P—B 4, is premature and must be considered the decisive mistake.

The correct move was 24. .... B—Q 5, followed by 25. ....B—Kt 3, with drawing chances for Black.

The continuation of this game, whose conclusion resembles a composed study, compensates in some degree for the monotony of its first phase.

25. K—Kt 3

Definitely depriving Black of the possibility of B—Q 5.

| 25. ...... | R—Q 2 |
| 26. R—R 5 ! | B—B 2 |

Again best, for if 26. ....R—Q 4; 27. B—B 3 !, R×R; 28. P×R and White wins the Queen-side Pawns. And if 26. ....P—B 3; 27. B—B 3, K—Q 1; 28. P—Kt 5, P×P; 29. R×P, K—B 1; 30. R—Kt 6, R—K 2; 31. K—B 4 and 32. K—Q 3, followed by the victorious advance of White's Queen-side Pawns.

| 27. R—R 5 | R—Q 7 |
| 28. B—B 3 | P—Kt 3 |

Clearly Black must at all costs maintain his Pawn.

29. R×P   R×P

Position after Black's 29th move.

30. B—R 5 !

The consequences of this move, which allows Black two very dangerous passed Pawns, had to be examined very accurately by the two opponents, for it held out, in appearance at least, as much danger for the one as for the other.

Finally White had the good fortune to foresee, in the critical position, the possibility of a problem-move, the only move to win.

| 30. ...... | R×P |
| 31. R×P ch | K—Q 1 ! |

After 31. ....K—Q 3; 32. R×P, Black, a Pawn down and with a bad position, would have lost slowly but surely.

INTERNATIONAL TOURNAMENT AT VIENNA

32. B—Kt 4 !   P—K 4 !

Forced, for the same reason as the previous move.

33. R—Q 7 ch   K—B 1
34. R—Q 2 dis ch   R×B
35. P×R   P—B 6 !

Position after Black's 35th move.

The hidden point of the combination commenced by 26. .... B—B 2. If 35. ....P—K 5 ; 36. R—Q 4 !, P—B 6 ; 37. R×P, P—B 7 ; 38. R—K 8 ch and 39. R—K B 8 wins easily.

What must White play now to avoid a draw or even the loss of the game in some contingencies?

Here are the leading variations to be considered :

I.—36. K—B 4, P—K 5 ; 37. K—Q 4, B—B 5 ; 38. R—K B 2, P—K 6 ; 39. R×P, P—K 7 and Black wins.

II.—36. K—B 2, P—K 5 ; 37. R—Q 4 !, P—K 6 ; 38. K—Q 1, B—Kt 6 ; 39. R—K 4, P—K 7 ch ; 40. K—Q 2, B—R 5 ; 41. R—K 5, B—Kt 6 and draws.

III.—36. P—K Kt 5, P—K 5 ; 37. R—Q 5 (if 37. P—Kt 6, B—K 4 followed by 38. ....P—K 6 and Black wins), P—B 7 ; 38. R—K B 5, P—K 6 ; 39. P—Kt 6, P—K 7 ; 40. P—Kt 7, P—B 8 = Q ; 41. P—Kt 8 = Q ch, K—Kt 2 ; 42. Q—Q 5 ch, K—R 2 and White cannot win, on account of the threats 43. .... P—K 8 = Q, and 43. ....Q—Q 8 ch.

IV.—36. R—R 2, P—K 5 ; 37. R—R 8 ch, K—Q 2 ; 38. R—K B 8, B—Kt 6 ! ; 39. P—Kt 5, B—Q 3 ! ; 40. R—B 6, B—K 4 ! ; 41. R—B 7 ch or R—B 5, K—K 3, and Black draws by chasing the White Rook along the K B file, which it dare not leave.

And yet the win is there !

36. R—Q 5 !

The variations springing from this rather unlikely move (it attacks one solidly defended Pawn and allows the immediate advance of the other) are quite simple when we have descried the basic idea : *The Black Pawns are inoffensive :*

(1) *When they occupy squares of the same colour as their Bishop*, for in that case White's King can hold them back without difficulty, by occupying the appropriate White squares.

(2) *When the Rook can be posted behind them*, as in the variation IV above, but *without loss of time*, and as the two main variations from the text-moves :

I.—36. ....P—B 7 ; 37. R—Q 1, P—K 5 ; 38. K—B 2, B—B 5 ; 39. R—K B 1 and 40. K—Q 1.

II.—36. ....P—K 5 ; 37. R—K B 5, B—Kt 6 ; 38. P—Kt 5, P—K 6 ; 39. R×P, P—K 7 ; 40. R—K 3,
answer the above aim, the victory is assured to White.

36. ......   P—K 5
37. R—K B 5   B—Kt 6
38. P—Kt 5   K—Q 2

This is the only possibility, for 38. ....P—K 6 has been shown to be inadequate in variation II above.

39. P—Kt 6	K—K 3
40. P—Kt 7	K×R
41. P—Kt 8=Q	B—B 5
42. Q—B 7 ch	K—Kt 5

If 42. ....K—K 4 White wins just as quickly by 43. P—B 4.

43. Q—Kt 6 ch	B—Kt 4
44. Q×P ch	K—Kt 6
45. Q—Kt 6	K—Kt 5
46. Q×P	Black resigns.

CHAPTER XX

TOURNAMENT AT MARGATE
APRIL, 1923

GAME 79

QUEEN'S GAMBIT DECLINED

White:	Black:
A. ALEKHIN.	A. MUFFANG.

1.	P—Q 4	P—Q 4
2.	P—Q B 4	P—K 3
3.	Kt—K B 3	Kt—K B 3
4.	Kt—B 3	B—K 2
5.	B—Kt 5	Q Kt—Q 2
6.	P—K 3	Castles
7.	R—B 1	P—B 3
8.	Q—B 2	P × P

This move has been adopted by Capablanca on several occasions, amongst others against myself in the London Tournament of 1922.

Without considering it bad we can affirm that it is certainly not the best, for there are numerous defensive resources available to Black which can later on yield him chances of a win.

Here is the continuation of my game against Capablanca: 9. B × P, Kt—Q 4; 10. B × B, Q × B; 11. Castles, Kt × Kt; 12. Q × Kt, P—Q Kt 3; 13. Q—Q 3. In this position White has the choice between several continuations which give him an excellent game, and the most Black can hope for is a draw. The game continued 13. ....P—Q B 4; 14. B—R 6, B × B; 15. Q × B, P × P; 16. Kt × P, Kt—B 4; 17. Q—Kt 5 and White has still a slight advantage owing to the weakness of the square at his Q B 6. This superiority is, however, not sufficient to force the win.

| 9. | B × P | Kt—Q 4 |
| 10. | Kt—K 4 | |

This move, of doubtful value in the variation 8. B—Q 3 (see Game No. 87), is still less commendable in the present position, because of the presence of the White Queen at Q B 2.

The only correct move is 10. B × B followed by 11. Castles.

| 10. | ...... | Q—R 4 ch ! |
| 11. | K—K 2 | |

The position of White's King is not safe, but 11. K—B 1 has the disadvantage of shutting in the K R.

| 11. | ...... | R—K 1 |

A serious loss of time which allows the opponent to maintain his advantage in position.

The line of play indicated was 11. ....P—B 3 !; 12. B—R 4, Kt (Q 2)—Kt 3, forcing the exchange of the adverse K B, for 13. B—Kt 3 would evidently be bad because of 13. ....Kt—Kt 5, threatening Q—R 3 ch or Q—Kt 4 ch.

Black by this manœuvre could have secured at least an equal game, which shows the inadequacy of 10. Kt—K 4.

12. K R—Q 1 !   Kt (Q 2)—Kt 3
13. B—Kt 3   Q—Kt 4 ch

Now 13. ... Kt—Kt 5 would not cause White any inconvenience, *e.g.*: 14. Q—Kt 1, Q—Kt 4 ch; 15. K—K 1, etc.

14. Q—Q 3

The exchange of Queens is forced, but it is entirely to the advantage of White, who had continually to reckon with the threats of the dangerous Black Queen.

14. ......   Q × Q ch
15. R × Q   B × B

The withdrawal of Black's K B to K B 1 would have prevented White's Knight from occupying Q 6, but in any case Black's game would have remained very cramped.

16. Kt (B 3) × B   Kt—B 3

Grünfeld in the Teplitz-Schönau Tournament-Book recommends here first 16. ....P—K R 3. Nevertheless, it seems doubtful whether this transposition of moves can be of great importance for the general valuation of a position in which Black has no compensation for his shut-in Q B.

17. Kt—Q 6   R—K 2
18. P—K 4   P—K R 3
19. Kt—B 3   R—Kt 1

In order to develop his Q B and subsequently dislodge the Knight on Q 6 by ....Kt—Q B 1.

White must therefore cast about for a very energetic line of play if he wishes to maintain his advantage.

Position after Black's 19th move.

20. P—Kt 4 !

This Pawn-sacrifice compels Black to modify his plan, for if now 20. ....B—Q 2; 21. P—Kt 5, P × P; 22. Kt × K Kt P, Kt—B 1; 23. Kt—B 4 with an overwhelming position for White.

It would be comparatively best for Black to resolve to maintain his Bishop in its blocked position and to continue 20. ....R—Q 2; 21. P—K 5, Kt (B 3)—Q 4; 22. K—Q 2 !, with 23. P—K R 4 and 24. P—Kt 5 to follow for White.

20. ......   Kt × P

On the contrary, the capture of the Pawn is rash, for the open lines of attack now available to White are heavy ransom for such sorry booty.

21. R—K Kt 1   Kt—B 3
22. Kt—K 5 !

Threatening, if 22. ....B—Q 2, to win by 23. R—K B 3, K—B 1; 24. Kt (K 5) × K B P !, R × Kt; 25. Kt × R, K × Kt ; 26. P—K 5.

22. ......   Kt (Kt 3)—Q 2

This move is not really an actual mistake. But in this laborious position all other moves would equally give the impression of being mistakes.

23. Kt (K 5) × K B P !

Regaining the Pawn sacrificed with a strong attack.

23. ......   Kt—R 4

If 23. ....R × Kt White wins by 24. B × P.

24. R—K B 3   K—R 2
25. P—K 5 !

Threatening 26. B—B 2 ch followed by 27. Kt × P ch.

25. ......   Kt—B 1
26. Kt × R P !   P—Q Kt 3

Indirectly defending the Knight by the threat of the Bishop's check at Q R 3.

27. Kt (R 6)—B 7   K—Kt 1
28. K—K 3

Threatening 29. R—R 3.

28. ......   P—Kt 3
29. B—B 2   K—Kt 2
30. R—Kt 5

After this move Black has no defence against the threatened 31. R × Kt ! and 32. R—Kt 3 ch.

Final Position.

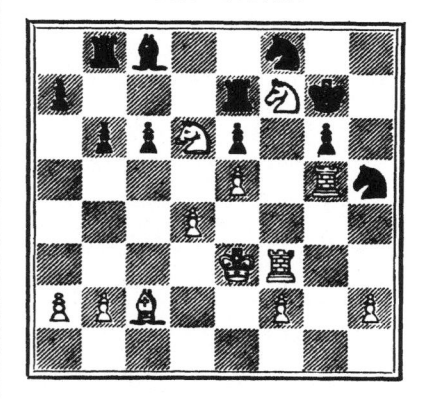

Black resigns.

CHAPTER XXI

INTERNATIONAL TOURNAMENT AT CARLSBAD
MAY, 1923

GAME 80

QUEEN'S GAMBIT DECLINED

Brilliancy Prize

White: Black:
A. ALEKHIN.   A. RUBINSTEIN.

1. P—Q 4	P—Q 4
2. P—Q B 4	P—K 3
3. Kt—K B 3	Kt—K B 3
4. Kt—B 3	B—K 2
5. B—Kt 5	Q Kt—Q 2
6. P—K 3	Castles
7. R—B 1	P—B 3
8. Q—B 2	

This move, which was very fashionable since the Ostend Tournaments of 1905–7 and which had almost completely superseded the old move, 8. B—Q 3, will soon become quite obsolete, for every International Tournament brings a fresh and sufficient line of play for Black.

In the Mährisch-Ostrau Tournament of 1923 Wolf played against the great theorist Grünfeld the simple continuation: 8. ....Kt—K 5; 9. B×B, Q×B; 10. B—Q 3 (10. Kt×Kt obviously leads to nothing, for if White captures the Pawn on K 4 he loses his Q Kt P). 10. ....Kt×Kt, with a very defendable game which resulted in a draw.

But apart from 8. ....Kt—K 5 there are available to Black at least four replies whose inadequacy has not yet been demonstrated: (a) 8. ....P×P; (b) 8. ....P—B 4; (c) 8. ....R—K 1; and (d) last but not least, 8. ....P—Q R 3!

8. ....   P—Q R 3!

In my opinion better than 8. ....P—K R 3, upon which White could have replied advantageously 9. B—B 4, *e.g.*: 9. ....R—K 1 (if 9. ....Kt—K 5, then 10. B—Q 3!, P—K B 4; 11. P—K R 4 followed at need by P—K Kt 3 and Kt—K 5, with advantage to White; but not 10. Kt×Kt, P×Kt; 11. Q×P, B—Kt 5 ch; 12. Kt—Q 2, Q—R 4; 13. Q—B 2, P—K 4!; 14. P×P, Kt—B 4 and Black has a strong attack); 10. B—Q 3, P×P; 11. B×P, P—Q Kt 4; 12. B—Q 3, P—R 3; 13. P—Q R 4!, etc.

The game Alekhin—Teichmann (Carlsbad, 1923) unfolded itself in the following way: 13. ....B—Kt 2; 14. Castles, R—B 1; 15. Q—Kt 3, Q—Kt 3; 16. Kt—K 5, K R—Q 1; 17. Kt—Kt 6!; B—B 1; 18. Kt×B, Kt×Kt; 19. Kt—K 4, Kt×Kt; 20. B×Kt, Kt—Q 2; 21. B—Q 6!, Kt—B 3; 22. B—Q B 5, Q—B 2; 23. B—B 3, P—Q R 4, and White by playing for example 24. K R—K 1 or 24.

R—B 2, instead of accepting the Pawn sacrificed, which only led to a draw, would have retained a winning position.

8. ....P—B 4 usually results in the isolation of White's Q P, but on the other hand it allows White to undertake a rather dangerous attack on the King-side. This variation admits of a complicated and very difficult game, with nearly equal chances.

Concerning 8. ....R—K 1 and 8. ....P×P, see Games No. 79 (Alekhin-Muffang) and 69 (Alekhin-Yates) respectively.

9. P—Q R 4

As this identical variation had yielded me a win the previous evening against Grünfeld, who played here 9. P—Q R 3 (see Game No. 81), I wished to avoid fighting against the defence which I considered then, and still consider now, the best.

This is the reason which decided me in favour of 9. P—Q R 4, a move which Rubinstein, my present adversary, had adopted against me, without conspicuous success, in a similar position in the Hastings Tournament of 1922.

The game continued as follows:
8. ....P—K R 3 ; 9. B—R 4, P—R 3 ; 10. P—Q R 4, P—B 4 ; 11. B—Q 3, B P×P ; 12. K P×P, P×P ; 13. B×P, Kt—Kt 3 ; 14. B—R 2, Q Kt—Q 4 ; 15. B—Kt 1, Kt—Q Kt 5 ; 16. Q—K 2, B—Q 2 ; 17. Castles, B—B 3 ; 18. K R—Q 1, R—B 1 ; 19. Kt—K 5, K Kt—Q 4 ; 20. B—Kt 3, B—K Kt 4 ; 21. P—B 4 !, B—R 5 ; 22. Kt×B, R×Kt ; 23. Kt×Kt, R×R ; 24. R×R, Kt×Kt ; 25. Q—K 4, P—K Kt 3 ; 26. B×B, Q×B ; 27. P—B 5 ?, Q—Kt 4 ! and Black wins easily.

It is manifest that thè move 9. P—Q R 4 cannot pretend to yield any advantage, since Black can answer it by 9. ....Kt—K 5 ! with greater force than on the preceding move, White's Queen-side being now slightly weak.

Rubinstein, however, seeks to take advantage of the weakness by a different method.

9. ...... R—K 1

If 9. ....P—R 3 White replies 10. B—B 4 with advantage.

10. B—Q 3   P×P
11. B×P   Kt—Q 4

We now realize the idea conceived by Black—a fusion of the new defensive system (....P—Q R 3) with the old system (....P×P and ....Kt—Q 4), in the hope of thus profiting by the weakening of the square Q Kt 5 created by the advance of White's Q R P.

Position after Black's 11th move.

12. B—B 4 !

White in his turn deviates from the beaten track. The text-move is here much stronger than in the analogous position where I played it against Selesnieff at Pistyan, 1922 (see Game No. 54) for the following reasons :

(1) After 12. ....Kt×B ; 13. P×Kt the position of the Black Rook at K 1 is less favourable than on K B 1, where it hinders a subsequent attack on the point K B 2.

(2) The manœuvre Kt—Kt 3—Q 4 which, in the game cited, allowed Black to undertake a counter-attack, loses its sting because White's Queen is at Q B 2 and he can therefore gain a *tempo* by B—Q 3, threatening the K R P.

In addition the move P—Q R 4, unfavourable in other cases, here affords him the possibility of B—R 2 and B—Kt 1, a manœuvre analogous to the Grünfeld variation (9. P—Q R 3), but still more effective here because of the opening of the King's file.

We can therefore anticipate a slight advantage in position for White, after the ensuing exchange.

12. ......   Kt×B
13. P×Kt   P—Q B 4

This move, which goes against *the general principle of not opening up fresh lines to a better-developed opponent*, is dictated by the wish to eliminate White's troublesome Pawn on K B 5.

White, who has not yet Castled, can scarcely oppose this plan, and the game speedily assumes a most animated appearance.

14. P×P

Forced, for if 14. Castles, then 14. ....P×P and 15. ....Kt—Kt 3.

14. ......   Q—B 2 !

The usual complement to the previous move. If now 15. P—K Kt 3, Q—B 3 ; 16. B—K 2, P—K 4 ! and Black would have freed himself once and for all.

15. Castles !   Q×K B P

The capture of the Q B P would also be insufficient to maintain equality, *e.g.* : 15. ....B×P ; 16. B—Q 3, Kt—B 3 ; 17. Kt—K 4 ! ; or 15. ....Kt×P ; 16. Kt—K 5.

Position after Black's 15th move.

16. Kt—K 4 !

This Pawn sacrifice is the only way to keep the initiative.

The attempt to defend the Q B P by P—Q Kt 4 would be inadequate, for the Q Kt P could not be supported by the Q R P, *e.g.* : 16. Kt—K 2, Q—R 3 ; 17. P—Q Kt 4, P—R 4 !

16. ......   Kt×P

If 16. ....B×P : 17. Q Kt—Kt 5, P—K Kt 3 (forced, since if 17. ....Kt—B 1 White wins by 18. B—Q 3) ; 18. K R—K 1 !, Kt—B 3 ; 19. P—K Kt 3, Q—Q 3 ; 20. K R—Q 1, Q—K 2 ; 21. Kt—K 5 with an overwhelming attack for White.

The text-move simplifies the game and allows Black some chances of salvation.

17. Kt×Kt   B×Kt
18. B—Q 3   P—Q Kt 3

If 18. ... B—Q 3, then 19. B×P ch and 20. K R—Q 1, threatening R—Q 4.

19. B×P ch   K—R 1

This seemingly plausible move (and not the next move, as the majority of annotators have thought) is the decisive mistake! After 19. ....K—B 1! Black's King would be less endangered than after the text-move, and it would have been very difficult for White to show how he could win, despite his positional superiority.

20. B—K 4

Position after White's 20th move.

20. ......   R—R 2

Better was 20. ....R—Kt 1, although in this case White would have obtained a decisive superiority by the following lines of play:—

I.—21. P—K Kt 3, Q—B 3; 22. P—Q Kt 4, B—Q 3 (else 23. Q—B 7! follows); 23. K R—Q 1, Q—K 2; 24. B—B 6, R—Q 1; 25. R—Q 4, P—Kt 3; 26. Q—Q 2!, K—Kt 2; 27. R—Q 1 and White wins.

II.—21. P—K Kt 3, Q—Q 3; 22. K R—Q 1, Q—K 2; 23. Kt—K 5, Q—B 2; 24. Q—B 3!, P—Q R 4; 25. Kt—B 6, and 26. Q—B 3, winning for White.

21. P—Q Kt 4!

From this point up to the end of the game Black has not a moment's respite.
Obviously he cannot capture the Q Kt P, because of 22. Q×B! and wins.

21. ......   B—B 1

Therefore this retreat is absolutely forced.

22. Q—B 6

Attacking both the Rook and the Q Kt P. Black's reply is the only way to parry temporarily this double threat.

22. ......   R—Q 2
23. P—Kt 3!

Position after White's 23rd move.

23. ......   Q—Kt 1

The alternative was 23. ....Q—Q 3, after which White had the choice between two winning lines:

I.—24. K R—Q 1, Q×R ch (or 24. ...Q×Q; 25. B×Q, R×R ch; 26. R×R, R—K 2; 27. R—Q 8 and wins); 25. R×Q, R×R ch; 26. K—Kt 2, B—Q 2; 27. Q×Kt P, B×R P; 28. Q×R P, B—Q 2; 29. Kt—Kt 5, K—Kt 1; 30. Q—K 2 and White wins.

II.—24. Q—B 4, K—Kt 1 (or 24. ....Q—K 2; 25. Kt—K 5 !, R—Q 3; 26. B—B 6 ! and wins); 25. B—B 6, R—B 2; 26. K R—Q 1, Q—K 2; 27. Q—Q 3 ! and White wins.

24. Kt—Kt 5 !

Threatening 25. Kt × P ch !

24. ...... R (K 1)—Q 1

Position after Black's 24th move.

25. B—Kt 6 ! !

The *coup de grâce*. Should Black capture this Bishop, the following mating variation would ensue :

26. Q—K 4 !, B × P; 27. Q—R 4 ch, K—Kt 1; 28. Q—R 7 ch, K—B 1; 29. Q—R 8 ch, K—K 2; 30. Q × P ch, K—K 1 (or 30. ....K—Q 3; 31. K R—Q 1 ch and mates next move); 31. Q—Kt 8 ch, B—B 1; 32. Q × Kt P ch, K—K 2; 33. Q × P mate.

On the other hand 25. ....B—Kt 2; 26. Q—B 4 ! would transpose into identical variations.

Black is consequently forced to sacrifice the Exchange, after which his game is hopeless.

25.	......	Q—K 4
26.	Kt × P ch	R × Kt
27.	B × R	Q—K B 4
28.	K R—Q 1 !	

Simple and decisive.

28.	......	R × R ch
29.	R × R	Q × B
30.	Q × B	K—R 2
31.	Q × R P	Q—B 6
32.	Q—Q 3 ch !	Black resigns.

GAME 81

QUEEN'S GAMBIT DECLINED

Brilliancy Prize

White : Black :
E. GRÜNFELD. A. ALEKHIN.

1.	P—Q 4	Kt—K B 3
2.	P—Q B 4	P—K 3
3.	Kt—K B 3	P—Q 4
4.	Kt—B 3	B—K 2
5.	B—Kt 5	Q Kt—Q 2
6.	P—K 3	Castles
7.	R—B 1	P—B 3
8.	Q—B 2	P—Q R 3 !
9.	P—Q R 3	

Grünfeld is probably correct in affirming that this move is the best here, but this assertion simply demonstrates that White's whole system, or rather 8. Q—B 2, yields no more than equality.

9. ...... P—R 3

This advance should not be made until Black has definitely made up his mind between the two systems of defence : ....P × P, followed by P—Q Kt 4 and P—Q B 4; or .... P × P, followed by Kt—Q 4.

But although this move has the advantage of weakening the attack on the point K R 2, when White succeeds in posting his K B on Q Kt 1 (Grünfeld's variation), it is, on the other hand, insufficient after ....P×P and ....Kt—Q 4, since it affords White the opportunity to retain his Q B by B—K Kt 3, which thereby leaves Black's pieces in their confined positions.

10. B—R 4   R—K 1 !

An important improvement on the line of play adopted by Maróczy against Grünfeld in the Vienna Tournament of 1922.

This game continued 10. ....P×P; 11. B×P, P—Q Kt 4; 12. B—R 2, B—Kt 2; 13. B—Kt 1, R—K 1; 14. Kt—K 5 !, Kt—B 1; 15. Castles, and White has far the better game.

The text-move gains an extremely important move by eliminating the subsequent mating threat at K R 2 and thereby enables Black to free his game speedily by ....P—Q B 4 !

11. B—Q 3

White could have played 11. P—R 3 without loss of time, seeing that Black has nothing better than the following capture of the Q B P.

The question is whether this move would in the end prove useful or detrimental to him.

In my game against Chajes (see Game No. 85) I wished to try this experiment, but my opponent, who adopted an altogether abnormal system of defence, did not give me the chance.

11. ......   P×P
12. B×P   P—Q Kt 4
13. B—R 2   P—B 4

The liberating move !
See Diagram.

14. R—Q 1

Upon 14. P×P, Black would have replied 14. ....Kt×P, and if 15. B—Kt 1, B—Kt 2 !, for the variation 16. B×Kt, B×B; 17. Q—

Position after Black's 13th move.

R 7 ch, K—B 1; 18. Kt×P, P×Kt; 19. R×Kt, B×P would be completely in his favour.

After the text-move Black gradually succeeds in seizing the initiative. 14. Castles, P×P (14. ....Q—Kt 3 is also worthy of consideration); 15. P×P was a little better, as played by Réti and Grünfeld against Teichmann in the same tournament.

Here is the continuation of the game Grünfeld—Teichmann: 15. ....B—Kt 2; 16. K R—Q 1, Q—Kt 3; 17. Kt—K 5, and instead of the passive move 17. ....Kt—B 1 Black could have obtained a slight advantage in position by a pretty combination discovered by Victor Kahn: 17. ....Kt×Kt !; 18. P×Kt, Q—B 3 !; 19. P—B 3, Kt—Kt 5 !; 20. Kt—Q 5 ! (White has nothing better, for 20. B×B is refuted by 20. ....Q—Kt 3 ch), 20. ....P×Kt; 21. Q×Q, B×Q; 22. P×Kt (not 22. B×B, Kt×K P; 23. B—Q 6, Kt—B 5), 22. ...B×B; 23. R×B, R×P; 24. P—K Kt 3 ! (not 24. B×P, Q R—Q 1), 24. ....B—B 3 or B—Kt 4; 25. R×P, R—K 8 ch followed by Q R—K 1, with advantage to Black.

This variation shows once again the frailty of the variation 8. Q—B 2 and 9. P—Q R 3.

14. ......   P×P

Simplest, for after the removal of the Rook from the Q B file Black could not with certainty visualize a counter-attack on the Queen-side.

15. Kt×Q P

Hoping to break through with his attack by a subsequent sacrifice of the Exchange on Q 7.

15. ......   Q—Kt 3
16. B—Kt 1

This move appears to prevent the reply 15. ....B—Kt 2 owing to the possibility of 16. Kt (Q 4)×Kt P, P×Kt; 17. R×Kt!, with a winning attack for White.

But . . . . . .

Position after White's 16th move.

16. ......   B—Kt 2!

Black plays this move all the same, for 17. Kt (Q 4)×Kt P would be refuted by 17. ....Q—B 3!!; 18. Kt—Q 4 (forced), Q×P, with a strong counter-attack.
In this way Black has successfully completed his development. There consequently remains nothing else for White than Castling, after the failure of his premature attack.

17. Castles   Q R—B 1
18. Q—Q 2

Hindering the double threat B—K 5 or Kt—K 5. 18. Q—K 2 would be insufficient on account of 18. ....B×R P; 19. Kt (B 3 or Q 4)×Kt P, B—Kt 5! and Black wins a Pawn.

18. ......   Kt—K 4!

This Knight will occupy the square Q B 5, thereby fixing the weakness of the Queen-side, induced by 9. P—Q R 3.

19. B×Kt

In order to exchange Black's dangerous Q B, White's next manœuvre is finely conceived, but insufficient to equalize.

19. ......   B×B
20. Q—B 2   P—Kt 3

Not at all to prevent a harmless check at K R 2 but rather to secure a retreat subsequently for his K B, whose action on the long diagonal will be very powerful.

21. Q—K 2   Kt—B 5
22. B—K 4!

Feeling himself in a strategic inferiority, Grünfeld attempts to save himself by tactical skirmishing.
Having provoked 20. ....P—Kt 3 he now hopes for the variation: 22. ....Kt×R P; 23. Q—B 3!, B×B; 24. Kt×B, B×Kt; 25. P×B, etc., which would ensure him the gain of the Exchange.

22. ......   B—Kt 2!

But by this simple move, which is part of his plan, Black retains his advantage.

23. B×B   Q×B
24. R—B 1

The threat 24. ....Kt×R P compels White to retrace his 14th move.

24. ......   P—K 4 !

This advance of the K P will give Black's Knight a new out-post on Q 6, still more irksome for the opponent than its present position.

25. Kt—Kt 3   P—K 5

Renewing the threat 26. .... Kt×R P.

26. Kt—Q 4   K R—Q 1 !

To make the following Knight-manœuvre still more effective, for now when it reaches Q 6 it will intercept the defence of the White Knight by the Rook.

27. K R—Q 1   Kt—K 4
28. Kt—R 2

After this move, which removes the Knight from the field of action, White is definitely lost. Comparatively better was 28. P—B 3, upon which Black would have continued 28. ....P×P; 29. P×P, Kt—B 5 with attacking chances on both flanks, and a probable win after a long and difficult struggle.

28. ......   Kt—Q 6
29. R×R   Q×R
30. P—B 3

Too late ! But already there was no satisfactory reply, e.g. : after 30. Kt—B 3, P—B 4; 31. P—B 3, Black would have gained the victory by the same sacrifice which occurred in the actual game : 31. ... R×Kt !; 32. P×R, B×P ch; 33. K—B 1, Kt—B 5; 34. Q—Q 2, Q—B 5 ch; 35. Kt—K 2, P—K 6 !; 36. Q—K 1, B×P; 37. R—Q 8 ch, K—B 2; 38. Q—Q 1, B×P !; 39. Q—Q 7 ch, B—K 2; 40. Q—K 8 ch, K—B 3; 41. Q—R 8 ch, K—Kt 4; 42. P—R 4 ch, K—R 4; 43. P—Kt 4 ch, P×P; 44. Q—K 5 ch, P—Kt 4 !! and Black wins.

Position after White's 30th move.

30. ......   R×Kt !
31. P×P

If 31. P×R, B×P ch ; 32. K—B 1, Kt—B 5; 33. Q×P (or 33. Q—Q 2, Q—B 5 ch ; 34. K—K 1, P—K 6 ! and wins), Q—B 5 ch ; 34. K—K 1, Kt×P ch ; 35. K—Q 2, B—K 6 ch and Black wins.

White, who does not perceive the hidden point of the sacrifice, hopes to save himself by the text-move.

31. ......   Kt—B 5 !
32. P×Kt

Evidently forced.

32. ......   Q—B 5 !!

Winning at least a piece ; but White chooses the speediest death.

33. Q×Q   R×R ch
34. Q—B 1   B—Q 5 ch

and mates next move.

GAME 82

RUY LOPEZ

White :   *Black :*
Dr. S. Tarrasch.   A. Alekhin.

1. P—K 4   P—K 4
2. Kt—K B 3   Kt—Q B 3
3. B—Kt 5   P—K Kt 3

Pillsbury's favourite defence, with which he opened at the Hastings Tournament and gained several fine wins; but modern theory not unreasonably considers it inferior.

If I adopted it in the present game, doubtless for the last time, it was solely to verify in practice a variation indicated by Rubinstein in Collijn's *Lärobok*, and then, should White play 4. Kt—B 3 to try out the new move 4. ....Kt—Q 5 !, which seems to give Black complete equality: 5. Kt×P ?, Q—Kt 4.; or 5. Kt×Kt, P×Kt; 6. Kt—K 2 ?, Q—Kt 4 !; 7. Kt×P, B—Kt 2; 8. P—Q 3, Q—Q B 4 ! and Black wins a piece.

4. P—Q 4 !   Kt×P

If 4. ....P×P; 5. B—Kt 5, P—B 3; 6. B—K R 4 and White will recover his Pawn in a few moves, with a strong attacking position.

5. Kt×Kt   P×Kt
6. Q×P   Q—B 3

Position after Black's 6th move.

7. Q—Q 3

Without the slightest doubt the correct move here is 7. P—K 5, after which 7. .... Q—Kt 3 (recommended in the *Lärobok*)

would be quite bad, because of 8. Q×Q !, R P×Q ; 9. Kt—B 3, B—Kt 2 ; 10. B—K B 4 !, and Black would experience great difficulty in developing his Queen-side.

Likewise after 7. ....Q—K 2 White can lead into very interesting complications, which appear to result in his favour, *e.g.*: 8. Kt—B 3, P—Q B 3 (or 8. ....B—Kt 2 ; 9. Kt—Q 5 !, Q×P ch; 10. Q×Q, B×Q; 11. Castles, threatening 12. R—K 1, with a good attack for the Pawn) ; 9. Kt—K 4 !, B—Kt 2 ! (if 9. ....P×B, then 10. Kt—Q 6 ch, K—Q 1; 11. B—K 3 [threatening mate in two by Q—Kt 6 ch !], 11. ....Q—K 3 ; 12. Castles K R and White has a winning attack) ; 10. Kt—Q 6 ch, K—B 1; 11. B—K B 4, P×B (or 11. ....P—B 3 ; 12. Kt×B, R×Kt ; 13. P—K 6 !, Q×P ch ; 14. B—K 2, and White recovers the Pawn sacrificed with an obvious advantage in position); 12. Castles K R, Kt—R 3; 13. B×Kt !, B×B ; 14. P—B 4, B—Kt 2; 15. Q R—K 1, with an overwhelming attack for White.

On the contrary, the move actually chosen by White does not occasion his opponent any difficulty, and even allows him shortly to seize the initiative.

7. ......   B—Kt 2
8. Kt—B 3   P—B 3
9. B—Q B 4   Kt—K 2
10. B—K 3

10. Castles was preferable, for after the text-move White will be compelled to protect his Q Kt P by withdrawing his Knight to Q 1, where it remains immobile.

10. ......   P—Q Kt 4 !
11. B—Kt 3   P—Q R 4

See Diagram.

12. P—Q R 4

12. P—Q R 3 was a little better, although in this case also the reply

Position after Black's 11th move.

12. ....B—Q R 3 would have forced the disadvantageous retreat of White's Knight, *e.g.*:
12. ....B—Q R 3; 13. Kt—Q 1, Castles K R !; 14. Castles K R (if 14. Q×P, K R—Q 1; 15. Q—Kt 4, P—R 5; 16. B—R 2, P—Kt 5; 17. P×P, P—R 6; 18. P—B 3, P×P; 19. R—Q Kt 1, Q×P ch !; 20. Kt×Q, B×Kt ch; 21. B—Q 2, R×B and wins), 14. ....P—Q 4 ! with by far the superior game for Black.

The text-move results in the complete blockade of White's Queenside, which is strategically equivalent to the loss of the game.

Nevertheless, the tactical realization of victory is fraught with very serious difficulties, owing to the consummate skill with which Dr. Tarrasch defends himself.

| 12. ...... | P—Kt 5 |
| 13. Kt—Q 1 | |

Compulsory in order to protect the Q Kt P. However, the immobility of this Knight on a square on which it prevents communication between the White Rooks will soon have fatal consequences for White.

| 13. ...... | Castles |
| 14. Castles | P—Q 4 ! |

Much stronger than 14. ....B—Q R 3; 15. B—Q B 4, B×B; 16. Q×B, P—Q 4, after which White could still have avoided the decisive opening of the Q B file, by playing 17. Q—Q 3.

15. P×P	B—Q R 3
16. B—Q B 4	B×B
17. Q×B	P×P
18. Q—Q 3	P—Q 5 !

Opposing 19. P—Q B 3 and initiating an attack difficult to meet against the weak Q B P.

| 19. B—Q 2 | Q R—B 1 |
| 20. K R—K 1 | |

Temporarily preventing 20. ....Q—B 4.

| 20. ...... | R—B 2 |
| 21. P—Q Kt 3 | |

White hopes to free his unfortunate Knight and afterwards post it on Q B 4, but, as will be seen later on, Black will not leave him time for this.

| 21. ...... | K R—B 1 |
| 22. R—Q B 1 | |

Position after White's 22nd move.

22. ...... Q—B 4!

This move, which White could not escape, at once settles the fate of the backward Pawn. Obviously White cannot exchange Queens without losing the Pawn subsequently.

On the other hand, the interposition of the White Rook at K 4 will favour the successful entry of Black's Knight at Q B 6, thereby forcing the exchange of White's Q B, his best defensive piece.

23. R—K 4   Kt—Q 4
24. Kt—Kt 2   Kt—B 6
25. B × Kt

Forced, for if 25. R—K 1, Q × Q; 26. Kt × Q, Kt—R 7, winning the Pawn; or 26. P × Q, Kt—K 7 ch.

25. ......   R × B
26. Q—K 2   B—R 3!

The final point of the attack against White's Q B P, initiated by 14. ....P—Q 4!

27. P—Kt 4

A desperate counter-attack, the refutation of which leads to very interesting positions.

27. ......   Q—B 3
28. R—K 8 ch   R × R
29. Q × R ch   K—Kt 2
30. R—B 1   R × B P

At last!

31. Kt—Q 3
    See Diagram.

31. ......   Q—B 6!

This move, which is no doubt the most difficult in the whole game, is based on the following considerations:

White threatens to consolidate his position by 32. Q—K 4 and 33.

Position after White's 31st move.

P—B 4, after which the win would be very difficult for Black, because of the unfavourable position of his K B.

On the other hand, the possible end-game resulting from 31. .... Q—K 3; 32. Q × Q, P × Q; 33. R—Q 1! is not without resources for White, *e.g.*: 33. ....K—B 3; 34. P—B 4, P—Kt 4; 35. P—R 4!

Therefore 32. Q—K 4 or 32. P—B 4 must be prevented.

The text-move alone answers this end.

32. Kt—K 5

The capture of the Q P by 32. Q—K 5 ch, K—Kt 1; 33. Q × Q P would have facilitated Black's victory, *e.g.*: 33. ....R—Q 7; 34. Kt—K 5 (or 34. Q—Q 8 ch, B—B 1; 35. Kt—K 5, Q—B 5!; 36. Q—Kt 8, K—Kt 2, followed by 37. ....B—Q 3 and Black wins), 34. ....Q × P; 35. Q—R 7; Q—Q 4, followed by 37. ....P—Kt 6, and wins.

32. ......   Q—Q 4
33. Kt—Q 7

Now White threatens mate on the move!

33. ....   Q—Q 3
34. R—Q

Preventing the advance of the Q P, and threatening 35. R×P! But Black's next move puts things in their proper place.

Position after White's 34th move.

34. ......   B—K 6!

White is compelled to bring his Rook back again to its starting point, for if 35. P×B, Q×P ch and mates next move; or if 35. Q×B, P×Q; 36. R×Q, P—K 7 and wins.

35. R—K B 1   B—Kt 4

Threatening now 36. ....B—K 2 followed by 37. ....P—Q 6, which threat forces the exchange of Queens.

36. Q—K 5 ch   Q×Q
37. Kt×Q   B—B 5

The ensuing end-game is undoubtedly won for Black, but it still requires very precise tactics.

38. Kt—B 4   P—Q 6
39. R—Q 1   R—B 6!

Not 39. ....P—Q 7, which would appreciably diminish the strength of the passed Q P, after 40. K—B 1.

40. Kt×P   K—B 3!

It is much more interesting to bring the King to the centre of the board without delay, rather than to recover the lost Pawn by 40. .... B—B 2. Moreover, White cannot protect his Q Kt P for ever.

41. P—R 4   K—K 4
42. K—Kt 2   K—Q 5
43. K—B 3   B—B 2
44. Kt—B 4   R×P
45. Kt—K 3   R—B 6
46. R—Q Kt 1   B—R 4
47. Kt—Q 1   R—R 6
48. Kt—K 3   R×P
49. P—Kt 5   R—R 6
50. R—Kt 1   P—Kt 6
51. R—Kt 4 ch   K—B 4
52. R—B 4 ch   K—Kt 4
53. R—B 8   R—R 8!

Avoiding White's last trap, 53. ....P—Kt 7; 54. R—Kt 8 ch, B—Kt 3; 55. R×B ch, followed by 56. Kt—B 4 ch and 57. Kt×R.

54. R—Kt 8 ch   B—Kt 3!

If now 55. Kt—Q 5, then simply 55. ....P—Q 7!, etc.

White resigns.

GAME 83

QUEEN'S GAMBIT DECLINED

White :   *Black :*
A. ALEKHIN.   G. MARÓCZY.

1. P—Q 4   Kt—K B 3
2. P—Q B 4   P—K 3
3. Kt—K B 3   P—Q 4
4. Kt—B 3   B—K 2
5. B—Kt 5   Castles
6. P—K 3   Kt—K 5

A defence practised on several occasions by Dr. Em. Lasker, and subsequently by Capablanca, in their respective matches with Marshall.

It is doubtless no worse than other defences, and has the advantage of simplifying the game, without creating weaknesses in Black's camp.

In the London Tournament of 1922 Maróczy tried against me 6. ....P—B 4, recommended by Rubinstein in Collijn's *Lärobok*, and obtained a very inferior game. Here is the instructive continuation of the game.

6. ....P—B 4; 7. B P×P, K P×P; 8. P×P, B—K 3; 9. B—Kt 5!, B×P; 10. Castles, Kt—B 3; 11. R—B 1, B—K 2; 12. B×Q Kt !, P×B; 13. Kt—Q R 4, R—B 1; 14. Kt—Q 4, B—Q 2; 15. B×Kt !, B×B; 16. Kt—Q B 5, B—K 1; 17. Q—Kt 4, R—Kt 1; 18. P—Q Kt 3, P—Kt 3; 19. R—B 2, Q—Q 3; 20. K R—B 1, B—K 4; 21. Kt—B 3 !, B—Kt 2; 22. Q—Q R 4, Q—K 2; 23. Kt—Q 4, R—Kt 3; 24. P—K R 3, B—K 4; 25. Kt—Q 3 !, B×Kt ; 26. P×B, R—Kt 2; 27. R—K 1, Q—Kt 4 and by 28. R—K 5 White could have easily maintained a winning advantage in position.

7. B×B   Q×B
8. Q—Kt 3

In order to avoid the variation 8. P×P, Kt×Kt ; 9. P×Kt, P×P; 10. Q—Kt 3, R—Q 1; 11. P—B 4, Kt—B 3 !, which seems to yield Black equality.

But with this idea 8. Q—B 2 is certainly preferable, for after the text-move Black need not have captured the Knight, and could first have played 7. ....P—Q B 3, and continued by 8. ....P—K B 4, etc.

8. ......   Kt×Kt
9. Q×Kt   P—Q B 3

At New York, 1924, in an identical position, Maróczy played against me 9. ....P—Q B 4, but after 10. B P×P, B P×P ; 11. Kt×P, White has an evident advantage owing to the weakness of Black's Q P and control of the open Q B file.

10. B—Q 3   Kt—Q 2
11. Castles K R P—K B 4

The "Stonewall" formation is here quite without value, for even supposing that Black's Q Kt were to occupy the square K 5, it could be dislodged by P—K B 3, or else exchanged against White's K B. On the other hand, the square K 5 will furnish White with an impregnable position for his K Kt, Black's Q B being of a different colour from that of the square mentioned.

12. Q R—B 1 !

Anticipating the manœuvre 12. ....Kt—B 3 followed by 13. ....Kt—K 5, to which he would have replied 13. Kt—K 5, White seizes his moment's respite to complete his development.

12. ......   P—K Kt 4

But this attack, quite astonishing from a master of Maróczy's reputation, hopelessly compromises the already insecure position of the Black King.

13. Kt—Q 2 !   R—B 2

As inexplicable as the previous move. Comparatively better was 13. ....Kt—B 3 followed by 14. ....B—Q 2, etc.

14. P—B 3   P—K 4

In the hope of forcing exchange of Queens on the 18th move, but without sufficiently appreciating the reply 19. Q—B 7 !, although in any case the game was lost for Black.

15. B P × P	B P × P	4. B—Kt 5	Kt—Q 5
16. P—K 4 !	B P × P	5. Kt × Kt	P × Kt
17. B P × P	R × R ch	6. Kt—Q 5	
18. R × R	K P × P		

Still reckoning on 19. Q × P, Q—B 4, etc. But White's next move shatters this last illusion.

Position after Black's 18th move.

19. Q—B 7 !

Paralysing in a single move all the Black pieces, after which Black's position becomes hopeless.

19.	K—Kt 2
20. R—B 5 !	P × P
21. Kt × P	Q—Kt 5

Surrendering to the inevitable. If 21. ....P—K R 3 White wins easily by 22. P—R 3, followed by 23. K—R 2 and 24. Kt—Q 6.

22. R × P ch   Black resigns.

GAME 84

FOUR KNIGHTS' GAME

White: H. WOLF.   *Black:* A. ALEKHIN.

1. P—K 4	P—K 4
2. Kt—K B 3	Kt—Q B 3
3. Kt—B 3	Kt—B 3

This move, introduced by Selesnieff in his game against Spielmann in the Pistyan Tournament of 1922, does not achieve its object, namely, an easy draw, as the present game shows.

Best here is 6. P—K 5, P × Kt ; 7. P × Kt, Q × P ; 8. Q P × P, B—K 2 ; 9. Castles, Castles ; 10. Q—Q 4 with a satisfactory game for White.

6.	Kt × Kt
7. P × Kt	Q—B 3 !

Avoiding the exchange of Queens, which White could have forced after 7. ....B—K 2 ; 8. Q—Kt 4, B—B 3 ; 9. Q—K 4 ch.

8. Castles	B—K 2
9. P—K B 4	

White is not sufficiently developed to be able to anticipate a lasting initiative which could alone justify this advance.

He would have been better advised to recognize the inadequacy of his 6th move, namely to play 9. B—K 2, followed by 10. P—Q B 4 and 11. P—Q 3, with approximate equality.

9.	Castles
10. Q—B 3	P—B 4 !

Definitely securing the position of his Q P, which would have been troublesome had he at once played 10. ....P—Q 3.

11. P—Q Kt 3

Preparing the fianchetto development of the Q B, so as not to restrict the action of his K B attendant upon 11. P—Q 3 or 11. P—B 4.

11.	P—Q 3
12. B—Kt 2	B—B 4
13. Q R—K 1	

Upon 13. B—Q 3 Black would have retained his slight advantage in position by 13. ....Q—Kt 3!

13.	B—Q 1!

In order to post this Bishop on Q R 4, an especially favourable position as White cannot screen his Q P from its attack, because of the unfavourable position of his K B.

14. B—Q 3	B—R 4
15. R—K 2	Q R—K 1
16. P—Kt 3	

White could still have avoided immediate material loss by playing 16. B—B 1, but in any event his game remained obviously inferior.

Position after White's 16th move.

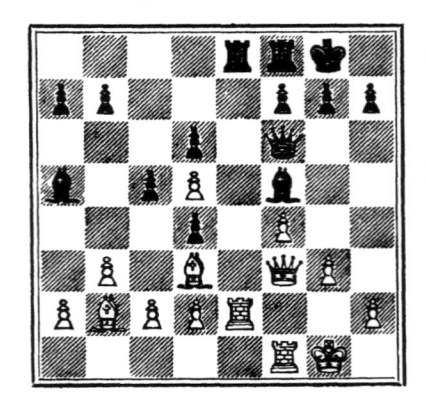

16.	B×B!

This exchange secures Black a decisive advantage in position, White being unable to recapture with the Queen on account of 17. ....R×R ; 18. Q×R, P—Q 6! and Black wins a piece; nor 17. R×R, B×R; 18. R×R ch, K×R; 19. K×B, B×P with an easy win.

17. P×B	R×R
18. Q×R	Q—B 4
19. R—B 2	

The end-game a Pawn to the bad resulting from 19. Q—K 4, Q×Q; 20. P×Q, B×P would not afford White any drawing chances.

19.	Q×P (Q 4)
20. Q—K 4	Q—K 3!

Preventing undoubling of the adverse Pawns, which would have allowed White's Q B sooner or later to join in the defence.

21. P—B 5

If 21. Q×P, then 21. ....B×P! and wins.

21.	Q—K 4!
22. Q×Q!	

The best alternative. After the exchange, the absence of open lines for Black's Rook and the advantageous position of White's King will occasion Black not a few technical difficulties, even though White's Q B remains imprisoned.

22.	P×Q
23. K—Kt 2	P—B 3
24. K—B 3	B—Q 1!

The Bishop has played its part at Q R 4, and it is important to barricade the Queen-side with Pawns promptly, in order to deprive White's Q B of all hopes of escape.

25. K—K 4	B—K 2
26. R—B 1	

After 26. K—Q 5, R—Q 1 ch; 27. K—B 4 (if 27. K—K 6, K—B 1! and mates next move), P—Q R 3; 28. P—Q R 4, K—B 2, Black would have penetrated the hostile position on the King-side still more easily than in the actual game, White's King being doomed to inactivity.

26. ...... R—Q 1
27. R—B 1 P—Q R 4 !

Not 27. P—Kt 3 because of 28. Q Kt 4 !

28. B—R 3 P—Q Kt 3
29. P—K Kt 4

In his turn hoping to block the King-side, after which the draw would be forced ; but Black at once prevents this.

29. ...... K—B 2
30. P—R 4 P—Kt 3
31. R—B 1

Or 31. P—R 5, P×R P ; 32. P×P, R—K Kt 1 ! ; 33. K—Q 5, R—Kt 6 ; 34. K—B 6, R×P ; 35. K×P, R×Q P ; 36. B×P, P—K 5, and Black's passed Pawns win easily.

Position after White's 31st move.

31. ...... P—R 4 !

Compelling the White King to relinquish its dominating position, and consequently to abandon the passive resistance upon which White had built his hopes.

32. P×P ch

Or 32. P—Kt 5. P×P ; 33. P×P, B×P ; 34. P×P ch, K×P ; 35. K×P, P—K R 5 and wins.

32. ...... K×P
33. P×P ch K—B 2 !

The point ! After 33. ....K×P ; 34. K—B 5, a win for Black would be very difficult, if not impossible.

34. P—R 6

Or 34. K—B 5, R—K R 1 ; 35. K—Kt 4, K—K 3.

34. ...... K—K 3 !
35. R—K Kt 1 R—K R 1
36. R—Kt 6 B—B 1
White resigns.

GAME 85

QUEEN'S GAMBIT DECLINED

White : *Black :*
A. ALEKHIN. O. CHAJES.

1. P—Q 4 Kt—K B 3
2. P—Q B 4 P—K 3
3. Kt—K B 3 P—Q 4
4. Kt—B 3 Q Kt—Q 2

After this move White, apart from the text-move (5. B—Kt 5), could very well have replied 5. P×P, P×P ; 6. B—B 4 !, etc., with an excellent position. This is the reason why 4. ....B—K 2 is considered better.

5. B—Kt 5 B—K 2

After 5. ....P—B 3 ; 6. P—K 3, Q—R 4 ; 7. Kt—Q 2, B—Kt 5 ; 8. Q—B 2, Castles, White, should he wish to avoid the variation played in the game Grünfeld — Bogoljuboff (Mährisch-Ostrau, 1923), namely, 9. B—K 2, P—K 4 ! ; 10. P×P, Kt—K 5 !, could continue simply 9. B×Kt, Kt×B ; 10. B—Q 3, R—Q 1 ; 11. Castles K R, with a slight advantage in position, as played by Johner against Dr. Tarrasch at Trieste, 1923.

6. P—K 3	Castles
7. R—B 1	P—B 3
8. Q—B 2	P—Q R 3 !
9. P—Q R 3	R—K 1
10. P—R 3	

In order to avoid the loss of a move by 10. B—Q 3, which would have transposed into a position in the game Grünfeld—Alekhin which is perfectly safe for Black (see Game No. 81) after 10. ....P—R 3 ; 11. B—R 4.

Position after White's 10th move.

10.	P—Kt 4

A very interesting idea which may actually have some future for it. But its tactical realization here lacks precision. It is on the 9th move before 10. P—K R 3, if such was his intention, that Black should have played 9. ....P—Kt 4, for in that case he could have answered 10. P—B 5 by 10. .... P—K 4 ; 11. P×P, Kt—Kt 5, with a very promising game.

On the other hand, should White, instead of 11. P×K P, open the Q B P file by 11. P×Q P or 11. P× Kt P, this would ultimately turn in Black's favour, White having to lose two moves to bring his King into safety.

This example emphasizes once again the numerous resources afforded by the defence 8. ....P— Q R 3 ! in this variation.

11. P—B 5 !

Whereas now Black will not succeed in breaking through in the centre, and the weakness of his Q B P will make itself felt sooner or later. It is, however, without immediate consequences, on account of the blocked position of the two adversaries and the difficulties experienced by White in penetrating the hostile lines.

11.	Kt—R 4
12. B—K B 4 !	

The only logical reply. White must at all cost retain control of the square K 5.

12.	Kt×B
13. P×Kt	P—Q R 4
14. B—Q 3	P—Kt 3 !

The best line of defence. Black guards against the possibility of P— B 5 and prepares a solid defensive position.

15. P—K R 4 !

Not with the illusion of a mating attack, but simply to secure at the right moment, the opening of the K R file which will later on become a winning factor for White.

15.	B—B 3
16. P—R 5	Kt—B 1
17. P—K Kt 3	

Quietly strengthening a position which Black can scarcely modify appreciably.

17.	R—R 2
18. Kt—Q 1 !	

Threatening to post this Knight on K Kt 4. Black's next move is intended to prepare the double advance of the K B P and thus to shut out White's Knight from the coveted square.

18. ......   B—K Kt 2
19. Kt—K 3   P—B 4

If this move has the advantage of further strengthening the Castled position, it does on the other hand leave Black with indifferent chances for the end-game.

20. Q—K 2 !

Preparing to occupy the square K 5 with a White piece.

Position after White's 20th move.

20. ......   P—R 5

This is the only move of Black's in the game which can be criticized, seeing that without apparent reason it abandons the square Q Kt 4 to the adverse Knights.
If Black had not modified the Pawn-position, White's right plan would have been Kt—B 2, K—B 1, Q Kt—K 1, B—Kt 1, Kt—Q 3 and Kt (Q 3)—K 5.

21. Kt—B 2

Now this Knight can at need be brought to K 5 via Q Kt 4 and Q 3, saving time.

21. ......   R (R 2)—K 2
22. K—B 1

In order to render innocuous the threat ....B—Q 2 followed by ....B × P ! and ....P—K 4, should White play, *e.g.*: 22. Kt—Kt 4, Q—B 2.

22. ......   B—B 3
23. Kt—K 5

This move to be sure compromises nothing, but the logical continuation was 23. Kt—Kt 4, followed by B—Kt 1, Kt—Q 3 and Kt (Q 3)—K 5.
Had Black made the correct reply White would have been forced to return to this plan.

23. ......   B × Kt

Better was 23. ....Q—B 2 ! followed by 24. ....B × Kt, forcing White either to recapture the Bishop with the Queen, which would have led to an exchange of Queens, or else to recapture it with one of the Pawns ; in both cases his chances of winning would have been reduced to vanishing point.
In these circumstances White would have withdrawn his Knight to K B 3, intending to carry out in perfect safety the manœuvre sketched above.

24. Q × B

This exchange, provoking the weakening of the Black squares in the hostile position, yields White new winning chances.

24. ......   Q—B 2
25. Q—B 6 !

An excellent manœuvre intended to create a new weakness at the adversary's K R 2.

| 25. | ...... | R—B 2 |
| 26. | Q—R 4 | Q—K 2 |

Position after Black's 26th move.

Position after Black's 32nd move.

27. P×P!

The right moment for this exchange has come at last, for Black cannot recapture with the Pawn, which would allow him to oppose his Rooks on the K R file.

Now White has a strategic advantage sufficient for victory, but its tactical realization is far from easy.

| 27. | ...... | Kt×P |
| 28. | Q—R 5! | |

White must avoid every exchange which would simplify Black's defence.

| 28. | ...... | Q—B 3 |
| 29. | B—K 2 | |

White's following moves are intended to reduce to a minimum the mobility of the Black pieces, in order to undertake a long range manœuvre with his King.

29.	......	R—K Kt 2
30.	Q—B 3	Kt—B 1
31.	Q—K 3	R (K 1)—K 2
32.	Kt—Kt 4	B—Q 2

33. B—R 5!

This move leads to a curious position in which Black's Queen, both Rooks and the Bishop are immobilized.

The problem still requires to be solved, for at present the doubling and even the trebling of the White pieces on the K R file would lead to nothing.

The rather complicated plan which White will strive to pursue, which must, of course, be modified in accordance with his adversary's manœuvres, can be summarized as follows:

1st phase.—Bringing the King to the centre where, after the subsequent exchange of Queens and Rooks on the K R file, it will threaten a rapid penetration of the hostile camp via Q R 5.

These tactics will logically induce a corresponding displacement of the Black King, the more plausible since its presence in the centre will consolidate the weak points Q B 3 and K 3.

2nd phase.—Compelling the Black pieces to remove themselves in succession from the King-side, by the tactical threats aimed either at the King himself or at the adverse Pawns (39th and 41st moves).

The prospect of the occupation of the square K 5 by a White Knight, thereby immobilizing the Black Knight at Q 2, increases still more the difficulty of concerted action by the Black pieces, which is already difficult enough on account of the limited space available to them.

3rd phase.—Finally, at an opportune moment, namely, when the Black pieces are at their greatest distance from the King-side, doubling the Rooks on the K R file. The Rooks, after the forced exchange of Queens and Bishops, will penetrate into the heart of the hostile position.

As we shall see by the sequel, the execution of this strategic plan requires not less than twenty-eight moves !

| 33. | ...... | Kt—Kt 3 |
| 34. | Kt—Q 3 | |

Not at once 34. K—K 2, on account of 34. ....P—K 4 !

34.	......	B—K 1
35.	K—K 2	K—B 1
36.	K—Q 2	R—Kt 2

Making way for the King.

37.	B—B 3	K—K 2
38.	K R—K 1	Kt—B 1
39.	Kt—Kt 4	

Threatening 40. B×P, etc.

39.	......	K—Q 1
40.	K—Q 3	R (K Kt 2)—K 2
41.	Q—Q 2 !	

Threatening, after 42. Kt—R 6 !, the entry of the Queen at Q R 5.

| 41. | ...... | R—R 2 |
| 42. | R—K R 1 | R (K 2)—Q B 2 |

In order to utilize the Bishop for the defence of the K R P when the Knight abandons it to guard the square K 4.

| 43. | R—R 2 | B—Kt 3 |
| 44. | Q—K 3 | K—B 1 |

Black, in order to make his Rooks available for the defence of the King-side, proposes to defend his Q B P with his King, but this manœuvre demands far too much time, and White is now ready for the assault.

45.	Q R—K R 1	K—Kt 2
46.	K—Q 2	R—K 2
47.	Kt—Q 3	Kt—Q 2
48.	B—R 5 !	

By this exchange of Black's best piece for the defence of his weak points, White takes an important step forward.

| 48. | ...... | R—R 1 |
| 49. | B×B | P×B |

After 49. ....Q×B his K R P would later on prove difficult to defend.

| 50. | R—R 7 | R (R 1)—K 1 |

For the moment Black's defence is still adequate, but White's next move discloses the difficulties of the hostile position.

Position after Black's 50th move.

51. Kt—K 5 !

The point of this move rests in the fact that for the first time in this game White can profitably consider the *recapture at K 5 with a Pawn*.

In fact, if 51. ....Kt×Kt ; 52. B P×Kt, Q—B 1 ; 53. Q—Kt 5 ! and White wins the K Kt P to start with.

Black's reply is therefore forced.

51. ......   Kt—B 1
52. R—R 8 !

Now the position demands exchange of Queens and not of Rooks.

52. ......   R—Kt 2
53. Kt—B 3 !   R—Q Kt 1

To secure freedom of movement for the Knight, in case of need.

54. Kt—Kt 5   R—K 2

Black is defenceless against White's next move.

55. Q—K 5 !

After the compulsory exchange of Queens, the doubling of the Rooks on the eighth rank will be decisive.

55. ......   Q×Q
56. B P×Q   K—R 1
57. R—Kt 8   P—Kt 5

In the hope of obtaining some last chance after R P×P, R (K 2)—Kt 2.

58. R (R 1)—R 8 ! R (K 2)—K 1
59. P×P   K—R 2
60. K—B 3   K—R 3
61. Kt—B 7 !

More energetic than the plausible move 60. Kt×P. White now goes straight for mate.

61. ......   R—R 1
62. Kt—Q 6   R (K 1)—Kt 1
63. R—R 1 !   Kt—Q 2
64. R—R 1 ! !   Black resigns.

Final Position.

GAME 86

QUEEN'S PAWN GAME

White :   *Black :*
A. ALEKHIN.   SIR G. A. THOMAS.

1. P—Q 4   Kt—K B 3
2. P—Q B 4   P—Q 3
3. Kt—K B 3   P—K Kt 3

This old defence is at present very fashionable in England. The two English champions, F. D. Yates and Sir George Thomas, have shown a predilection for it, justified by numerous successes.

4. P—K Kt 3   B—Kt 2
5. B—Kt 2   Castles
6. Castles   Kt—B 3

This move, suggested by Burn in place of 6. ....Q Kt—Q 2, adopted up till then, is aimed at forcing White to disclose his intentions in the centre as soon as possible.

Nevertheless, it does not seem sufficient to equalize.

7. P—Q 5

The most energetic and also the best continuation.

The defeat inflicted on me by Yates, in particularly sparkling style, during a previous round of the same tournament, did not in the least shake my opinion as to the value of this move, seeing that I lost an advantage in position which had been already acquired, solely on account of several tactical errors.

| 7. | ...... | Kt—Kt 1 |
| 8. | Kt—B 3 | P—K 4 |

This apparently plausible move is certainly not best, for it allows White to open up the game by an exchange in the centre, and thus to profit by his superior development.

More in accordance with the spirit of the opening was 8. .... P—Q R 4, followed by 9. .... Q Kt—Q 2 or Kt—R 3 and 10. .. Kt—B 4, as played by Yates in an analogous position in the game cited.

9. P × P e. p.!

This frees Black's game only in appearance, for if he retakes with the Bishop, White replies 10. Kt—Q 4! with marked advantage; and if he retakes with the Pawn he will sooner or later be forced to play P—K 4, to free his Q B, which will weaken the square Q 4 and will give White distinct chances in the centre and on the Queen's wing.

| 9. | ...... | P × P |
| 10. | B—Kt 5 | |

In order to exchange Bishops by 11. Q—Q 2 and B—R 6, or else to provoke the reply 10. ....P—K R 3. In both cases the position of Black's King is weakened.

10.	......	Kt—B 3
11.	Q—Q 2	Q—K 1
12.	Q R—Q 1	

In order to meet 12. ....B—Q 2 with 13. P—B 5!

12.	......	R—Kt 1
13.	B—R 6	Q—B 2
14.	B × B	Q × B

Position after Black's 14th move.

15. Kt—K Kt 5!

A very strong position for this Knight, which cannot be dislodged without compromising the position of Black's King.

In addition, this move will be the prelude to an offensive in the centre, commencing with P—K B 4, which will bring about a contact of the Pawns, Black's reply P—K 4 being practically forced.

| 15. | ...... | P—K 4 |
| 16. | Kt—Q 5 | Kt—Q 5 |

In order to provoke P—K 3 and thus to develop his Q B with the gain of a move.

| 17. | P—K 3 | Kt—B 3 |

After 17. ....Kt—K 3 the reply 18. P—B 4! would have been still stronger, e.g.: 17. ....Kt—K 3; 18. P—B 4!, Kt × Kt (Kt 4); 19. P × Kt, Kt × Kt; 20. B × Kt ch, K—R 1; 21. R × R ch, Q × R; 22. R—K B 1 and White has a winning position.

18.	P—B 4!	B—Kt 5
19.	Q R—K 1	Q R—K 1
20.	P—Q Kt 4!	

With the object of dislodging the adverse Q Kt, in order to give White's K B its maximum efficiency.

230 MY BEST GAMES OF CHESS

| 20. ...... | P—K R 3 |

To defend his Queen-side successfully Black has nothing better than to expel the White pieces from their threatening positions.

21. Kt×Kt ch	R×Kt
22. Kt—K 4	R (B 3)—B 1
23. P—Kt 5	Kt—Q 1
24. P—B 5 !	

Much better than attempting to win a Pawn by 25. Q—R 5, which would have yielded Black sufficient counter-chances, e.g.: 24. .....P×P; 25. Kt P×P, B—B 4 ; 26. Kt —B 2, B—K 3 !

24.	Q P×P
25. Kt×P	B—B 1
26. P—Q R 4	

White now exercises strong pressure on the Queen-side, for which Black has no compensation.

Nevertheless, had he on the next move played 26. ....K—R 2 he would have propounded a problem of great difficulty for his opponent, whereas against his actual reply White can undertake a forcible offensive.

| 26. ...... | P—B 3 |
| 27. Q—Q 6 ! | |

This entry of White's Queen is very dangerous. White now threatens 28. Q—Kt 8 !

| 27. ...... | P—Kt 3 |
| 28. Kt—K 4 ! | K P×P |

There is no longer any good move. 28. ....B P×P or 28. ....P—B 4, indicated by many annotators with surprising unanimity, would lead to an immeditae catastrophe after 29. P×K P ! threatening 30. Kt—B 6 ch.

29. P×Q B P !

This Pawn, defended by the K B, will decide the game in White's favour.

| 29. ...... | R—K 3 |
| 30. Q—Q 5 | |

Threatening 31. B—R 3.

| 30. ...... | K—R 2 |

Position after Black's 30th move.

31. Kt—Q 6 !

The winning move, of which the consequences, in the leading variation, had to be analysed twelve and fifteen moves ahead.

| 31. ...... | B—R 3 ! |

The reply creating most difficulty for White.

If 31. ....Q—Q B 2, then simply 32. R—Q 1 ! retaining the passed Pawn, with a winning position.

| 32. R×P | R×R |
| 33. Kt P×R | |

See Diagram.

| 33. ...... | Q—K 2 |

As in Game No. 66, my opponent facilitated my task, and rendered superfluous my detailed analysis, which had taken more than half-an-hour.

The principal variation considered by me was the following :

33. ....Q—B 6 !; 34. R—Q 1 !, R×P ! (if 34. ....Q×P ch ; 35.

Position after White's 33rd move.

Kt—K 4 !, R—B 8 ch ; 38. K—B 2, Kt × P ; 39. R—Q 7 ch, K—Kt 1 !; 40. Kt—B 6 ch, K—B 1 ; 41. B—Q 5, Kt—K 2 ; 42. R—Q 8 ch, K—Kt 2 ; 43. Kt—K 8 ch, K—R 2 ; 44. R—Q 7, R—B 7 ch ; 45. K—B 3, R—K 7 ; 46. B—K 4 and White wins a piece and the game.

34. R—Q 1	R × P
35. Kt—K 4 !	Kt—K 3
36. Q—K 5 !	

Winning at least the Exchange.

36.	R—Q 6
37. R × R	B × R
38. Kt—B 6 ch	K—R 1
39. Kt—Q 5 ch	Q—Kt 2
40. Q × Kt	Black resigns.

K—R 1 and wins) ; 35. Q—Q 2 !, Q × Q (if 35. ....Q—B 4 ; 36. Q—K B 2) ; 36. R × Q, R—Q B 6 ; 37.

CHAPTER XXII

MAJOR OPEN TOURNAMENT AT PORTSMOUTH
AUGUST, 1923

GAME 87

QUEEN'S GAMBIT DECLINED

White :	Black :
A. ALEKHIN.	DR. A. VAJDA.
1. P—Q 4	Kt—K B 3
2. P—Q B 4	P—K 3
3. Kt—K B 3	P—Q 4
4. Kt—B 3	B—K 2
5. B—Kt 5	Q Kt—Q 2
6. P—K 3	Castles
7. R—B 1	P—B 3
8. B—Q 3	P×P
9. B×P	Kt—Q 4
10. Kt—K 4	

10. B×B, Q×B ; 11. Castles does not yield White any advantage and also 10. B—B 4, tried by me against Selesnieff in the Pistyan Tournament of 1922 (see Game No. 54) is scarcely any better ; I therefore hoped to secure an advantage with the text-move.

But although in the present game the result was favourable to me, because of the tame reply of my opponent, later analysis has convinced me that 10. Kt—K 4 allows Black sufficient chances.

10. ...... P—K R 3

After this move White, without running any risks, attains his object, which is to conserve at least temporarily three minor pieces, an important consideration on account of his opponent's cramped position.

The correct continuation was : 10. ....Q—R 4 ch ; 11. K—B 1 ! (if 11. K—K 2 the ensuing variation is even stronger), 11. ....P—B 3 !; 12. B—R 4, Kt (Q 2)—Kt 3 ; 13. B—Kt 3, Kt—Kt 5 ! and Black has the initiative.

This is the reason why 10. Kt—K 4 is hardly commendable. It is, however, playable after 10. B×B, Q×B (not 10. ....Kt×Kt ; 11. B×Q, Kt×Q ; 12. B—K 7, R—K 1 ; 13. B—R 3 and wins); 11. Kt—K 4, Q—Kt 5 ch ; 12. Q—Q 2, Q×Q ch ; 13. K×Q, and White's game is, of course, preferable. (Compare Alekhin—Treybal, Baden-Baden, 1925).

It cannot be denied, however, that the exchange of Queens in this variation increases Black's chances of drawing.

11. B×B	Q×B
12. Castles	P—Q Kt 3
13. Kt—Kt 3	

Preparing P—K 4 later on.

13. ...... R—Q 1

Position after Black's 13th move.

14. B×Kt

Yielding to the influence of certain critics who have maintained that I seek complications "at all costs," to the detriment of clear and simple solutions, I was here the victim of deliberate simplification. But the exaggeration of this quality is not always favourable, for the advantage secured by White after the text-move, thanks to the control of the Q B file, would have been insufficient for victory against an absolutely correct defence.

On the contrary, the continuation 14. P—K 4, Kt (Q 4)—B 3 (or 14. ....Kt—B 5 ; 15. Q—Q 2) ; 15. R—K 1 threatening later P—Q 5, or also 15. P—K 5 followed by Kt—K 4—Q 6, would have afforded more favourable although less definite prospects than those in the actual game.

The choice between the two variations is above all a question of style and I ought to have dropped a half-point through not following my natural inclination on this occasion.

14.	B P×B
15. Q—R 4 !	

Preventing 15. ....B—R 3, and threatening 16. R—B 7, which would not have been effective on the 15th move because of 15. .... Q—Q 3.

15.	Kt—B 1
16. Kt—K 5	B—Kt 2
17. R—B 3	P—B 3

This slight weakening of the Castled position was inevitable, as the White Knight was in a dominating position on K 5 ; but Black's position is solid enough to stand this weakness.

18. Kt—Q 3	Q—Q 2

In order to oppose his Rooks on the open Q B file, which would enable him to equalize if accomplished without inconvenience.

19. Q—R 3	B—B 3
20. K R—B 1	K R—B 1
21. P—R 3 !	

Absolutely essential, as will be seen later.

21.	B—Kt 4
22. Kt—B 4	

Threatening to win the Q R P after all the Rooks are exchanged.

22.	P—Q R 4

It is curious that this plausible move leads to the inevitable loss of the game. 22. P—K 4 would also be bad, because of 23. Kt×P !, etc.

On the other hand, 22. ....R×R ; 23. Q×R, B—R 3 !, or 23. R×R, P—K 4, would have yielded Black a satisfactory defence, temporarily at least.

23. R×R !	R×R
24. R×R	Q×R
25. Q—Q 6 !	

The White Queen enters the adverse game with decisive effect.

Black is unable to dislodge it, his mobility being restricted by the necessity of defending his weak K P and Q Kt P.

25. ......   B—B 3

Or 25. ....Q—B 3 ; 26. Q—Q 8, etc.

Position after Black's 25th move.

26. Kt (Kt 3)—R 5 !

An unexpected mating-attack commencing 27. Kt×Kt P !, K×Kt ; 28. Q—K 7 ch, K moves ; 29. Kt—R 5 and wins.
As a direct result of this move the White Queen will occupy the square Q Kt 8, which his opponent will be compelled to yield to him ; and as an indirect result Black must advance his Q Kt P, which abandons the square Q B 5 to the White Knights.

26. ......   Q—Q 2
27. Q—Kt 8   P—Q Kt 4

If 27. ....Q—Kt 2, then 28. Q—Q 8, K—B 2 ; 29. P—K Kt 4 threatening 30. P—K R 4 and 31. P—Kt 5, with a strong attack.

28. P—Kt 4 !

Not at once 28. Kt—Q 3 because of the possible reply 28. ....Q—K 1.

28. ......   K—B 2
29. Kt—Q 3

Threatening to win a Pawn by 29. Kt—B 5, Q—K 2 ; 30. Q—Kt 6, etc.

29. ......   P—R 5
30. Kt—B 5   Q—K 2
31. Q—Kt 6   B—K 1

Black's pieces are clustered round his King like a flock of sheep round the ram before the tempest !

32. Kt—B 4 !

The second White Knight takes the same road as the first in order to enter the adverse position by the open breach on the Queen-side (Q B 5).

32. ......   P—Kt 4

A despairing manœuvre.

33. Kt (B 4)—Q 3   P—R 4
34. Kt—Kt 7   P×P
35. P×P   K—Kt 2
36. Kt (Q 3)—B 5 !

White reserves the option of winning a Pawn by Kt—Q 6, a threat which Black cannot evade and which is made still more definite by the text-move.

36. ......   P—K 4
37. Kt—Q 6   B—Kt 3
38. Kt×Kt P   Kt—Q 2
39. Q—B 7   B—K 1
40. Kt—Q 6   K—B 1
41. Kt—B 5   Q—R 2

Or 41. ....Q—B 2 ; 42. Q—Q 6 ch and 43. Kt—R 6 ch wins the Queen.

42. Kt—K 6 ch   K—B 2
43. Q—Q 8 !   Black resigns.

Final Position.

fear the variation ....Q—R 4 ch ; K—K 2 or B 1.

| 11. ...... | B×B |
| 12. Kt (B 3)×B | Kt (Q 2)—B 3 |

If 12. ....P—K B 4 ; 13. Q—R 5 !, P—K R 3 ; 14. Q—B 7 ch, K—R 1 ; 15. Kt—Q 6, R—K 2 ; 16. Kt×B P !

13. Kt—Kt 3 !

When possessing greater freedom of movement than the opponent—and this is the case for White here—*it is good strategy to retain the greatest possible number of pieces on the board, in order to reap the greatest profit from this freedom.*

13.	P—K R 3
14. Kt—B 3	Kt—Kt 3
15. B—Kt 3	Kt (Kt 3)—Q 2

Black wishes to enforce the move ....P—K 4 all the same, but, as we shall see, it is much too late !

In an exhibition game played at Paris in February, 1922, Znosko-Borovski adopted 15. ....B—Q 2 against me, but also without satisfactory results.

Here is the continuation of that game :—

16. Kt—K 5, Q—K 2 ; 17. P—B 4, Q R—B 1 ; 18. Q—B 3, R—B 2 ; 19. Kt—K 2 !, B—B 1 ; 20. Kt—Q 3, Kt (Kt 3)—Q 2 ; 21. Kt—B 3, and White threatens a strong King-side attack commencing P—K Kt 4, etc.

16. P—K 4

White not only does not attempt to prevent the following reply by 17. P—K R 3, but on the contrary, having recognized its futility, he seeks to provoke it.

16. ......   P—K 4

Facilitating his opponent's task, although in any case White's game was won strategically.

GAME 88

QUEEN'S GAMBIT DECLINED

| White : | Black : |
| A. ALEKHIN. | A. WEST. |

1. P—Q 4	Kt—K B 3
2. P—Q B 4	P—K 3
3. Kt—K B 3	P—Q 4
4. Kt—B 3	B—K 2
5. B—Kt 5	Q Kt—Q 2
6. P—K 3	Castles
7. R—B 1	P—B 3
8. B—Q 3	R—K 1

Black lets slip the opportunity of playing 8. ....P×P followed by 9. ....Kt—Q 4 before White has Castled, for after the text-move he will not succeed in freeing himself by ....P—K 4.

The move R—K 1 is only to be considered before White's K B has moved, e.g. if White should play 8. Q—B 2.

9. Castles	P×P
10. B×P	Kt—Q 4
11. Kt—K 4 !	

A very natural move. As he has already Castled, White need not

17. P×P Kt—Kt 5
18. P—K 6 !

Simplest. The Black Pawn at K 3 is a fresh stumbling-block in the way of Black's already laborious development.

18. ...... P×P
19. Kt—Q 4 Kt (Q 2)—K 4
20. P—K R 3 Kt—B 3
21. P—B 4 Kt—B 2

Position after Black's 21st move.

K—R 1

This and the next move, incomprehensible at first sight, form the necessary preparation for the decisive attack. They arise from the following reasoning :
(1) White must win the game if he can attain the formation : Kt at K R 5 and Q at K Kt 4. But this plan is at present impracticable, for the opponent, after 22. P—K 5, Kt—Q 4, threatens Kt—K 6.
(2) On the other hand when played would no longer defend the White Queen on Q 4, which Black would threaten to capture with a check.
Therefore the text-move avoids this latter contingency, and the next move prevents the threat of the Black Knight (Kt—K 6).

After this explanation the final manœuvre reveals itself without difficulty.

22. ...... P—Q R 4

Hopeless, like every other move.

23. R—Q B 3 ! Q—Kt 3
24. P—K 5 Kt—Q 4
25. Kt—R 5 !

The point of the decisive manœuvre. If 25. ....Kt×R ; 26. Q—Kt 4, P—Kt 4 ; 27. Kt—B 6 ch, K—B 1 ; 28. P×Kt and White wins.

25. ...... R—K 2
26. R—Kt 3 Kt—R 1
27. Q—Q 3

Threatening 28. B—B 2 or B × Kt, against which Black is defenceless.

27. ...... Q—B 2

Position after Black's 27th move.

28. B×Kt !

Falling under the spell of a beautiful variation in mind, I was tempted to continue here by 28. B—Q 1, Kt—Kt 5 ; 29. Q—R 7 ch ! !, K×Q ; 30. R×P ch !, R×R ; 31. Kt—B 6 ch, K—Kt 3 ; 32. B—R 5 mate.

But as, first, the move 28. ....Kt—Kt 5 is not at all forced, and moreover, the text-move equally leads to mate, I decided in favour of a forced and logical continuation.

28. ......   K P × B
29. Kt—B 6 ch

If now 29. ....K—B 1 ; 30. Q—R 7, or if 29. ...K—B 2 ; 30. R × P ch, and mates in two moves.

Black resigns.

GAME 89

IRREGULAR OPENING

White :   *Black :*
A. ALEKHIN.   J. A. J. DREWITT.

1. Kt—K B 3   P—Q 4
2. P—Q Kt 4

An innovation of the Hypermodern School (Réti, Bogoljuboff, Grünfeld, Sämisch), which has a predilection (at times carried to excess) for the development of the Bishops on the long diagonals.

The move 2. P—Q Kt 4 is intended to establish a fianchetto in an enlarged form. Should Black, as in the present game, reply with P—Q B 4, White can secure the majority of Pawns in the centre by 3. P × P. This is of far greater moment than the majority of Pawns on the Queen-side, of which so much is made, although it only offers very problematical chances for the end-game.

2. ......   P—K 3
3. B—Kt 2   Kt—K B 3
4. P—Q R 3   P—B 4
5. P × P   B × P
6. P—K 3   Castles
7. P—B 4   Kt—B 3
8. P—Q 4   B—Kt 3

8. ....B—Q 3 seems more plausible, although in this case also White obtains a very good game by 9. Q Kt—Q 2, R—K 1 ; 10. P—B 5, B—B 2 ; 11. B—Kt 5 !

9. Q Kt—Q 2   Q—K 2
10. B—Q 3   R—Q 1

If 10. ....B—B 2, preparing ....P—K 4, White has the choice between the complications resulting from 11. Kt—K 5 and the simpler move 11. P—K 4.

11. Castles   B—Q 2
12. Kt—K 5 !

Taking advantage of the fact that the best square of retreat for Black's K Kt will be occupied by his Q B (after 12. ....Kt × Kt ; 13. P × Kt).

12. ......   B—K 1
13. P—B 4   Q R—B 1
14. Q R—B 1   Kt—Q 2

This move will allow White to obtain a decisive advantage. Black, threatened on every side, has already no adequate plan of defence.

Position after Black's 14th move.

15. Kt × Kt (B 6) !

By this unexpected exchange of his best placed piece White takes immediate advantage of the cramped position of Black's piece.

15. ...... R×Kt

If 15. ....P×Kt, then 16. P—B 5, B—R 4 (or 16. ....B—B 2; 17. Q—R 4); 17. Kt—Kt 3, B—B 2; 18. B—B 3, R—Kt 1; 19. Kt—R 5, Kt—B 1; 20. Q—R 4, and the exploitation of White's strategic advantage on the Queenside is merely a question of technique.

Black by the text-move prepares a sacrifice of the Knight which at first sight seems not devoid of chances.

16. P—B 5   Kt×P

Practically forced, for if 16. ....B—R 4 then 17. Kt—Kt 3, B—B 2; 18. B—Kt 5 winning the Exchange.

17. P×Kt   B×P

Black has secured two Pawns for the piece and appears certain to capture yet another Pawn, but White speedily concludes the game by the following sacrifice, which is the point of the 15th move, Kt×Kt (B 6).

18. R—K B 3!   B×P
19. R×R   B×R

See Diagram.

20. B×P ch!

This sacrifice of both Bishops has its precedents in the games Lasker—Bauer, Amsterdam, 1889, and

Position after Black's 19th move.

Niemzovitch—Tarrasch, St. Petersburg, 1914.

In the present game its interest rests solely in the way in which White has masked his plan of attack up to the last moment, by occupying his opponent with a demonstration on the opposite wing.

20. ......   K×B
21. R—R 3 ch   K—Kt 1
22. B×P!

If now 22. ....P—B 3 White would not be satisfied to win the Queen for Rook and Bishop, but would play:

23. B—R 6!, Q—R 2; 24. Q—R 5, B—B 1; 25. Q—Kt 4 ch, B—Kt 2; 26. B×B and White wins.

Black resigns.

CHAPTER XXIII

EXHIBITION GAMES AND SIMULTANEOUS GAMES

GAME 90

KING'S GAMBIT DECLINED
(by transposition of moves)

The second of a series of match-games* played at Berlin, June, 1921.

White :	Black :
A. ALEKHIN.	R. TEICHMANN.

1. P—K 4   P—K 4
2. Kt—Q B 3   Kt—Q B 3

As we have already mentioned, the best move is 2. ....Kt—K B 3 followed, if 3. B—B 4, by 3. .... Kt×P !

3. B—B 4   Kt—B 3
4. P—Q 3   B—B 4
5. P—B 4   P—Q 3
6. Kt—B 3

By transposition of moves White has led into a safe and very promising position in the King's Gambit Declined.

6. ......   B—Kt 5

Stronger was 6. ....B—K 3 and if 7. B—Kt 5, then 7. ....P—Q R 3; 8. B×Kt ch, P×B; 9. Q—K 2, P×P!, with approximate equality

* Result : 2 wins, 2 draws, 2 losses.

(Spielmann—Dr. Tarrasch, Pistyan, 1922).
After the text-move White obtains a slight advantage in position.

7. Kt—Q R 4

The only correct move.
On the other hand, the old move 7. P—K R 3 is inadequate, on account of 7. ....B×Kt; 8. Q×B, P×P! (but not 8. ....Kt—Q 5; 9. Q—Kt 3!, Q—K 2!; 10. P×P, P×P ; 11. K—Q 1 with the better game); 9. Q×P (if 9. B×P, Kt—Q 5!; 10. Q—Kt 3, Kt—R 4), Kt—K 4, and White, in view of the threat 10. ....Kt—R 4, has no way to avoid the exchange of his K B, after which Black has emerged from all the difficulties of the opening.

7. ......   P—Q R 3

Hardly customary, and certainly not best. His opponent's previous move clearly showed his intention to eliminate the Q B, and it was therefore futile to force him to do that.
An interesting variation, which is, however, advantageous for White, was 7. ....B×Kt; 8. Q×B, Kt—Q 5; 9. Q—Q 1, P—Q Kt 4; 10. B×P ch, K×B; 11. Kt×B,

P × Kt ; 12. P × P followed by 13. Castles ch, and White would have formidable attacking chances, apart from the two Pawns for the sacrificed piece.

In a game Alekhin—O. Tenner (a Berlin amateur), played at Cologne in 1907, the latter continued 7. ....P × P ; 8. Kt × B, P × Kt ; 9. B × P, Kt—K R 4 ; 10. B—K 3, Kt—K 4 ? ; 11. Kt × Kt, B × Q ; 12. B × P ch, K—K 2 ; 13. B × P ch, K—B 3 ; 14. Castles ch, K × Kt ; 15. R—B 5 mate.

Comparatively best was 7. .... B—Kt 3 or 7. ....Castles.

8. Kt × B	P × Kt
9. Castles	Q—K 2
10. P—K R 3	

Securing the advantage of two Bishops against two Knights.

10.	B × Kt
11. Q × B	Castles K R
12. B—K 3	P × P
13. Q × P	Kt—K 4
14. B—Kt 3	Q R—K 1

Further loss of time, which seriously compromises Black's game. The following was equally disadvantageous : 14. ....P—B 5 ; 15. P × P, Kt—Kt 3 ; 16. Q—Kt 5 !, Q × P ; 17. Q R—K 1 with the better game.

On the other hand 14. ....Q R—Q 1 would clearly have been better, as it would make the advance of White s centre Pawns more difficult.

15. Q—B 2 !

With the double threat 16. B × P and 16. B—Kt 5.

15.	Kt (B 3)—Q 2
16. Q R—Q 1	P—Q Kt 3
17. P—B 3	

Preparing 18. P—Q 4, against which there is no defence. The loss of the present game by Black can be attributed to the fact that his Knights lack bases in the centre, and that in positions of this character the possession of the two Bishops constitutes a decisive advantage for the opponent.

17. ......   Kt—Kt 3

Position after Black's 17th move.

18. Q—B 5 !

The first move of a new regrouping, the completion of which will give White a won-game. White's Q B is to be posted on K Kt 3, whence it will exercise pressure on Black's Pawn at his Q B 2, which will be weakened still more by the imminent opening of the Q B file after White's P—Q 4.

Throughout the execution of this plan Black will find himself reduced to absolute passivity.

18.	K—R 1
19. B—K B 2 !	R—Q 1
20. B—Kt 3	Kt (Q 2)—K 4
21. P—Q 4	P × P
22. P × P	Kt—B 3
23. P—Q 5	Kt (B 3)—K 4
24. P—K R 4 !	

This threat to win a piece compels Black to weaken his position still more, thus enabling White's Rook to break through into his game.

24. ......   Q—B 4 ch
25. K—R 2

Not 25. B—B 2 on account of 25. ....Q—Q 3.

25. ......   P—B 3

Evidently forced.

26. R—B 1   Q—Q 3
27. R—B 6   Q—K 2

If 27. ....Q—Q 2; 28. Q×Q, R×Q; 29. P—R 5, Kt—Kt 5 ch; 30. K—R 3, Kt (Kt 3)—K 4; 31. K R—B 1! and wins.

28. R—K 6!   Q—Q 2
29. P—R 5   Kt—K 2
30. Q—R 3   Kt—B 2

Again forced, because of the double threat 31. B×Kt and 31. P—R 6.

31. B—K B 4   P—R 3
32. Q—Q B 3!   Kt—Q 3

Allowing a decisive sacrifice. 32. ....R—B 1 was a little better, upon which White would have continued his winning attack by 33. Q—Kt 4 and 34. B—R 4.

Position after Black's 32nd move.

33. B×P!

Putting an end to all resistance, for if 33. ....P×B; 34. R (B 1) ×P, K—Kt 1; 35. Q—Kt 3 ch and mates in a few moves.

33. ......   Kt×K P

A desperate move.

34. R×Kt   Kt×P
35. Q—B 1!

If now 35. ....P×B; 36. B×Kt, Q×B; 37. Q×P ch, K—Kt 1; 38. R—Kt 4 ch, K—B 2; 39. Q×P ch and wins.

Black resigns.

GAME 91

RUY LOPEZ

Fourth of a series of match-games played at Berlin, June, 1921.

White :   *Black :*
A. ALEKHIN.   R. TEICHMANN.

1. P—K 4   P—K 4
2. Kt—K B 3   Kt—Q B 3
3. B—Kt 5   P—Q R 3
4. B—R 4   Kt—B 3
5. Castles   Kt×P
6. P—Q 4   P—Q Kt 4
7. B—Kt 3   P—Q 4
8. P×P   B—K 3
9. P—B 3   B—K 2
10. B—K 3!   Castles
11. Q Kt—Q 2   B—K Kt 5

This line of defence is inadequate, on account of White's following manœuvre, invented by the Dutch amateur, Van Gelder.

11. ....Kt×Kt and 12. ....Kt—R 4 is preferable. On the other hand, 11. ....P—K B 4 is not advisable, by reason of 12. P×P e. p., Kt×P (B 3); 13. Kt—Kt 5!, B—K B 4; 14. Kt (Q 2)—K 4!, with advantage to White.

12. Kt×Kt   P×Kt
13. Q—Q 5!   Q×Q

If 13. ....P×Kt; 14. Q×Kt, P×P; 15. Q×K Kt P, Q—Q 2; 16. Q—Kt 3 and White has excellent prospects of attack on the open K Kt file.

After the present exchange of Queens, White's game remains a little superior, thanks to the weakness of the hostile Queen-side.

14. B×Q	P×Kt
15. B×Kt	P×P
16. K×P	Q R—Q 1
17. P—Q R 4 !	

As soon as White succeeds in playing this move without immediate inconvenience in this variation of the Lopez, he obtains the advantage.

17. ......   P—B 3 !

Black rightly prefers to attempt a counter-attack, based on the somewhat exposed situation of White's King, rather than a laborious and unpromising defence by 17. ....B—Q 2.

18. R P×P

Naturally not 18. P×B P, R×P; 19. P×P, P×P; 20. B×P, R—K Kt 3 !

18.	R P×P
19. B×P	P×P
20. B—B 4 ch	

With the double aim of:

(1) Removing Black's King from the centre, with a view to the end-game.

(2) Preventing Black's Q B from withdrawing to K 3.

20.	K—R 1
21. P—B 3	B—R 4
22. R—R 5	

By this move, which incidentally attacks Black's K P, White in reality intends to consolidate the position of his King by B—Q 5 and B—K 4, and later on to make use of his majority of Pawns on the Queen-side.

To thwart this scheme Black discovers an ingenious resource which is nevertheless insufficient to equalize the game.

22. ......   R—Q 8 !

Apparently as discreet as it is elegant, since it is difficult to foresee how White, with the little material left to him, can secure the victory in the end-game, against equal forces.

Position after Black's 22nd move.

23. B—Q 5 !

The only way to maintain the advantage, because the capture of the K P would lead only to a draw: 23. R×P, R×R; 24. K×R, R×P ch; 25. B—B 2, B—R 5; 26. R×B, R×B ch; 27. K—Kt 1, R—B 5.

23.	R×R
24. K×R	B×P
25. B×B	R×B ch
26. K—K 2	R—B 1
27. K—Q 3 !	

The first move of a strategic winning plan—White, instead of capturing the hostile K P, prefers to immobilize it and to make use of it to limit the range of action of Black's K B, after which the advance of his Queen-side Pawns will decide the game in White's favour.

27. ......   K—Kt 1

If Black had recognized in time his opponent's intentions, and the dangers to which he is exposed, it is probable that he would immediately have rid himself of the embarrassing Pawn by 27. ....P—K 5 ch !, which would have afforded him some drawing chances.

28. K—K 4!   R—Kt 1

After this useless move Black's game becomes hopeless. But even the best move would in the end be shown up as inadequate, for example : 28. ....R—B 8 ; 29. K—Q 5 (not 29. R—R 7, R—K 8, threatening 30. ....R × B ch), K—B 2 ; 30. R—R 7.

29. P—Kt 4   K—B 2
30. P—Kt 5

The advance of the Pawns now becomes irresistible.

30. ......   K—K 3
31. P—B 4   K—Q 2
32. R—R 7   B—Q 3

In the vain hope of sacrificing the Bishop for two Pawns, after 33. P—B 5.

33. K—Q 5 !

Preparing the next move which, if played at once, would not be so strong on account of the reply : 33. ....K—B 3.

33. ......   P—K 5

Too late !

Position after Black's 33rd move.

34. P—Kt 6 !

Decisive, for if 34. ....B × P ; 35. P—B 5, K—B 1 ; 36. K—B 6, P × P ; 37. R × P ! and wins.

34. ......   R—K B 1
35. P—B 5   R—B 4 ch
36. K—B 4   Black resigns

GAME 92

ENGLISH OPENING

Exhibition Game played at Berlin, July, 1921.

White :   *Black :*
A. ALEKHIN.   F. SÄMISCH.

1. P—Q B 4   P—K 4

By answering 1. P—Q B 4 with 1. ....P—K 4 Black accommodates White in his desire to play a Sicilian with a move ahead. As a reply to White's first move Black has the choice between several good continuations : 1. ....Kt—K B 3, 1. ....P—K 3, 1. ....P—Q B 4 and 1. ....P—K B 4, the Dutch Defence being more playable for him by the fact that White has already advanced his Pawn to Q B 4.

2. Kt—Q B 3   Kt—K B 3

2. ....Kt—Q B 3, with the intention of developing his K Kt at K 2 after the fianchetto of Black's K B, was also to be considered.
It is true that against this move White is not compelled to answer 3. P—K Kt 3, seeing that 3. Kt—B 3, followed by 4. P—Q 4, seems preferable.

3. P—K Kt 3   P—K Kt 3

Regarding 3. ....P—Q 4 see Game No. 8.

4. B—Kt 2   B—Kt 2
5. Kt—B 3   P—Q 3
6. P—Q 4   P×P

It was preferable to keep the Pawn-position intact by playing 6. ....Q Kt—Q 2, free to disturb it at a more opportune moment.

7. Kt×P   Castles
8. Castles   Q Kt—Q 2
9. P—Kt 3!

In an analogous position, save that the exchange of centre-Pawns had not occurred, I played the weaker move 8. Q—B 2, against Réti at Pistyan, 1922, after which Black equalized the game by 8. .... P×P; 9. Kt×P, Kt—Kt 3; 10. Q—Q 3, P—Q 4!
9. P—Kt 3 is probably the only move to maintain an appreciable advantage.

9. ......   Kt—B 4
10. B—Kt 2   R—K 1
11. Q—B 2   Kt—K 3
12. Q R—Q 1

12. Kt—B 3 was better. Black's position is so hemmed-in that White should seek to avoid every exchange capable of alleviating this constraint.

12. ......   Q—K 2

For the above reason, 12. .... Kt×Kt was the best alternative.

13. K R—K 1   R—Kt 1
14. Kt—B 3!   Q—B 1

Black's position, although free from weaknesses, is almost without resource, on account of the lack of range of his pieces, which obstruct each other. Under such conditions it is generally impossible to establish an adequate plan of defence, and the loss of the game is only a question of time.

15. P—K 4   Kt—Q 2

Position after Black's 15th move.

16. B—Q R 3!

The commencement of the decisive manœuvre, which finally ends in the win of a Pawn, with a dominating position.
White now threatens on the one hand 17. P—K 5, and on the other hand 17. Kt—Q 5 or Q Kt 5, followed by 18. Kt×Q B P and 19. B × P. Black's next moves are therefore forced.

16. ......   Kt—K 4
17. Kt×Kt   B×Kt
18. P—B 4   B—Q 5 ch
19. K—R 1   Q—Kt 2

Black was threatened with 20. P—K B 5.

20. Kt—Q 5!   B—B 3

EXHIBITION GAMES, ETC.

Or 20. ....P—Q B 4; 21. P—B 5, Kt—B 1; 22. P×P, R P×P; 23. R×B, P×R (if 23. ....Q×R; 24. B—Kt 2); 24. B×P and White recovers the Exchange with a Pawn ahead.

21. Kt×B ch	Q×Kt
22. B—Kt 2	Q—K 2
23. Q—B 3	

The simplest. White leads into an end-game with two Bishops and a Pawn against Bishop and Knight.

23.	P—B 3
24. Q×P	Q×Q
25. B×Q	P—Q Kt 4

A desperate attempt to free his pieces, but in reality merely easing White's task.

26. P×P	R×P
27. P—K 5	P×P
28. B×P	

Not 28. B—B 6, B—Kt 2.

28.	B—Kt 2
29. B×B	R×B
30. R—Q 7	P—K R 4
31. K R—Q 1 !	

Instead of playing 31. R—K B 1 White temporizes, reserving this possibility until after Black's plausible move, K—B 1, when he no longer has the defence ....R—K B 1 at his disposal.

| 31. ...... | K—B 1 |
| 32. R—K B 1 | R—K 2 |

See Diagram.

33. P—B 5 !

Winning a second Pawn and therefore the game.

| 33. ...... | P×P |

Clearly forced, since if 33. .... R×R; 34. P×Kt ch would win a piece.

Position after Black's 32nd move.

34. R×P ch	K—K 1
35. R×R ch	K×R
36. R×P	Black resigns

GAME 93

SICILIAN DEFENCE

Consultation Game played at Berlin, December, 1921.

White :   *Black :*
Messrs. Wegemund.   A. Alekhin.
    Brennert.
    Friedrich.
    Deissner.

1. P—K 4	P—Q B 4
2. Kt—K B 3	P—K 3
3. P—Q 4	P×P
4. Kt×P	Kt—K B 3
5. B—Q 3	

This allows Black to obtain at least an equal game by the advance of the centre Pawns. The correct move is 5. Kt—Q B 3 (see Game No. 60).

5.	Kt—B 3
6. B—K 3	P—Q 4
7. Kt—Q 2	P—K 4
8. Kt (Q 4)—B 3	P—K R 3 !

A good move. The threat 8. ..... P—Q 5 compels White to weaken his position by the advance of his Q B P, unless he cares to abandon his centre immediately by 9. P×P.

9. P—B 3	B—K 2
10. Castles	Castles
11. Q—K 2	B—K 3
12. K R—Q 1	Q—B 2
13. P×P	

Practically forced, as Black threatens 13. ....P×P ; 14. Q Kt × P, Kt×Kt ; 15. B×Kt, P—B 4 with formidable attacking prospects.

| 13. ...... | Kt×P |
| 14. Kt—K 4 | Kt—R 4 ! |

14. ....P—K B 4 was premature, since after 15. Kt—B 5, B×Kt ; 16. B×B, Kt—B 5 ; 17. Q—B 1, Black would have no appreciable advantage, whereas after the text-move the threat P—B 4 becomes still more objectionable.

15. B—Q 2 !

If 15. P—Q Kt 4 Black's Knight would simply withdraw to Q B 3, and White would merely have weakened his Queen-side. The text-move conceals a trap. If, for example, 15. ....P—B 4, then 16. Kt—Kt 3, P—K 5 ; 17. Kt×K P !, P×Kt ; 18. Q×P and wins.

| 15. ...... | Q R—K 1 ! |

This move strengthens the position in the centre, and its purpose will soon become clear.

| 16. Kt—Kt 3 | B—Q 3 |
| 17. Kt—B 5 | |

White, engrossed by the latent threat P—B 4, does not perceive another danger. The best move here was 17. Kt—R 4, Kt—K B 5 ; 18. B×Kt, P×B ; 19. Kt—K 4, B—K 2 ; 20. Kt—B 3, B—K Kt 5 !, after which Black would obtain the better game on account of his two Bishops.

17.	B×Kt
18. B×B	P—K 5 !
19. Kt—Q 4	

If 19. B×K P, then 19. .... Kt—K B 3 wins a piece.

| 19. ...... | B×P ch |
| 20. K—R 1 | B—B 5 |

Black has won a Pawn, but the win is not without difficulties. White by his next move introduces fresh complications, and seeks to fish in troubled waters.

Position after Black's 20th move.

21. P—B 4 !

After 21. B×P victory would have been quite easy for Black : 21. B×P, B×B ; 22. R×B, Kt—Q B 5 ; 23. R—B 2, Kt (Q 4)—K 6 ; 24. P×Kt, R×B ; 25. Kt—B 5, Q—K 4 ; 26. Q—B 3, Kt×K P ; 27. R—K 2, Kt—B 8 ! and wins.

Whereas, after the text-move, Black is compelled to make lengthy and elaborate calculations before deciding upon the ensuing sacrificial variation.

| 21. ...... | Kt×P ! |
| 22. Q R—B 1 | P—Q Kt 4 ! |

EXHIBITION GAMES, ETC.

The necessary preliminary to the following counter-attack. If now 23. Kt×P, then 23. ....Q—K 4 ! and Black is out of all his difficulties, with a Pawn ahead.

23. P—Q Kt 3

Position after White's 23rd move.

23. ...... P—K 6 !

Saving the threatened piece, and at the same time imperilling the position of White's King, which allows him to undertake a mating-attack.

24. P × P   Kt (Q 4) × P
25. B × Kt   B × B
26. Kt × P   Q—Kt 6 !

The point of the combination. On the contrary, 26. ....Q—K 4 would be insufficient, on account of 27. R × Kt, Q × Kt ; 28. B—Q 7, winning the Exchange; or 27. ....Q × B ; 28. Kt—Q 6.

27. Q × Kt

It is manifest that if 27. R or P × Kt, Black's next move would win at once.

27. ...... B—B 5
28. K—Kt 1

Now White is a piece ahead and Black seems to have only perpetual check by 28. ....B—K 6 ch ; 29. K—R 1, B—B 5 ; 30. K—Kt 1, since 28. ....Q—R 7 ch ; 29. K—B 2, B—Kt 6 ch ; 30. K—B 3 is indecisive.

By his next two moves Black, however, demonstrates the whole import of his sacrifice of the Knight.

28. ...... R—K 4 !

In order to occupy K R 4 with this Rook. White cannot prevent this plan without submitting to a decisive loss of material.

29. Kt—Q 6

If 29. Q—Q 3, Q—R 7 ch ; 30. K—B 2, B × R followed by 31. ....Q—B 5 ch and wins.

Position after White's 29th move.

29. ...... P—Kt 3 !

This quiet move wins at once. White is compelled either to leave the Bishop *en prise* (which would weaken Black's attack only momentarily) or to allow Black to continue the plan which he has mapped out for himself.

30. B—R 3   B—K 6 ch
31. K—R 1   R—R 4

And White is defenceless against the threatened 32. ....R×B ch. If 32. Q—K 2 or Q—B 1, then 32. ....B—B 5; 33. K—Kt 1, R×B and mates in a few moves.

White resigns.

GAME 94

SCOTCH GAME

Played in a *séance* of four consultation games at Basle, March, 1922.

White:	Black:
DR. FLEISSIG MESSRS. AD. & H. STAEHELIN.	A. ALEKHIN.

1. P—K 4	P—K 4
2. Kt—K B 3	Kt—Q B 3
3. P—Q 4	P×P
4. Kt×P	B—B 4

This move is more ancient and on the whole less certain than 4. ....Kt—B 3, which leads to equality, but on the other hand it has the advantage of engendering more lively variations.

5. B—K 3	B—Kt 3

Introduced by Lasker against Mieses at St. Petersburg, 1909, in place of the usual continuation up till then, 5. ....Q—B 3; 6. P—Q B 3, K Kt—K 2. It should be remarked that Blumenfeld's move 6. Kt—Kt 5 (instead of 6. P—Q B 3) is inadequate, on account of the following variation: 6. ....B×B; 7. P×B, Q—R 5 ch; 8. P—Kt 3, Q×K P; 9. Kt×P ch, K—Q 1; 10. Kt×R, Q×R; 11. Q—Q 6, Kt—B 3!; 12. Kt—Q 2, Kt—K 1; 13. Q—R 3, Q×P; 14. Castles, Q×P, with advantage to Black.

6. P—Q B 3	

But in the present position this move is no longer necessary, and merely obstructs the best square of development for the Q Kt. He should play 6. Kt—Q B 3, K Kt—K 2; 7. B—K 2 followed by 8. Q—Q 2 and later Castles Q R with a very fine game (Spielmann—Dr. Tarrasch, Breslau, 1912).

6.	K Kt—K 2
7. B—K 2	Castles
8. Castles	P—Q 3
9. Kt—Q 2	P—B 4 !

The opening of the K B file yields Black an initiative of long duration, without any ill results.

10. P×P	B×P
11. R—K 1	

The command of the King-file, however, is only of little value for White, as we shall recognize later on. But even after 11. Kt×B, Kt×Kt; 12. B×B, R P×B, White would remain with the inferior game.

11.	Kt×Kt
12. B×Kt	B×B

Not 12. ....P—B 4; 13. B—K 3, P—Q 4 on account of 14. B—K Kt 5.

13. P×B	K—R 1

Black was threatened with 14. Q—Kt 3 ch followed by 15. Q×P.

14. Kt—B 3	P—B 3 !

Preventing 15. P—Q 5, followed by the manœuvre of White's Knight with the square K 6 as an objective.

15. R—Q B 1	Kt—Kt 3
16. R—B 3	Q—B 3

Black mobilizes all his available forces before unleashing an attack against the weak points of the hostile position (K B 2 and K Kt 2).

17. B—Q 3	

EXHIBITION GAMES, ETC.   249

In order to exchange the dangerous Knight should Black play 17. ....B—Kt 5 immediately.

17.	Kt—B 5 !
18. B—B 2	

This allows Black to force the win in a few moves. 18. B×B was somewhat better, although in this case also Black's attack must inevitably end in victory.

18.	B—Kt 5

18. ....Q—Kt 3 would be inadequate against 19. Kt—R 4 !

19. R (B 3)—K 3

Now White finds himself defenceless against the next manœuvre.

19.	Kt—R 6 ch !
20. K—B 1	

Position after White's 20th move.

20.	Q—R 5 !

The only move which forces an immediate win. 20. ....Kt—Kt 4 would be insufficient, on account of 21. Q—Q 3 !, P—K Kt 3 ; 22. B—Q 1.

21. Q—K 2

Or 21. Q—Q 2, B×Kt ; 22. R×B, R×R ; 23. P×R, Kt—B 5 and wins. If 21. P—K Kt 3, Q—R 4 followed by 22. ....Kt—Kt 4.

21.	Q—R 4

Threatening 22. ....Kt—Kt 4 and 22. ....Kt—B 5, against which White is defenceless.

22. Q—Q 3	Kt—B 5
23. Q—K 4	Kt×P !

If now 24. K×Kt, Q—R 6 ch ; 25. K—Kt 1, B×Kt ; 26. R×B, R×R ; 27. Q—K 8 ch, R—B 1 and wins.

White resigns.

GAME 95

QUEEN'S PAWN GAME

Exhibition Game played at Madrid, May, 1922.

White :   Black :
A. ALEKHIN.   M. GOLMAYO.

1. P—Q 4	Kt—K B 3
2. P—Q B 4	P—Q 3
3. Kt—K B 3	Q Kt—Q 2

The usual continuation in practice is 3. ....P—K Kt 3 followed by 4. ....B—Kt 2, 5. ....Castles and 6. ....Kt—B 3.

4. Kt—B 3	P—K 4
5. P—K Kt 3 !	

The best system of development in this variation.

5.	B—K 2
6. B—Kt 2	Castles
7. Castles	R—K 1
8. P—Kt 3	P—B 3

Threatening 9. ....P—K 5 followed by 10. ....P—Q 4, which White at once prevents.

9. Q—B 2	B—B 1
10. P—K 4 !	P×P

Black is already obliged to surrender the centre, in order to disentangle his pieces and develop his Queen-side.

11. Kt×P   Q—B 2
12. B—Kt 2 P—Q R 4

Clearly with the object of securing the square Q B 4 for his Knight, without allowing it to be dislodged by P—Q Kt 4.

13. P—K R 3   Kt—B 4
14. Q R—K 1   B—Q 2
15. P—B 4   Kt—K 3
16. Kt—B 5!

Having the greater freedom of action, White should avoid any exchange capable of relieving the enemy's game.

16. ......   Kt—B 4
17. Kt—K 3

But here 17. P—K Kt 4, instead of the withdrawal of the Knight, would have been simpler and would ultimately have led to a winning attack, without great complications.

Whereas after the text-move Black succeeds in evolving a very interesting counter-attack.

17. ......   R—K 2!
18. P—K Kt 4

There is, nevertheless, nothing better than this move.

18. ......   Q R—K 1
19. Kt—B 5

As we can see, White has lost two moves. The second phase of the game will be only the more lively by reason of this.

19. ......   B×Kt
20. Kt P×B   P—Q Kt 4!

Bold, but very accurately calculated. White is compelled to play very cautiously to maintain his advantage.

21. P×P   P×P

If now 22. Kt×P, Q—Kt 3 with advantage to Black.

Position after Black's 21st move.

22. P—K 5!

The correct reply to the manœuvre commenced by 20. ....P—Q Kt 4. If now 22. ....P×P; 23. P×P, R×P then 24. Kt×P, Q—Kt 3; 25. R×R, R×R; 26. R×R and Black's discovered check would be perfectly harmless, on account of the answer 27. B—Q 4.

Black's next move is therefore again best.

22. ......   Kt (B 4)—Q 2!
23. Q—B 2

With the double threat 24. Kt×P and 24. P×Kt; Black has accordingly no choice of reply.

23. ......   P×P
24. Kt×P   Q—Kt 1

If 24. ....Q—Q 1 or Q—B 1, then clearly 25. Kt—Q 6.

See Diagram.

25. Kt—R 7!

The point of the manœuvre initiated by 22. P—K 5! Black must lose at least the Exchange, but

Position after Black's 24th move.

Position after Black's 31st move.

he rightly prefers to sacrifice the Queen for Rook and Bishop, which would indeed have yielded him some defensive resources had occasion offered.

25.	......	P×P
26.	Kt—B 6	R×R !
27.	Kt×Q	R (K 8)—K 7
28.	Kt×Kt !	Kt×Kt

If 28. ....R×Q, then 29. Kt× Kt ch, P×Kt ; 30. R×R (but not 30. K×R, B—B 4 ch ; 31. K—B 3, R—K 6 ch ; 32. K×P, R—K 7), B—B 4 ; 31. K—B 1 and White wins without difficulty.

| 29. | Q×P | R×B |
| 30. | B—B 6 ! | |

The only move to win.

| 30. | ...... | B—B 4 ch |
| 31. | K—R 1 | R—K 2 |

31. ....R—K 6 would have been a little better, although in this case also White would have won as follows :

32. Q—R 4 !, R (K 6)—K 7 !; 33. Q—Q 8 ch, Kt—B 1 ; 34. Q—B 7 !, R—K 6 ; 35. B—B 3, R—Q B 7 ; 36. Q×P.

32. P—B 6 !

White wins another piece by this pretty move.

32.	......	P×P
33.	B×Kt	R×B
34.	Q—Kt 4 ch	Black resigns

GAME 96

RUY LOPEZ

Exhibition Game played at Seville, June, 1922.

White :   *Black :*
Dr. Torres.   A. Alekhin.

1.	P—K 4	P—K 4
2.	Kt—K B 3	Kt—Q B 3
3.	B—Kt 5	P—Q R 3
4.	B—R 4	Kt—B 3.
5.	Castles	P—Q 3

This move, commended by Rubinstein, seems to me less sound than 5. ....B—K 2, as White has at his disposal several good continuations and as he can obtain a draw by a forced variation (compare the next note).

6. B×Kt ch

This exchange, however, is not to be commended. White would do better to adopt one of the following continuations:

(1) 6. P—B 3 and if 6. ...Kt×P; 7. P—Q 4, with a fine attack.

(2) 6. Q—K 2.

(3) 6. P—Q 4 and if 6. ....P—Q Kt 4; 7. B—Kt 3, P×P; 8. P—B 3 !, sacrificing a Pawn for the attack. This line of play was successfully played by Yates against Rubinstein on two occasions (London, 1922, and Carlsbad, 1923).

(4) 6. R—K 1, P—Q Kt 4; 7. B—Kt 3, Kt—Q R 4. A game Aurbach—Alekhin, played in Paris in October, 1922, continued thus: 8. P—Q 4, Kt×B; 9. R P×Kt, B—Kt 2; 10. P×P, Kt×P; 11. P×P, B×P; 12. Q—Q 4 !, Q—K 2; 13. Kt—B 3 ! (not 13. Q×P ?, Castles; 14. B—Kt 5. Kt×B ! and wins), P—K B 4; 14. B—Kt 5, Q—Q 2 (if 14. ....Q—B 2, given in Collijn's *Lärobok*, 15. Kt×Kt, P×Kt; 16. R×P ch !, B×R ; 17. Q×B ch, K—Q 2; 18. R—Q 1 and wins); 15. Kt×Kt, P×Kt.

Position after Black's 15th move in sub-variation.

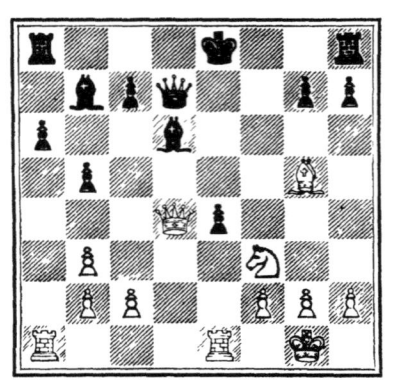

16. R×P ch !, B×R; 17. Q×B ch, K—B 2; 18. R—K 1 !, Q R—K 1 !; 19. Q—Q 5 ch, K—B 1; 20. R—K 5 !, R×R; 21. Kt×R, Q—K 1; 22. Q—B 3 ch, K—Kt 1; 23. Q—Q 5 ch and White draws by perpetual check.

6.	P×B
7. P—Q 4	Kt×P !
8. R—K 1	P—B 4
9. P×P	P—Q 4

Now Black has undoubtedly the better game, with his two Bishops and his strongly-posted Knight in the centre.

10. Kt—Q 4	B—B 4
11. P—Q B 3	

Sooner or later necessary in order to develop the Q Kt at Q 2, without leaving the K Kt *en prise* to Black's K B.

11.	Castles
12. P—K B 4	

It would have been rather better to dislodge the Black Knight by 12. P—B 3 and then to play 13. P—K B 4. Nevertheless, in this blocked position the gain of a *tempo* is hardly capable of improving his game sufficiently.

12.	Q—K 1
13. B—K 3	B—Kt 3
14. Kt—Q 2	B—Kt 2

In perfect safety Black prepares the advance of his centre Pawns, thus enabling his Bishops to exercise pressure on the hostile King.

15. Kt (Q 2)—B 3	Q R—Q 1
16. Q—B 2	P—B 4
17. Kt—Kt 3	

17. Kt—K 2 at once was preferable, upon which Black would probably have continued 17. ....P—R 3, followed by 18. ....K×R 1 and 19. ....R—K Kt 1, preparing to open the K Kt file by ....P—Kt 4.

The text-move allows him to increase his pressure on the centre to a still greater extent.

17.	P—B 5 !

Profiting by the fact that White cannot play 18. B×B on account of 18. ....P×Kt.

18. Kt(Kt 3)—Q 4   P—B 4
19. Kt—K 2   Q—B 3
20. Q R—Q 1   P—R 3 !

In continuation of the above-mentioned plan.

21. R—K B 1   K—R 1 !

In order that the Q B P shall not be captured by the hostile Queen with a check, in the event of .... P—Q 5, a precaution whose purpose will appear later on.

22. K—R 1   Q—Kt 3

Black intends to occupy K R 4 with his Queen, which would make the advance of the Kt P still more effective.

23. Kt (K 2)—Kt 1

By attempting to prevent this strategically decisive advance White allows his opponent to conclude the game with a pretty combination, based upon the hidden action of his Q B on the long diagonal.

23. ......   Q—R 4
24. Kt—R 3

Position after White's 24th move.

24. ......   P—Q 5 !

Allowing the sacrifice of the Queen on the 28th move, thanks to which Black wins a piece or forces mate.

25. P×P   P×P
26. B×P   B×B
27. R×B   R×R
28. Kt×R   Q×Kt !
29. P×Q   Kt—B 7 ch
30. K—Kt 1   Kt×P mate

GAME 97

SICILIAN DEFENCE

Exhibition Game played at Berlin, February, 1923.

White :   Black :
A. ALEKHIN.   F. SAMISCH.

1. P—K 4   P—Q B 4
2. Kt—K B 3   Kt—Q B 3
3. B—K 2

In the Vienna Tournament of 1922, playing against the same opponent, I had played 3. P—Q 4 (see Game No. 76).

The text-move indicates White's intention to Castle, before undertaking any action in the centre.

3. ......   P—K 3
4. Castles   P—Q 3

After 4. ....P—Q 4 ; 5. P×P, P×P ; 6. P—Q 4, Black's Q P would be isolated and therefore weak.

5. P—Q 4   P×P
6. Kt×P   Kt—B 3
7. B—B 3 !

White delays the plausible move 7. Kt—Q B 3 in order to play first P—Q B 4 thus preventing all counter-attack on the Q B file.

7. ......   Kt—K 4

To secure the advantage of the two Bishops, which is rather illusory in this position. But this manœuvre loses valuable time which would be better utilized in playing B—K 2, Castles and B—Q 2, etc.

```
 8. P—B 4 !      Kt × B ch
 9. Q × Kt       B—K 2
10. Kt—B 3       Castles
11. P—Q Kt 3
```

The occupation of the long diagonal being threatening, Black prepares to oppose his K B, a manœuvre which, however, implies a further loss of time.

```
11. ......       Kt—Q 2
12. B—Kt 2       B—B 3
13. Q R—Q 1      P—Q R 3
```

Preventing the threatened Kt (Q 4) —Kt 5, but in any case his Q P remains permanently weak.

```
14. Q—Kt 3       Q—B 2
15. K—R 1 !
```

An essential preliminary to the decisive manœuvre commencing by the advance of the K B P.

```
15. ......       R—Q 1
16. P—B 4        P—Q Kt 3
17. P—B 5 !
```

White's advantage in position and attacking chances are already so great that the abandoning of the square K 5 to the opponent cannot present any strategic inconvenience.

Moreover the text-move, if Black answers it in the most plausible manner, is shown to be the prelude to a beautiful final combination.

```
17. ......       B—K 4
```

Black's game is untenable, for White's attack is already too strong, e.g.: 17. ....B × Kt; 18. R × B, Kt—K 4; 19. P—B 6, Kt—Kt 3; 20. B—R 3 ! with decisive advantage for White.

Position after Black's 17th move.

18. P × K P !!

The Queen-sacrifice, which Black is compelled to accept, decides the game in a few moves.

```
18. ......       B × Q
```

If 18. ....P × P; 19. Kt × P.

```
19. P × P ch     K—R 1
```

Also forced.

```
20. Kt—Q 5 !!
```

Position after White's 20th move

The whole point of the sacrifice ! 20. Kt—K 6 would not be so good, because of 20. ....Q—Kt 1 ; 21. Kt—Q 5, B—K 4, and Black could still defend himself, whereas after the text-move he remains defenceless, as the following variations show:

I.—20. ....Q—Kt 1; 21. Kt—Q B 6, B—K 4 (if 21. ....Q—Kt 2; 22. Kt×R, etc.); 22. B×B, P×B; 23. Kt×Q, R×Kt; 24. Kt—B 7!, R—B 1; 25. Kt—K 6 followed by 26. Kt×R and 27. R—Q 8, and White wins.

II.—20. ....Q—R 2; 21. Kt—Q B 6, B—K 4; 22. B×B, P×B; 23. Kt×Q, R×Kt; 24. Kt×P, R—B 1; 25. Kt×B, R×Kt; 26. R×Kt and White wins.

III.—20. ......Q—Kt 2; 21. Kt—K 6!, B—K 4; 22. Kt×R and White wins.

IV.—20. ....Q—B 4; 21. Kt—K 6, B—K 4; 22. B×B, P×B; 23. Kt×Q, P×Kt; 24. Kt—B 7, R—Q Kt 1; 25. Kt—K 8! and White wins.

As can be seen, in all these variations White's K B P is stronger than Black's Queen!

Black resigns.

GAME 98

RUY LOPEZ

Played in a *séance* of six consultation games at Antwerp, February, 1923.

White:	Black:
A. ALEKHIN.	MESSRS. PRILS & BLAUT.

1. P—K 4   P—K 4
2. Kt—K B 3   Kt—Q B 3
3. B—Kt 5   P—Q R 3
4. B—R 4   Kt—B 3
5. Kt—B 3

This move, especially recommended by Dr. Tarrasch, gives White a safe and solid game, but Black, truth to tell, has nothing much to fear in this variation.

5. ......   B—K 2

He has also the choice between this move, which is in practice the most usual, and 5. ....B—B 4, which is equally playable (see Game No. 74).

6. Castles   P—Q Kt 4
7. B—Kt 3   P—Q 3
8. P—Q R 4

The main object of this move is to avoid the exchange of White's K B against Black's Q Kt, an exchange which would be inevitable after 8. P—Q 3, Kt—Q R 4; but the loss of time which it entails creates new troubles for White. It is therefore admissible that Svenonius' manœuvre, 8. Kt—K 2, B—Kt 5; 9. P—B 3, is preferable to the text-move.

8. ......   P—Kt 5!

Much better than 8. ....R—Q Kt 1, which surrenders the Q R file to White (see Game No. 66).

9. Kt—Q 5

Position after White's 9th move.

9. ......   Castles

Simplest, and perhaps also best. Apart from Castles, Black could also have adopted one of the following three variations:

I.—9. ....Kt×P; 10. P—Q 4, Castles; 11. R—K 1, Kt—B 3; 12. Kt×B ch, Kt×Kt (if 12. ....Q×Kt; 13. B—Kt 5 with the better game); 13. P×P, P×P; 14. Q×Q, R×Q; 15. Kt×P with advantage to White.

II.—9. ....R—Q Kt 1; 10. P—Q 4, B—Kt 5; 11. P—B 3, Castles; 12. B—Q B 4! (but not 12. R—K 1, Kt P×P; 13. Kt P×P, P×P; 14. P×P, B×Kt; 15. P×B, Kt×P, winning a Pawn for Black, but giving White a slight advantage in position: Marco—Alekhin, Pistyan, 1922).

III.—9. ....Kt—Q R 4; 10. Kt×B! (not 10. B—R 2, Kt×Kt; 11. B×Kt, P—Q B 3; 12. B—R 2, P—Q B 4!; 13. P—B 3, R—Q Kt 1; 14. B—Q 5, Castles; 15. P—Q 4, K P×P; 16. P×Q P, P—B 5, with marked advantage to Black, Alekhin — Bogoljuboff, Pistyan, 1922), Q×Kt; 11. P—Q 4!, Kt×B; 12. P×Kt, Kt×P!; 13. P×P, B—Kt 2; 14. P×P, Q×P, with an equal game.

10. P—Q 4

This move is premature in the present position. White will soon find himself under the necessity of sacrificing a Pawn for a problematical initiative.

Collijn's *Lärobok* here rightly recommends 10. R—K 1, and if 10. ....B—Kt 5 then 11. P—B 3 (preparing 12. P—Q 4), with a satisfactory game.

10. ......   B—Kt 5
11. P—B 3

11. P×P, Q Kt×P would avoid the loss of the Pawn, but would transfer the attack to Black. By the text-move White, while maintaining his pressure on the centre, hopes later to profit by a certain weakness in the adverse Queen-side.

11. ......   Kt P×P
12. Kt P×P   Kt×K P
13. R—K 1

If 13. Kt×B ch Black could have answered 13. ....Q×Kt, for if then 14. B—Q 5 ?, Kt×Q B P.

13. ......   Kt—B 3
14. P—R 3

Compelling the opponent, should he wish to maintain the Pawn which he has won, to abandon the idea of utilizing his Q B later on to secure the defence of the weak squares on his Queen's wing.

14. ......   B—R 4
15. Kt×Kt ch

The attempt to regain the Pawn by 15. P—Kt 4, B—Kt 3; 16. Kt×B ch, Q×Kt; 17. P×P, Kt×K P; 18. Kt×Kt, P×Kt; 19. B—R 3, P—B 4; 20. P—K B 4, K R—Q 1; 21. Q—B 1, Q—Kt 2! would ultimately end in White's discomfiture.

By the move chosen he definitely abandons this, but has prospects of a positional advantage resulting from the following:

15. ......   B×Kt
16. B—Q 5   Q—Q 2
17. P—R 5

Threatening to win a piece by 18. Q—R 4.

17. ......   Q R—Q 1
18. Q—Q 3   Kt—Kt 1

The remoteness of this Knight, which remains on this useless square until the conclusion of the game, is a substantial compensation for White's material inferiority.

19. B—R 3   K R—K 1
20. B—K 4

Having already in mind the following sacrifice of a second Pawn.

20. ......   B—Kt 3

Not 20. ....P—R 3 on account of 21. P—Kt 4.

21. B×B   R P×B
22. P—Q 5!

Position after White's 22nd move.

22. ......   P—K 5

The critical moment of the game. Black who, up to the present, has played in irreproachable style, allows himself to be led astray by a fresh capture which in the end will prove fatal for him.

He would do better to attempt to free his Queen-side by 22. ....P—B 3, after which the game would probably have resulted in a draw; for example: 22. ....P—B 3; 23. Q R—Q 1, P×P (if 23. ....P—B 4; 24. R—K 4!, followed by 25. R—Kt 1); 24. Q×Q P, Q—B 3; 25. Q×Q, Kt×Q; 26. R—Q 5! (better than 26. R×P) and even if Black could maintain his material advantage he would have only the slightest chances of winning, in view of the position of White's pieces.

23. R×P   R×R
24. Q×R   B×P

Now White's Q R P is untenable, for if 25. R—R 2, B×P; 26. B×P, B—Kt 3! and Black in the end would win the Q P.

But its capture will remove from the King-side the only piece which could secure him an adequate defence, and White will profit by this *tempo* to undertake a very strong attack against the weakened position of the Black King.

25. R—B 1!   B×P

After 25. ....B—B 3 the Pawns on Q R 3 and Q B 2 would obviously be very weak.

26. B—Kt 2!

Threatening 27. Kt—Kt 5, as Black's reply 27. ....B—Q 7, previously feasible, would no longer be so, on account of 28. Q—Q 4!

26. ......   R—K 1

In order to play 27. ....P—K B 3.

27. Q—K R 4 P—K B 3
28. Kt—Q 4!

White does not fear an exchange of Rooks, since after 29. ....R—K 8 ch; 30. R×R, B×R; 31. Q—K 4! he would regain one of the sacrificed Pawns, while maintaining his powerful pressure upon the adverse position.

28. ......   K—B 2

Recognizing the danger threatened by the inroad of White's Knight at K 6, Black merely prepares to sacrifice the Exchange. Indeed, after 29. Kt—K 6, R×Kt; 30. P×R ch, Q×P, White would no longer have any satisfactory continuation of the attack, and Black's two centre Pawns would win ultimately.

Position after Black's 28th move.

29. R—B 4 !!

This move, which is the result of a close examination, is the only one which offers prospects of a winning attack, because it prevents the sacrifice of the Exchange. For example, 30. Kt—K 6, R×Kt ; 31. P×R ch, Q×P ; 32. R—K 4 !, Q—B 4 (or anywhere else) ; 33. B×P ! and wins.

Black therefore can no longer prevent White's Knight from occupying K 6, and from this moment White's attack becomes irresistible.

29. ...... R—K 4
30. Kt—K 6 ! R—R 4

If 30. .... R×P, White wins by 31. Kt×Kt P !

31. Q—K 4 Q—K 2

And if now, or on the next move, R×P, then 32. Kt—Q 8 ch ! wins a Rook.

32. Q—Q 3 !

Preparing the decisive action of the Rook on the fourth rank.

32. ...... B—Kt 3

Or 32. ... Kt—Q 2 ; 33. R—K 4, Kt—K 4 ; 34. Q×P, B—Kt 3 ;

35. Q—B 8 with a winning attack for White.

33. R—K 4 Q—Q 2
34. P—Kt 4 ! R—R 1
35. R—K B 4 !

This move leaves Black defenceless against the threats 36. B×P, 36. Kt×Kt P and 36. P—Kt 5.

35. ...... R—K 1

Position after Black's 35th move.

36. B×P ! P×B

This capture leads to mate. Black could have escaped immediate danger by 36. .... R×Kt, but after 37. P×R ch, Q×P ; 38. B—Q 4 ch, K—Kt 1 ; 39. B×B, P×B ; 40. R—Q 4 ! his game would be hopeless.

37. R×P ch ! K×R

If 37. .... K—K 2 ; 38. Q×Kt P ! and mates in two moves. Or if 37. .... K—Kt 1 ; 38. Q×P ch, K—R 1 ; 39. Q—R 5 ch, K—Kt 1 ; 40. R—Kt 6 ch and mates.

After the text-move White mates in three moves by 38. Q—Q B 3 ch, B—Q 5 ; 39. Q×B ch, K moves ; 40. Q—Kt 7 mate.

GAME 99

QUEEN'S GAMBIT DECLINED

First game of a match at Paris, February, 1923.

White:	Black:
A. ALEKHIN.	A. MUFFANG.

1. P—Q 4   P—Q 4
2. P—Q B 4   P—K 3
3. Kt—K B 3   P—Q B 4

This variation, favoured by Tarrasch, is disadvantageous for Black should White adopt Rubinstein's system (P—K Kt 3 and B—Kt 2), as in the present game.

4. B P×P   K P×P
5. P—K Kt 3   Kt—Q B 3
6. B—Kt 2   Kt—B 3
7. Castles   B—K 3

After 7. ....B—K 2 White has the choice between the line of play adopted in this game, and the continuation 8. P×P, B×P; 9. Q Kt—Q 2 followed by 10. Kt—Kt 3, successfully put into practice by Sämisch against Dr. Tarrasch (Carlsbad Tournament, 1923).

8. Kt—B 3   B—K 2
9. P×P   B×P
10. Kt—Q R 4 !

This new continuation, introduced by Réti against Dr. Tarrasch in the Pistyan Tournament of 1922, aims at occupying, once and for all, the square Q 4, of vital importance in the Tarrasch variation.

This innovation, in my opinion, constitutes a notable strengthening of the Rubinstein variation.

10. ......   B—K 2
11. B—K 3   Castles

Dr. Tarrasch continued 11. ....P—Q Kt 3 in his game against Réti, without, however, obtaining a satisfactory game. Here is the continuation of the game: 12. Kt—Q 4, Kt×Kt; 13. B×Kt, Q—Q 2; 14. Kt—B 3, R—Q 1; 15. Q—Kt 3, Castles; 16. K R—Q 1 and White's advantage is obvious.

12. Kt—B 5

This move is sufficient to yield White a slight advantage. It is, however, probable that 12. Kt—Q 4 first would have given a more marked advantage.

12. ......   Kt—K 5 !

Comparatively best. White evidently cannot capture the Q Kt P, because of 13. Q—B 2.

The ensuing liquidation reduces White's winning chances, which will consist solely in the weakness of the adverse centre Pawns and the slight advantage of a Bishop against a Knight in this type of position, where it is not blocked by Pawns.

13. Kt×B   P×Kt
14. Kt—Q 4   Kt×Kt
15. Q B×Kt

On the other hand, the advantage of the two Bishops is illusory, for it is clear that after ....B—B 3 White cannot avoid the exchange of his Q B.

15. ......   Kt—Q 3
16. Q—Kt 3 !

Already threatening 17. P—K 4.

16. ......   B—B 3
17. Q R—Q 1   B×B
18. R×B   Q—B 3
19. P—K 3 !

Preparing 20. R—K B 4! which would not be so strong if played at once, because of 19. ....Q—K 4.

19. ......   Q R—B 1
20. R—K B 4 !   Q—K 2

The weakness of the grouping of Black's Pawns on K 3 and Q 4 is felt the more as the hostile K B dominates the White squares.

The plausible move 20. ....Q—K 4 would be quite bad because of the subtle reply 21. Q—R 4! attacking the Q R P and threatening to enter at Q 7 with decisive effect.

21. R×R ch   K×R

Again best. If 21. ....Q×R; then 22. P—K 4! or if 21. .... R×R; 22. R—Q B 1, R—B 1; 23. R×R ch, Kt×R; 24. P—K 4! and White's K B enters into action with very great effect.

22. R—Q 1   K—Kt 1

This retreat of the Black King to the square it originally occupied is intended to hinder the threatened 23. Q—Q 3 followed by 24. P—K 4, etc.

It will, however, enable White to force the gain of a Pawn by a hidden manœuvre.

Better was 22. ....P—Q R 3, prolonging the resistance.

23. Q—R 3!

After this move Black has no defence against the double threat, 24. Q×P and 24. P—K 4!

23. ......   R—B 7

Position after Black's 23rd move.

24. P—K 4!

Attacking the centre and thereby enabling his Queen to join in the defence of the King-side, since it will protect the K B P after capturing the Q R P.

24. ......   Q—B 1
25. Q×P   Kt—Kt 4

Reckoning to secure a passed Pawn on Q 5, but the realization of this plan necessitates an immobility of the Black pieces of which White will take advantage to conclude the game by a direct attack.

On the other hand, it was scarcely possible for Black to entertain other continuations, *e.g.*:

I.—25. ....Kt×P; 26. B×Kt, P×B; 27. Q—Kt 6!

II.—25. ....P×P; 26. Q—Kt 6, R—B 3; 27. Q—Kt 4.

With an easy win for White in both variations.

26. Q—Kt 6   P—Q 5

Threatening mate in two.

27. R—K B 1!   Q—Q B 4
28. Q×P ch   K—B 1
29. P—K 5!

Enabling White's K B to enter into the adverse game with decisive effect.

29. ......   Q—B 1
30. Q—Q Kt 6 R×Kt P

See Diagram.

31. B—Q 5!

Not 31. P—Q R 4 because of 31. ....Q—B 2, whereas now White threatens inevitably 32. P—Q R 4, Q—B 2; 33. Q—K 6.

31. ......   Q—Q 2
32. B—B 4   R—Kt 5
33. Q—B 5 ch   Q—K 2
34. Q—B 8 ch   Q—K 1
35. Q—K B 5 ch K—K 2
36. Q—K 6 ch   K—B 1

Position after Black's 30th move.

If 36. ....K—Q 1, then 37. Q—Kt 6 ch, K—B 1 ; 38. Q—B 5 ch, winning the Rook.

37. Q—Kt 8 ch	K—K 2
38. Q×P ch	K—Q 1
39. Q×Kt P !	Q×P
40. R—B 1	Black resigns

GAME 100

FRENCH DEFENCE

Second game of a match at Paris, February, 1923.

White :	Black :
A. MUFFANG.	A. ALEKHIN.
1. P—K 4	P—K 3
2. P—Q 4	P—Q 4
3. P—K 5	

Steinitz's move, reintroduced by Niemzovitch a few years ago. It leads to a very complicated game, not disadvantageous for Black.

3.	P—Q B 4
4. P—Q B 3	Kt—Q B 3
5. Kt—B 3	P—B 3

In an analogous position at St. Petersburg, 1914, Dr. Lasker played 5. ....P—B 4.against Dr. Tarrasch.

The text-move, although perhaps less solid, aims at creating a tension in the centre which necessitates perfectly correct play on the part of his opponent.

6. B—Q 3   B—Q 2

More prudent was here 6. .... Q—B 2 ; 7. B—K B 4, Q—Kt 3 !, for after the text-move White could have introduced complications equally dangerous for both players by 7. Kt—Kt 5 !?, e.g.: 7. Kt—Kt 5 !?, P—B 4 ; 8. P—K Kt 4 !, P×Q P ; 9. P×B P, Kt×P ; 10. P×K P, B—B 3 ; 11. P×P, Kt×B ch ; 12. Q×Kt, Q—B 3 ; 13. Castles, Kt—R 3, followed by Castles Q R, and in spite of White's Pawn plus the chances can be considered approximately equal, since the position of White's King is compromised by the opening of the K Kt file.

7. Q—B 2

As White's Queen cannot be maintained on this file, it was useless to lose a move to provoke a reply which would sooner or later be forced on account of the dangers arising from Kt—Kt 5.
It was therefore better to play 7. Q—K 2 at once.

| 7. ...... | P—B 4 |
| 8. P—K Kt 4 | |

Very energetic . . . . . but as will be seen subsequently, the opening of the K Kt file is rather to the advantage of his opponent.

8.	P—K Kt 3
9. Kt P×P	Kt P×P
10. P×P	

Once again best. He must prevent the threatened exchange of Knight against the Pawns, leading to the opening of the Q B file and the weakening of White's square at Q 4.

| 10. ...... | B×P |
| 11. Q—K 2 | |

Threatening a demonstration on the right wing, commencing 12. Kt—Kt 5, but Black opposes it by the following move.

11.	Q—B 2 !
12. Q Kt—Q 2	K Kt—K 2
13. Kt—Kt 3	B—Kt 3
14. Kt (Kt 3)—Q 4	

This move should not have been played until his Q B had been developed, which would have enabled White to occupy the Q B file in the event of an exchange.
Better was 14. B—K Kt 5, with the probable continuation 14. .... Castles Q R ; 15. B—B 6, K R—Kt 1 ; 16. Kt (Kt 3)—Q 4, B×Kt ; 17. P×B, Q R—K 1 ; 18. R—Q B 1, K—Kt 1, with a slight advantage to Black, whereas after the text-move he secures a practically won position after a few moves.

14.	B×Kt !
15. P×B	Q—Kt 3
16. Q—K 3	

If 16. B—K 3, the reply 16. .... Kt—Kt 5 would be still more disagreeable.

16.	Kt—Kt 5
17. B—Kt 1	R—Q B 1
18. B—Q 2	

While the position of Black's King is sufficiently protected, that of White's King appears seriously compromised.
White should have taken the chance to Castle, thereby securing some prospects of a satisfactory defence.

| 18. ...... | Kt—B 7 ch |
| 19. B×Kt | Q×Kt P ! |

The entry of the Black Queen into the enemy's game should speedily terminate the game.

| 20. R—Q Kt 1 | Q×B |
| 21. R×P | |

Position after White's 21st move.

| 21. ...... | Q×P |

This useless capture makes the win difficult again, as White can temporarily bring his King into safety.
The right move was 21. .... R—K Kt 1, definitely preventing Castling by White, after which the victory would have been fairly easy, *e.g.*:
22. Q—Kt 3, Q—K 5 ch ; 23. Q—K 3, P—B 5 ; 24. Q—K 2, P—Q R 3 ! and White has not sufficient defence against 25. ....B—Kt 4, which will have fatal consequences.

| 22. Castles ! | R—Kt 1 ch |
| 23. K—R 1 | |

See Diagram.

| 23. ...... | Q—B 7 ! |

Black, in order to retain his slight advantage in position, has no other resource than to provoke an exchange of Queens on K 5, for all other manœuvres, tending to maintain his material advantage, would have turned in the adversary's favour, *e.g.*:

I.—23. ....Q—R 3 ; 24. R (B 1)—Q Kt 1, R—B 8 ch ; 25. R×R

EXHIBITION GAMES, ETC

Position after White's 23rd move.

(if 25. B×R ?, Q—B 8 ch and mates next move), Q×R ; 26. Q—R 6 and White has a strong attack.

II.—23. ....P—B 5 ; 24. Q×P, R—B 1 ; 25. Q—K 3, R×Kt ; 26. Q×R, Q×B ; 27. Q—R 5 ch, K—Q 1 ; 28. Q—B 7 !, Q—R 3 ; 29. R—K Kt 1 and White should win.

24. Kt—Kt 5

This move only results in the improvement of Black's position, Black's Rook being better placed for the defence on K Kt 2 than on K Kt 1.

A little better was 24. R×P at once, although in this case Black's position would have been preferable after 24. ....Q—K 5.

24.	R—Kt 2
25. R×P	P—R 3 !
26. Kt—B 3	

The Knight is compelled to retreat, for if 26. R—B 1, P—B 5 ! ; 27. R×Q (or 27. Q×P, P×Kt), P×Q ; 28. R×R ch, Kt×R, and White has three pieces *en prise*.

26. ......   P—B 5 !

The initial move of the decisive attack. White cannot capture this Pawn because of 27. Q×P, Q—Q 6 !,

followed by 28. ....R—K B 2, and Black wins.

27. Q—K 2   Q—K 5 !
28. Q—Q 1

If 28. R—K 1, Q×Q ; 29. R×Q, B—Kt 4 ; 30. R—K 1, B—Q 6 followed by 31. ....B—K 5, and Black has a winning position.

28. ......   Kt—B 3

Position after White's 29th move.

29. R—K 1

The game could not be saved, *e.g.*:

I.—29. R—R 4, Kt×K P, etc.

II.—29. R—R 3, Kt×Q P ; 30. R—K 1, Kt×Kt ! ; 31. R×Q, P×R ; 32. R×Kt, P×R ; 33. B×P, R—Kt 5 ; 34. B—Kt 3 (or 34. Q—Q 2, R—Q Kt 1 !), R (Kt 5)—Q B 5, and Black wins.

29. ......   Kt×R !

This Queen-sacrifice is the logical sequel to the preceding moves. It enables Black's Q B at last to take an active part in the attack against the opposing King.

30. R×Q   P×R
31. Kt—R 4   P—K 6 !

The point! White's Knight will now be hopelessly pinned by Black's Q B on the long diagonal, after which the gain of this piece will be merely a question of time.

32. Q—R 5 ch	K—B 1
33. P×P	P×P
34. B×P	

Or 34. Q—B 3 ch, K—Kt 1; 35. Q×P, B—B 3 ch; 36. Kt—B 3, R—B 1, and wins.

| 34. ...... | B—B 3 ch |
| 35. Kt—B 3 | K—Kt 1 |

Still simpler was 35. R—Q Kt 1!; 36. P—R 4, R—Q Kt 6. However, the text-move is quite sufficient to win.

36. Q—R 3!	B—Q 4
37. B×P	R—Kt 3
38. Q—R 5	B—K 5!
39. B—Kt 5	R—B 1
40. K—Kt 1	R×Kt
41. Q—Kt 4	Kt—Kt 4!
42. P—R 4	

Obviously 42. Q×B would lead to mate in three moves.

42.	Kt—B 6
43. K—R 2	R—B 7 ch
44. K—R 3	B—B 4

White resigns.

INDEX OF OPENINGS

Note:—The Numbers in heavy type denote the games in which Alekhin had White.

	PAGE
Alekhin's Defence	145
Bishop's Gambit	**105**
Bishop's Opening	29, 124
Centre Game	50
Danish Gambit	**125**
English Opening	**19, 20,** 243
Four Knights' Game	**12,** 60, 221
French Defence	6, 69, **84,** 119, 200, 261
Giuoco Piano	**79,** 82
Irregular Opening	**237**
Kieseritski Gambit	**87**
King's Gambit Declined	**66, 239**
King's Knight's Opening	109
Petroff's Defence	**64,** 122
Philidor's Defence	23, 97, 116
Queen's Fianchetto Defence	**96**
Queen's Gambit Declined	9, 32, 59, 110, **140,** 153, **160, 165,** 171, 176, 179, **183, 185,** 196, **205, 208,** 212, **219, 223, 232, 235, 259**
Queen's Pawn Game	35, **103, 115,** 129, 132, **137, 143, 148,** 158, 162, **173, 185,** 199, **228,** 249
Ruy Lopez	4, 40, **43,** 45, 48, **54, 56,** 73, 77, 93, **100,** 168, **192,** 215, 241, 251, **255**
Scotch Game	25, 114, 248
Sicilian Defence	37, 102, 150, **197,** 245, **253**
Three Knights' Game	15
Vienna Game	**1,** 91, **107, 111**

INDEX OF NAMES

Note:—*The Numbers in heavy type denote the games in which Alekhin had White.*

	PAGE
Alapin	15
Allies	245, 248, **255**
Balla (von)	**148**
Bernstein	**32, 37**
Blumenfeld	97
Bogoljuboff	**137, 143, 185,** 187
Chajes	**19,** 223
Cohn, E.	25
Drewitt	237
Duras	**43,** 73
Dus-Chotimirski	20
Euwe	173
Evenssohn	116
Fahrni	**84**
Feldt	**119**
Flamberg	77
Freymann (von)	59, **100**
Gofmeister	**120**
Golmayo	**249**
Gonssiorovski	124
Gregory	1
Grünfeld	212
Hromadka	**171**
Issakoff	**125**
Johner	162
Jonkovski (de)	87
Kmoch	196
König	**199**
Lasker, Ed.	**111**
Lasker, Em.	**114**
Levitski	**105,** 107
Lövenfisch	40, **54,** 103
Marco	23
Maróczy	219
Marshall	**64**

	PAGE
Mieses	50, 82
Muffang	**205, 259,** 261
Niemzovitch	35, **56,** 60
Olland	48
Potemkin	102
Prat	**110**
Rabinovitch, A.	122
Rabinovitch, E.	129
Réti	**192**
Rodzynski (de)	109
Rosanoff	96
Rubinstein	153, 179, **208**
Sämisch	**197, 243,** 253
Selesnieff	132, **160**
Speyer	6
Spielmann	29
Steiner	145
Sterk	**140**
Tarrasch	66, 69, **79,** 158, 183, 215
Tartakover	**200**
Teichmann	**239,** 241
Thomas	**228**
Torres	251
Treybal	168
Vajda	**232**
Verlinski	4
Vidmar	12
West	**235**
Wjakhireff	91
Wolf	**165,** 221
Wygodchikoff	93
Yates	9, 150, **176**
Znosko-Borovski	45
Zubareff	**115**

Printed in Great Britain
by Amazon